# iPad and iPhone Tips and Tricks

## FOURTH EDITION

Jason R. Rich

800 East 96th Street,
Indianapolis, Indiana 46240

# iPAD® AND iPHONE® TIPS AND TRICKS
## FOURTH EDITION

## COPYRIGHT © 2015 BY PEARSON EDUCATION, INC.

All rights reserved. No part of this book shall be reproduced, stored in a retrieval system, or transmitted by any means, electronic, mechanical, photocopying, recording, or otherwise, without written permission from the publisher. No patent liability is assumed with respect to the use of the information contained herein. Although every precaution has been taken in the preparation of this book, the publisher and author assume no responsibility for errors or omissions. Nor is any liability assumed for damages resulting from the use of the information contained herein.

ISBN-13: 978-0-7897-5355-7

ISBN-10: 0-7897-5355-3

Library of Congress Control Number: 2014952763

Printed in the United States of America

First Printing: November 2014

## TRADEMARKS

All terms mentioned in this book that are known to be trademarks or service marks have been appropriately capitalized. Que Publishing cannot attest to the accuracy of this information. Use of a term in this book should not be regarded as affecting the validity of any trademark or service mark.

iPad and iPhone are registered trademarks of Apple, Inc.

## WARNING AND DISCLAIMER

Every effort has been made to make this book as complete and as accurate as possible, but no warranty or fitness is implied. The information provided is on an "as is" basis. The author and the publisher shall have neither liability nor responsibility to any person or entity with respect to any loss or damages arising from the information contained in this book.

## SPECIAL SALES

For information about buying this title in bulk quantities, or for special sales opportunities (which may include electronic versions; custom cover designs; and content particular to your business, training goals, marketing focus, or branding interests), please contact our corporate sales department at corpsales@pearsoned.com or (800) 382-3419.

For government sales inquiries, please contact governmentsales@pearsoned.com.

For questions about sales outside the U.S., please contact international@pearsoned.com.

EDITOR-IN-CHIEF
Greg Wiegand

SENIOR ACQUISITIONS EDITOR
Laura Norman

DEVELOPMENT EDITOR
Jennifer Ackerman-Kettell

MANAGING EDITOR
Sandra Schroeder

SENIOR PROJECT EDITOR
Tonya Simpson

INDEXER
WordWise Publishing Services

PROOFREADER
Dan Knott

TECHNICAL EDITOR
Greg Kettell

EDITORIAL ASSISTANT
Kristen Watterson

INTERIOR DESIGNER
Anne Jones

COVER DESIGNER
Mark Shirar

COMPOSITOR
Mary Sudul

# CONTENTS AT A GLANCE

# TABLE OF CONTENTS

# ABOUT THE AUTHOR

**Jason R. Rich** (www.JasonRich.com) is the bestselling author of more than 55 books, as well as a frequent contributor to a handful of major daily newspapers, national magazines, and popular websites. He also is an accomplished photographer and avid Apple iPhone, iPad, Apple TV, and Mac user.

Jason R. Rich is the author of the books *Your iPad at Work*, Fourth Edition, as well as *iPad and iPhone Digital Photography Tips and Tricks*, both published by Que Publishing. Also for Que, he has produced the *Using Your GoPro Hero3+: Learn to Shoot Better Photos and Videos* video course.

Some of his other books include *How To Do Everything MacBook Air*, *How To Do Everything iCloud*, Second Edition, and *How To Do Everything iPhone 5* for McGraw-Hill, *Ultimate Guide to YouTube For Business* for Entrepreneur Press, and *The Crowd Funding Services Handbook* for Wiley.

More than 225 feature-length how-to articles by Jason R. Rich, covering the Apple iPhone and iPad, can be read for free online at the Que Publishing website. Visit www.iOSArticles.com and click on the Articles tab. Additionally, more than 40 free how-to videos by Jason R. Rich can be found on Que's YouTube channel (www.youtube.com/QuePublishing).

Please follow Jason on Twitter (@JasonRich7), or read his blog, called *Jason Rich's Featured App of the Week*, to learn about new and useful iPhone and iPad apps (www.FeaturedAppOfTheWeek.com).

# DEDICATION

*I am honored to dedicate this book to Steve Jobs (1955–2011), a true visionary, entrepreneur, and pioneer who forever changed the world. This book is also dedicated to my close friends and family, including my wonderful niece, Natalie.*

# ACKNOWLEDGMENTS

Thanks once again to Laura Norman at Que Publishing for inviting me to work on all four editions of this book, and for all of her guidance as I've worked on this project. My gratitude also goes out to Greg Wiegand, Todd Brakke, Kristen Watterson, Tonya Simpson, Cindy Teeters, Jennifer Ackerman-Kettell, Greg Kettell, and Paul Boger, as well as everyone else at Que Publishing/Pearson who contributed their expertise, hard work, and creativity to the creation of this all-new edition of *iPad and iPhone Tips and Tricks*.

Finally, thanks to you, the reader. I hope this book helps you fully utilize your iOS mobile device in every aspect of your life and take full advantage of the power and functionality your iPhone and/or iPad offers.

# WE WANT TO HEAR FROM YOU!

As the reader of this book, *you* are our most important critic and commentator. We value your opinion and want to know what we're doing right, what we could do better, what areas you'd like to see us publish in, and any other words of wisdom you're willing to pass our way.

We welcome your comments. You can email or write to let us know what you did or didn't like about this book—as well as what we can do to make our books better.

*Please note that we cannot help you with technical problems related to the topic of this book.*

When you write, please be sure to include this book's title and author as well as your name and email address. We will carefully review your comments and share them with the author and editors who worked on the book.

**Email:**  feedback@quepublishing.com

**Mail:**   Que Publishing
ATTN: Reader Feedback
800 East 96th Street
Indianapolis, IN 46240 USA

# READER SERVICES

Visit our website and register this book at quepublishing.com/register for convenient access to any updates, downloads, or errata that might be available for this book.

# Introduction

Whether you're making the transition from an older Apple iPhone or iPad model that was running iOS 7 (or an earlier version of Apple's iOS) and upgrading to a new device running iOS 8, or you're keeping your current device but upgrading to iOS 8, the word that best describes the biggest changes you should expect from iOS 8 is *continuity*.

Apple has implemented hundreds of new features and functions, not just into iOS 8 itself, but into the core apps that come preinstalled with your mobile device—like Contacts, Calendar, Reminders, Notes, Safari, Mail, Messages, and so on—and you'll learn how to use many of these new features shortly. If you use a Mac, as well as an iPhone and/or iPad, you'll discover that all of your Apple computers and mobile devices now work more seamlessly together, thanks to iCloud and other technologies, so your content and data are always available when and where it's needed, and you can communicate more effectively, regardless of which computer or mobile device you happen to be using at any given time.

Thanks to iOS 8's Continuity and Handoff features, you can begin using one application on your iPhone, for example, and then pick up exactly where you left off on your iPad or Mac. This now happens automatically if you want it to.

Plus, it's now possible to answer incoming calls made to your iPhone from your iPad or Mac, as long as your smartphone is nearby and wirelessly linked with your other computers and devices. This is just a preview of the Handoff-related features you can soon be utilizing and that will be explained shortly.

Apple's iPhone smartphones and iPad tablets continue to revolutionize the way people communicate and handle their everyday computing and communications needs. These devices have also altered our perception about what a smartphone and tablet is and what they're capable of.

The fact is, in just over six years, hundreds of millions of people around the world have somehow incorporated an Apple iOS mobile device into their lives. With each new iPhone or iPad model that Apple introduces, and each revision of the iOS operating system, these mobile devices become more powerful, and they introduce us to new features and functionality that seem as if they have been lifted directly from the pages of science-fiction novels and made a reality.

This year, with the release of the latest iPhone 6, iPhone 6 Plus, and new iPad models, as well as the early-2015 release of the much-anticipated Apple Watch, the launch of the Apple Pay service, and enhancements made to Apple's iCloud service, our ability to utilize these devices and technologies in our everyday lives has once again taken a giant leap forward. This book will help you prepare yourself for this latest evolution.

> **NOTE** Throughout this book, an "iOS mobile device" refers to any Apple iPhone, iPad, or Apple mobile device that's running the iOS 8 operating system. If you plan to continue using iOS 7 with your iOS mobile device, pick up a copy of *iPad and iPhone Tips and Tricks*, Third Edition, which focuses on the older version of Apple's mobile device operating system.

If you're a veteran iPhone or iPad user, when you upgrade from iOS 7 to iOS 8, you'll discover that the graphical interface is pretty similar to what you're already accustomed to. However, based on how you tap, swipe, or hold the mobile device, you'll be able to easily take advantage of some of iOS 8's newest features and functions.

For those first-time iPhone or iPad users, congratulations! Now is the perfect time to introduce yourself to these mobile devices or switch from another smartphone or tablet to what Apple has to offer. Not only can you expect an exciting experience as you begin using your new iPhone or iPad hardware that's running the iOS 8 operating system, but you have the opportunity to access the App Store to utilize any of the more than 1.3 million apps that can greatly expand the capabilities of these mobile devices.

> **(iOS 8) WHAT'S NEW** It's now possible to use the official Microsoft Word, Excel, PowerPoint, or OneNote apps, and/or Outlook Web App (OWA) on your iPhone or iPad to view, create, edit, and manage Microsoft Office–related documents and files that are fully compatible with the version of Microsoft Office you have running on your Mac or PC. These documents and files sync with your other computers and devices when used with your paid Office 365 subscription and Microsoft OneDrive account.

Whether you're a veteran iPhone or iPad user or are just learning how to use an iOS mobile device, this book will teach you what you need to know to quickly become proficient using the device itself, as well as the majority of the apps that come bundled with it. The focus of this all-new fourth edition of *iPad and iPhone Tips and Tricks* is to quickly get you acquainted with iOS 8 and help you adapt to this new version of the operating system while learning how to best utilize the newest features and functions it offers.

> **NOTE** The iOS 8 operating system is compatible with the iPhone 4s, iPhone 5, iPhone 5c, iPhone 5s, iPhone 6, and iPhone 6 Plus, as well as the iPad 2, iPad 3rd Generation, iPad 4th Generation, iPad Air, iPad mini, iPad mini with Retina Display, the newest iPad models released by Apple in late 2014, and the iPod touch (5th generation or later).
>
> If you purchased a new iPhone, iPad, or iPod touch after September 2014, iOS 8 came pre-installed on your mobile device, but you might be able to upgrade to an updated version of iOS 8, such as iOS 8.1.

# HOW TO UPGRADE FROM iOS 7 TO iOS 8

Anyone who purchased an iPhone, iPad, or iPod touch before September 2014 will need to upgrade to iOS 8. The easiest way to do this is to use your mobile device to access any Wi-Fi hotspot or wireless home network to establish a high-speed Internet connection. Then, from the Home screen, launch Settings.

> **☑ TIP** Before upgrading your iOS mobile device from iOS 6 or iOS 7 to iOS 8, be sure to create a backup of your iPhone or iPad using the iTunes Sync Backup feature or, better yet, the iCloud Backup feature. After you install the iOS 8 operating system, all of your apps and related data will automatically be fully restored.

Next, tap on the General option from the main Settings menu, and then tap on the Software Update option (shown in Figure I.1). If your device is running iOS 6 or iOS 7, a message will appear indicating that an operating system upgrade is available. Follow the onscreen prompts to download and install iOS 8 for free. The upgrade process will take between 20 and 45 minutes, depending on which iPhone or iPad model you're using, its internal storage capacity, and how much information is currently stored on your device.

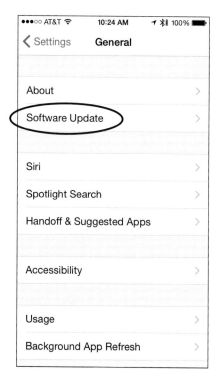

**FIGURE I.1**

*The easiest way to upgrade your iPhone or iPad from iOS 7 to iOS 8 is to use Wi-Fi and access the Software Update option from within Settings.*

☑ **TIP**   Every few months, Apple updates the iOS to add new features to your iPhone or iPad. When a free iOS update is required, a message appears on your device's screen, plus a Badge icon appears within the Settings app icon on your Home screen. For example, iOS 8 was released on September 17, 2014; however, Apple had already announced a planned iOS 8 update in October 2014 to add the Apple Pay functionality to the iPhone 6 and iPhone 6 Plus.

# INTERACTING WITH YOUR iPHONE OR iPAD

If you're a veteran iPhone or iPad user, you already know that Apple's iOS mobile operating system enables you to interact with your mobile device using its touchscreen. Data entry, for example, is typically done using the virtual keyboard that is displayed on the screen when it's needed. Based on the type of information you're entering and the app you're using, the keyboard's layout adapts automatically.

(iOS 8) **WHAT'S NEW**   Among the improvements made to iOS 8 is the introduction of the QuickType virtual keyboards. From an appearance standpoint, the virtual keyboard that appears on your iPhone or iPad's screen might initially look similar to what you're used to, but app developers now can modify virtual keyboard layouts to make apps easier and more intuitive to use.

Plus, iOS 8 is designed to better predict what you're typing, as you're typing it, so as you're using the virtual keyboard, data entry can occur faster and be more accurate than ever before.

When not using the virtual keyboard, much of your interaction with the iPhone or iPad is done using a series of taps, swipes, and other finger gestures on the Multi-Touch display. However, you can also communicate with your iPhone or iPad using your voice, thanks to Apple's Siri (which also has some added and improved functionality) and the Dictation feature, or utilize an optional external keyboard and/or pen-shaped stylus.

# TOUCHSCREEN TECHNIQUES YOU'LL NEED TO MASTER

To navigate your way around iOS 8 on your iPhone or iPad, you need to master a series of basic taps and finger gestures. For the most part, these taps and figure gestures are pretty much the same as they were before, with occasional usage differences.

> **iOS 8 WHAT'S NEW** When using the Mail app to review your Inbox(es), when you swipe from right to left across a message listing, a new menu appears giving you the option to quickly Move, Flag, or Trash that message. If you swipe across the listing from left to right, you can mark the message as read, or by tapping on the message, you can open and read it.

As you learn more about iOS 8's new features, throughout this book you'll also discover how to best utilize them by executing the necessary taps, swipes, pinches, and other finger gestures.

Just as when using previous editions of the iOS with an iPhone or iPad, from the moment you turn on your device (or take it out of Sleep mode), aside from pressing the Home button, virtually all of your interaction with the smartphone or tablet is done through the following finger movements and taps on the device's highly sensitive multitouch display:

- **Tap**—Tapping an icon, button, or link that's displayed on your device's screen serves the same purpose as clicking the mouse when you use your main computer. And, just as when you use a computer, you can single-tap or double-tap, which is equivalent to a single- or double-click of the mouse.

- **Hold**—Instead of a quick tap, in some cases, it is necessary to press and hold your finger on an icon or onscreen command option. When a hold action is required, place your finger on the appropriate icon or command option, and hold it there with a slight pressure. There's never a need to press down hard on the smartphone or tablet's screen.

- **Swipe**—A swipe refers to quickly moving your finger along the screen from right to left, left to right, top to bottom, or bottom to top, in order to scroll left, right, up, or down, depending on which app you're using.

- **Pinch**—Using your thumb and index finger (the finger next to your thumb), perform a pinch motion on the touchscreen to zoom out when using certain apps. Or "unpinch" (by moving your fingers apart quickly) to zoom in on what you're looking at on the screen when using many apps.

☑ **TIP** Another way to zoom in or out when looking at the device's screen is to double-tap the area of the screen on which you want to zoom in. This works when you're surfing the Web in Safari or looking at photos using the Photos app, as well as within most other apps that support the zoom in/out feature. To zoom out again, double-tap the screen a second time.

■ **Pull-down**—Using your finger, swipe it from the very top of the iPhone or iPad's screen quickly in a downward direction. This causes the Notification Center window to appear. You can be holding the device in portrait or landscape mode for this to work. As you'll discover in Chapter 1, "Tips and Tricks for Customizing Settings," the functionality of Notification Center, and what information you can access from it, has been enhanced in iOS 8 and is more customizable than before.

(iOS 8) **WHAT'S NEW** The pull-down gesture is also used to access the enhanced Spotlight Search feature. Use a pull-down gesture that starts in the *middle* of the iPhone or iPad's Home screen to access iOS 8's Spotlight Search feature. One use of Spotlight Search is to quickly find any information that's stored in your mobile device, such as a Contacts entry, Calendar event, or content in an email message. Enter a keyword or search phrase into the Search field that appears, tap on the Search key on the virtual keyword, and then tap on one of the search result listings to access the related data or content by automatically launching whichever app it relates to.

When your iPhone or iPad has Internet access, Spotlight Search utilizes online-based resources automatically to give you access to Wikipedia, news, information about nearby places, the iTunes Store, App Store, iBooks Store, relevant suggested websites, movie show times, and other content based on what you're searching for (shown in Figure I.2).

**FIGURE I.2**

*The Spotlight Search feature gives you fast access to a broader range of information and content that's stored in your mobile device and that's available from the Internet.*

- **Swipe up**—From the bottom of the iPhone or iPad's screen at any time, swipe your finger in an upward direction to make the Control Center appear. From here, you can access a handful of functions, such as Airplane Mode, Wi-Fi, Bluetooth, the Do Not Disturb feature, and the Screen Rotation Lock, plus access screen brightness controls, Music app controls, utilize AirDrop and AirPlay functions, and access commonly used core apps, such as Clock, Calculator, and Camera. On the iPhone, you can also quickly turn on/off the Flashlight function. How to use Control Center is also covered in Chapter 2, "Using Siri, Dictation, and CarPlay to Interact with Your Mobile Device."

- **Five-finger pinch (iPad only)**—To exit out of any app and return to the Home screen, place all five fingers of one hand on the screen so that they're spread out, and then draw your fingers together, as if you're grabbing something. Be sure, however, that the Multitasking Gestures are turned on in the Settings app (found under the General heading).

> **TIP**  Return to the Home screen anytime by pressing the Home button once, regardless of which app is being used.

- **Multi-finger horizontal swipe (iPad only)**—When multiple apps are simultaneously running, swipe several fingers from left to right or from right to left on the screen to switch between the active app and the other apps that are currently running in the background (using the app switcher). Alternatively, iPad and iPhone users alike can access the app switcher to quickly switch between apps by quickly pressing the Home button twice.

**TIP** Apple continues to make navigating around your favorite apps with taps, figure gestures, and swipes easy. For example, on any screen where you're scrolling downward, such as when you're surfing the Web with Safari, you can simply tap on the time that's displayed at the top center of the screen to quickly return to the top of the page or screen.

Meanwhile, if you're in the process of typing something on your iPhone and don't like what you typed, instead of pressing and holding the Delete key to delete your text, simply shake the smartphone in your hand for a second or two to "undo" your typing.

**WHAT'S NEW** With iOS 8, Apple has incorporated ways to more easily interact with the iPhone using just one hand. On the iPhone 6 and iPhone 6 Plus, the Sleep/Wake button is now positioned on the side, as opposed to the top of the phone.

When using the iPhone 6 or iPhone 6 Plus, double touch the Home button, and everything that's displayed on the screen shifts downward, so you can more easily reach it with your thumb. Plus, as you're reading emails, you can use your thumb (on the hand you're holding the iPhone with) to swipe left or right across an Inbox message listing to manage that incoming message.

## HOME BUTTON QUICK TIPS

Positioned on the front of your iPhone or iPad, below the main touchscreen, is the Home button. Here's how to use some of the Home button's main functions when using iOS 8:

- **Activate Siri**—Press down and hold the Home button for 2 seconds from the Home screen or when using any app.

■ **Access the app switcher**—From any app (or from the Home screen), quickly press the Home button twice. Press the Home button again to exit the app switcher.

■ **Exit an app and return to the Home screen**—When using any app, press the Home button once to exit it and return to the Home screen. Keep in mind, in most cases this does not shut down the app; it will continue running in the background.

■ **Reboot the device** (without deleting any of your apps or data)—Press and hold the Home button simultaneously with the Sleep/Wake button for about 5 seconds, until the Apple logo appears on the screen.

■ **Return to the main Home screen**—When viewing any of the Home screens on your mobile device, press the Home button once to return to the main Home screen.

■ **Wake up the device from Sleep mode**—Press the Home button once when your iPhone or iPad is in Sleep mode. If the device is powered down, press and hold the Power button for several seconds instead.

■ **Readjust what's displayed for one-handed iPhone operation**—Double touch the Home button to shift everything that's displayed on the iPhone's screen downward, so you can interact with that content using the same hand you're holding the smartphone with. (This works with the newer iPhone models only.)

Use the Touch ID that's built in to the Home button (available in the more recently released iOS mobile devices) to unlock the device or confirm a payment using Apple Pay, or when making a content purchase from the App Store, iTunes Store, iBookstore, or Newsstand.

## HOW TO MAKE THE BEST USE OF THE VIRTUAL KEYBOARD

Whenever you need to enter data into your iPhone or iPad, you almost always use the virtual keyboard that pops up on the bottom portion of the screen when it's needed. The virtual keyboard typically resembles a typewriter or computer keyboard; however, certain onscreen keys have different purposes, depending on which app you're using.

For example, when you access the Spotlight Search screen (refer to Figure I.2), you will notice the large Search key on the right side of the keyboard. However, when you use the Pages or Microsoft Word apps, the Search key becomes the Return key. When you surf the Web using Safari, the Search key becomes the Go key in certain situations, and other keys along the bottom row of the virtual keyboard change as well.

When you're using an app that involves numeric data entry, such as Numbers, the layout and design of the virtual keyboard can change dramatically.

## VIRTUAL KEYBOARD QUICK TIPS

Use these tips to help you more easily work with the virtual keyboard on your iPhone or iPad.

- **Divide the virtual keyboard in half** (iPad and iPad mini only)—Make it easier to type on the virtual keyboard with your two thumbs while holding the device. To split the keyboard, use the index fingers on your right and left hand simultaneously, place them in the center of the virtual keyboard when it's visible, and then move them apart.

- **Unlock and move the virtual keyboard upward** (iPad and iPad mini only)—Hold down the Hide Keyboard key (displayed in the lower-right corner of the keyboard). You'll be given the opportunity to split or merge the keyboard, as well as unlock the keyboard.

- **Turn on/off the keyboard's key click sound**—Launch Settings, tap on the Sounds option, and then from the Sounds menu, scroll down and turn on or off the virtual switch associated with Keyboard Clicks.

- **Adjust auto-capitalization, autocorrection, check spelling, enable caps lock, predictive, split keyboard (iPad only), and the keyboard shortcuts options**—Launch Settings, tap on the General option, and then tap on the Keyboard option to access the Keyboard menu. Turn on or off the virtual switch associated with each option.

- **Access alternate keys within the virtual keyboard**—When you press and hold down certain keys, it's possible to access alternative letters, characters or symbols. For example, this works when you press and hold down the A, C, E, I, N, O, U, S, Y, or Z keys. When using Safari, press and hold down the period (".") for a second or two to access the .us, .org, .edu, .net, and .com extensions.

> **TIP** When using the virtual keyboard, to turn on Caps Lock, quickly double tap the Shift key (it displays an upward-pointing arrow). Tap the key again to turn off Caps Lock as you're typing or doing data entry.

- **Make the virtual keyboard disappear**—You can often tap anywhere on the screen except on the virtual keyboard itself, or you can tap on the Hide Keyboard key (iPad and iPad mini only), which is always located in the lower-right corner of the keyboard.

- **Make the virtual keyboard appear**—If you need to enter data into your iPhone or iPad but the virtual keyboard doesn't appear automatically, simply tap on an empty data field. An appropriately formatted virtual keyboard will appear.

- **Make the keys on the virtual keyboard larger**—For some people, this makes it easier to type. Simply rotate the iPhone or iPad from portrait to landscape mode. Keep in mind that not all apps enable you to rotate the screen.

- **Create keyboard shortcuts**—If there's a sentence, paragraph, or phrase you need to enter repeatedly when using an app, it's possible to enter that text just once and save it as a keyboard shortcut. Then, instead of typing a whole sentence, you can simply type a three-letter code that you assign to that shortcut, and the virtual keyboard will insert the complete sentence. To create your own keyboard shortcuts, follow these steps:

  1. Launch Settings and tap on the General option followed by the Keyboard option.

  2. From the Keyboard menu, tap on the Shortcuts option.

  3. When the Shortcut window appears (shown in Figure I.3), press the "+" icon to add a new shortcut.

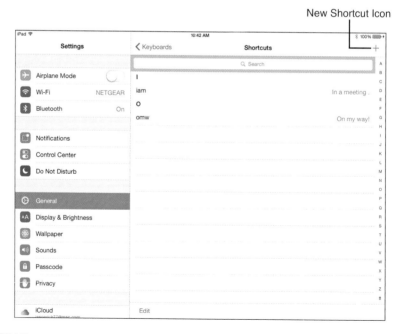

FIGURE I.3

*Create keyboard shortcuts that can later save you time and help improve accuracy as you enter text into your iPhone or iPad via the virtual keyboard.*

4. Fill in the Phrase field with the complete sentence you want to include, such as, "I am in a meeting and will call you back later."

5. In the Shortcut field, enter a three-letter combination to use as the keyboard shortcut, such as "IAM" (representing In A Meeting).

6. Now, anytime the virtual keyboard is displayed (when using any app), simply type IAM to input the sentence, "I am in a meeting and will call you back later."

- **Change keyboard layouts**—Built in to iOS are a handful of alternate keyboard layouts, some offering emoticons, such as Emoji, and some that offer characters from various foreign languages. To add an alternate keyboard to your phone or tablet, from the Keyboard menu, follow these steps:

1. In Settings, tap on the General option.

2. From the General menu, tap on the Keyboard option.

3. From the Keyboards menu, tap the Keyboards option (near the top of the screen), and then from the submenu, tap on the Add New Keyboard option.

4. The Add New Keyboard screen displays a long list of alternate keyboards. Select one of them by tapping on it. It will appear on the Keyboards list.

5. Exit out of Settings.

6. From this point forward, when you access the virtual keyboard, a new key with a globe icon will appear between the 123 and Dictation key. Tap on this key (shown in Figure I.4) to replace the current keyboard with the newly added one, and then tap the key with a globe-shaped icon again to return to the default keyboard layout.

New QuickType Word Suggestions

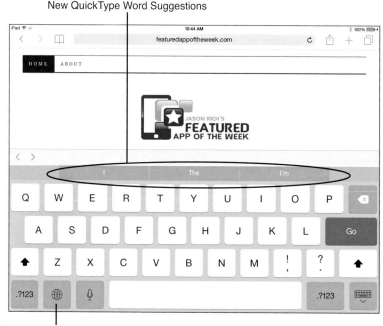

Alternate Keyboard Key

**FIGURE I.4**

*Tap on the alternate keyboard key (which looks like a globe) to switch between preloaded keyboard layouts.*

## SOMETIMES AN OPTIONAL EXTERNAL KEYBOARD OR STYLUS WORKS BETTER

If you expect to do a lot of data entry or word processing on your iOS mobile device, instead of using the virtual keyboard, you can purchase an optional external keyboard that connects to the smartphone or tablet using a wireless Bluetooth connection or the device's Lightning port.

🔍 MORE INFO   Apple (http://store.apple.com), Brookstone (www.brookstone.com), Logitech (www.logitech.com), and Zagg (www.zagg.com) are just a sampling of companies that offer external iPhone or iPad keyboards. Some of these keyboards are built in to phone or tablet cases that also double as stands.

Some apps for the iPhone or iPad enable users to handwrite or draw on the phone or tablet's screen using an optional stylus (a pen-shaped device with a special tip that's designed to work with the touchscreen display). In the past year, several pressure-sensitive stylus pens that work with a growing number of drawing, handwriting, art-related, photo editing, and PDF file annotation apps have been released. Much less expensive, nonpressure-sensitive styluses are also available.

**TIP** The Siri and Dictation features in iOS 8 have also been enhanced. Discover tips and strategies that focus on how to "communicate" with your iPhone or iPad using your voice in Chapter 2.

# HOW TO TURN THE iPHONE OR iPAD ON OR OFF, VERSUS PLACING IT INTO SLEEP MODE

Your iOS mobile device can be turned on, turned off, placed into Sleep mode, or placed into Airplane mode.

- **Turned on**—When your phone or tablet is turned on, it can run apps and perform all the tasks it was designed to do. The touchscreen is active, as is its capability to communicate. To turn on the iPhone or iPad when it is powered off, press and hold the Power button that's located near the top-right corner of the device for about 5 seconds, until the Apple logo appears on the screen. Release the Power button, and then wait a few additional seconds while the device boots up. When the Lock Screen appears, you're ready to begin using the iPhone or iPad.

**WHAT'S NEW** The location of the Sleep/Wake (or Power) button on the iPhone 6 and iPhone 6 Plus has been moved to the side of the handset.

- **Turned off**—When your iPhone or iPad is turned off and powered down, it is not capable of any form of communication, and all apps that were running are shut down. The device is dormant. To turn off your phone or tablet, press down and hold the Power button for about 5 seconds, until the Slide To Power Off banner appears on the screen. Swipe your finger along this red-and-white banner from left to right. The device will shut down.

■ **Sleep mode**—To place your iPhone or iPad into Sleep mode, press and release the Power button once. To wake up the device, you can press the Power button or the Home button. In Sleep mode, your device's screen is turned off but the phone or tablet can still connect to the Internet, receive incoming calls (iPhone) or text messages, retrieve emails, and run apps in the background. Notification Center also remains fully operational, so you can be alerted of pre-set alarms, for example. Sleep mode offers a way to conserve battery life when you're not actively using your phone or tablet.

**NOTE**  By default, your iPhone or iPad will go into Sleep mode and Auto-Lock after 5 minutes. To adjust this time interval or turn off the Auto-Lock feature, launch Settings, tap on the General option, and then tap on the Auto-Lock feature. Options then include activating Auto-Lock after 1, 2, 3, 4, or 5 minutes, or never.

**TIP**  On the iPad, you can place the tablet into Sleep mode by placing an Apple Smart Cover (or compatible cover) over the screen, assuming the iPad Cover Lock/Unlock option is turned on from the General menu within Settings. When in Sleep mode, an iPad will "wake up" for an incoming call (when used with iOS 8's Continuity feature), a FaceTime call, or an incoming text message.

■ **Airplane mode**—This mode enables your device to remain fully functional, except it can't communicate in any way using a 3G or 4G (LTE) cellular connection (and the iPhone cannot make or receive calls). Apps that do not require Internet access continue to function normally. So, if you're aboard an airplane, you can switch into Airplane mode and continue reading an eBook, playing a game, word processing, watching a movie that you've downloaded from the iTunes Store, or working with a wide range of other apps. After switching into Airplane mode, it is possible to turn Wi-Fi Internet access back on, yet keep the cellular connection turned off. This is useful if you're traveling abroad, for example, and don't want to incur international cellular roaming charges, or if you're aboard an airplane that offers Wi-Fi service.

**TIP**  To turn on/off Airplane mode, launch Settings, and from the main Settings menu, tap on the virtual switch that's associated with Airplane mode. Alternatively, launch Control Center and tap on the Airplane mode icon.

On the iPhone, you can also place the device into Do Not Disturb mode. This automatically routes incoming calls directly to voice mail. As you'll discover, you can customize the Do Not Disturb feature to allow certain people that you preselect to reach you, when you otherwise want to be left alone.

**TIP** To activate and customize the Do Not Disturb feature, launch Settings and tap on the Do Not Disturb option. To later turn on or off the feature, access the Control Center and tap on the crescent moon-shaped icon (shown in Figure I.5).

When turned on, a moon icon is displayed on the iPhone or iPad's Status Bar, and all calls and alerts are silenced. This feature can be turned on or off at anytime, or you can preschedule specific times you want Do Not Disturb to be activated, such as between 11:00 p.m. and 7:00 a.m. on weekdays. From the Do Not Disturb menu within Settings (shown in Figure I.6), you can also determine whether certain callers are allowed to reach you when the phone is in Do Not Disturb mode.

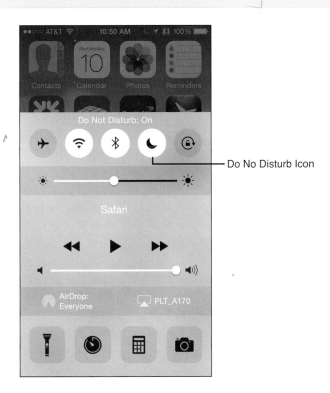

Do No Disturb Icon

**FIGURE I.5**

*Turning on or off the Do Not Disturb feature is now much easier using Control Center in iOS 8.*

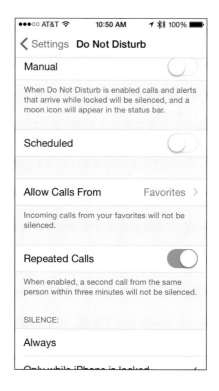

**FIGURE I.6**

*From the Do Not Disturb menu screen within Settings, be sure to customize this feature so it best meets your needs and schedule, based on when you want to be left alone.*

Keep in mind that when your iPhone is turned off, all incoming calls are forwarded directly to voicemail, and it is not possible to initiate an outgoing call. Likewise, incoming text messages, FaceTime calls, and other communications from the outside world cannot be accepted when an iPhone or iPad is turned off. Instead, when you turn on the device, notifications for these missed messages are displayed in Notification Center, within their respective apps, and potentially on the Lock Screen, depending on how you set up Notification Center.

# DISCOVER WHAT'S NEW IN iOS 8

Among the major enhancements to iOS 8 are the ways it enables your iPhone or iPad to communicate and easily share data and information wirelessly with others. You'll also discover better integration with online social networking services, as well as with Apple's own iCloud service. Plus, thanks to Handoff and iCloud integration, your iPhone, iPad, and Mac more seamlessly work with each other.

Let's take a quick look at some of the major new features and enhancements made to iOS 8. You'll learn strategies for best utilizing the majority of these features later in the book. But first, here's a rundown of what's new and noteworthy about iOS 8:

- **Camera**—The Camera app on the iPhone has several new features, like a Time-Lapse and Timer shooting mode. On the iPad, several Camera app features that were previously available only on the iPhone can now be used when snapping photos with the tablet's built-in camera, including the Pano (panoramic) shooting mode. Chapter 8, "Shoot, Edit, and Share Photos and Videos," focuses on using the Camera app to take awesome photos.

- **Photos**—In addition to providing a more powerful collection of photo editing and organizational tools, the Photos app now works with iCloud's Family Sharing feature, so you can share images and videos with up to five other family members. Plus, in 2015, Apple will be changing iCloud's My Photo Stream and Shared Photo Stream features, making them easier to use. Thus, sharing photos with others via the Internet will be easier than ever using a new feature called iCloud Photo Library.

- **Messages**—In addition to giving you greater control over your text messaging, iOS 8 makes it easier to participate in group conversations and withdraw from group conversations that no longer interest you. Plus, you can now send sound (see Figure I.7) and/or video clips as a text message, more easily share your location with others during a conversation, see attachments sent and received during a text message conversation on one scrollable screen, and send multiple photos or video clips at once.

**FIGURE I.7**

*The Messages app now enables you to record and send sound as a text message.*

- **QuickType**—Whenever you use the iPhone or iPad's virtual keyboard, not only does it better anticipate what you're typing, it understands context and adjusts word or phrase suggestions accordingly.

- **Family Sharing**—Now, up to six family members can share iTunes Store, iBookstore, and App Store content purchases, plus share photos. Yet, each person can have their own (private) iCloud account that utilizes their own Apple ID and password. So, while selected content can be shared, other data and content stored in an iCloud account or iOS mobile device can be kept private.

- **iCloud Drive**—In addition to app-specific data and files, it's now possible to manually or automatically back up or sync other types of files, data, and documents using a personal iCloud account. This feature works more like other cloud-based file sharing services, such as Dropbox.

- **Health**—Using the iPhone's new Health app with third-party apps, the Apple Watch, and/or other optional equipment, you can manage aspects of your health, fitness, diet, sleep, and daily activity, so you can lead a healthier lifestyle.

- **Handoff**—Your iPhone, iPad, and Mac(s) now work more seamlessly together, so you can always have access to the information you need, when and where you need it. Plus, you can communicate more efficiently. For example, it's now possible to answer an incoming phone call (to your iPhone) from your nearby iPad or Mac (running OS X Yosemite), as shown in Figure I.8.

**FIGURE I.8**

*When turned on, if your iPhone and iPad are within wireless range of each other (about 33 feet), you can answer incoming calls to your iPhone on your iPad, and then use your tablet as a speakerphone.*

- **Enhanced Notification Center**—Notification Center (shown in Figure I.9) offers a centralized place where your iPhone or iPad keeps track of alerts, alarms, and notifications related to the apps you're running and functions you're using. Thanks to iOS 8, additional information, such as the current weather forecast and/or local traffic conditions, can now be displayed as part of Notification Center's Today screen. In Chapter 1, discover strategies for managing Notification Center and learn how to customize the information it tracks and displays.

**FIGURE I.9**

*Additional and customizable information can now be displayed on the Notification Center's various screens.*

**WHAT'S NEW** To access the Notification Center window, regardless of which app you're working with or what you're doing on your iOS mobile device, simply swipe your finger from the top of the screen in a downward direction. To begin customizing how Notification Center functions on your device, launch Settings, and then tap on the Notifications option listed in the main Settings menu.

Additional customization options can be accessed by launching Notification Center, tapping on the Today tab, and then scrolling down to the bottom of the screen. Tap on the Edit button to determine what information should appear within this screen and rearrange the order in which information is displayed.

- **Enhanced multitasking**—Your iPhone or iPad has the capability to run multiple apps simultaneously, although on the screen, you can be working with only one app at a time. The rest continue running in the background. To quickly switch between apps that are running, or shut down one or more apps, enter the app switcher on your device. To do this, press the Home button twice quickly.

The app switcher displays icons for all the apps currently running on your device along the bottom of the screen, and in the main area of the screen are thumbnail images representing the apps that are running.

Scroll from right to left or from left to right (using a swipe motion with your finger) to see all the apps that are running. To switch to a different app and make it active, tap on its thumbnail or app icon.

To shut down an app while in the app switcher, swipe your finger in an upward direction along the thumbnail image for the app you want to close.

**iOS 8 WHAT'S NEW** When you access the app switcher, displayed along the top are thumbnail images representing people you've recently communicated with. To reconnect with any of these people via phone call, FaceTime call, or text message, tap on his or her thumbnail image.

**NOTE** After you launch most apps, they continue running in the background if you simply press the Home button to exit out of them to return to the Home screen. You can shut down an app from the app switcher or by turning off your iPhone or iPad altogether. If an app was running before you turned off your device, however, it automatically reopens in the background when you restart the device.

- **AirDrop**—Instead of just being able to wirelessly send certain types of content, such as photos, from one nearby iOS mobile device to another, the AirDrop feature now works between iPhones, iPads, and Macs and can be used with more types of files and content.

- **New Web surfing features in Safari**—The Safari web browser that comes bundled with iOS 8 has also been enhanced, giving users more features that make surfing the Web, as well as organizing and sharing Bookmarks and related information, much easier and more efficient. Be sure to read Chapter 12, "Surf the Web More Efficiently Using Safari," to discover strategies for using all of Safari's newest features.

- **Improved Siri functionality**—Siri has been given additional functionality with iOS 8. When you ask Siri a question, the feature can now access more online sources to quickly find you the answer. You can also use Siri to control more iPhone or iPad functions, such as playing music, accessing voicemails, or controlling iTunes Radio. The focus of Chapter 2 is on how to effectively "talk" to Siri.

**iOS 8 WHAT'S NEW**   If you own a 2013 or later model year vehicle from one of more than a dozen car manufacturers, including General Motors, your vehicle can probably link with your iPhone or iPad via Bluetooth, or the vehicle might have a CarPlay Lightning port built in.

Using Siri Eyes Free and other iOS 8 CarPlay functionality, it's possible to control certain features and functions of your iPhone through your car's in-dash infotainment system and issue commands using your voice, while never taking your eyes off the road to look at the iPhone's screen. For example, you can listen to music stored on your iOS device, have Siri read incoming emails or text messages, access details about your contacts or schedule, and perform a wide range of other tasks verbally while driving.

■ **New features in all of iOS 8's core apps**—Your iPhone or iPad comes with a handful of preinstalled apps, such as Contacts, Calendar, Reminders, Notes, Mail, Safari, Maps, App Store, iTunes Store, Music, Weather, Messages, and Passbook. The iOS 8 versions of these and other preinstalled apps have all been redesigned and enhanced with new features and functions that will be explained throughout this book. In addition, Apple's iWork apps (Pages, Numbers, and Keynote) and iLife apps (including iMovie) have been enhanced for use with iOS 8 and some of iCloud's newest functions.

■ **Better integration with iCloud**—In addition to serving as an online-based file sharing and data backup service, iCloud works seamlessly with many core iPhone and iPad functions built in to iOS 8, as well as many of the apps that come bundled with the operating system. With iOS 8, Apple has introduced Family Sharing, iCloud Drive, and iCloud Photo Library (coming in 2015) to make this online-based service even more powerful.

**NOTE**   Some iCloud-related functions can be utilized from your iPhone or iPad using a 3G or 4G (LTE) cellular data connection. However, to utilize some of iCloud's other features, such as iCloud Backup, a Wi-Fi connection is required.

■ **Improved communication tools through iOS 8's app-related sharing buttons**—Certain apps that come preinstalled with iOS 8, such as Contacts and Photos, enable you to share app-specific data with others. The latest versions of these and other apps offer enhancements in terms of how you can share app-specific data via the Mail or Messages app, Facebook or Twitter, or the AirDrop feature. You'll discover these improvements in most apps that feature a Share button, including the optional iWork for iOS apps (Pages, Numbers, and Keynote).

Figure I.10 shows the Share menu screen that's displayed on the iPad Air after tapping on the Share icon in the Photos app. As you can see, digital images stored on an iOS mobile device can now be shared via AirDrop, Messages, Mail, iCloud Photo Sharing, Twitter, Facebook, or Flickr. From this menu screen, the Copy, Slideshow, Airplay, Assign to Contact, Use as Wallpaper, and Print commands are also available, and thumbnails of selected images are displayed.

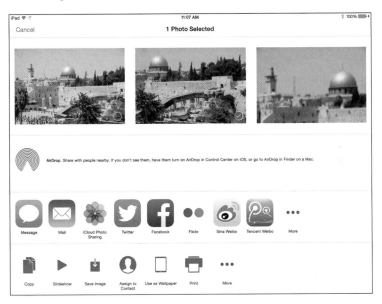

**FIGURE I.10**

*The newly expanded Share menu screen in the iOS 8 version of the Photos app.*

## APPLE PAY OFFERS A NEW WAY TO PAY FOR THINGS

Built in to iOS 8, Apple Pay is available when using the iPhone 6, iPhone 6 Plus, Apple Watch, and perhaps the newest iPad models released in late 2014. Apple Pay is a new way to pay for purchases in retail stores throughout the United States and online.

With Apple Pay, your iPhone is used to scan each of your credit or debit cards just once. This information is then securely stored in a special chip built in to your iOS mobile device. Then, when you're visiting a participating retail store, simply hold your compatible iOS mobile device (or Apple Watch) up to a special scanner that's connected to a cash register, place your thumb or finger on the Touch ID sensor that's built in to the mobile device, and within seconds, you can initiate a credit or debit card purchase in an extremely secure fashion.

The merchant doesn't actually gain access to your credit card number or your name, and Apple does not collect any personal details related to the purchase transaction. If your iOS mobile device gets lost or stolen, simply use the Find My iPhone feature to lock down the device. Your stored credit/debit card details can't be used by an iPhone thief, because their fingerprint will not be recognized by the Touch ID sensor, and because Apple Pay does not retain your actual credit/debit card numbers, there's no need to contact your bank to cancel the cards and have them reissued.

Apple Pay works with the Passbook app that comes preinstalled on the iPhone with iOS 8, and the service supports Visa, MasterCard, and American Express credit and debit cards. When the Apple Pay service launched in October 2014, it was immediately supported at more than 220,000 retail and fast food locations.

Currently, Apple Pay is accepted at Macy's, Bloomingdales, Walgreen's, Subway, McDonald's, Whole Foods, Disney Stores, Walt Disney World, PetCo, Toys 'R Us, Apple Stores, and many other retail chains, with more stores incorporating the Apple Pay technology into their cash registers every week.

## SECURING YOUR iOS MOBILE DEVICE WITH A PASSCODE

If you're worried about other people being able to pick up your iPhone or iPad and access your confidential information or use it to access your favorite websites by signing in using your username, it continues to be possible to password protect your iOS mobile device. When the Passcode Lock feature is turned on, you must manually enter a four-digit passcode (or a longer password) that you preselect to get past the device's Lock Screen.

To turn on the Passcode Lock feature, launch Settings and tap on the General option. From the General menu, tap on Passcode Lock. Then, from the Passcode Lock screen, tap on the Turn Passcode On option. You will be promoted to create a four-digit passcode for your device and reenter it twice.

**CAUTION** When creating a passcode, do not use something obvious, like 1234, 4321, 1111, or your birthdate.

From the Passcode Lock screen, you can then customize Passcode Lock functionality. For example, you can restrict certain iPhone/iPad features from being accessible from the Lock Screen. Plus, by turning on the Erase Data option, you can set up the device to automatically delete its contents if someone enters the wrong passcode 10 times in a row.

**TIP** If you don't think a four-digit passcode is secure enough for your iPhone or iPad, turn off the Simple Passcode option that's displayed as part of the Passcode Lock menu screen within Settings. You'll now be able to create a more complex alphanumeric password for your device.

**WHAT'S NEW** With iOS 8, more iOS mobile devices (including the iPhone 5s, iPhone 6, iPhone 6 Plus, iPad Air 2, and iPad mini 3) have a Touch ID sensor built in to the Home button. This enables the device to be unlocked using a fingerprint scan, as opposed to a four-digit passcode. This same Touch ID can be used to authorize purchases.

## FIND YOUR LOST OR STOLEN DEVICE USING THE FIND MY iPHONE/iPAD FEATURE

The Find My iPhone/iPad feature enables you to quickly pinpoint the exact location of your device if it gets lost or stolen, and then offers tools to help you lock down, erase, and/or retrieve your device. At the same time, if the device does get stolen, you can render the device absolutely useless unless someone knows your Apple ID and password.

For the Find My iPhone/iPad feature to work, however, it must be turned on and activated once. Then, to pinpoint the location of your phone or tablet, it will need to be turned on and be able to connect to the Internet (that is, not be in Airplane mode).

To activate Find My iPhone/iPad, as soon as you install iOS 8 or anytime thereafter, access Settings and tap on the iCloud option from the main Settings menu. Then, from the iCloud menu, make sure the virtual switch associated with Find My iPhone is turned on.

Now, if you ever need to locate your iPhone or iPad, you have several options. First, you can use the free Find My iPhone app that's available from the App Store. Launch the app and sign in using your Apple ID and password. The location of your device will then be displayed on a detailed map.

Tap on the virtual pushpin on the map, or any of the command buttons displayed at the bottom of the app's screen, to then use online-based tools to help you locate, lock down, or erase your mobile device remotely.

Another way to locate your iOS mobile device is to use any computer's web browser and visit www.icloud.com/#find. Sign in to the website using your Apple and ID and password. The same tools for locating and protecting your iOS mobile device are then made available to you online—from anywhere. The Find My feature can also be set up to work with iCloud's Family Sharing function, so you can use a family member's Apple equipment to pinpoint the location of your iPhone or iPad.

> ✓ **TIP**   Be sure you turn on Find My iPhone/iPad on your mobile device immediately. If this feature is not active, you will not be able to use the tools Apple offers to locate, lock down, or remotely erase your device if it later gets lost or stolen.
>
> Even if the device is not turned on or connected to the Internet when it's initially lost or stolen, the Find My iPhone/iPad feature can alert you the moment someone finds or tries to turn on your device.

## MAINTAIN A BACKUP OF YOUR DEVICE

Using Apple's iCloud service, it is possible to set up your iPhone or iPad to automatically back itself up once per day, as long as you turn on the auto backup feature. For this feature to work, the device needs access to a Wi-Fi Internet connection. It also must be locked and plugged in to an external power source to auto-initiate the backup process.

To set up the iCloud Backup feature, which needs to be done only once, follow these steps:

1. Launch Settings and tap on the iCloud option.

2. Make sure Wi-Fi is turned on and your device can link to the wireless network in your home or office.

3. From the iCloud menu screen, tap on the Backup option.

4. From the Backup menu screen, turn on the virtual switch that's associated with the iCloud Backup option (shown in Figure I.11).

**FIGURE I.11**

*After turning on the virtual switch that's associated with the iCloud Backup option in Settings, it's possible to manually initiate a backup by tapping on the Back Up Now option.*

> **TIP**    At anytime, you can initiate a manual backup of your device. Access the Backup menu screen within Settings, and then tap on the Back Up Now option. You'll notice that the time and date of the last successful backup is displayed on this screen.

Later, if you need to reset your iPhone or iPad and erase its contents, or you need to replace your phone or tablet, you can easily restore your data using the last successful iCloud backup. When using this backup method, the backup files associated with your mobile device are stored "in the cloud" within your iCloud account.

### iTUNES SYNC IS ALSO A VIABLE BACKUP OPTION

When it comes to syncing data between your primary computer(s) and other iOS mobile device(s), as well as maintaining a backup of your iPhone or iPad, this can be done by connecting your iOS mobile device(s) directly to your primary computer via the supplied USB cable, and then by using the iTunes Sync process.

Because iOS 8 is fully integrated with iCloud, maintaining a backup of your device and syncing app-specific data, as well as transferring data, files, photos and content between your Mac(s), PC(s), and other iOS mobile device(s), can now much more easily be done using iCloud. When you use iCloud Backup, for example, your iPhone or iPad's backup files are stored online "in the cloud," and not on your primary computer's hard drive. Because this is the more popular way to back up and sync data, it's the approach we'll focus on in this book.

🔍 **MORE INFO**   To use the iTunes Sync process between your iPhone or iPad and a Mac or Windows-based PC, download and install the latest version of the iTunes software onto your computer. To do this, visit www.apple.com/itunes.

To learn more about using the iTunes Sync process to transfer, sync, and back up apps, data, content, and photos, visit www.apple.com/support/itunes.

## WHAT THIS BOOK OFFERS

This all-new fourth edition of *iPad and iPhone Tips and Tricks* will help you quickly discover all the important new features and functions of iOS 8 and show you how to begin fully utilizing this operating system and its bundled apps so that you can transform your iPhone, iPad, iPad mini, or iPod touch into the most versatile, useful, and fun-to-use tool possible.

Each chapter of this book focuses on using various aspects of iOS 8 or the apps that come preinstalled with it. You'll also discover strategies for finding and installing optional third-party apps from the App Store, plus learn all about how to experience various other types of content—from music, TV shows, and movies, to eBooks and digital editions of magazines, plus learn how to best organize, view, and share your own digital photos.

In terms of using your iPhone or iPad as a powerful communications tool, you'll discover strategies for efficiently making and receiving calls (iPhone only), sending and receiving text messages, participating in FaceTime calls (videoconferencing), and participating on the online social networking services (like Facebook and Twitter), while simultaneously making full use of iOS 8's latest features. The book also explores how to take full control of and customize your phone or tablet using the tools and features available from Settings, Control Center, and Notification Center.

In *iPad and iPhone Tips and Tricks*, Fourth Edition, you'll also discover tricks for utilizing iCloud with your iOS mobile device, plus learn all about how to use the most popular apps that come bundled with the iOS 8 operating system (including Contacts, Calendar, Reminders, Notes, Mail, Messages, Safari, Camera, Photos, Maps, Music, Videos, Newsstand, FaceTime, and the iTunes Store), as well as popular apps released by Apple and third parties that enhance the capabilities of your device, including Find My iPhone, YouTube, iPhoto, Facebook, and Twitter.

For the first time, this fourth edition of the book offers details about how to manage your health and automate your home using new iOS 8 features and functions. For this, see Chapter 10, "Improve Your Health and Automate Your Home Using Your iOS Mobile Device."

Plus, this edition of the book includes an introduction to Apple Watch and explains how this wearable device, which will be released in early 2015, can be used with your iPhone and various apps.

> **NOTE** Now that the iPhones and iPads come with a variety of different screen sizes, based on the model you choose, iOS 8 automatically adjusts all apps to best utilize available screen space. Thus, as you're looking at screenshots throughout this book, keep in mind that what you see on your device's screen may vary slightly if you're using a different model iPhone or iPad than what was used to create the screenshot.

## ATTENTION, PLEASE...

Throughout the book, look for What's New, Tip, Note, Caution, and More Info boxes that convey useful tidbits of information relevant to the chapter you're reading. Within each chapter, you'll also discover Quick Tips sections, which quickly outline how to perform a series of common tasks related to the iOS 8 features, functions, or app(s) that are being discussed.

The What's New boxes, for example, highlight new features or functionality introduced in iOS 8, while the More Info boxes provide website URLs or list additional resources that you can use to obtain more information about a particular topic.

# TIPS AND TRICKS FOR CUSTOMIZING SETTINGS

Thanks to iOS 8, the functionality of your iPhone or iPad is more customizable than ever before. You can adjust many device and app-related options from within Settings, plus use Notification Center to help you manage alerts, alarms, notifications, and other informative content in one centralized location. Meanwhile, iOS 8's Control Center gives you quick access to a handful of commonly used features and functions.

This chapter focuses on personalizing and customizing your iOS mobile device and getting you acquainted with using Settings, Control Center, and Notification Center.

**TIP** To access Settings, simply tap on the Settings app icon from the Home screen (shown in Figure 1.1).

Settings App Icon

**FIGURE 1.1**

*To launch Settings, tap on the Settings icon from the iPhone or iPad's Home screen.*

In Settings, it's possible to personalize and customize many different options that give you more control than ever over how your iPhone or iPad responds to you, while managing your apps, files, content, and data.

After iOS 8 is installed and fully operational on your iPhone or iPad, you'll definitely want to manually adjust some of the options in Settings, as opposed to relying entirely on their default settings.

> **TIP**  As you install additional apps onto your iPhone or iPad, if those apps enable you to customize specific features within the app, those customization options are often available to you from within Settings as well.

> **WHAT'S NEW**  To customize new iCloud-related functions that are associated with iCloud, including Family Sharing and iCloud Drive, launch Settings and tap on the iCloud menu option. More about using iCloud with your iOS mobile device is covered in Chapter 5, "Ways to Use iCloud's Latest Features with Your iPhone and/or iPad."

# USING THE SETTINGS APP

After you launch Settings, the menus and submenus are displayed in a hierarchical structure. Under the main Settings heading are a handful of main menu options relating to various apps and functions offered by your iPhone or iPad (shown in Figure 1.2). When you tap on many of these options, a submenu often displays with additional related options.

> **TIP** When you access Settings (shown in Figure 1.3), you'll immediately discover some new menu options that were not available in iOS 7. Keep in mind that when an option's virtual switch is positioned to the right and you see green, that option is turned on. When the switch is positioned to the left, it's turned off.

**FIGURE 1.2**

*On the iPad, the left side of the screen shows the main Settings menu. To the right are available submenu options.*

This virtual switch is turned off.

This virtual switch is turned on.

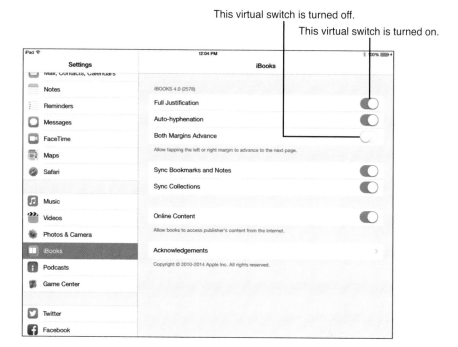

**FIGURE 1.3**

*To turn on a feature, the switch should be positioned to the right and green should be showing.*

**NOTE** The user-customizable options available from within Settings vary based on which model of iOS device you're using and whether it offers 3G/4G (LTE) cellular Internet connectivity.

For example, if you tap on the Wallpaper option (which is now a standalone menu option), the submenus associated with customizing your device's Lock and Home screens appear. By tapping on the wallpaper thumbnails displayed under the Wallpaper heading, additional submenu options are displayed.

As you work your way deeper into each submenu, a left-pointing arrow icon appears near the upper-left corner of each submenu screen that enables you to exit out of each Settings submenu and move a step back toward the main Settings menu. At any time, tap on this left-pointing arrow icon to exit out of the submenu you're in (before or after you've made adjustments to the various option settings). If you opt to make adjustments, those changes are automatically saved when you exit out of the menu or submenu within Settings. If you exit out of a menu or submenu without making any changes, nothing is altered.

# MAIN OPTIONS AVAILABLE FROM THE SETTINGS APP

The following is a summary of the main options available from the Settings app, which will vary slightly based on whether you're using an iPhone, an iPad, or another iOS device.

> ## 📝 NOTE
> If you're using an iPhone 5s, iPhone6, and iPhone 6 Plus, or an iPad model released after September 2014, additional options pertaining to the Touch ID sensor (Home button), as well as the built-in cameras are offered within Settings.

## AIRPLANE MODE (iPHONE/iPAD CELLULAR + WI-FI MODELS)

The Airplane mode option has no submenu; it simply offers one virtual on/off switch. In Airplane mode, a small airplane icon appears in the upper-left corner of the iPhone or iPad's screen, as shown in Figure 1.4.

**FIGURE 1.4**

*In Airplane mode, a small airplane icon appears in the upper-left corner of your iPhone or iPad's screen.*

Even while your device is in Airplane mode, you can still turn on Wi-Fi and/or Bluetooth, enabling the iOS device to access the Web via a Wi-Fi hotspot (to utilize the wireless web access available on some commercial aircrafts, for example), and also communicate with a Bluetooth-enabled wireless keyboard or headset.

> **☑ TIP**  When you turn on Airplane mode, the Wi-Fi and Bluetooth features of your iPhone or iPad get turned off automatically. You can, however, turn them back on manually while still in Airplane mode. This can be done from within Settings or the Control Center.

In Figure 1.4, the iPhone is in Airplane mode (the airplane icon is displayed in the upper-left corner of the screen). However, the smartphone is also connected to a Wi-Fi network. You can see the Wi-Fi signal strength icon displayed in the upper-left corner of the screen, near the Airplane Mode icon. In addition, this iPhone has Bluetooth turned on and a Bluetooth headset. You can tell this from the Bluetooth icons displayed in the upper-right corner of the screen, next to the battery indicator icon and percentage meter.

> **☑ TIP**  Turn on Airplane mode on your iPhone or iPad when plugging it in to recharge to speed up the charging process. Keep in mind, however, that this prohibits the smartphone from receiving calls (they go straight to voice mail), and the iPhone or iPad does not receive incoming text messages, emails, or FaceTime calls until Airplane mode is turned off.

## WI-FI (iPHONE/iPAD)

Located directly below the Airplane Mode option is the Wi-Fi option. When you tap this option, a submenu containing a virtual on/off switch is displayed. When it's turned on, a listing of available Wi-Fi networks (hotspots) is displayed directly below the Choose a Network heading.

☑ **TIP**   When you're reviewing a list of available Wi-Fi networks, look to the right side of each listing to determine whether a lock icon also appears. This indicates that the Wi-Fi hotspot is password protected. Tap on a hotspot that does not display a lock icon unless you possess the password for that network.

Also on the right side of each listing is the signal strength of each Wi-Fi hotspot in your immediate area.

To choose any Wi-Fi hotspot listed, simply tap on it. In a few seconds, a check mark appears to the left of your selected Wi-Fi hotspot, and a Wi-Fi signal indicator appears in the upper-left corner of your device's screen, indicating that a Wi-Fi connection has been established.

If you select a Wi-Fi network that is password protected, when you tap on it, an Enter Password window appears on your screen. Using the device's virtual keyboard, enter the correct password to connect to the Wi-Fi network you selected. You will often have to do this when connecting to a Wi-Fi hotspot offered in a hotel, for example.

📝 **NOTE**   If you attempt to access a public Wi-Fi hotspot—in an airport, library, or school, for example—you might be required to accept terms of a user agreement before Internet access is granted. In this case, your iOS device will say it's connected to a Wi-Fi hotspot, but until you launch Safari and accept the user agreement terms, your various apps will not be able to access the Internet.

## BENEFITS OF CONNECTING TO A WI-FI HOTSPOT TO ACCESS THE WEB

There are several benefits to connecting to the Internet using a Wi-Fi connection, as opposed to a cellular-based 3G/4G (LTE) connection (if you're using an iPhone or iPad Cellular + Wi-Fi model), including the following:

- A Wi-Fi connection is typically faster than a 3G/4G (LTE) connection. (Although if you're within a 4G LTE coverage area, you might experience faster connectivity using it as opposed to Wi-Fi.)
- When connected to the Internet via Wi-Fi, you can send and receive as much data as you'd like without worrying about using up the monthly wireless data allocation that's associated with your cellular data plan.

■ Using a Wi-Fi connection, you can download large files, such as movies and TV show episodes, from the iTunes Store directly onto your device. You also can create wireless backups of your iPhone or iPad that are stored on iCloud.

> **NOTE** The main drawback to using a Wi-Fi connection is that a Wi-Fi hotspot must be present, and you must stay within the radius of that hotspot to remain connected to the Internet. The signal of most Wi-Fi hotspots extends for only several hundred feet from the wireless access point (the Internet router). When you go beyond this signal radius, your Internet connection will be lost.

If you leave the Wi-Fi option turned on, your iPhone or iPad can automatically find and connect to an available Wi-Fi hotspot based on whether you have the Ask to Join Networks option turned on or off. When the Ask To Join Networks feature is turned off, your iPhone or iPad reconnects automatically to wireless networks and Wi-Fi hotspots that you have connected to previously, such as each time you return to your home or office.

> **TIP** By turning off the Ask To Join Networks option found in the Wi-Fi submenu of Settings, your iOS mobile device automatically joins known Wi-Fi networks without first asking you for permission.

## BLUETOOTH (iPHONE/iPAD)

Turn on Bluetooth functionality to use compatible Bluetooth devices, such as a wireless headset, external keyboard, or wireless speakers, with your iOS mobile device. Bluetooth is also needed to use AirDrop and certain iOS 8 Continuity features that enable your iPhone or iPad to communicate with other iOS mobile devices and/or Macs.

In Settings, tap Bluetooth and then turn on the virtual switch in the submenu. The first time you use a particular Bluetooth device with your iOS mobile device, you will probably need to pair it. Follow the directions that came with the device or accessory for performing this initial setup task. Some Bluetooth 4.0 devices automatically pair with your iOS device. The pairing process should take only about a minute or two. Multiple Bluetooth devices can be used simultaneously with your iPhone or iPad.

> **NOTE** After an optional device has been paired once, as long as it's turned on and in close proximity to your iOS device and the iOS device has the Bluetooth feature turned on, the two devices will automatically establish a wireless connection and work together.

> **TIP** If you're using your iPhone or iPad without having a Bluetooth device connected, turn off the Bluetooth feature altogether. This helps extend the battery life of your iOS device. When you turn on this feature, your iPhone or iPad automatically seeks out any Bluetooth-compatible devices in the vicinity.

## CELLULAR (iPHONE) OR CELLULAR DATA (iPAD WITH CELLULAR + WI-FI)

When the Cellular or Cellular Data option is turned on, your iOS mobile device can access the wireless data network from the wireless service provider to which you're subscribed. When this option is turned off, your device can access the Internet only via a Wi-Fi connection, assuming that a Wi-Fi hotspot is present.

The Data Roaming option appears on the Cellular submenu. When turned on, Data Roaming enables your iPhone or iPad to connect to a cellular network outside the one you subscribe to through your wireless service provider. The capability to tap into another wireless data network might be useful if you must connect to the Internet, there's no Wi-Fi hotspot present, and you're outside your own service provider's coverage area (such as when traveling abroad).

> **CAUTION** When your iPhone or iPad is permitted to roam, you will incur hefty roaming charges, often as high as $20 per megabyte (MB). Refrain from using this feature unless you've prepurchased a cellular data roaming plan through your service provider, or be prepared to pay a fortune to access the Web.

From the Cellular menu within Settings, you can determine which apps and iPhone or iPad features can use your phone or tablet's cellular data network to connect to the Internet. Scroll down and set the virtual switch that's associated with each app or device feature to turn it on or off. When turned on, Internet access via a cellular data network and/or Wi-Fi is granted. When turned off, only Wi-Fi Internet access is granted.

Depending on your service provider, you might be able to transform your iOS device into a personal hotspot so other devices can connect wirelessly to the Internet via Wi-Fi using your iPhone or iPad's cellular data connection. If your provider allows, this option is available from the main Settings menu or within the Cellular submenu.

> **NOTE** To use iOS 8's Continuity and Handoff functions, your iPhone can establish a private wireless hotspot that can be utilized by your own iPad and Mac that are in the immediate area. This enables you to answer incoming calls to your iPhone from your iPad or Mac, for example. This feature is covered in Chapter 4, "Sync, Share, and Print Files Using AirDrop, AirPlay, AirPrint, and Handoff."

The Cellular menu also enables you to track call time (on the iPhone) and cellular data usage.

## NOTIFICATIONS (iPHONE/iPAD)

This Settings option (shown in Figure 1.5) enables you to determine which apps function with Notification Center, plus it enables you to determine the other ways in which apps that generate alerts, alarms, or notifications notify you.

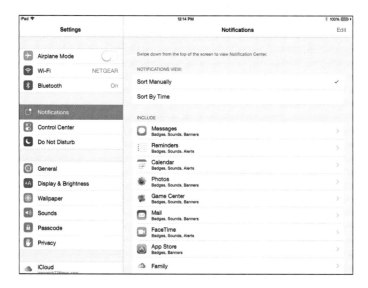

**FIGURE 1.5**

*Apps that are set to exchange data with Notification Center are listed under the heading Include when you select the Notifications option from within the Settings app.*

**WHAT'S NEW** Thanks to iOS 8, you can now customize additional content that's displayed in the Notification Center window, beyond just how alerts, alarms, and notifications are presented. It's now possible to toggle between and personalize the appearance of the Today and Notifications screens, which are part of the Notification Center feature.

Displayed near the top of the Notification Center window are two tabs. The Today tab displays a summary of the day's weather forecast, along with an overview of your appointments and tasks for the day that are stored in the Calendar and Reminders apps. The Notifications tab reveals a listing of alerts and notifications generated by all the apps that Notification Center is monitoring. This includes notification of missed calls and text messages.

When you tap on the Notifications option within Settings and scroll down, a section of the submenu under the Include heading lists apps currently installed on your iPhone or iPad that are compatible with Notification Center, and that are set to automatically share data with Notification Center.

These apps include Phone (iPhone only), Messages, Passbook (iPhone only), Calendar, Reminders, Game Center, Photos, FaceTime, Mail, App Store, Family, Health, Tips, and iTunes Store, which all come preinstalled with iOS 8. However, additional apps that you install later might also be compatible with Notification Center, and will ultimately be listed here as well.

Below the Include heading is another heading, Do Not Include. Here, other apps that are capable of generating alerts, alarms, badges, or notifications are listed. However, the apps listed here are not currently set to exchange data with the Notification Center app.

**TIP** To move an app between the Include and Do Not Include section, tap on its listing under the heading it currently appears, and toggle the virtual switch associated with Allow Notifications to the on or off position. When turned on, the app is monitored by Notification Center and listed under the Include heading. When turned off, the app is ignored by Notification Center and included under the Do Not Include heading.

When the Allow Notifications option is turned on, you'll often see a Show in Notification Center option below it. Tap on this to determine how many app-specific alerts, alarms, or notifications can be displayed at once. Your options include none, 1, 5, 10, or 20 items. If you select the None option, the selected app will not be included in the Allow Notifications section.

As you review each app listed under the Include or the Do Not Include heading, you can tap on it to reveal a secondary submenu pertaining specifically to that app.

The submenu associated with each app related to Notification Center enables you to fully customize how alerts, sounds, and badges generated by that specific app are presented to you. These options vary based on the app listing you select. From here, you can also determine whether app-specific notifications appear on your device's Lock screen and/or whether Badge icons (if applicable) are displayed.

Notifications can be viewed as a banner or alert when using your smartphone or tablet, on the Lock screen, and/or as a badge on the app icon (displayed on the Home screen).

From the Notification Center submenu, one at a time, tap on an app that's listed under the Include menu, such as Calendar (which offers a different selection of options than Messages, for example). Then, adjust the settings listed in its respective submenu screen.

From the Calendar submenu under Notifications (shown in Figure 1.6), once you turn on the virtual switch that's associated with Allow Notifications, and then set the Show in Notification Center option, tap on the Upcoming Events, Invitations, Invitee Responses, and Shared Calendar Changes options one at a time. The new submenu that appears (shown in Figure 1.7) enables you to determine where related notifications are displayed, plus which Alert Style should be used.

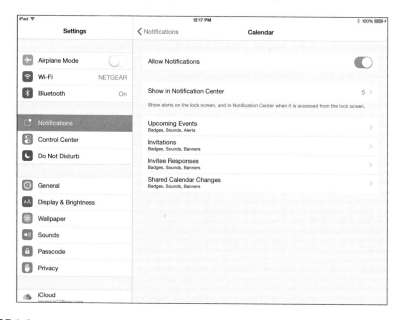

**FIGURE 1.6**

*Depending on the app, there can be several levels of submenus that enable you to customize how each app exchanges information with iOS 8's Notification Center.*

**FIGURE 1.7**

*New options give you greater control over what information is displayed by Notification Center, plus you can choose how, when, and where that information gets displayed.*

By selecting an Alert Style, you can choose whether a banner or alert should be displayed on the screen, even when you are using another app.

If you choose Banners, a pop-up window appears at the top of the screen with the alert-related information. It appears for a few seconds and then automatically disappears. The alert style for the Messages app, for example, defaults to a banner.

If you choose the Alerts option, a pop-up window displays on the iPhone or iPad's screen until you tap on it to dismiss or address the alarm. The Calendar app generates alerts by default if you set an alarm for an upcoming event.

If you select the None option, no app-specific banner or alert is displayed while you're using the iPhone or iPad. A notification can still be displayed in the Notification Center window, however, if the app appears in the Include list in the Notification Center Settings submenu.

By turning on the virtual switch associated with the Badge App Icon option, the app you're customizing can display a badge on the Home screen along with its app icon. Some, but not all, apps can utilize Home screen badges.

NOTE   A badge (as shown in Figure 1.8) is a small red-and-white circular graphic that can appear in the upper-right corner of an app icon on your device's Home screen. The badge contains a number used to graphically show you that something relating to a specific app has changed. For example, a badge appears on your Mail app icon when you've received new incoming email messages, indicating how many new messages were received.

**FIGURE 1.8**

*On this iPhone 5s Home screen, the Phone, Mail, Messages, Facebook, and Apple Insider app icons are all displaying badges.*

Also from the submenu associated with customizing app-specific Notification Center options, you can adjust the Notification Sound that's generated if that app is capable of playing sounds with alerts, alarms, or notifications. From the Calendar submenu in the Notification Center settings, tap on the Upcoming Events option, for example, and then tap on the Notification Sound option to access another submenu that enables you to choose a sound to be associated with event alarms. The default sound for this specific option is called Chord.

Turn on the virtual switch associated with Show In Notification Center if you want alerts related to that app to be displayed in the Notification Center window. Then, when applicable, tap on the Show in Notification Center option to determine how many related alerts generated by the selected app will be listed at any given time in the Notification Center window (shown in Figure 1.9).

**FIGURE 1.9**

*First turn on the Allow Notifications option for an app, and then tap on the Show in Notification Center option to determine how many items may be displayed for that app in the Notification Center window.*

As you're first starting to use this feature, keep the number of alerts manageable by selecting just five per app. You can always add more for specific apps that are more important to you.

Finally, you can determine whether notifications generated by a particular app should be displayed on the Lock screen when your device is otherwise in Sleep mode. When enabled, the phone or tablet is woken up automatically to display new notifications on the Lock screen for anyone to see, without the device first needing to be unlocked.

## NOTIFICATION CENTER QUICK TIPS

- To avoid getting bombarded by excessive notifications from apps that aren't too important to you, manually set the capability of Notification Center to work with specific apps that are important to you.

- At the bottom of the Notification Center settings are two features: AMBER alerts and Emergency Alerts. When turned on, if the government issues an AMBER alert in your area or a message is broadcast over the emergency broadcast system, an alert appears on your device. These features work only with iPhones.

- To protect your privacy, you can set up Notification Center to refrain from having alerts displayed on your Lock screen. To do this, tap on each app under the Include heading, and turn off the Show On Lock Screen option.

- As you customize how Notification Center displays notifications, the options available to you vary by app. For example, for the Messages app, you can assign Notification Center to repeat alerts between one and ten times, at two-minute intervals, to get your attention. You also can opt to preview an incoming message in alerts and banners and in the Notification Center window, plus decide whether you want to be alerted to all incoming messages or just messages from people who have entries in your Contacts database.

## CONTROL CENTER (iPHONE/iPAD)

The Control Center grants you quick access to a handful of smartphone- or tablet-related functions and apps. In the Settings app, tap the Control Center option to choose whether to make the Control Center accessible from the Lock screen or while using an app.

When the Access on Lock Screen option is turned on, you can swipe your finger from the bottom of the screen up to display Control Center from the Lock screen. When the option is turned off, Control Center is accessible only after the device is unlocked. If Access Within Apps is turned off, you can access Control Center from the Home screen but not while you're using an app.

> **TIP**  If you play a lot of games that require a lot of onscreen tapping or swiping at the bottom of the screen, you might want to disable the Control Center option to keep it from opening accidently and disrupting your game. To do this, launch Settings, tap on the Control Center option, and then turn off the virtual switch that's associated with the Access within Apps option.

## DO NOT DISTURB (iPHONE/iPAD)

This feature enables you to temporarily turn off your iPhone or iPad's capability to disturb you with notifications of incoming calls or text messages, as well as app-specific alerts, alarms, or notifications. From the Do Not Disturb menu option within Settings, it's possible to fully customize this feature.

At any time, you can manually turn on the Do Not Disturb feature by turning on the virtual switch that's labeled Manual (shown in Figure 1.10). This feature can also be manually turned on from the Control Center.

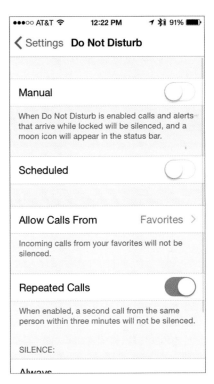

**FIGURE 1.10**

*It's possible to manually turn on the Do Not Disturb feature anytime from the Do Not Disturb submenu within Settings by turning on the Manual virtual switch.*

## GENERAL (iPHONE/iPAD)

When you tap the General option in the Settings app, various other options become available. Unless otherwise noted, each option is available using an iPhone or iPad. Because many of these options remain consistent from iOS 7, only the most important or new settings are discussed here. Thus, some of the General options include the following:

- **Software Update**—Use this option to update the iOS operating system wirelessly, without having to connect your iPhone or iPad to your primary computer and use the iTunes sync procedure.

- **Siri**—Enable or disable Siri functionality on compatible devices, and adjust specific settings related to this feature. See Chapter 2, "Using Siri, Dictation, and CarPlay to Interact with Your Mobile Device," for more information about using Siri.

**TIP** The iPhone offers a Raise To Speak option. When this is turned on, Siri engages anytime you physically pick up the iPhone and hold it up to your ear. Otherwise, you must press and hold down the Home button for about 2 seconds to activate Siri.

**TIP** From the Siri menu in Settings, you can give Siri a male or female voice. To do this, launch the Settings app, access the General menu, and then tap on the Siri option, followed by the Voice Gender option.

- **Spotlight Search**—When you tap this option, you can determine which portions of your iPhone or iPad are searched when you use the Spotlight Search feature built in to the device. In addition, you can now choose to display Internet-related search results by adding a checkmark to the Bing Web Results option displayed as part of the Spotlight Search submenu.

**TIP** To access Spotlight Search from the Home screen, perform a swipe downward that originates from the center of the screen to make the Spotlight Search screen appear. If you swipe from the top of the screen, you open the Notification Center, so be sure your swipe originates from the center. Separate Search fields also appear in some other apps.

**WHAT'S NEW**   With Spotlight Search, turn on the Location Services feature. This enables you to locate nearby businesses or points of interest as part of your Spotlight Search results. For example, if you enter "Chinese Food" in the Spotlight Search field, listings for local Chinese food restaurants are displayed (shown in Figure 1.11). Tap on one of these listings to launch the Maps app and learn more about it.

**FIGURE 1.11**

*Spotlight Search now gathers information from the Internet based on the words or phrases you enter into the Search field. So, if you enter "Chinese Food," for example, the locations of local Chinese restaurants are displayed.*

■ **Handoff & Suggested Apps**—This new iOS 8 feature enables you to start performing a task on one iOS mobile device (or Mac) and continue it on another Mac or iOS mobile device that's linked to the same iCloud account. This feature must be turned on from within Settings. Turn on the virtual switch associated with the Handoff option. From this submenu, you can also turn on or off the Suggested Apps feature, which enables the App Store to recommend specific apps based on your location or that are relevant to what you're working on. These recommendations appear in the app switcher.

■ **Multitasking Gestures (iPad)**—There are several iPad-exclusive finger gestures for interacting with the multitouch display. You can opt to turn on or off recognition of these gestures by adjusting the virtual on/off switch that's associated with the Multitasking Gestures option. The gestures are listed on the General submenu beneath this option.

■ **Use Side Switch To (iPad)**—Located on the right side of your iPad just above the volume button is a tiny switch. From the General Settings menu, you can set this switch to be used as either a Lock Rotation switch or a Mute switch.

If you choose Lock Rotation, when the switch is turned on, you can physically rotate your iPad but the screen does not automatically switch between landscape and portrait mode.

When it's used as a Mute switch, this turns off the iPad's built-in speaker so that no sounds are heard, such as alarms. This is useful when using your iPad in a meeting or in a quiet area, such as a library.

> ☑ **TIP**  On the iPhone, the Ring/Silent switch silences call-related ringers and many alert sounds that your iPhone is capable of generating. It is located on the left side of the handset, above the Volume Up and Volume Down buttons.

> ☑ **TIP**  You can also turn on/off Lock Rotation from Control Center (iPhone or iPad). To do this, swipe your finger upward from the bottom of the screen to access Control Center, and then tap on the Rotation Lock icon.

■ **Usage**—Tap on this option to see how the storage capacity of your device and your iCloud account are being utilized. From the Battery Usage option displayed on this screen, you can choose to display your device's battery life as a numeric percentage (for example, 73%) alongside the battery icon graphic.

■ **Background App Refresh**—This enhanced feature enables you to control the capability of apps to automatically access the Internet to refresh app-specific content and/or Location Services data when the device has Internet access.

■ **Auto-Lock**—Anytime your iPhone or iPad is turned on, if you don't do anything for a predetermined amount of time, it can be set to automatically switch into Sleep mode to conserve battery life and secure it.

■ **Restrictions**—This feature provides a way to "childproof" your iPhone or iPad by enabling a user to gain access to only specific apps or content. To activate it, tap the Restrictions option and then tap Enable Restrictions from the submenu. Set a passcode for the restrictions. You can then customize which apps are allowed, block the installation or deletion of apps, prevent in-app purchases, or set ratings limits for content.

**! CAUTION** If you choose to utilize this feature, make sure you remember the passcode you associate with it. If you forget the passcode, it might be necessary to erase your entire iOS device and reload everything from scratch.

■ **Keyboard**—You can make certain customizations from the Settings screen that impact how your virtual keyboard responds as you're typing. Tap on the Keyboard option when using the Settings app to discover whether several customizable settings, such as whether Auto-Capitalization, Auto-Correction, and Check Spelling, are turned on.

**(iOS 8) WHAT'S NEW** From the Keyboards submenu within Settings, it's possible to turn on/off the new Predictive (also referred to as QuickType) feature. This enables your iPhone or iPad to automatically figure out what you're typing and make intelligent suggestions that are context specific.

■ **Reset (iPhone/iPad)**—Every so often, you might run in to a problem with your iPhone or iPad such that the system crashes or you need to reset specific settings. For example, to restore your iPhone or iPad to its factory default settings and erase everything stored on it, tap on the Reset option, and then tap on the Erase All Content and Settings option. In general, you should refrain from using any of these settings unless you're instructed to do so by an Apple Genius or a technical support person.

**! CAUTION** Before using any of the options found under the Settings Reset option, which could potentially erase important data from your iPhone or iPad, be sure to perform an iTunes sync or back up your device wirelessly to iCloud and create a reliable backup of your device's contents. See Chapter 5 for step-by-step directions for how to do this.

You'll probably never need to tinker with or adjust several options found under the General heading. Leave them at their default settings. Others you'll need to utilize often as you use your iPhone or iPad for different tasks.

## DISPLAY & BRIGHTNESS (iPHONE/iPAD)

The Display & Brightness options enable you to control the brightness of your iPhone or iPad's screen, plus customize the default text size and typestyle. In general, you should leave the virtual switch for the Auto-Brightness feature turned on, and then only use the Brightness slider when you manually need to adjust the screen to accommodate a specific lighting situation.

Drag the white dot on the Auto-Brightness slider to the right to make the screen brighter or to the left to make the screen darker.

When the Auto-Brightness virtual switch is turned on, your device takes into account the surrounding lighting where you're using your Phone or iPad, and then adjusts the screen's brightness accordingly. This can also be set from the Control Center. In addition, some apps, such as iBooks, have their own Brightness sliders built in to the app.

## WALLPAPER (iPHONE/iPAD)

The capability to choose a custom graphic to be used as the wallpaper behind your device's Lock and Home screen now has its own option within Settings. From the main Settings menu, tap on the Wallpaper option to adjust this.

Your iPhone or iPad has more than two dozen preinstalled wallpaper designs built in, plus you can use any digital images stored on your device (in the Photos app) as your Lock screen or Home screen wallpaper. In Figure 1.12, you see a thumbnail graphic of your iPhone or iPad's Lock screen (left) and its Home screen (right).

To change the Wallpaper, tap on the Choose a New Wallpaper option. Then you have three options. Tap on the Dynamic or Stills thumbnail to reveal iOS 8's built-in Wallpaper options, or select a photo from an Album that's listed under the Photos heading (shown in Figure 1.13).

**FIGURE 1.12**

*Tap on the Choose a New Wallpaper option to select a new graphic or photo to be used behind your Lock and/or Home screen as a Wallpaper.*

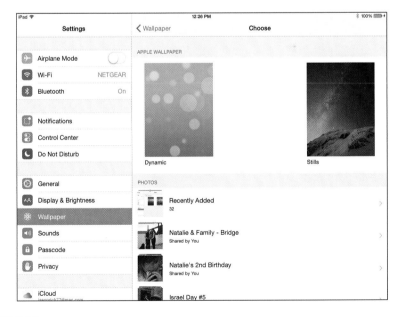

**FIGURE 1.13**

*Tap on Dynamic, Stills, or an Album thumbnail that's displayed under the Photos heading to select a specific graphic or image to use as your wallpaper.*

> ## NOTE
> If you select an Apple wallpaper for your Lock screen or Home screen, you can choose between a dynamic or still wallpaper. The dynamic wallpapers are animated and appear multidimensional, while the still images are static.

Next, the graphic or image you select is displayed in full-screen mode. In the bottom-right corner of the iPad screen are three command options, labeled Set Lock Screen, Set Home Screen, and Set Both.

On the iPhone, after tapping on your wallpaper selection, tap the Set button, and then select whether to set the Lock screen, Home screen, or both to display that graphic.

After making your selection, when you return to the iPhone or iPad's Lock screen or Home screen, you see your newly selected wallpaper graphic displayed.

Instead of choosing one of the preinstalled wallpaper graphics, you also have the option of using photos you've transferred to your iOS device and have stored in the Photos app or photos you've shot using the Camera app. To select one of your own photos to use as your Lock screen or Home screen wallpaper, tap on the Wallpaper option in Settings, followed by the Choose a New Wallpaper option. Next, tap on an Album thumbnail that's listed under the Photos heading.

When the thumbnails related to the contents of the image Album you selected are displayed, tap on the thumbnail that represents the image you want to use as your Wallpaper. As soon as a preview screen is displayed, if necessary, use your finger to move the image around on the screen. You can also zoom in or out, in some cases. When this is possible, the Perspective Zoom On/Off option will be displayed in the lower-right corner of the preview screen.

Now, tap on the Set Lock Screen, Set Home Screen, or Set Both option to save your selection. Figure 1.14 shows a custom Lock screen on an iPhone, while Figure 1.15 shows a custom Home screen on an iPad.

> ## CAUTION
> If the image you opt to use is not sized appropriately for both the portrait and landscape aspect ratio on the iOS mobile device's screen, the image can appear distorted or not fill the entire screen when you rotate your device.

**FIGURE 1.14**

*A newly selected Lock screen graphic, chosen from a photo stored on the iPhone 5s in the Photos app.*

**(iOS 8) WHAT'S NEW** To see which apps require the most battery power at any given time, launch Settings, tap on the General option, tap on the Usage option, and then tap in the Battery Usage option that's displayed near the top of the Usage submenu screen. When the Battery Usage screen appears, you will see a listing of apps that are actively draining your iPhone or iPad's battery.

**FIGURE 1.15**

*A still wallpaper selected from within Settings is now displayed as the Home screen wallpaper, behind the app icons (shown here on the iPad).*

## SOUNDS (iPHONE/iPAD)

Tap on this option to adjust the overall volume of the iPhone or iPad's built-in speaker (or the volume of the audio you hear through headsets), as well as to turn on or off various audible tones and alarms your phone or tablet generates.

From this menu, you can also assign specific audio tones, sounds, or ringtones to specific types of app-specific alerts and alarms, plus turn on or off the click noise associated with pressing keys on the iPhone or iPad's virtual keyboard.

It's also possible to turn on the Vibrate mode so that the iPhone handset shakes, instead of or in addition to playing a ringtone. You can control the ringer volume using an onscreen slider and adjust the custom ringtones and audio alerts associated with various features and functions of your iPhone. Your iPhone has an all-new library of different audio alarms and alerts, as well as ringtones built in, plus you can download additional ringtones from iTunes.

> **TIP** In addition to customizing ringtones and the wallpaper, it's possible to customize the vibration patterns used by your device, such as when an incoming call is received. To do this, launch Settings, tap on the Sounds option, and from under the Sounds and Vibration Patterns heading, tap on any of the listed options, such as Ringtone or New Mail.
>
> Next, tap on the Vibration option that's displayed at the top of the submenu for the option you selected. Choose one of the patterns from the Vibration submenu, or tap on Create New Vibration to create your own pattern for the selected option.

> **TIP** On your iPhone, you can manually adjust the ringer and speaker volume using the Volume Up and Volume Down buttons located on the left side of your handset. You also can control the vibration of the phone and choose different vibration patterns to alert you of different things. This can be customized from the Sounds menu within Settings. Volume controls are also accessible from the Control Center.

## TOUCH ID & PASSCODE (NEWER iPHONES AND iPADS)

Determine whether your iOS mobile device's Touch ID (Home button sensor) can be used to identify your fingerprint and unlock the device and/or approve online purchases. A separate option must be turned on when using the iPhone 6 or iPhone 6 Plus to activate the Apple Pay feature. Tap on one of the Finger options displayed as part of this menu to scan and store your fingerprint(s).

> **TIP** Consider storing the fingerprint for the thumb and index finger on both of your hands, so you can use Touch ID with any of those fingers based on how you're holding the device.

## PRIVACY (iPHONE/iPAD)

This menu option in Settings gives you much greater privacy control in terms of how information is shared between apps and shared with other people.

From this Settings submenu screen, you can control specifically which apps have access to the iOS device's Location Services feature, for example, plus which other apps can share data with certain pre-installed apps (including Contacts, Calendar, Reminders, and Photos).

Certain apps and services, such as Maps, HomeKit, or Find My iPhone (or Find My iPad), utilize the capability to pinpoint your exact location. It's important to customize the Location Services options if you're concerned that certain apps can potentially share this information.

When the master virtual switch for Location Services option is turned on, your iPhone or iPad can fully utilize its GPS capabilities, in addition to crowd-sourced Wi-Fi hotspots and cell towers, to determine your exact location. When it's turned off, your device cannot determine (or broadcast) your location. However, some of your apps will not function properly.

> **TIP**   When the Location Services option is turned on and you snap a photo or shoot video using the Camera app, the exact location where that photo or video was shot is recorded and saved. This feature is deactivated if you turn off the Location Services option. You can also leave the master Location Services feature for your device turned on, but turn off this feature with specific apps, such as the Camera app.

> **NOTE**   From the Privacy menu within Settings, you determine which apps can share information with each other and with the public when you use Facebook, Twitter, or other online social networking apps. Click on the Advertising option from the Privacy menu to turn off the Limit Ad Tracking option. Ad Tracking helps to determine which ads you see in Safari when surfing the Web or which in-app ads are displayed when using advertiser-supported apps based on your past web searches and activity.

## iCLOUD (iPHONE/iPAD)

You learn all about using iCloud with your iPhone or iPad in Chapter 5.

## iTUNES & APP STORE (iPHONE/iPAD)

From this menu within Settings, you can determine whether you see all iTunes content you own when you use the Music or Video app, or if only content that is currently stored in your device is displayed. Plus, you can turn on/off the optional (fee-based) iTunes Match service on the device you're using.

From under the Automatic Downloads heading, turn on or off the virtual switches associated with Music, Apps, Books, and Updates to determine whether each type of content should automatically be downloaded to the device you're currently using, even if it's purchased on other Mac or iOS mobile devices that are linked to the same iCloud account (or Family Sharing account).

It's also possible to turn on/off the Suggested Apps option, which enables your device to recommend optional apps based on your location or what you're currently doing.

## MAIL, CONTACTS, CALENDARS (iPHONE/iPAD)

If you use your iPhone or iPad on the job, three apps you probably rely on heavily are Mail, Contacts, and Calendars. From the Settings app, you can customize a handful of options pertaining to each of these apps. From here, you also must set up your existing email account(s) to work with your smartphone or tablet.

For information about how to use the Settings app to customize the Mail app-related settings, see Chapter 11, "Send and Receive Emails, Texts, and Instant Messages with the Mail and Messages Apps." You can find details about customizing the settings of the Contacts and Calendar apps in Chapter 13, "Tips for Using Calendar, Contacts, Reminders, and Notes."

**TIP** Under the Calendars heading of the Mail, Contacts, Calendars option, one useful setting is Default Alert Time. Tapping on this option reveals the Default Alert Times menu screen, from which you can automatically set advance alarms for birthdays, events, and all-day events stored in your Calendar app. Each of these options can be individually set to alert you at 9:00 a.m. on the day of the event, one or two days prior, or one week before the event, based on your preference.

If you fill in the Birthday field as you create contact entries in the Contacts app, these dates can automatically be displayed in the Calendar app to remind you of birthdays. The advance warning of a birthday gives you ample time to send a card or a gift.

## MORE APP-SPECIFIC OPTIONS WITHIN SETTINGS

As you scroll down on the main Settings menu on your iPhone or iPad, you'll see specific apps listed, including some of the core preinstalled apps (such as Notes, Reminders, Messages, FaceTime, Maps, Safari, Music, Videos, Photos & Camera, iBooks, Podcasts, and Game Center).

As you continue scrolling down, listings for Twitter, Facebook, Flickr, and Vimeo lead to submenus that offer the capability to fully customize integration with these online social networking services with many of the apps you'll soon be using.

**(iOS 8) WHAT'S NEW** Podcasts and iBooks were previously optional apps available from the App Store. These two apps now come preinstalled on your iPhone or iPad as part of iOS 8. Podcasts is used to subscribe and listen to free, on-demand audio- or video-based podcasts. The iBooks app enables you to acquire, manage, and read eBooks on your iPhone or iPad.

The iPhone also comes with the new Health app preinstalled. Learn more about this cutting-edge app, and how it can be used with an Apple Watch, in Chapter 10, "Improve Your Health and Automate Your Home Using Your iOS Mobile Device."

### USER-INSTALLED APPS

By scrolling toward the bottom of the Settings menu, you'll discover a listing of other individual apps that you have installed on your iPhone or iPad and that have user-adjustable options or settings available. Tap on one app listing at a time to modify these settings. Remember, as you install new apps in the future, additional app listings will be added to this section of the Settings menu and can be modified accordingly.

## CONTROL CENTER GIVES YOU QUICK ACCESS TO POPULAR FEATURES AND FUNCTIONS

At any time, regardless of what you're doing on your iPhone or iPad, it's possible to access the Control Center. To do this, simply place your finger near the bottom of the screen and swipe upward. This causes the Control Center window to appear (shown in Figure 1.16).

**(iOS 8) WHAT'S NEW** If you are using an iPhone 6, iPhone 6 Plus, iPad Air 2, or iPad mini 3, a new option available from Settings, called Passbook and Apple Pay, enables you to set up and customize the new Apple Pay service to work with your mobile device.

**FIGURE 1.16**

*The Control Center window on the iPhone.*

On the iPhone, several circular icons appear near the top of the Control Center window, each of which enables you to control a frequently used iPhone feature. From left to right, the icons include

■ **Airplane Mode**—Quickly place your iPhone or iPad into Airplane mode.

■ **Wi-Fi**—Turn Wi-Fi on or off with a single tap, without having to access Settings.

■ **Bluetooth**—Turn Bluetooth on or off so that your iPhone or iPad can link to Bluetooth devices it has already been paired with.

■ **Do Not Disturb**—Manually turn on the Do Not Disturb feature after you've customized this option from within Settings.

■ **Rotation Lock**—Normally, when you rotate your iPhone sideways, the screen automatically switches from portrait to landscape mode. To prevent this from happening when the phone is rotated, turn on the Rotation Lock feature by tapping on its icon.

> **!CAUTION**    If you turn on the Rotation Lock, this could prevent you from accessing certain app-specific features or views, depending on which app you're using. For example, turning on Rotation Lock prevents you from using the Week view in the Calendar app.

Displayed below these icons is the screen brightness slider, and below that are the Music app controls, which enable you to play currently selected music (or Playlists) without launching the Music app.

Moving down within Control Center, there are two additional command buttons, labeled AirDrop (left) and AirPlay (right). Tap on AirDrop to quickly activate this feature and determine which content or data you want to wirelessly share with nearby iPhone or iPad users. Tap the AirPlay button to select where AirPlay-compatible apps will direct content.

> **TIP**    When AirDrop is turned on, your iPhone or iPad is discoverable by any iPhone, iPad, or Mac user that's in your immediate vicinity that also has the AirDrop feature turned on (or just by people included in your Contacts database). You can then wirelessly transfer data from certain apps, such as Contacts and Photos. To protect your privacy when out in public, consider keeping this feature turned off unless you specifically want to use it.

Displayed along the bottom of the Control Center window on the iPhone are four app-related icons. Tap on the flashlight icon to turn on the iPhone's flash so that it serves as a bright flashlight. Tap on the alarm icon to set and manage alarms. This serves as a shortcut to the Clock app. Tap on the Calculator icon to launch the Calculator app quickly. Finally, tapping on the Camera icon offers yet another way to quickly launch the Camera app and begin snapping photos.

The Control Center on the iPad is similar to that of the iPhone; however, as you can see from Figure 1.17, the layout of the options is different. The Control Center on the tablet is displayed as a bar across the bottom of the screen.

**FIGURE 1.17**

*The Control Center feature on the iPad.*

The Music controls and volume slider are displayed on the left, the five command icons (Airplane Mode, Wi-Fi, Bluetooth, Do Not Disturb, and Rotation Lock) are displayed near the center, and the Clock/Alarm and Camera app icons and screen brightness slider can be found on the right. The AirDrop and AirPlay icons are displayed near the bottom center of the Control Center window.

To close the Control Center window, tap anywhere near the top of the iPhone's screen, or tap on the down-pointing arrow icon that's displayed near the top of the window.

# ORGANIZE APPS ON YOUR HOME SCREEN WITH FOLDERS

If you're like most iPhone and iPad users, you'll probably be loading a handful of third-party apps onto your device. After all, there are 1.3 million third-party apps to choose from. To make finding and organizing your apps easier from the iPhone or iPad's Home screen, and to reduce onscreen clutter, you can place app icons in folders.

Utilizing the Folders feature is easy. From the Home screen, press and hold down any app icon until all the app icons begin shaking on the Home screen. Using your finger, drag one app icon on top of another, to automatically place both of those apps into a new folder.

You can organize your apps in folders based on categories, like Games, Travel, or Productivity (shown in Figure 1.18), or you can enter your own folder names, and then drag and drop the additional app icons into the folders you create. After your app icons are organized, simply press the Home button again on the iPhone or iPad to save your folders and display them on your Home screen.

Games Folder

**FIGURE 1.18**

*On this iPad, a Games folder has been created.*

To open a folder, tap on its icon that's displayed on the Home screen. Tap on any of the contained app icons to launch one of the apps. Figure 1.19 shows a Games folder that contains eight popular game apps.

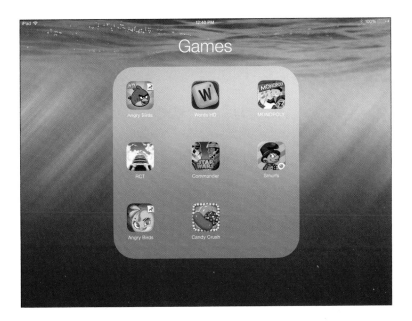

**FIGURE 1.19**

*This Games folder was created to organize the eight game apps currently installed on this iPad Air. Using folders helps to eliminate clutter on your Home screen.*

> **NOTE** As you're creating app folders, you are no longer limited in terms of how many apps you can place into each folder.

If you later want to remove an app icon from a folder so that it appears as a standalone app icon on your Home screen, simply press and hold any of the folder icons until all the onscreen icons start to shake. The folder's contents are displayed.

When the app icons are shaking, simply drag the app icons, one at a time, back onto the Home screen. Each is then removed from the folder. Press the Home button to finalize this action.

## MOVING APP ICONS AROUND ON THE HOME SCREEN

To move app icons around and reorganize them on the Home screen, press and hold down any app icon with your finger. When the app icons start to shake, you can use your finger to drag one app icon at a time around on the Home screen.

Your iPhone or iPad can extend the Home screen across multiple pages. (Switch pages by swiping your finger from left to right, or right to left when viewing the Home screen.) To move an app icon to another Home screen page, while it's shaking, hold it down with your finger and slowly drag it to the extreme right or left, off of the screen, so that it bounces onto another of the Home screen's pages.

When you switch pages, the row of up to four app icons displayed at the very bottom of the iPhone's screen (or up to six app icons on the iPad's screen) remains constant. Place your most frequently used apps in these positions so that they're always visible from the Home screen.

As the app icons are shaking on the Home screen, you can delete the icons that display a black-and-white "X" in the upper-left corner from your iPhone or iPad by pressing that "X" icon. The preinstalled (core) apps related to iOS 8, such as Contacts, Calendar, Reminders, Notes, App Store, and Settings, cannot be deleted. They can only be moved.

> **TIP**  Although it is not possible to delete any of the apps that come preinstalled on your iPhone or iPad, you can place the core apps that you seldom or never use in a separate folder to remove unwanted clutter from your Home screen.

# ADD FREQUENTLY USED WEB PAGE ICONS TO YOUR HOME SCREEN

Many people constantly return to their favorite websites for updates throughout the day or week. Instead of first accessing the Safari browser on your iPhone or iPad, and then choosing your favorite sites from your Bookmarks list, it's possible to create individual icons for your favorite web pages and display them on your Home screen. This enables you to access that web page with a single tap of the finger from the Home screen.

Depending on the website, when you create a web page icon, it either uses a thumbnail image from the website itself or a predesigned logo or graphic. In Figure 1.20, the Jason Rich's Featured App of the Week icon shows a thumbnail for this iPhone/iPad-related blog, while the CNN icon is for CNN.com.

CNN.com Web Page Icon

Jason Rich's Featured App of
the Week Blog Web Page Icon

**FIGURE 1.20**

*A web page icon (such as the one for Jason Rich's Featured App of the Week blog or CNN.com)
on your Home screen looks similar to an app icon; however, when you tap it, Safari is launched
and the web page that the icon is associated with is loaded automatically.*

To create a web page icon on your Home screen, access Safari and visit your
favorite web page. Next, tap the Share icon that's located to the immediate right
of the Address Bar, and tap the Add to Home Screen option that appears (shown
in Figure 1.21).

**FIGURE 1.21**

*To create a web page icon that appears on your Home screen, use the Add to Home Screen command displayed when you tap the Share icon in Safari (shown here on the iPhone 5s).*

The menu that appears when you tap on the Share icon contains several features, which you'll learn more about in Chapter 12, "Surf the Web More Efficiently Using Safari."

When you return to your Home screen, the icon for that web page is now displayed and looks very much like an app icon. To access that web page in the future, simply tap the appropriate icon on the Home screen.

# DISCOVER WHAT'S NOW POSSIBLE FROM THE LOCK SCREEN

iOS 8 offers additional functionality that you can access directly from the Lock screen. From within Settings, however, you can opt to turn off most of this functionality to protect your privacy. Thus, if you turn on Passcode Lock, strangers cannot pick up and use your phone or tablet or access any content from it.

The Lock screen automatically displays the current time and date, the Slide To Unlock feature, as well as the Camera icon. You can also set it up so app-specific alerts or banners are displayed on the Lock screen when applicable, plus you can decide whether you want the ability to access the Control Center directly from the Lock screen. These features can be customized from within Settings.

(iOS 8) **WHAT'S NEW** To unlock the Lock screen and access your Home screen, it's now possible to swipe anywhere on the screen from left to right. You no longer have to place your finger directly on the Slide To Unlock slider.

# MANAGE YOUR CUSTOMIZED NOTIFICATION CENTER SCREEN

Accessing the Notification Center window/screen from the iPhone or iPad at anytime continues to be possible simply by placing your finger near the top of the screen and swiping downward. From the newly designed Notification Center, you can see all alerts, alarms, and notifications generated by your device in one place.

As you now know, the Notification Center screen displays additional content beyond just app-specific notifications. For example, along the top of the Notification Center are two commands: Today and Notifications. Tap on Today to see the current day and date, along with the weather forecast, plus a preview of upcoming appointments from the Calendar app. Scroll down on this screen to see a preview of tomorrow's schedule.

Tap on the Notifications tab to see items recently generated by all compatible apps running on your phone or tablet. The name and app icon for each compatible app is displayed, followed by the preselected number of alerts, alarms, or notifications related to that app. (Keep in mind that which apps are displayed and how many alerts, alarms, or notifications from each app can be customized from within Settings.)

To clear all notifications related to an app that's displayed in Notification Center, tap on the small "X" icon that's displayed to the right of the app's name and icon.

**☑️ TIP** To control the order in which app-related alerts, alarms, and notifications are displayed in the Notification Center window/screen, launch Settings, select the Notifications option, and then under the Notifications View, tap on the Sort Manually option. Then, tap on the Edit option (near the top-right corner of the screen) and use your finger to move apps listed under the Include heading either up or down on the list. To do this, hold your finger on the Move icon that's displayed to the right of each app listing, and then drag it.

To view this information by the date and time each alert, alarm, or notification was generated, select the Sort By Time option instead.

**(iOS 8) WHAT'S NEW** When viewing a notification, swipe upward to dismiss the alert, alarm, or notification, or swipe downward on the item to launch the appropriate app and view whatever the alert, alarm, or notification was related to.

For example, if you swipe downward on an alert for an incoming text message, the Messages app launches, the incoming message is displayed, and you can immediately respond to it.

When viewing an item from within Notification Center, swipe sideways to access a mini-menu of available options, or tap on the item to launch the related app to review the item. When looking at incoming email message items from within Notification Center (shown in Figure 1.22), for example, swipe from right to left across the listing to reveal an "X," Mark As Read, and Trash button pertaining to that message. Menu options vary based on what app the item is related to.

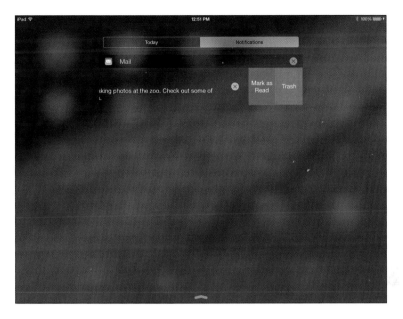

**FIGURE 1.22**

*New mini menus are available from the Notification Center window when you swipe sideways (right to left) across an item listing.*

**(iOS 8) WHAT'S NEW** If you turn on the Handoff feature, you can begin using an app on your Mac or another iOS mobile device, and then pick up exactly where you left off on the mobile device you are currently using. If the Handoff feature is available when you begin using an iPhone or iPad, an icon for the active app you were previously using on another device will be displayed in the bottom-left corner of the Lock screen. Place your finger on this icon and flick upward to launch that app.

## IN THIS CHAPTER

- Introduce yourself to Siri
- How to use Siri with your iPhone or iPad
- Use the Dictation feature as an alternative to the virtual keyboard
- Use your iPhone "Siri Eyes Free" with CarPlay in your vehicle

2

# USING SIRI, DICTATION, AND CARPLAY TO INTERACT WITH YOUR MOBILE DEVICE

Siri is designed to be a virtual assistant that responds to commands, questions, and requests that you say, as opposed to type into your mobile device. Siri has access to the content stored in your iPhone or iPad, as well as an arsenal of Internet-based resources that can be used to quickly gather information that you need within seconds after you state your request.

**iOS 8 WHAT'S NEW** Siri is constantly evolving. The biggest iOS 8 enhancement is the "Hey Siri" feature. When your iPhone or iPad is plugged in to an external power source, simply say, "Hey Siri," to activate Siri. When you do this, the familiar, "What can I help you with?" screen appears and you hear Siri's "ready" tone.

Of course, you can also press and hold down the Home button for 2 seconds or turn on the Raise to Speak feature on your iPhone to activate Siri.

It's possible to deactivate this feature from the Siri menu within Settings. Simply turn off the virtual switch that's associated with the Allow "Hey Siri" option.

Thanks to Siri, instead of having to utilize the touchscreen to interact with your phone or tablet, simply use your voice and speak using normal sentences after the feature has been activated. There are no commands to memorize.

It's important to realize that Siri does not understand everything, and this feature does have its limitations in terms of what it can do and which apps it works with. When you get accustomed to working with Siri, however, this feature can make you more efficient when using your iPhone or iPad.

In addition to using cutting-edge voice recognition, Siri uses advanced artificial intelligence, so it doesn't just understand what you say, it interprets and comprehends what you mean, and then translates your speech to text. And if you don't initially provide the information Siri needs to complete your request or command, you're prompted for more information.

**TIP** To get the most out of the Siri feature, turn on your iOS device's master Location Services functionality, and then make sure Location Services is set up to work with Siri.

To do this, launch Settings, tap on the Privacy option, and then tap on the Location Services option. Turn on the virtual switch that's associated with Location Services, as well as the virtual switch that's associated with the Siri option.

## WHAT YOU SHOULD KNOW BEFORE USING SIRI

For Siri to operate, your phone or tablet must have access to the Internet via a cellular or Wi-Fi connection. Every time you make a request or issue a command to Siri, your iOS mobile device connects to Apple's data center. Thus, if you're using a cellular data connection, some of your monthly wireless data allocation gets used up (if cellular data allocation, such as 2GB per month, is imposed by your wireless service provider).

> ☑ **TIP**   Because a Wi-Fi connection is typically significantly faster than a cellular data connection, Siri often responds faster to your requests and commands when you use a Wi-Fi connection.

You should also understand that heavy use of the Internet, especially when connected via a cellular data connection, depletes the battery life of the iPhone or iPad faster. So, if you constantly rely on Siri throughout the day, the battery life of your device will be shorter.

> **! CAUTION**   If your iPhone or iPad is placed in Airplane mode (and Wi-Fi connectivity is turned off), Siri does not function. You'll receive a verbal message stating that Siri is unavailable.

## CUSTOMIZING SIRI

To customize the Siri feature, launch Settings, tap on the General option, and then tap on the Siri option. From the Siri submenu (shown in Figure 2.1), there's a master switch for turning on/off this feature. You can also turn on/off the "Hey Siri" function with the virtual switch that's labeled Voice Activation.

**FIGURE 2.1**

*You can customize Siri from within Settings. This needs to be done only once; however, you can alter these settings whenever you wish.*

Tap the Language option to select your native language, and then tap on the Voice Gender option to choose between giving Siri a male or female voice. Siri functions the same as a male or female, so which voice you choose is a matter of personal preference.

The Voice Feedback option enables you to control whether Siri speaks its responses to each request, or just displays related content on the iPhone or iPad's screen. When using the hands-free capabilities of Siri in your car, no content is displayed on the screen. Siri says everything, so you can keep your eyes on the road.

It's important that Siri be able to greet you properly. Thus, tap on the My Info option and then select your own entry from your Contacts database. Within this entry, be sure to include as much information as possible because Siri uses this information to assist you. For example, if you have a Home and Work address in your own Contacts entry, from anywhere you are, you can activate Siri and say, "How do I get home from here?" or "How do I get to work from here?," and Siri knows exactly where you're talking about.

> **✓ TIP** By default, Siri addresses you by your first name, based on the information in your own Contacts entry. However, at anytime, you can activate Siri and say, "Siri, call me [insert nickname]." Siri remembers your request and addresses you by that name in the future.

At the bottom of the Siri menu on the iPhone, the Raise To Speak option is listed. When the switch is turned on, Siri automatically activates when you pick up the phone and hold it up to your ear.

> **✓ TIP** Siri also utilizes information stored in the Related Name fields as you create or edit a contact in the Contacts app. By tapping on this field, you can add a relationship title, such as mother, father, brother, or sister. Then, when using Siri, if you say, "Call Mom at home," Siri knows exactly to whom you're referring. Otherwise, if you activate Siri and say, "Call my mom at home," the first time you use Siri for this task, you're asked who your mother is. As long as you have a Contact entry for your mother stored in the Contacts app, when you say your mother's real name, Siri links the appropriate contact and remembers this information. This applies to any nickname or title you have for other people, such as "wife," "son," "mother," "dad," or even "Uncle Jack."

## WAYS TO ACTIVATE SIRI

If you want to use the Siri feature, you first must activate it. There are five ways to do this:

- Use the "Hey Siri" function when your iOS mobile device is plugged in. As long as your iPhone or iPad is turned on, anytime you say, "Hey Siri," the device activates Siri. This works when the device is in Sleep mode but not when the iPhone or iPad is powered off altogether.
- Press and hold the Home button on your iPhone or iPad for 2 seconds.
- Pick up your iPhone and hold it up to your ear. Siri activates automatically, assuming this feature has been turned on in Settings.
- Press and hold the Call button on your wireless Bluetooth headset that is paired with your iPhone or iPad. This enables you to speak to Siri on your device from up to 30 feet away.
- If you're using Apple EarPods or an original Apple headset (headphones), press the middle button on the controls found on the cable.

> ☑ TIP   If you're using your iOS device with a Bluetooth headset, when you activate Siri, to the right of the microphone icon will be a Bluetooth icon. Tap on it to choose between using the iPhone's built-in microphone or your headset's microphone when talking to Siri.

When Siri is activated, the message, "What can I help you with?" displays on the screen, along with a circular microphone icon. You'll simultaneously hear Siri's activation tone. As you're speaking, the microphone icon transforms into an animated sound wave graphic (shown in Figure 2.2).

**FIGURE 2.2**

*When Siri is activated, the "What can I help you with?" message appears, and you hear Siri's activation tone.*

Do not start speaking to Siri until this tone is heard. Then, you have about 5 seconds to begin speaking before the microphone deactivates. To reactivate it, simply tap on the microphone icon or repeat one of the previously mentioned steps.

As soon as you hear Siri's activation tone, speak your question, command, or request. For the most accurate results when using Siri, speak directly into the iPhone, iPad, or headset. Try to avoid being in areas with excessive background noise. Also, speak as clearly as possible so Siri can understand each word in your sentences.

# DISCOVER HOW SIRI CAN HELP YOU

The great thing about Siri is that you don't have to think too much about how you phrase a command, question, or request. Siri automatically interprets what you say.

**(iOS 8) WHAT'S NEW** When you're in a quiet area, you can press and hold down the Home button for 2 seconds to activate Siri, and then speak your question, command, or request. Simply stop speaking when you're finished, and Siri responds accordingly.

However, if you're in a noisy area, Siri might have trouble determining when you've stopped speaking. To avoid this problem, press and hold down the Home button as you speak to Siri. When you're finished speaking, release the Home button so Siri can process your request.

To get the most out of using Siri—with the least amount of frustration as a result of Siri not being able to comply with your requests—you must develop a basic understanding of which apps this feature works with and how Siri can be used with those apps.

In general, Siri can be used with most of the apps that come preinstalled with iOS 8, plus Siri can find information on the Internet by performing web searches. You can use Dictation mode, however, in any app where the microphone key appears on the iPhone or iPad's virtual keyboard.

**NOTE** Dictation mode offers an easy way to speak into your iPhone or iPad and have what you say translated into text and inserted into the app you're using, instead of typing.

The following sections provide a sampling of what Siri can be used for and tips for how to use Siri effectively. Apple and third-party app developers are continuously working to upgrade Siri's capabilities, so you might discover additional functionality as you begin using Siri with various apps.

## SIRI QUICK TIPS

- Siri is one of the few features that work from the Lock screen. Thus, even if you have the Passcode Lock feature turned on, someone can potentially pick up your device and access your data using Siri without your permission. To keep this from happening, set up the Passcode feature on your device. Then, turn off the Siri option in the TouchID & Passcode options of the Settings app.

- Siri can be used to verbally launch any app. To do this, activate Siri and say, "Launch [app name]." If it's a game you want to play, simply say, "Play [game name]." Another option is to say, "Open [app name]."

- For more information about how Siri can be used, activate Siri and say, "What can you do?" or tap on the Help ("?") icon that's displayed on the screen when Siri is activated.

> **(iOS 8) WHAT'S NEW** Siri is compatible with FaceTime, Messages, Calendar, Maps, Twitter, Facebook, Music, Mail, Weather, Stocks, Clock, Contacts, Notes, Settings, Safari, iTunes, iBooks, and Podcasts. By accessing the Internet, Siri can also respond to requests related to almost anything having to do with sports, movies, restaurants, music, or stocks.
>
> Plus, Siri can look up information when you pose almost any type of question or can be used to verbally control almost any iPhone/iPad-related feature that's adjustable from within Settings or Control Center. For example, you can activate Siri and say, "Turn on Airplane mode." or "Turn off Do Not Disturb."

# FIND, DISPLAY, OR USE INFORMATION RELATED TO YOUR CONTACTS

Your Contacts database can store a vast amount of information about people or companies. Every field within a Contact's entry is searchable and can be accessed by Siri. Or you can ask Siri to look up a specific contact for you and display that contact's Info screen.

Again, the more information you include in each entry stored in your Contacts database, the more helpful Siri can be. To have Siri look up and display information stored in Contacts, say something like the following:

- "Look up John Doe in Contacts."
- "What is John Doe's phone number?"
- "What is John Doe's home phone number?" (See Figure 2.3.)

**FIGURE 2.3**

*When you ask, "What is John Doe's home phone number?" the appropriate number from your Contacts database displays. Tap it to initiate a call from your iPhone.*

- "What is John Doe's work address?"
- "Where does John Doe live?"
- "Where does John Doe work?"

> **TIP**  When Siri displays the Info screen for a Contact, it is interactive; therefore, you can tap on a displayed phone number to initiate a call (iPhone only), or tap on an email address to launch the Mail app to send email to that address. If you tap on a regular address, the Maps app launches, and if you tap on a website URL, Safari launches and opens that web page.

Siri can also use information stored in your Contacts database to comply with various other requests, such as

- **"Send John Doe a text message"**—This works if you have an iPhone-labeled phone number or iMessage username or email address saved in John Doe's Contacts entry. On the iPhone, it also works with the phone's SMS text messaging feature if you have a phone number in someone's Contacts entry that's associated with the "mobile" label.

- **"Send John Doe an email"**—This works if you have an email address saved in John Doe's Contacts entry.

- **"How do I get to John Doe's home?"**—This works if you have a home address saved in John Doe's Contacts entry. The Maps app launches, and directions from your current location are displayed.

- **"When is John Doe's birthday?"**—This works if you have a date saved in the Birthday field in John Doe's Contacts entry.

- **"What is John Doe's wife's name?"**—This works if you have a spouse's name saved in John Doe's Contacts entry.

## INITIATE A CALL

On the iPhone, you can initiate a call by activating Siri and then saying, "Call [name] at home," or "Call [name] at work." This works if that person has a Contacts entry associated with their name, as well as a phone number labeled Home or Work, respectively. You could also say, "Call [name]'s mobile phone," or "Call [name]'s iPhone." If you just use the command call, and that person has several phone numbers in their Contacts entry, Siri gives you the option to select which number you want to call.

If you request someone's work phone number and Siri finds a contact's name but not a corresponding phone number, Siri responds with, "There is no work number for John Doe in your contacts." This is followed by a listing of whichever phone numbers are available for that contact.

> **NOTE** When issuing a command to Siri, you have flexibility in terms of what you say. For example, say, "Call John Doe at work," "Call John Doe work," or "Call the work number for John Doe," and in all these cases, Siri initiates a call to John Doe's work number.

Alternatively, if someone's contact information or phone number is not stored in your iPhone, you can say, "Call" or "Dial" followed by each digit of a phone number. Thus, you'd say, "Call 212 555 1212."

> ☑ **TIP**    You can also ask Siri to look up a business phone number or address by saying, "Look up [business name] in [city, state]." Or, you could say, "Look up [business type, such as a dry cleaner] in [city, state]."

On the iPhone, when Siri finds the phone number you're looking for, Siri says, "Calling [name] at [location]," and then automatically initiates a call to that number by launching the Phone app. Siri also has the capability to initiate FaceTime video calls. Use a command, such as, "FaceTime with [name]."

> ☑ **TIP**    On the iPhone or iPad, Siri works with FaceTime, so you can say, "FaceTime Natalie," or "Make a FaceTime call to Natalie" to initiate a video call. You can also use FaceTime to initiate an audio-only call by saying, "Make a FaceTime audio call to Natalie."

## FIND YOUR FRIENDS

The optional Find My Friends app is available free from the App Store. If you install it and begin following friends, coworkers, or family members (with their permission), at any time, you can ask Siri, "Where is [name]?" or say, "Find [name]," and Siri finds that person and displays a map showing that person's exact whereabouts. This feature is great for keeping tabs on your kids or teenagers, especially if they miss a curfew or claim to be studying at the library on a Friday evening.

For this feature to work, however, you must be logged in to your free Find My Friends account via the app.

> ❗ **CAUTION**    If you're using the Find My Friends app to track your kid's whereabouts, be sure to activate the Restrictions feature on their iOS device so they cannot deactivate the Find My Friends app. To do this, launch Settings, tap on the General option, and then select the Restrictions option. Adjust the Location Services feature and the Find My Friends feature so your child can't change those settings.

## SET UP REMINDERS AND TO-DO ITEMS

If you constantly jot down reminders to yourself on scrap pieces of paper or sticky notes, or manually enter to-do items into the Reminders app, this is one Siri-related feature you'll truly appreciate.

To create a reminder (to be utilized by the Reminders app), complete with an alarm, simply activate Siri and say something like, "Remind me to pick up my dry cleaning tomorrow at 3 p.m." Siri then creates the to-do item, displays it on the screen for your approval, and then saves it in the Reminders app. At the appropriate time and day, an alarm sounds and the reminder message is displayed.

**TIP** When creating a Reminder using Siri, you can provide a specific date and time, such as "tomorrow at 3 p.m." or "Friday at 1 p.m." or "July 7th at noon." You can also include a location that Siri knows, such as "Home" or "Work." For example, you could say, "Remind me to feed the dog when I get home," or "Remind me to call Emily when I get to work."

## READ OR SEND TEXT MESSAGES

When you receive a new text message but can't look at the screen (such as when you're driving), activate Siri and say, "Read new text message." After Siri reads the incoming message, you're given the opportunity to reply to that message and dictate your response.

Using Siri with the Messages app, you can also compose and send a text/instant message to anyone in your Contacts database by saying something like, "Compose a text message to John Doe."

You are asked to select an email address or mobile phone number to use. To bypass this step, say, "Send a text message to John Doe's mobile phone," or "Send a text message to John Doe's iPhone." Then, Siri says, "What do you want to say to John Doe?" Dictate your text message.

When you're finished speaking, Siri says, "I updated your message. Ready to send it?" The transcribed message is displayed on the screen, along with Cancel and Send icons. You can tap an icon or speak your reply.

# CHECK THE WEATHER OR YOUR INVESTMENTS

The Weather app can display an extended weather forecast for your immediate area or any city in the world, and the Stocks app (on the iPhone) can be used to track your investments. However, Siri has the capability to automatically access the Web and obtain weather information for any city, as well as stock-related information about any stock or mutual fund.

After activating Siri, ask a weather-related question, such as

- **"What is today's weather forecast?"**—Siri pinpoints your location and provides a current forecast.
- **"What is the weather forecast for New York City?"**—Of course, you can insert any city and state in your request.
- **"Is it going to rain tomorrow?"**—Siri accesses and interprets the weather forecast, and then vocalizes, as well as displays a response. Siri determines your current location before providing a forecast.
- **"Should I bring an umbrella to work?"**—Siri knows the location of your work and can access and then interpret the weather forecast to offer a vocalized and displayed response.

If you have stock-related questions (using the iPhone or iPad), you can ask about specific stocks by saying something like

- "What is [company name]'s stock at?"
- "What is [company]'s stock price?"
- "How is [company name]'s stock performing?"
- "Show me [company name] stock."

When you request stock information, you get a verbal response from Siri along with information about that stock displayed on the iPhone or iPad's screen, as you can see in Figure 2.4.

**FIGURE 2.4**

*Just by asking, Siri can tell you how a specific stock is performing.*

## FIND INFORMATION ON THE WEB OR GET ANSWERS TO QUESTIONS

If you want to perform a web search, you can manually launch the Safari browser, and then use a keyboard to find what you're looking for in the Search field. Or, you can ask Siri to perform the search for you by saying something like

- "Look up the [company] website."
- "Access the website cnn.com."
- "Find [topic] on the web."
- "Search the web for [topic]."
- "Google information about [topic]."
- "Search Wikipedia for [topic]."
- "Bing [topic]." (Bing is a popular search engine operated by Microsoft.)

You also can ask a question, and Siri seeks out the appropriate information on the Web.

> **NOTE** When you ask Siri a question that requires your iPhone or iPad to seek out the answer on the Internet, this is done through Apple using Wolfram Alpha. To learn more about the vast topics you can ask Siri about, from unit conversions to historical data, visit www.wolframalpha.com/examples.

## SCHEDULE AND MANAGE MEETINGS AND EVENTS

Like many of the apps that come preinstalled with iOS 8, the Calendar app is fully compatible with Siri, which means it's possible to use Siri to create or modify appointments, meetings, or events by using your voice. To do this, some of the things you can say include

- "Set up a meeting at 10:30 a.m."
- "Set up a meeting with Ryan at noon tomorrow."
- "Meet with Emily for lunch at 1 p.m."
- "Set up a meeting with Rusty about third-quarter sales projections at 4 p.m. on December 12th."

> **TIP** Siri can also be used to reschedule or cancel events in the Calendar app. For example, you could say, "Move my 2 p.m. meeting to 4:00 p.m.," or "Cancel my 6:00 p.m. dinner with Rusty."
>
> To obtain an overview of your schedule, ask a question like, "What does the rest of my day look like?," or "When is my next appointment?" You can ask about a specific event as well, by asking, "When is my next meeting with Kevin?" or "Where is my next meeting?"
>
> Siri can also tap the Calendar and Maps app simultaneously if you ask a question like, "How do I get to my next meeting?" This works if you've filled in the Location field when creating an event in the Calendar app.

## SEND EMAIL AND ACCESS NEW (INCOMING) EMAIL

If you want to compose an email to someone, activate Siri and say, "Send an email to [name]." If that person's email address is listed in your Contacts database, Siri addresses a new message to that person. Siri then says, "What is the subject of your email?" Speak the subject line for your email. When you stop speaking, Siri says, "Okay, what would you like the email to say?" You can now dictate the body of your email message.

When you're finished speaking, Siri composes the message, displays it on the screen, and then says, "Here is your email to [name]. Ready to send it?" You can now respond "yes" to send the email message, or say "cancel" to abort the message. If the message isn't what you want to say, you can edit it using the virtual keyboard, or ask Siri to "Change the text to…".

## SET AN ALARM OR TIMER

Siri can control the Clock app that comes preinstalled on your iOS device so that it serves as an alarm clock or timer. You can say something like, "Set an alarm for 7:30 a.m. tomorrow" or "Set a recurring wakeup call for 7:30 a.m." to create a new alarm. Or, to set a 30-minute timer, say, "Set a timer for 30 minutes." A countdown timer is displayed on the iPhone or iPad's screen, and an alarm sounds when the timer reaches zero.

You can also simply ask Siri, "What's today's date?" or "What time is it?" if you're too busy to look at the iPhone or iPad's screen, such as when you're driving.

## GET DIRECTIONS USING THE MAPS APP

Pretty much any feature you can use the Maps app for—whether it's to find the location or phone number for a business, obtain turn-by-turn directions between two addresses, or map out a specific address location—you can access using Siri.

To use Maps-related functions, say things like the following:

- "How do I get to [location]?"
- "Show [address]."
- "Directions to [contact name or location]."
- "Find a [business type, such as gas station] near [location]."
- "Find a [business or service name, such as Starbucks Coffee] near where I am."
- "Where is the closest [business type, such as post office]?"
- "Find a [cuisine type, such as Chinese] restaurant near me."

If multiple businesses or locations are found that are directly related to your request, Siri asks you to select one, or all related matches are displayed on a detailed map.

## CONTROL THE MUSIC APP

In the mood to hear a specific song that's stored on your iPhone or iPad? Maybe you want to begin playing a specific playlist, you want to hear all the music stored on your iOS device by a particular artist, or you want to play a specific album? Well, just ask Siri. You can control the Music app using your voice by saying things like the following:

- "Play [song title]."
- "Play [album title]."
- "Play [playlist title]."
- "Play [artist's name]."
- "Play [music genre, such as pop, rock, or blues]."

You can also issue specific commands, such as "Shuffle my [title] playlist," or speak commands, such as "Pause" or "Skip" as music is playing. However, Siri is unable to search for and display song or album listings. For example, if you say, "Show music," or "Show song playlists," Siri responds by saying, "Sorry, [your name], I can't search that content." Thus, to use Siri to control your music, you must know what music is stored on your iPhone or iPad.

## FORGET STICKY NOTES—DICTATE NOTES TO YOURSELF

The Notes app that comes preinstalled with iOS 8 is used to compose notes using a text editor (as opposed to a full-featured word processor, such as Pages or Microsoft Word). Siri is compatible with the Notes app and enables you to create and dictate notes.

To create a new note, activate Siri and begin a sentence by saying, "Note that I… " You can also say, "Note: [sentence]." What you dictate is saved as a new note in the Notes app.

**NOTE** When using the Siri or dictation feature, your iPhone or iPad can capture and process up to 30 seconds of your speech at a time.

# SIRI KNOWS ALL ABOUT SPORTS, MOVIES, AND RESTAURANTS, TOO

If you're looking for the latest scores related to your favorite professional team or sporting event, just ask Siri. It's also possible to ask sports-related questions and then have Siri quickly research the answers via the Internet. When it comes to sports, here are some sample questions or requests you can use with Siri:

■ "Did the Yankee's win their last game?"

■ "What was the score of last night's Patriots game?"

■ "What was the score the last time the Yankees and Red Sox played?"

■ "Show me the baseball scores from last night."

■ "When do the Dallas Cowboys play next?"

■ "Who has the most home runs on the New York Mets?"

■ "Show me the roster for the Patriots."

■ "Are any of the Bruins players currently injured?"

When it comes to movies, Siri can also help you decide what to go see, determine where movies are playing, look up movie times, and provide details about almost any movie ever made. Here are some sample questions or requests you can use with Siri that relate to movies:

■ "Where is [movie title] playing?"

■ "What's playing at [movie theater]."

■ "Who directed the movie [movie title]."

■ "Show me the cast from [movie title]."

■ "What's playing at the movies tonight?"

■ "Find the closest movie theater."

■ "Show me the reviews for [movie title]."

■ "What movie won Best Picture in [year]?"

■ "Buy two tickets to see [movie title] tonight at the [movie theater name]."

If you're looking to try out a new restaurant or want to learn more about a local dining establishment, Siri knows all about restaurants too. Plus, thanks to Yelp! and Open Table integration, you can view detailed information about restaurants, make dining reservations, or read reviews.

Here are some examples of how Siri can be used when you want to know more about restaurants:

■ "Where's the closest Japanese restaurant?

■ "Find a good Italian restaurant in Boston."

- "Table for two at Palm Restaurant in Boston for 7 p.m."
- "Show me reviews for [restaurant name] in [city]."

As you can see from Figure 2.5, when Siri locates restaurant information, thanks to Yelp!, details about that establishment, including it's location, phone number, hours of operation, entree price range, and a star-based rating, are displayed.

**FIGURE 2.5**
*The restaurant information Siri displays is interactive. For example, tap on the phone number to initiate a call to that restaurant or tap on the listed address to launch the Maps app and get detailed directions.*

## MORE SIRI QUICK TIPS

- Siri is a mathematical genius. Simply say the mathematical calculation you need solved, and Siri presents the answer in seconds. For example, say, "What is 10 plus 10?", "What's the square root of 24?", or "What is 20 percent of 500?" This feature is particularly useful for helping you calculate the server's tip when you receive the check at a restaurant.

- When asking Siri to look up businesses, landmarks, popular destinations, or restaurants, in addition to just displaying a location on a map, Siri integrates with the Yelp! online service to provide much more detailed information about many businesses and restaurants.

- Send a Tweet or update your Facebook status using your voice. Activate Siri and say something like, "Send a Tweet that says, 'I am at Starbucks, come join me.'" To update your Facebook status, say something like, "Write on my wall, 'I just landed in New York City and I am leaving the airport now.'"

  When dictating a Tweet, you can add the phrase, "Tweet with my location," to have Siri publish your current location with the outgoing Tweet you're dictating.

- If you need to turn on or off certain iPhone or iPad features, activate Siri and say, "Turn on Wi-Fi" or "Turn off Bluetooth."

- In addition to controlling the Music app, Siri can be used to verbally control iTunes Radio. Start with a command like, "Launch iTunes Radio," after you've activated this service from the Music app.

## PRACTICE (WITH SIRI) MAKES PERFECT

Right from the start, Siri will probably understand most of what you say. However, as you begin using this feature often, you will become acquainted with the best and most efficient ways to communicate questions, commands, and requests to generate the desired response.

Keep in mind that Siri translates what you say phonetically, so periodically, you might encounter names or commands that Siri can't understand or match up with correctly spelled information stored on your iPhone or iPad. This occurs most frequently with unusual names that sound vastly different from how they're spelled or used.

**! CAUTION** Before allowing Siri to send any message or text, be sure to proofread it carefully on your device's screen. Keep in mind that some words sound the same when spoken, and Siri might choose the wrong word when translating your speech to text. This could lead to embarrassing situations or dramatically change the meaning of what you intended to say.

Siri can streamline how you interact with your device and make certain tasks much easier to accomplish. Based on the questions you ask, you might also discover that Siri has a sense of humor. For example, try asking, "Siri, what do you look like?", "Siri, are you attractive?", or "What is the best smartphone on the market?"

# USE DICTATION MODE INSTEAD OF THE VIRTUAL KEYBOARD

Even if you're using an app that Siri is not yet compatible with, chances are you can still use your iPhone or iPad's Dictation mode. In many situations when the iPhone or iPad's virtual keyboard appears, a microphone key is located to the left of the spacebar. When you tap on this microphone key, Dictation mode is activated (shown in Figure 2.6). An animated sound wave graphic displays on the screen as you speak.

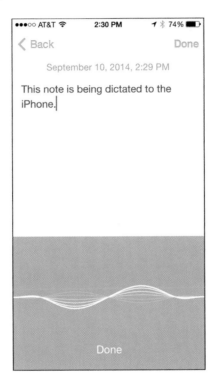

**FIGURE 2.6**

*Use Dictation mode to enter text using your voice, instead of typing on the virtual keyboard.*

You can now say whatever text you were going to manually type using the virtual keyboard. You can speak for up to 30 seconds at a time. When you're finished speaking, it's necessary to tap the Done key so that your device can translate your speech into text and insert it into the appropriate onscreen field.

For the fastest and most accurate results, speak one to three sentences at a time, and have your device connected to a Wi-Fi Internet connection.

> ☑ **TIP**  While using Dictation mode, you can easily add punctuation just by saying it. For example, you can say, "This is a sample dictation period," and Siri adds the period (".") at the end of the sentence. You can also use words like "open parenthesis" or "close parenthesis," "open quotes" or "close quotes," or "comma," "semicolon," or "colon" as you dictate.

# CONNECT OR LINK YOUR IPHONE TO YOUR CAR TO USE THE CARPLAY FEATURE

Over the past few years, Apple has worked with several dozen car manufacturers to integrate the iPhone with the stereo system or infotainment system that's built in to many vehicles. This functionality varies depending on the make, model, and year of your car.

In some cases, if your vehicle is CarPlay compatible, there is a Lightning port for your iPhone built in to the car. When you plug in your iPhone, your smartphone charges, plus it integrates directly with the car's in-dash infotainment system. This enables you to tap the iPhone's navigation capabilities, Siri functionality, and music capabilities by pressing the CarPlay button that's built in to your steering wheel or dashboard, for example.

In other cases, your vehicle establishes a wireless Bluetooth connection with your car and enables you to play music that's stored in your iPhone via your car's stereo or use the Phone feature to make and receive calls hands-free while you're driving.

Every vehicle manufacturer is implementing iPhone integration differently, and this functionality is only built in to 2013, 2014, or 2015 model year vehicles. If you have an older car, you must use third-party accessories to link your iPhone to the vehicle.

Typically, when you use Siri, information that's requested is displayed on the iOS device's screen. Siri Eyes Free, however, offers much of the same functionality as Siri but turns off the iPhone's screen altogether. Thus, it offers only verbal responses to a user's requests, commands, and questions.

Siri Eyes Free offers a solution to drivers who must pay attention to the road yet want to access content from their Internet-connected iOS mobile device to initiate calls, look up information, access email or text messages, or obtain turn-by-turn driving directions to a specific location.

When an iPhone is paired with a compatible car, you can press the Siri or voice recognition button that's built in to your steering wheel or your car's in-dash infotainment system. This activates Siri Eyes Free on the iPhone while the phone remains in your pocket, purse, or glove compartment. There is never a need for you to even momentarily divert your eyes to the phone's screen.

Thanks to Siri Eyes Free, all compatible cars now have access to GPS navigation; can utilize Internet connectivity; and be used for a growing selection of voice-activated tasks, such as accessing weather forecasts, finding nearby gas stations, looking up or adding appointments, obtaining sports scores, locating nearby restaurants, and playing music that's stored on the iOS device.

Siri Eyes Free does not handle features that would ordinarily require Siri to display content on the screen. For example, if you ask for a weather forecast, Siri Eyes Free says the current temperature but does not display a graphic-intensive extended forecast on the screen.

Likewise, Siri Eyes Free can read aloud an incoming email or text message and allow a response to be verbally created, but the message does not appear on your screen as you're driving.

When using Siri Eyes Free and CarPlay functionality, handling certain tasks, such as initiating a call, are straightforward.

Other tasks that you can utilize via Siri, such as finding a restaurant and then making a reservation or accessing movie listings and finding the closet theater that's playing a certain movie, are handled slightly differently using Siri Eyes Free. For example, if you ask a question such as, "What does the state flag of Massachusetts look like?", Siri displays the flag on the iPhone's screen, but Siri Eyes Free informs you that the requested task is not possible while you're driving.

Any time you leave your vehicle or manually activate a Bluetooth headset to use with your iPhone, Siri Eyes Free automatically deactivates and gives you full access to all of Siri's regular features, including the full use of the iPhone's touchscreen.

 **WHAT'S NEW** If you plan to invest in an Apple Watch in early 2015, you will have full access to Siri from the watch when it is linked to your iPhone. The Dictation feature can also be used directly from the Apple Watch to dictate text messages, for example.

IN THIS CHAPTER

- Install optional apps onto your iOS mobile device from the App Store
- Pinpoint the apps that are of interest to you or relevant to your needs
- Learn the difference between iPhone-specific, iPad-specific, and hybrid apps

3

# STRATEGIES FOR FINDING, BUYING, AND USING THIRD-PARTY APPS

The collection of preinstalled apps that comes with iOS 8 enables you to begin utilizing your iPhone or iPad for a wide range of popular tasks without first having to find and install additional apps. However, one of the things that has set the iPhone and iPad apart from its competition and made these devices among the most sought-after and popular throughout much of the world is the vast library of optional apps available for them.

Whereas other smartphones or tablets might offer a collection of a few hundred or even a few thousand optional apps, third-party developers have created an ever-growing collection of iPhone and iPad apps that's now in excess of 1.3 million. An additional selection of optional apps is or will soon be available for the Apple Watch.

All the apps currently available for your iOS device can be obtained from Apple's online-based App Store. Then, as needed, iOS 8 can automatically update your apps to ensure you're always working with the most recently released version.

> **NOTE** Although some apps are tweaked to work exceptionally well on the latest iPhone or iPad models, such as the iPhone 6 Plus, all iPhone-specific apps can scale themselves automatically to accommodate the iPhone model you're using, whether it has a 4", 4.7", or 5.5" display. Likewise, apps for the iPad (as well as hybrid iPhone/iPad apps) automatically adapt to the screen size of the device you're using.

> **TIP** From the App Store, several Apple-created (or endorsed) iPhone and iPad apps are available. Some of these free apps include Find My Friends (for tracking the whereabouts of your friends and family and allowing them to track your location in real time), iTunes U (for accessing the incredible collection of personal enrichment and educational content compiled by Apple), the official Twitter app, the official Facebook app, and Find My iPhone.

## APP STORE BASICS

There are two ways to access the App Store: directly from your iPhone or iPad (using the App Store app that comes preinstalled on your device) or using the iTunes software on your primary computer.

The App Store app is used exclusively for finding, purchasing (if applicable), downloading, and installing apps directly onto your device from the App Store. Other apps are used to access additional types of content. iTunes on your primary computer is used to access the App Store as well as many other types of content.

### HOW NEW APPS INSTALL THEMSELVES

If you're shopping for apps directly from your iPhone or iPad, tap on the Price icon, followed by the Buy icon, to make a purchase. You might be asked to supply your Apple ID password to confirm the transaction. The app automatically downloads and installs itself on your device. After it is installed, its app icon appears on your iPhone or iPad's Home screen and is ready to use.

You can also shop for apps from your primary computer and transfer them to your iPhone or iPad, or sync apps between your various mobile devices using the iTunes Sync process or iCloud.

> ☑ **TIP** Instead of manually entering your Apple ID password to confirm an app purchase (or acquire a free app), if your iOS mobile device is equipped with a Touch ID sensor as part of its Home button, you can simply scan your fingerprint to approve the transaction. For this to work, the feature must be turned on once from within Settings. To do this, launch Settings, tap on the Touch ID & Passcode option, and then turn on the virtual switch that's associated with the iTunes & App Store option.

## FREE OR PURCHASED?

Some apps available from the App Store are free. To download them, you go through the same process as you do for purchasing an app; however, instead of tapping on the Price icon, followed by the Buy icon, you must tap on the Free icon associated with the app, followed by the Install icon. You are not charged for downloading a free app. You do, however, still need to supply your Apple ID password to confirm the transaction.

In addition to apps, you can add a wide range of content to your iPhone or iPad, such as music, movies, TV shows, podcasts, audiobooks, and eBooks. How to acquire and enjoy this content is mentioned later in this chapter.

## RESTORING OR REINSTALLING APPS YOU'VE ALREADY DOWNLOADED

If you have Family Sharing set up via iCloud (see Chapter 5, "Ways to Use iCloud's Latest Features with Your iPhone and/or iPad"), you can share apps you acquire with up to five other family members without having to repurchase that app. With or without Family Sharing, you can also install the app on all of your own iOS mobile devices that are linked to the same iCloud account, as long as the app is compatible with each device.

To download an app onto your iPad that has already been purchased or downloaded onto another computer or device, tap on the Purchased icon that's displayed at the bottom of the screen in the App Store app. On the iPhone, tap on the Updates icon, and then tap on the Purchased option that's displayed near the top of the Updates screen. All your app purchases to date are displayed.

> **TIP** As an app is downloading from the App Store to your mobile device, to pause the process, tap on the Download icon that's displayed in the app description or app preview box in the App Store, or tap on the app icon as it's installing on the Home screen. To resume the download and installation process, tap the icon again.

> **NOTE** At the top of the Purchased screen on the iPhone or iPad, tap on the All tab to view all of the apps you've purchase to date for that device. You also have the option to tap on the Not On This iPhone/Not On This iPad tab to view apps you've acquired in the past but that are not currently installed on the device you're using.

Instead of a Free or Price icon being associated with each app description, an iCloud icon indicates the app is available through your iCloud account. Tap on the iCloud icon to download the app (without having to pay for it again) to the iOS device you're currently using. You can only install already purchased apps that are compatible with that iOS device. For example, you can't install an iPad-specific app onto an iPhone or iPod touch. You can, however, install iPhone-specific or hybrid apps onto an iPad or iPad mini.

> **TIP** From the Settings app, you have the option of having your iOS device automatically download and install any new (and compatible) apps, music, or eBooks purchased using your Apple ID on any other computer or device. To set this up, launch Settings, select the iTunes & App Store option from the main Settings menu, and then adjust the Automatic Downloads options, which include Music, Apps, and Books. You also can decide whether this feature works with a cellular data Internet connection or just when a Wi-Fi connection is available.

## WHERE TO FIND APPS, MUSIC, AND MORE

If you're shopping for apps, music, movies, TV shows, podcasts, audiobooks, eBooks, ringtones, or other content from your primary computer, with the goal of transferring what you acquire to your iPhone or iPad later via the iTunes sync process or via iCloud, use the latest version of the iTunes software on your Mac or PC computer.

However, from your iPhone or iPad, acquiring and then enjoying different types of content is done using a handful of different apps. Table 3.1 explains which app you should use to acquire and then enjoy various types of content on your iOS device.

**Table 3.1**   How to Acquire and Enjoy Various Types of Content on Your iPhone or iPad

| Content Type | Buy with App | Run with App |
|---|---|---|
| Apps | App Store | The app itself that you download and install |
| Digital editions of publications (including newspapers and magazines) | Newsstand | The digital publication's proprietary app |
| Music | iTunes Store | Music |
| Movies | iTunes Store | Videos |
| TV Shows | iTunes Store | Videos |
| Podcasts | Podcasts | Podcasts |
| Audiobooks | iTunes (or the optional Audible app) | Music (or the optional Audible app) |
| eBooks* | iBooks (to access iBookstore) | iBooks |
| PDF files | Mail, iCloud, iTunes Sync | iBooks or another PDF reader app |
| iTunes U Personal Enrichment and Educational Content | iTunes U** | iTunes U |
| Ringtones (and Alert Tones) | iTunes Store | Phone, FaceTime, Messages (or other apps that generate audible alarms or ringtones) |

*  eBooks can also be purchased from Amazon.com and read using the free Kindle app, or purchased from BN.com and read using the free Nook app.

**  The iTunes U app serves as a gateway to a vast selection of personal enrichment and educational courses, lectures, workshops, and information sessions that have been produced by leading educators, universities, and other philanthropic organizations. All iTunes U content is provided for free.

# EVERYTHING YOU NEED TO KNOW ABOUT APPS

Apps are individual programs that you install on your iPhone or iPad to give it additional functionality, just as you utilize different programs on your primary computer. For the iPhone or iPad, all apps are available from one central (online-based) location, called the App Store.

When you begin exploring the App Store, you'll discover right away that there are in excess of 1.3 million apps to choose from. They are divided into different categories to help make it easier and faster to find what you're looking for.

The App Store's app categories include Games, Kids, Newsstand, Books, Business, Catalogs, Education, Entertainment, Finance, Food & Drink, Health & Fitness, Lifestyle, Medical, Music, Navigation, News, Photo & Video, Productivity, Reference, Social networking, Sport, Travel, Utilities, and Weather.

## COMPATIBILITY: DOES THE APP RUN ON MULTIPLE DEVICES?

In terms of compatibility, all iOS apps fall into one of these three categories:

1. **iPhone-specific**—These are apps designed exclusively for the various iPhone models that might not function properly on the iPad. Most iPhone-specific apps will run on an iPad but will not take advantage of the tablet's larger screen. Some iPhone-specific apps have been optimized to work with the larger screen of the iPhone 5s, iPhone 6, and/or iPhone 6 Plus.

2. **iPad-specific**—These are apps designed exclusively for the iPad. They fully utilize the tablet's larger display and do not function on the iPhone or on other iOS devices. All iPad-specific apps do, however, function flawlessly on all iPad and iPad mini models.

3. **Hybrid**—Although you might encounter a few exceptions, these are apps designed to work on all iOS devices, including the iPhone and iPad. These apps detect which device they're running on and adapt.

> ☑ **TIP** When reading the App Store description of any app, tap on the Details tab and scroll down to the Information heading. Here, you can see a listing of which iOS devices the app is compatible with. Look for the Compatibility listing that's found under the Information heading (see Figure 3.1).

**FIGURE 3.1**

*From an app's Description screen, you can see which iOS mobile devices the app is compatible with. Look for the Compatibility heading.*

> ☑ **TIP**   If you own two or more iOS devices, such as an iPhone and an iPad (or an iPod touch), and all the devices are linked to the same Apple ID (iCloud) account, you can purchase a hybrid (or iPhone-specific) app once but install it on all of your iOS devices. This can be done through iTunes Sync or via iCloud after an app is initially purchased or downloaded.

When you're browsing the App Store from your iPhone, by default it displays all iPhone-specific apps followed by hybrid apps, but it does not display iPad apps. When you're browsing the App Store from your iPad, iPad-specific, hybrid, and iPhone-specific apps are all listed. Tap on the Phone or iPad tab that's displayed near the top center of the screen when viewing many areas of the App Store.

If you're shopping for apps using the iTunes software on your primary computer, click the iPhone or iPad tab that's displayed near the top center of the iTunes screen (shown in Figure 3.2) to select which format apps you're looking for.

App Store Device Tabs

**FIGURE 3.2**

*When shopping for apps using iTunes on your primary computer (in this case, an iMac), click the appropriate tab to indicate which format apps you're looking for, keeping in mind that iPhone-specific apps will run on an iPad (but not take advantage of the tablet's larger screen), but iPad-specific apps do not run on an iPhone.*

> **TIP** Because some app developers release the same app in both an iPhone-specific and an iPad-specific format, many iPad-specific apps have "HD" for High-Definition in their title, to help differentiate them from iPhone or hybrid apps. Some iPad-specific apps include the words "for iPad" in their title.

## QUICK GUIDE TO APP PRICING

Regardless of whether you use the App Store app from your device or visit the App Store using the iTunes software on your primary computer, you must set up an Apple ID account and have a major credit card or debit card linked to the account to make purchases.

> **TIP** If you don't have a major credit card or debit card that you want to link with your Apple ID account, you can purchase prepaid iTunes Gift Cards from Apple or most places that sell prepaid gift cards.
>
> iTunes Gift Cards are available in a variety of denominations and can be used to make app and other content purchases. They are distinct from Apple Gift Cards, which are only redeemable at Apple Stores or Apple.com.

The first time you access the App Store and attempt to make a purchase, you are prompted to enter your Apple ID account username and password or set up a new Apple ID account, which requires you to supply your name, address, email, and credit card information. For all subsequent online app purchases, you simply need to enter your Apple ID password, and the purchase is automatically billed to your credit or debit card or deducted from your iTunes Gift Card balance.

> **TIP** An Apple ID account can also be referred to as an iTunes Store account. To learn more about how an Apple ID account works or to manage your account, visit www.apple.com/support/appleid. The same Apple ID you use to make purchases can also be used as your username when you're using FaceTime for video calling, Messages to access the iMessage service, or to access your iCloud account.

Originally, when the App Store opened, there were two types of apps: free apps and paid apps. The free apps were often demo versions of paid apps (with limited functionality) or fully functional apps that displayed ads in the app. Paid apps were typically priced between $.99 and $9.99.

As the App Store has evolved, additional payment options and fee structures for apps have been introduced, giving app developers new ways to generate revenue and iPhone and iPad users different methods of paying for apps and content.

The following sections summarize the different types of apps from a pricing standpoint.

## FREE APPS

Free apps cost nothing to download and install on your phone or tablet. Some programmers and developers release apps for free out of pure kindness to share their creations with the iPhone- and/or iPad-using public. These are fully functional apps.

There are also free apps that serve as demo versions of paid apps. In some cases, certain features or functions of the app are locked in the free version, but are later made available if you upgrade to the paid or premium version of the app.

A third category of free apps comprises fully functional apps that display ads as part of their content. In exchange for using the app, you must view ads. These ads typically offer the option to click on special offers from within the app or learn more about a product or service being advertised.

**NOTE** Many free apps that contain ads also have a paid app counterpart that's ad-free.

A fourth category of free apps serves as a shell for premium (paid) content that must be loaded into the app to make it fully functional. For example, many newspaper and magazine publishers offer free apps related to their specific publications but require users to pay for the actual content of the newspaper or magazine, which later gets downloaded into the app.

The final type of free app enables the user to make in-app purchases to add features or functionality to the app or unlock premium content. The core app, without the extra content, is free, however.

**TIP** Some fully functional apps are free because they're designed to promote a specific company or work with a specific service. For example, to use the free HBOGo app, you must be a paid subscriber of the HBO premium cable channel through your cable TV or satellite provider.

Likewise, to use the free Netflix app, you must be a paid subscriber to this streaming movie service. The AmEx app is useful only to people with an American Express Card, but the free Target app is useful to anyone who shops at Target stores.

When you're looking at an app listing or description in the App Store, if the app is free, it has a Free icon instead of a Price icon, associated with it (as shown in Figure 3.3). Read a free app's description carefully. Look for the heading In-App Purchases. This indicates that optional in-app purchases are available, and in some cases, these purchases are required to fully use the app.

Free Icon

**FIGURE 3.3**

*A free app has a Free icon displayed in its App Store listing or description.*

## PAID APPS

After you purchase an app, you own it and can use it as often as you'd like, usually without incurring additional fees (although in-app purchases might be possible). You simply pay a fee for the app upfront, which is often between $.99 and $9.99. Typically, future upgrades of the app are free of charge.

## SUBSCRIPTION-BASED APPS

Digital editions of magazines and newspapers can be purchased from the Newsstand app that comes preinstalled on your device. These publications each require their own proprietary app (also available from the App Store) to access and read the publication's content. Digital editions of many popular publications are available from the Newsstand app.

These apps are typically free, and then you pay a recurring subscription fee for content, which automatically gets downloaded into the app. Many digital editions of newspapers, such as the *New York Times* and the *Wall Street Journal*, utilize a subscription app model, as do hundreds of different magazines.

Typically, the main content of the digital and printed version of a publication are identical. However, you can view the digital edition on your iPhone or iPad and take advantage of added interactive elements built in to the app. If you're already a subscriber to the print version of a newspaper or magazine, some publishers offer the digital edition free, while others charge an extra fee to subscribe to the digital edition as well. Or you can subscribe to just the digital edition of a publication.

With some magazines, you can download the free app for a specific publication and then, in the app, purchase one issue at a time, including past issues. There is no long-term subscription commitment, but individual issues of the publication still must be purchased and downloaded. Or you can purchase an ongoing (recurring) subscription and new issues of that publication will automatically be downloaded to your iPhone or iPad as they become available.

**(iOS 8) WHAT'S NEW** To utilize all of the features and functions built in to the Microsoft Word, Excel, PowerPoint, and OWA for iPad apps, a paid monthly subscription to Microsoft's Office 365 service is required. You also must set up a free Microsoft OneDrive account.

Likewise, some other popular apps, like Intuit's QuickBooks Online for iPad, also require a paid subscription to a corresponding service (in this case, QuickBooks Online) to function.

## IN-APP PURCHASES

This type of app might be free or might be a paid app. As you're actually using the app, you can purchase additional content or add new features and functionality by making in-app purchases. The capability to make in-app purchases has become very popular and is being used by app developers in a variety of ways.

As you read an app's description in the App Store, if an app requires in-app purchases, it is revealed in the text included in the app description screen. Look for the heading within an app's description that says In-App Purchases and tap on it.

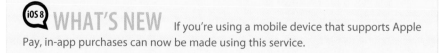
**(iOS 8) WHAT'S NEW** If you're using a mobile device that supports Apple Pay, in-app purchases can now be made using this service.

> **! CAUTION** The price you pay for an app does not translate directly to the quality or usefulness of that app. Some free or very inexpensive apps are extremely useful and packed with features and can really enhance your experience using your iPhone or iPad. There are also costly apps (priced at $4.99 or more) that are poorly designed, filled with bugs, or don't live up to expectations or to the description of the app offered by the app's developer or publisher.
>
> The price of each app is set by the developer or programmer that created or is selling the app. Instead of using the price as the only determining factor if you're evaluating several apps that appear to offer similar functionality, be sure to read the app's customer reviews carefully, and pay attention to the star-based rating the app has received. These user reviews and ratings are a much better indicator of the app's quality and usefulness than the price.

## HOW TO SHOP WITH THE APP STORE APP

From your iPhone or iPad's Home screen, to access the App Store, tap on the blue-and-white App Store app icon. Your device must have access to the Internet via a cellular or Wi-Fi connection.

When you access the App Store app (shown in Figure 3.4 on the iPad), a handful of command icons at the top and bottom of the screen are used to navigate your way around the online-based store.

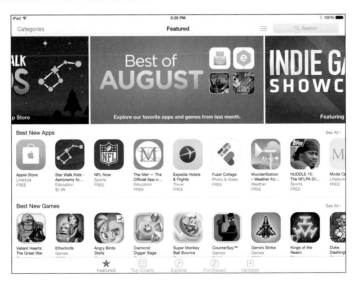

**FIGURE 3.4**
The main App Store app screen on the iPad. Find, purchase, download, and install apps directly from your tablet.

If you already know the name of the app you want to find, purchase, download, and install, tap on the Search field, which is located near the upper-right corner of the screen in the iPad version. On the iPhone, tap on the Search option displayed at the bottom of the App Store app's screen (as shown in Figure 3.5).

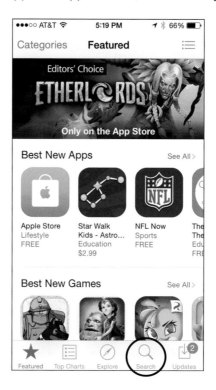

**FIGURE 3.5**

*From your iPhone, tap on the Search icon to search for any app in the App Store by name or keyword.*

Using the virtual keyboard, enter the name of the app. Tap the Search key on the virtual keyboard to begin the search. You can also perform a search based on a keyword or phrase, such as "word processing," "to-do lists," "time management," or "photo editing."

In a few seconds, matching results are displayed on the App Store screen in the form of app previews.

If you're shopping for apps from your iPad, as you browse the App Store, iPad-specific apps are displayed if you tap on the iPad tab near the top center of most areas in the App Store.

> **✓ TIP** At the bottom center of the main App Store screen on the iPad are several command icons, labeled Featured, Top Charts, Explore, Purchased, and Updates. On the iPhone, the icons along the bottom of the screen are labeled Featured, Top Charts, Explore, Search, and Updates. If you don't know the exact name of an app you're looking for, these command icons will help you browse the App Store and discover apps that might be of interest to you.

## THE FEATURED ICON

Tap on the Featured icon near the bottom of the App Store screen to see a listing of what Apple considers "Featured" apps. These are divided into a handful of categories. Either flick your finger from right to left to scroll horizontally through the apps listed, or tap on the See All option that's displayed to the right of the category heading.

Near the top of the screen are large graphic banners that constantly change. When you refer to Figure 3.4, for example, one of the banners says "Best of August"; however, it constantly scrolls and often showcases specific apps. These banner graphics sometimes promote what Apple considers the "App of the Week," as well as other noteworthy apps the company wants to promote.

## THE TOP CHARTS ICON

When you tap on the Top Charts command icon, located near the bottom center of the App Store app's screen, a listing of Paid, Free, and Top Grossing apps are displayed (shown in Figure 3.6). These charts are based on all app categories. To view charts related to a specific app category, such as Business or Games, first tap on the Top Charts button, and then tap on the Categories button and choose a category.

**FIGURE 3.6**

*From the App Store app on the iPad, tap on the Top Charts icon at the bottom of the screen to view a list of popular free, paid, and top-grossing apps.*

## MANAGE YOUR ACCOUNT AND REDEEM iTUNES GIFT CARDS

When you scroll down to the very bottom of the Featured screen in the App Store, you'll see several command buttons.

Tap on the Redeem button to redeem a prepaid iTunes Gift Card. Tap on the Apple ID [Your Apple ID Username] button to manage your Apple ID account and update your credit card information, for example. When the Apple ID window appears, tap on the View Apple ID option. When prompted, enter your password.

Tap on the Apple ID account button to manage your recurring paid subscriptions, as well. When the Account Settings screen is displayed (shown in Figure 3.7), scroll down to the Subscriptions heading and tap on the Manage button. You can then modify or cancel your paid recurring subscriptions to digital newspapers or magazines, for example. If you don't yet have any active subscriptions, this option does not appear.

**FIGURE 3.7**

*From the Account Settings menu, you can change or cancel your recurring paid subscriptions for digital editions of newspapers and magazines.*

Tap on the Send Gift option to send an iTunes Gift Card to someone else. Their gift will arrive via email and they can redeem it almost instantly from the App Store, iTunes Store, iBookstore, or Newsstand.

## FEATURES OF AN APP LISTING

As you browse the App Store, each screen is composed of many app listings (or more information-packed app previews). Each listing promotes a specific app and displays the app's title, graphic icon or logo, what category the app falls into, and its price.

Within an app preview (shown in Figure 3.8), the app's title, its logo/graphic, the app's developer, its average star-based rating, how many ratings the app has received (the number in parentheses), the price icon, and a sample screen shot from the app itself are displayed.

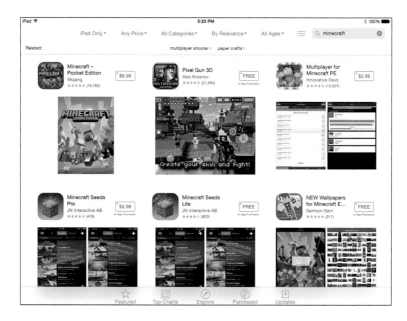

**FIGURE 3.8**

*A sample app preview contains important, at-a-glance details about that app, including its title and price. Here, a search was performed on the iPad using the game title "Minecraft" and app preview boxes for several Minecraft-related, iPad-specific search results are displayed.*

## LEARN BEFORE YOU BUY: ACCESSING THE APP'S DESCRIPTION PAGE

Before committing to a purchase, as you're looking at an app's listing or preview in the App Store, you can tap on its title or graphic icon to view a detailed description. When you do this on the iPhone, the App Store screen is replaced with a detailed description of the app. On the iPad, a new app description window is displayed over the App Store screen.

An app description screen (shown in Figure 3.9) displays the app's title and logo near the top of the screen, along with its price icon, average star-based rating, and the number of ratings it has received.

**FIGURE 3.9**
*From an app's description screen, you can learn all about a specific app. This information can help you decide whether it's of interest to you or relevant to your needs.*

You then see three command tabs, labeled Details, Reviews, and Related. Tap on the Details tab to view a detailed description of the app. Tap on the Reviews tab to view a star-based ratings chart for that app, as well as detailed text-based reviews written by your fellow iPhone and iPad users. Tap on the Related tab to view similar apps that are available from the App Store.

Displayed immediately below the Details, Reviews, and Related tab are sample screen shots from the app itself. Swipe your finger horizontally to scroll through the sample screen shots, or scroll down to view the Details, Reviews, or Related information, based on which command tab you've tapped.

## WHAT'S OFFERED WHEN YOU TAP THE DETAILS TAB

Immediately below the sample screen shots from the app is a text-based description of the app that has been written and supplied by the app's developer. This description is a sales tool that's designed to sell apps.

Below the description is information about what new features have been added to the app in the most recent version. Look for the What's New heading.

Displayed beneath the What's New heading, if applicable, is the Supports heading. Here, you can quickly determine whether the app is compatible with Apple's

Game Center online service. As you scroll down on this screen, the Information section offers more useful facts about the app.

Below the Information section, tap on the In-App Purchases option, if this option is available, to discover what in-app purchases are available and their cost.

Tap on the Version History option to see information about all revisions to the app that have been released since it was first introduced.

Tap on the Developer Info link to discover other apps available from the same developer or publisher. Tap on the Developer Website option to access the website operated by the app developer or the app-specific website. When you do this, Safari automatically launches and then loads the applicable website.

## WHAT'S OFFERED WHEN YOU TAP THE REVIEWS TAB

When you tap on the Reviews tab, the App Store Ratings chart is displayed (shown in Figure 3.10). This graphically shows how many ratings the app has received, its overall average rating, and the total number of ratings. A top rating is five stars.

**FIGURE 3.10**

*Every app description contains an average rating and a rating summary chart. Use it to quickly see what other users think about the app you're currently looking at.*

Below the App Store Ratings chart are text-based reviews that have been written by other App Store customers.

> **✓ TIP**  As you're looking at an app's Description screen, sharing details about an app with others are offered when you tap on the Share icon displayed near the top-right corner of the Description screen. For example, the Gift option enables you to purchase and send a paid app to someone else.

### WHAT'S OFFERED WHEN YOU TAP THE RELATED TAB

These are listings for other apps, usually similar in functionality to the app you're looking at.

On the iPhone, to exit an app's description page and continue browsing the App Store, tap on the left-pointing arrow icon that's displayed near the top-left corner of the screen. On the iPad, tap anywhere outside the app's description window.

### KEEP YOUR APPS CURRENT WITH THE UPDATES COMMAND ICON

One of the command icons that's constantly displayed at the bottom of the App Store app's screen is the Updates icon. This is used to keep your currently installed apps up to date. More information about this feature is included in the section, "Keep Your Apps Up to Date with the Latest Versions."

> **✎ NOTE**  If you opt to shop for apps using the iTunes software on your Mac or PC, you can transfer those apps to your iOS mobile device using the iTunes Sync process or download your purchases from iCloud by tapping on the Purchased option in the App Store app on your mobile device.
>
> To learn more about using the iTunes software on your computer and the iTunes Sync process, visit www.apple.com/support/itunes.

# QUICK TIPS FOR FINDING APPS RELEVANT TO YOU

As you explore the App Store, it's easy to get overwhelmed by the sheer number of apps that are available for your iOS device. If you're a new iPhone or iPad user, spending time browsing the App Store introduces you to the many types of apps that are available, and provides you with ideas about how your phone or tablet can be utilized in your personal or professional life.

However, you can save a lot of time searching for apps if you already know the app's exact title or if you know what type of app you're looking for. In this case, you can enter either the app's exact title or a keyword description of the app in the App Store's Search field to see a list of relevant matches. If you're looking for a word-processing app, you can either enter the search phrase "Pages" into the App Store's Search field, or enter the search phrase "word processor" to see a selection of word-processing apps.

If you're looking for vertical market apps with specialized functionality that caters to your industry or profession, enter that industry or profession (or keywords associated with it) in the Search field. For example, enter keywords like "medical imaging," "radiology," "plumbing," "telemarketing," or "sales."

> **TIP**   Many websites, blogs, and publications regularly publish detailed reviews of iPhone and iPad apps. One source for these app reviews is *Jason Rich's Featured App of the Week* (www.FeaturedAppOfTheWeek.com), which is a blog maintained by this book's author.

As you're evaluating an app before downloading it, use these tips to help you determine whether it's worth installing on your phone or tablet:

- Figure out what type of features or functionality you want to add to your iPhone or iPad.

- Using the Search field, find apps designed to handle the tasks you have in mind. Chances are, you can easily find a handful of apps created by different developers that are designed to perform the same basic functionality. You can then pick which is the best based on the description, screenshots, and list of features each app offers.

- Check the customer reviews and ratings for the app. This useful tool quickly determines whether the app actually works as described in its description. Keep in mind that an app's description in the App Store is written by the app's developer and is designed to sell apps. The customer reviews and star-based ratings are created by fellow iPhone or iPad users who have tried out the app firsthand. If an app has only a few ratings or reviews and they're mixed, you might need to try out the app for yourself to determine whether it will be useful to you.

- If an app offers a free version, download and test that first before purchasing the premium version. You can always delete any app that you try out but don't wind up liking or needing.

**iOS 8 WHAT'S NEW** One of the command icons displayed at the bottom of the App Store screen is labeled Explore. This option enables the App Store to recommend apps for you based on a variety of different criteria, including which apps you've previously purchased and your current location. For example, based on your current location, the App Store might recommend an app from a local TV, radio station, or newspaper, or an app that offers tourist information or shopping discounts related to your current whereabouts.

**TIP** If you discover an app that looks interesting but you don't want to purchase or install it right away, access the Description screen for that app, and then tap on its Share button. You can then either email yourself information about the app, or tap on the Add to Wish List button and add it to a list of apps you're interested in.

You can later view your Wish List by tapping on the Wish List icon that on the iPhone is displayed in the top-right corner of the App Store's Featured screen. On the iPad, the Wish List icon is located to the immediate left of the Search field (in the top-right corner of the App Store screen.)

# KEEP YOUR APPS UP TO DATE WITH THE LATEST VERSIONS

Periodically, app developers release new versions of their apps. iOS 8 can automatically update your installed apps as long as your iPhone or iPad has access to the Internet.

To customize this auto-update option, launch Settings and then tap on the iTunes & App Store option. From the iTunes & App Store menu, you can set up automatic downloads for Music, Apps, Books, and Updates. Make sure the virtual switch associated with the Updates option is turned on.

Next, scroll down to the Use Cellular Data option. Choose whether you want apps to update using a cellular data connection to the Internet. Keep in mind that some apps which have a large file size associated with them will require a Wi-Fi Internet connection to update.

At any time, you can see which apps have been updated and read a summary of what functionality or features have been added to the app update (as well as which bugs have been fixed) by launching the App Store app and tapping on the Updates option.

If an app listed on the Updates screen has an Open button associated with it, the app has been recently updated. The date of the update is listed. Tap on the app icon or its title to read about the update. Tap on the Open button to launch the app and use it on your iPhone or iPad.

From the Updates screen, if an Open button is not displayed, you might see a progress meter indicating the app is currently being updated and downloaded to your device. If an update is available but has not yet been downloaded and installed, an Update button, instead of an Open button, is displayed with that app.

As you're viewing the Updates screen, apps are listed in chronological order, based on when they were updated. Pending updates are displayed near the top of the screen (shown in Figure 3.11).

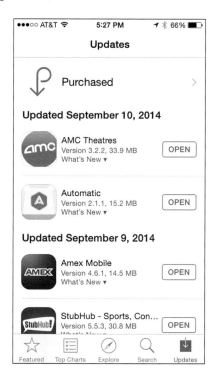

**FIGURE 3.11**

*iOS 8 can automatically download and install updates to apps. The Updates screen shows which apps have been recently updated and what's new in those updates.*

> **TIP** To see what's been added or changed to a newly updated app, from the App Store's Updates screen, tap on the What's New option displayed below each updated app's title, version number and file size (refer to Figure 3.11).

# MANAGE YOUR KIDS' APP ACQUISITIONS

Thanks to a variety of tools, as a parent, you can control what apps your child is allowed to purchase, install, and ultimately use on their iOS mobile device or yours. You can also control their online spending when it comes to apps and in-app purchases in several different ways.

To determine which apps and content your child is allowed to use on an iOS mobile device, activate the parental control options. To do this, launch Settings on the device, tap on the General option, and then tap on the Restrictions option.

From the Restrictions submenu, tap on Enable Restrictions, and then turn on the virtual switches associated with iTunes Store, iBooks Store, Installing Apps, Deleting Apps, and In-App Purchases to limit what your child can do.

Under the Allowed Content heading, tap on the Apps option and determine what apps your child will be able to access, based on the App Ratings.

When you set up iCloud's Family Sharing, it's possible to set up your child's iOS mobile device so he or she needs to ask you for permission (via a text message to your iPhone or iPad) before acquiring any new apps or content. This feature also gives parents greater control over apps installed on a child's device.

It's also possible to set up an iTunes Allowance for your child and give them a predetermined amount of money to spend in the App Store, iTunes Store, and iBookstore each month. To learn more about this option, visit www.apple.com/itunes/gifts.

## IN THIS CHAPTER

- Use AirDrop to share data with other nearby Mac, iPhone, and iPad users
- Utilize your iPhone or iPad with AirPlay-compatible equipment
- Print files wirelessly to a compatible AirPrint printer
- Discover iOS 8's new Handoff functionality

4

# SYNC, SHARE, AND PRINT FILES USING AIRDROP, AIRPLAY, AIRPRINT, AND HANDOFF

When it comes to syncing and sharing files and data (including app-specific data), your iOS mobile device is equipped with several tools, including AirDrop, AirPlay, AirPrint, and Handoff.

**iOS 8 WHAT'S NEW** iCloud's new features for syncing and sharing documents, files, photos, and data include Family Sharing and iCloud Drive, which are explained in greater detail in Chapter 5, "Ways to Use iCloud's Latest Features with Your iPhone and/or iPad."

The new Handoff feature built in to iOS 8 offers yet another way your iPhone, iPad, and Mac(s) linked to the same iCloud account can share information and functionality, enabling you to begin a task on one computer or device and seamlessly continue it on another.

The AirDrop tool enables your iPhone or iPad to wirelessly transfer certain types of files (including photos) and app-specific data to other iPhones, iPads, and Macs that are in close proximity and that also support the AirDrop function.

To turn on the AirDrop feature on your iPhone or iPad, launch Control Center by swiping your finger upward from the very bottom of the screen. When the Control Center appears, tap on the AirDrop icon.

From the AirDrop menu (shown in Figure 4.1), choose whether you want to utilize AirDrop to communicate with any other nearby users (Everyone) or only with people within your Contacts database (Contacts Only). It's also possible to turn off the feature altogether.

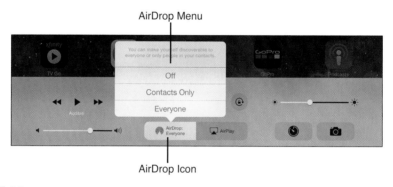

**FIGURE 4.1**

*Access the AirDrop menu from the Control Center. (Shown here on the iPad Air.)*

When it's turned on, use this feature to send content from the Share menu that's built in to compatible apps. For example, if you want to send a photo to another AirDrop user, launch Photos, view and select the photo(s) you want to send, and then tap on the Share icon.

When the Share menu is displayed (shown in Figure 4.2), thumbnails representing people in close proximity who have AirDrop turned on are displayed. Tap on the intended recipient, and the selected photos are wirelessly sent.

AirDrop Icon in Share Menu

**FIGURE 4.2**

*Select AirDrop from the Share menu of compatible apps to send app-specific content to other iOS mobile devices and Mac users.*

> 📝 **NOTE**  AirDrop is available only when using an iPhone 5/5c/5s, iPhone 6, iPhone 6 Plus, a fourth-generation iPad, iPad Air, iPad mini, iPad mini with Retina Display, or the newer iPad models released by Apple in late 2014.
>
> If you want to use AirDrop between an iOS mobile device and a Mac, the Mac must be running OS X Yosemite.

> ✓ **TIP**  In addition to the Photos app, the AirDrop feature is supported by the Share menu found in other apps, including Contacts, Maps, Notes, Safari, iBooks, and iTunes Store.

Regardless of what you're currently doing on your iPhone or iPad, if someone sends you something via AirDrop, a pop-up window appears on your screen that provides you with information about the sender and what's being sent. You then have the option to Accept or Decline the transmission (shown in Figure 4.3).

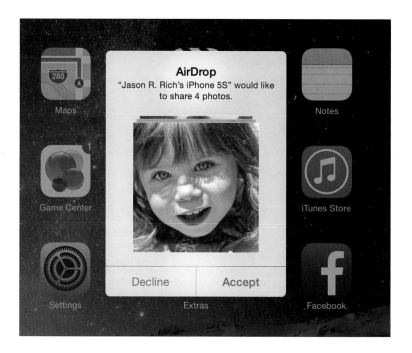

**FIGURE 4.3**
Receiving something sent by someone else via AirDrop is as easy as tapping on the Accept button that's displayed.

> **NOTE** After you receive content via AirDrop, to access that content, launch the relevant app. For example, to view, organize, or edit photos you receive, open the Camera Roll album in the Photos app. If you receive a Contacts entry, it is automatically added to your Contacts database and accessible from the Contacts app.

In addition to sharing app-specific content and photos with other people, AirDrop offers a quick and convenient way to share compatible content between your own iOS mobile device(s) and Mac(s).

## STREAM CONTENT FROM YOUR iPHONE OR iPAD TO OTHER COMPATIBLE DEVICES USING AIRPLAY

AirPlay is a wireless feature that enables your mobile device to stream content, such as photos, videos, or audio, to an AirPlay-compatible device, such as Apple TV, a Mac, or AirPlay-compatible speakers.

To use AirPlay, your iOS mobile device and the other AirPlay-compatible device must be connected to the same wireless home network (via Wi-Fi). Then, when you turn on the AirPlay feature, the two compatible devices automatically establish a wireless connection.

After the connection is made, an AirPlay icon appears within compatible apps, such as Music, Videos, and Photos, enabling you to transfer (stream) what you would otherwise see on your iPhone or iPad's screen, or what would be heard through the device's speaker, to another compatible device.

In addition to being able to stream photos and video (including iTunes Store TV show and movie purchases and rentals), you can use AirPlay to connect external speakers (without cables) to your iOS mobile device, and then stream music or audio (such as audiobooks or podcasts) from your device to those compatible speakers.

When it's available, one of the easiest ways to turn AirPlay on or off is to access it from Control Center. Tap on the AirPlay icon, and then choose where you want to stream the content to. In Figure 4.4, you'll see that an iPad Air is wirelessly connecting to Apple TV to stream a TV show that's saved in the iPad and display it on an HD television set via Apple TV.

AirPlay Menu

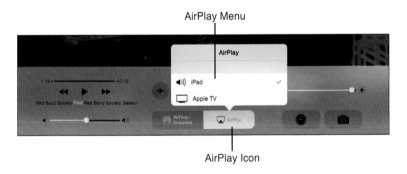

AirPlay Icon

**FIGURE 4.4**
*The AirPlay icon and menu found in Control Center.*

🔍 MORE INFO   AirPlay-compatible speakers are available from a handful of different companies, starting around $49.95. To learn about the AirPlay speakers available from the Apple Store and Apple.com, visit http://store.apple.com/us/ipad/ipad-accessories/speakers?m.tsOtherFeatures=airplay.

# PRINT FILES WIRELESSLY USING AN AIRPRINT-COMPATIBLE PRINTER

Another wireless feature built in to iOS 8 is AirPrint. It enables compatible apps to wirelessly send documents, data, or photos to be printed on an AirPrint-compatible laser, ink jet, or photo printer. For this feature to work, the iOS mobile device and the printer must be connected to the same wireless network.

Dozens of different AirPrint-compatible printers are now available, from companies such as Brother, HP, Canon, Lexmark, and Epson. To learn more about AirPrint-compatible printers, visit http://support.apple.com/kb/HT4356.

After you've set up an AirPrint-compatible printer, use the Print feature that's built in to many apps, such as Pages, Notes, Safari, Maps, and Photos. The Print option is often found in the Share menu of these apps, although this can vary.

> **TIP** When you have documents or files currently being printed, to access iOS 8's print queue, access the app switcher by pressing the Home button twice in quick succession, and then swipe from left to right, past the Home screen.

> **TIP** If you're not using an AirPrint-compatible printer, it's possible to install specialized software on your Mac, such as handyPrint (www.netputing.com/handyprint) or Printopia (http://ecamm.com/mac/Printopia), to enable your printer to work with the AirPrint feature of your iPhone or iPad as long as your Mac is turned on.

# CONTINUE A TASK ON ONE DEVICE EXACTLY WHERE YOU LEFT OFF ON ANOTHER USING HANDOFF

New to iOS 8 is a feature called Handoff. It works with several apps that come preinstalled with iOS 8, including Phone, Safari, Mail, Maps, Messages, Contacts, Calendar, and Reminders, as well as the iWork for iOS apps. It's also compatible with a growing number of third-party apps.

Basically, this feature enables you to begin a task on one of your Mac(s) or iOS mobile devices, and then pick up exactly where you left off on another Mac or iOS mobile device that's linked to the same iCloud account and is within Bluetooth range (which is about 33 feet).

> **⎘ NOTE** To use the Handoff feature between your iPhone and a Mac, the Mac must be running the latest version of OS X Yosemite.

To enable the Handoff feature, launch the Settings app, tap on General, and then tap on the Handoff & Suggested Apps option. Turn on the virtual switch associated with the Handoff option. This must be done on each of your iOS mobile devices.

When Handoff is turned on, start performing a compatible task on one of your Macs or iOS mobile devices. Then, to pick up what you were doing on a different iPhone or iPad, wake up the device, and from the Lock screen, place your finger on the app icon that's displayed in the lower-left corner of the screen and swipe upward (shown in Figure 4.5), or access the app switcher and swipe from left to right to scroll past the Home screen to access the handoff screen.

Handoff-Related
App Icon

**FIGURE 4.5**

*When it's possible to take advantage of the Handoff feature, upon waking up your iPhone or iPad, place your finger on the app icon that's displayed in the lower-left corner of the Lock screen and swipe upward.*

> **NOTE** When you attempt to use the Handoff feature from the Lock screen, it is still necessary to unlock the iPhone or iPad you're currently using, before accessing the app that you were using on your other computer or iOS mobile device.

> **NOTE** To pick up what you were previously doing while currently using a Mac, simply open the app you were previously using on your other Mac or iOS mobile device.

One of the coolest uses of the Handoff feature, if you're an iPhone user, is that when you receive an incoming call on your iPhone, when the Handoff feature is also active on your iPad and/or Mac, you can answer the incoming call and engage in the phone conversation from one of these other devices.

Your iPhone continues to host the call, but the wireless connection between your iPhone and iPad (or iPhone and Mac), enables you to use the Mac or iPad's built-in microphone and speaker(s) to use one of these devices as a speakerphone.

> **NOTE** For this aspect of the Handoff feature to work, your iPad or Mac must be linked to the same Wi-Fi network as your iPhone, plus both devices must be signed in to the same iCloud account.

When an incoming call is displayed on your iPad or Mac's screen, tap or click on the Answer icon to answer the call. If you want to initiate a call from your iPad or Mac (via your iPhone), tap or click on a phone number that's displayed in the Contacts, Calendar, or Safari apps, or tap on one of the recent contact thumbnails displayed in the app switcher.

Another nice feature of Handoff is that you can now send and receive SMS and MMS text messages via your cellular service provider's texting network (as opposed to Apple's Internet-based iMessage service) from your iPad or Mac(s). These incoming or outgoing messages use the Message app running on your iPhone as a conduit.

**NOTE** When AirDrop, AirPlay, AirPrint, Handoff, and the functionality now offered by iCloud are used together, your iPhone or iPad can not only sync and share content in a variety of ways, but you can use your smartphone or tablet to control other equipment or use the Find My... tools offered by iCloud to keep tabs on the whereabouts of your own devices remotely.

5

# WAYS TO USE iCLOUD'S LATEST FEATURES WITH YOUR iPHONE AND/OR iPAD

iCloud is Apple's cloud-based service, which has been designed from the ground up to work seamlessly with all iOS mobile devices and Macs. Functionality for using iCloud's various features and functions is built in to the iOS 8 operating system, as well as OS X Yosemite for the Mac.

As the technology related to Apple's iOS mobile devices continues to evolve, Apple has continuously worked to expand and enhance iCloud's capabilities. Now, more than ever, if you're an iPhone, iPad, and/or Mac user, setting up an iCloud account is essential in order to take full advantage of the latest features and functions built in to your smartphone, tablet, and/or computer.

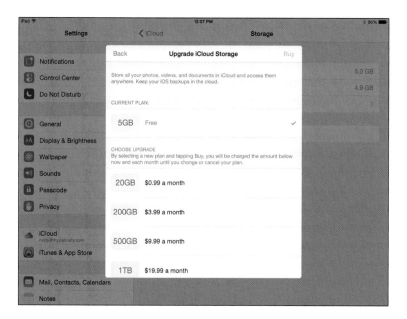

**WHAT'S NEW**  With the release of iOS 8 and OS X Yosemite, iCloud's newest features include iCloud Drive and Family Sharing, along with dramatic enhancements made to how photos are synced, stored, and shared. Improvements have also been made to many other iCloud features, such as Find My… and the iCloud.com service (which offers fully functional online editions of Contacts, Calendar, Reminders, Notes, Find My…, Pages, Numbers, and Keynote).

While setting up an iCloud account continues to be free, if you need to utilize more than the 5GB of online storage space that comes with each account, you must purchase additional online storage. The monthly fee structure for additional iCloud online storage space recently changed (as shown in Figure 5.1).

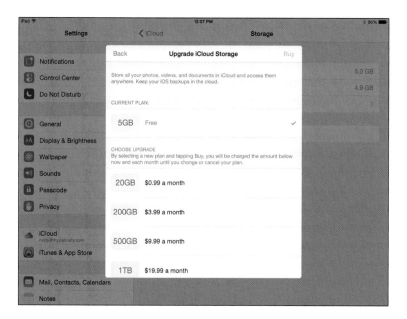

**FIGURE 5.1**

*To upgrade your iCloud account's online storage, launch Settings, tap on the iCloud option, tap on the Storage option, tap on the Storage option, and then tap on the Change Storage Plan option.*

(iOS 8) **WHAT'S NEW**   The included 5GB of online storage space, plus any additional space you pay for, can be utilized to store your app-specific data, backup files, photos, and your personal files (including those created using the iWork apps).

In the past, online storage needed to store your photos, as part of iCloud's My Photo Stream and Shared Photo Streams, was provided for free. With the transition to iCloud Photo Library, which is managed from the Photos app on your iPhone, iPad, and/or Macs, this is no longer the case. Photo storage via iCloud Photo Library now utilizes your 5GB allocation and any additional storage space you purchase.

However, the additional online storage space that's needed for your iTunes Store, App Store, iBookstore, and Newsstand content purchases continues to be free.

To see and manage how your iCloud online storage space is actually being utilized, launch Settings and tap on the iCloud option. Tap on the Storage option, and from the Storage submenu, tap on the Manage Storage option.

From the Manage Storage screen (shown in Figure 5.2), you can quickly see how much online storage space is currently available, as well as how much is being utilized by photos, backups, documents and data, and mail.

**FIGURE 5.2**
*The Manage Storage screen enables you to see how your iCloud account's online storage is currently being utilized.*

**TIP** Under the Documents & Data heading found on the Manage Storage screen (refer to Figure 5.2), you can see which third-party apps are storing app-specific data within your iCloud account. Tap on a listing to see additional detail. Then, from the Info screen, to delete unneeded data, documents, files or app-specific content, tap on the Edit option. Next, swipe your finger across a listing from left to right, and then tap on the Delete option.

Alternatively, tap on the Edit option, and then tap on the negative sign icon associated with a listing or tap on the Delete All option. This can be done to free up online storage space and remove content or files you no longer need to maintain a remote (cloud-based) backup of.

**TIP** To conserve online storage space within your iCloud account, delete iCloud Backup files for old devices, or backups that are redundant and no longer needed. As each new iCloud Backup is created, you can control what content is actually backed up to iCloud from within Settings.

To do this, launch Settings, tap on the iCloud option, tap on the Storage option, and then tap on the Manage Storage option. Under the Backups heading (shown in Figure 5.3), tap on any of your device-specific backup files. To delete that backup, tap on the Delete Backup option. Under the Backup Options heading, turn on or off the virtual switches associated with which apps you want to back up during the iCloud Backup process.

Each iCloud account also includes a free @icloud.com email account, which you can use to send and receive email from any devices that are linked to your iCloud account. Once it's set up, iCloud automatically keeps your email account synchronized via the Mail App.

**FIGURE 5.3**
*The iCloud Backup feature now lets you decide what content from your iPhone or iPad to include in the device backup. Select a device you're backing up, and view its iCloud-related Info screen from within Settings.*

> **NOTE** If you have an older Apple ID account that has an associated @mac.com or @me.com email address, its @icloud.com equivalent can automatically be used as the email address that's associated with your iCloud account.

# CONTENT SAVED TO iCLOUD IS AVAILABLE ANYWHERE

By default, as soon as you establish your free iCloud account, anytime you acquire and download content from the iTunes Store, App Store, iBookstore, or Newsstand, a copy of that content automatically gets saved in your iCloud account and immediately becomes available on all of your compatible computers and iOS mobile devices (including Apple TV) that are linked to that iCloud account. This includes all past purchases and downloads, as well.

So, if you hear an awesome new song on the radio (or on iTunes Radio), you can immediately purchase and download it from the iTunes Store using your iPhone.

As always, that song becomes available on your iPhone within a minute. Then, thanks to iCloud, you can access that same song from your primary computer, iPad, iPod touch, and/or Apple TV device, without having to repurchase it. This feature also works with TV shows and movies purchased from the iTunes Store.

**(iOS 8) WHAT'S NEW** Thanks to iCloud's Family Sharing feature, it's now possible for up to six family members to have their own independent iCloud accounts, but share some or all of their purchased content from the iTunes Store, App Store, and iBookstore. How to use Family Sharing is covered later in this chapter.

Another benefit to using iCloud is that syncing can be done from anywhere via the Internet, without using iTunes Sync or requiring a connection between your iOS mobile device and your primary computer.

**NOTE** The iTunes Sync process is also still possible by installing the iTunes software onto your primary computer, and then connecting your iOS mobile device using the supplied USB cable, but this process for backing up and syncing data is less convenient than using iCloud.

Because using the iTunes Sync process is now considered an antiquated way to sync and back up data, this book focuses on using iCloud. If you're still interested in using iTunes Sync, however, visit Apple's website (http://support.apple.com/kb/PH12117) for more information on how to use this feature.

It's still possible to use the Wireless iTunes Sync process between your iOS mobile device and primary computer that's running the iTunes software, as long as the iPhone or iPad and the computer are connected to the same wireless network.

If you ever opt to delete a purchase from your iOS mobile device, for whatever reason, you always have the option of downloading and installing it again, free, from iCloud.

☑ **TIP**   Depending on how you set up the iTunes Store, App Store, and iBookstore to work with iCloud, you can automatically have all of your computers and iOS mobile devices download all new music, app, and eBook content you purchase, or this can be done manually. To adjust these Automatic Downloads settings, launch Settings, select the iTunes & App Stores option, and then set the virtual switches associated with Music, Apps, and Books that are listed under the Automatic Downloads heading.

In iOS 8, it's possible to also set up your iPhone or iPad to automatically update all of your apps as new versions of previously installed apps get released. To do this, turn on the virtual switch associated with the Updates option that's listed below the Music, Apps, and Books options.

Due to their large file sizes, automatic downloads are not possible for TV show episodes, movies, or audiobooks acquired from the iTunes Store. However, you can download these purchases manually onto each of your computers and/or iOS mobile devices that are linked to the same iCloud account.

✐ **NOTE**   Although your iTunes Store music purchases might represent a portion of your overall personal digital music library, chances are that library also includes CDs (which you have ripped into digital format), as well as online music purchases and downloads from other sources (such as Amazon.com).

For an additional fee of $24.99 per year, you can upgrade your iCloud account by adding the iTunes Match services. This grants you full access to your entire personal digital music library (including non-iTunes Store purchases) from all of your computers and devices that are linked to your iCloud account. To learn more about iTunes Match, visit www.apple.com/itunes/itunes-match.

## ACCESS YOUR PURCHASED iTUNES STORE CONTENT FROM ANY DEVICE

If you do not have the Automatic Downloads option enabled, you can still manually load iTunes Store purchases onto your device by following these steps:

1. Make sure that your iOS device is connected to the Web via a cellular data or Wi-Fi connection.

2. Launch the iTunes Store app on your device. If prompted, when the Apple ID Password window pops up on your screen, use the virtual keyboard to enter your Apple ID password.

3. Tap on the Purchased icon near the lower-right corner of the iTunes app's screen. Then, near the top center of the screen, tap on the Music, Movies, or TV Shows tab.

> **NOTE**  On an iPhone, to access already purchased content, launch the iTunes Store app, tap on the More icon near the bottom-right corner of the screen, and then tap on the Purchased option. Select Music, Movies, or TV Shows; then choose the content you want to download onto the phone.

4. On the iPad, in a column on the left side of the screen is an alphabetic listing of artists, music groups, or TV shows, depending on which category of content you selected. Tap the one you want to see what is available under that listing. If you chose Movies in step 3, you can directly select a movie.

5. On the iPhone, after selecting a content type, past purchases are listed in alphabetical order. For example, Figure 5.4 shows purchased music on an iPhone. Tap on a song listing, and then tap on its iCloud icon to download that song onto the device you're currently using. On the iPad, this is possible from a single screen that displays both purchase listings and respective iCloud icons.

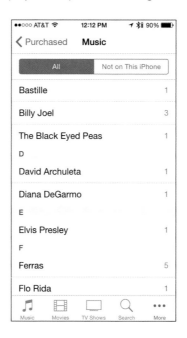

**FIGURE 5.4**

*From the iTunes Store app, access and download your previous purchases by tapping on the Purchased icon. Shown here is an alphabetical listing of purchased music on an iPhone 5s.*

> **☑ TIP** To see a listing of your most recent purchased content, tap on the category (Music, Movies, or TV shows, for example), and then tap on the Most Recent option on the iPad or the Recent Purchases option on the iPhone.

6. Tap on the iCloud icons, one at a time, to select content you want to download onto the iPhone or iPad you're currently using. Or to download all of the listed content, tap on the iCloud icon to the right of the Download All option at the top of the list.

> **☑ TIP** If you've acquired audiobooks, an additional tab is displayed alongside the Music, Movies, and TV Shows options. Below these tabs are two additional tabs, labeled All and Not On This iPad [iPhone]. Tapping on the All tab lists all content of that type you own, while tapping on the Not On This iPad [iPhone] tab displays only related content you own that's not already stored on the device you're using.

7. Within minutes, the content you selected to download is available to enjoy on the iOS mobile device you're currently using.

8. Exit the iTunes Store app by pressing the Home button.

9. Launch the Music or Videos app on your iOS mobile device to experience the newly downloaded (or re-downloaded) content.

## USE iCLOUD TO SYNC YOUR APP-SPECIFIC DATA, DOCUMENTS, AND FILES

Most cloud-based file-sharing services serve mainly as a place in cyberspace to remotely store files. However, you must manually transfer those files to and from the "cloud." Thanks to iCloud's integration with iOS 8, many of the core apps that come with the latest version of this mobile operating system, as well as a growing number of third-party apps, automatically keep data and files created or managed using those apps synchronized with other devices and computers linked to the same iCloud account.

From within Settings on your iPhone or iPad, turn on or off iCloud support for all compatible apps on your device. In terms of iOS 8's preinstalled apps, those compatible with iCloud data syncing include Contacts, Calendars, Reminders,

Safari, Notes, Photos, Passbook, and Mail (relating only to your free iCloud-related email account).

> **TIP** iCloud Keychain can automatically store the username, password, and credit card information (for online purchases) related to all the websites you visit. Thus, you no longer need to manually sign in to websites when you revisit them, nor do you need to remember each username and password you associated with a website-related account. When this feature is turned on once on each of your iOS mobile devices and Macs, your iCloud Keychain database syncs automatically with iCloud and all computers and iOS mobile devices linked to your iCloud account.

> **NOTE** Some bank- and personal finance-related websites, for example, purposely do not support the iCloud Keychain feature. When visiting these sites that require added security, iCloud Keychain might be able to remember your username, but it cannot automatically remember your password.

> **MORE INFO** iCloud is also fully compatible with Apple's optional iWork apps, which include Pages (word processing), Numbers (spreadsheet management), and Keynote (for digital slide presentations).

When you turn on the iCloud functionality related to the Contacts app, for example, your iOS mobile device automatically syncs your Contacts app database with iCloud. Thus, if you add or update an entry on your iPhone, it automatically synchronizes with the Contacts app running on your other iOS devices, as well as the compatible contact management software that's running on your primary computer (such as the Contacts app or Microsoft Outlook on your Mac). This is also true if you delete a Contacts entry from one device. It is almost instantly deleted from all of your other computers and iOS mobile devices linked to the same iCloud account. (Keep in mind, there is no "undo" option related to this feature.)

As you surf the Web using Safari, when you turn on iCloud syncing functionality related to this app, all of your Bookmarks and Bookmark Bar data, along with your Reading List information and open browser window/tabs data, are synced via iCloud.

To share your photos between iOS devices, your primary computer, and/or an Apple TV device, from the iCloud submenu within Settings, tap on the Photos option to turn on the iCloud Photo Library feature.

## CUSTOMIZING iCLOUD TO WORK WITH YOUR APPS

It's important to understand that the app-related synchronization feature offered by iCloud is different from iCloud Backup, which creates a complete backup of your iOS mobile device that gets stored online as part of your iCloud account.

When you set up iCloud to work with a specific compatible app, that app automatically accesses the Web, connects to iCloud, and then uploads or downloads app-related files, documents, or data as needed. iCloud then shares (syncs) that app-specific data with your other computers and devices that are linked to the same iCloud account.

To customize which of your compatible apps utilize iCloud functionality, follow these steps:

1. Launch Settings from your iPhone's or iPad's Home screen.

2. Tap on the iCloud option.

3. When the iCloud Control Panel screen appears (shown in Figure 5.5), at the top of the screen, make sure the Apple ID–linked email address that's associated with your iCloud account is displayed next to the Account option. If it's not, use your existing Apple ID to create or access an iCloud account by tapping on the Account option.

4. Below the Account option is a list of all preinstalled iCloud-compatible apps on your iOS device. To the right of each listing is a virtual on/off switch. To turn on the iCloud functionality associated with a specific app, set its related virtual switch to the on position.

5. When you have turned on the iCloud functionality for all the apps that you want to synchronize via iCloud, press the Home button to exit Settings and save your changes.

6. Repeat this process on each of your iOS mobile devices. If you have an iPhone and an iPad, you must turn on the iCloud functionality for Contacts, for example, on both devices to keep Contacts data synchronized via iCloud on both devices.

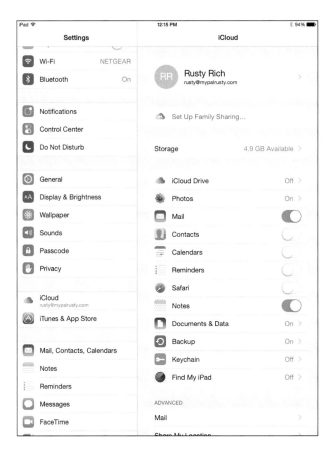

**FIGURE 5.5**
Turn iCloud functionality on or off for specific apps from the iCloud menu within Settings.

> **NOTE** After you've turned on the iCloud functionality for specific apps, to stay synchronized, each computer or device must have access to the Internet. For this use of iCloud on your iPhone or iPad, a cellular or a Wi-Fi Internet connection works fine. For certain other iCloud features, such as managing iCloud Photo Library functions or iCloud Backup, your iPhone or iPad requires a Wi-Fi Internet connection.

# ACCESS YOUR APP-SPECIFIC DATA ONLINE FROM iCLOUD.COM

Another benefit of using iCloud to sync your app-specific data is that using any computer or Internet-enabled device, you can visit www.iCloud.com, log in using your iCloud username and password (which is typically your Apple ID username and password), and then access Web versions of the Contacts, Calendar, Reminders, Notes, Find My…, Pages, Numbers, and Keynote apps. This is shown on a Mac using the Safari web browser in Figure 5.6. Your most up-to-date data automatically populates the online versions of these apps.

**FIGURE 5.6**

*Log in to www.iCloud.com to access your app-specific content using online versions of popular iPhone and iPad apps, including Contacts, Calendar, Reminders, Notes, Find My…, Pages, Numbers, and Keynote.*

If you forget your iPhone at home, for example, you can still access your complete Contacts database, your schedule, your to-do lists, and your notes from any Internet-enabled computer, whether or not that computer is typically linked to your iCloud account.

After you log in to iCloud.com, click on the onscreen app you want to access. The online apps are almost identical to the iPad versions of these apps.

**WHAT'S NEW**    From iCloud.com, it's now possible to access and manage files you manually store in the iCloud Drive portion of your iCloud account. This includes nonapp-specific files, as well as iWork documents and files. To do this, log in to iCloud.com and click on the iCloud Drive icon. You can then access or manage your files from the iCloud Drive screen (shown in Figure 5.7).

Displayed near the top center of the iCloud Drive screen, from left to right, are command icons for creating a new file folder, as well as uploading, downloading, or deleting selected files. This functionality of iCloud works in much the same way as competing cloud-based file sharing services, such as Dropbox.

**FIGURE 5.7**
*From the iCloud Drive screen accessible from iCloud.com, it's possible to access and manage files you've manually stored in this area of your iCloud account.*

**CAUTION**    If you plan to use the iCloud Drive feature with your Macs, as well as your iOS mobile devices, make sure the Macs are running the latest version of the OS X Yosemite operating system.

**CAUTION**    If you're using someone else's computer to access iCloud.com, be sure to log off from the iCloud service when you're finished. To do this, click on your username in the top-right corner of the screen, and click on the Sign Out option.

# AUTOMATICALLY TRANSFER DOCUMENTS USING iCLOUD

In addition to the iCloud compatibility built in to many of the core (preinstalled) apps that are included with iOS 8, a growing number of other apps also offer iCloud compatibility and enable you to easily and automatically transfer or synchronize app-related documents and files. For example, this functionality is built in to Apple's iWork apps. Be sure to upgrade your iWork for iOS apps to the latest versions for this functionality to work.

If you turn on iCloud functionality within Pages, Numbers, Keynote, or other compatible third-party apps, when you create or revise a document or file, that revision is stored on your iOS device and on iCloud. From iCloud, that same app running on your iOS device (or compatible software running on your primary computer) can access that most recent version of your files or documents within seconds.

So, if you're working with the Pages word processor on your iPhone, your iPad, or the Mac, you always know that when you access a specific Pages document from any compatible device, you're working with the most up-to-date version of that document. The synchronization process happens automatically behind the scenes, assuming that your iOS devices and primary computer are connected to the Internet.

> **NOTE** If you're using the Office for iOS apps, which include Microsoft Word, Microsoft Excel, Microsoft PowerPoint, Microsoft OneNote, and OWA (Outlook Web Application) for iPad, these apps are designed to automatically sync and share files via Microsoft's OneDrive service, not with iCloud.

The processes for turning on iCloud functionality within compatible apps on your mobile devices are almost identical. To begin, turn on the iCloud Drive option from the iCloud menu in Settings. Then, to turn on the iCloud functionality in Pages on an iPad, for example, follow these steps:

1. In the Settings app, scroll down the main menu until you find the listing of apps stored on your device.

2. Tap the listing for Pages (or the app of your choice).

3. In the Pages menu screen, tap on the virtual switch that's associated with the Use iCloud option, and switch it to the on position. If you turn this feature to

the off position, your documents are stored only on your device and are not automatically synchronized with other devices via iCloud.

4. Repeat this process for each iCloud-compatible app on each of your iOS devices.

> **NOTE** From your iPhone/iPad, to access iWork documents and files created on your Mac, it's necessary to store those documents in iCloud Drive. To do this, be sure to turn on iCloud syncing from the Mac version of Pages, as well as in the iCloud option of your Mac's System Preferences. You can also access your iWork documents and files from the iWork for iCloud apps (www.icloud.com).

# CREATE A PHOTO LIBRARY USING iCLOUD

With the release of iOS 8 for the iPhone and iPad, as well as OS X Yosemite for the Macs, Apple has redesigned and streamlined iCloud's photo sharing, back up, syncing, and sharing capabilities. Everything is now done through the iCloud Photo Library portion of your iCloud account and can be managed from the Photos app that comes bundled with iOS 8. This will be replacing the iPhoto and Aperture apps on the Mac starting in early 2015.

Using iCloud Photo Library, you can automatically sync your complete photo library with all the computers and mobile devices that are linked to the same iCloud account. You can opt to share specific albums with specific people, yet keep the rest of your photo library private.

To customize options related to iCloud Photo Library, launch Settings, tap on the iCloud option, and then tap on the Photos option. Turn on the virtual switch associated with iCloud Photo Library, and if you want to be able to share certain albums with others, turn on the iCloud Photo Sharing option.

All of the features and functions associated with iCloud Photo Library will not be fully implemented until early 2015. At that time, an update to the Photos app will be installed on your iPhone and/or iPad that supports all of iCloud Photo Library's options. Again, this will replace the My Photo Stream and Shared Photo Stream features, which will automatically be converted to work with iCloud Photo Library.

> **NOTE** One goal of iCloud Photo Library is to give you full online access to your entire digital images library, anytime, from any of your computers or iOS mobile devices. As a result of this content being readily available via the Internet, the need to store digital images on your mobile device will be reduced, so you will ultimately be able to free up internal storage space within your iPhone or iPad.
>
> Depending on the size of your entire digital photo library, it might become necessary to purchase additional iCloud online storage space in order to store all of your digital images.

## USING A UNIQUE APPLE ID FOR iCLOUD

When you first create an iCloud account, you're encouraged to use your existing Apple ID and username. This is to encourage Apple computer and device users to use the same Apple ID to make all of their iTunes Store, App Store, iBookstore, and Newsstand purchases, plus use that same Apple ID to access Apple's online-based iMessage instant messaging service, the FaceTime video calling service, and utilize all of iCloud's other functionality.

To create and manage your Apple ID account(s), visit https://appleid.apple.com from any computer or Internet-enabled device. When you set up iCloud, or use iMessage, FaceTime, or try to access the iTunes Store, iBookstore, or Newsstand for the first time, you also have the option to create a new Apple ID account.

> **TIP** From your iPhone or iPad, to view and manage your Apple ID account, launch Settings, tap on the iTunes & App Stores option, and then tap on the Apple ID option that's displayed near the top of the iTunes & App Store menu screen. Tap on the View Apple ID option to access and manage your account, or tap on the iForgot option to recover a forgotten Apple ID username or password.

## BACKING UP WITH iCLOUD

Another useful feature of iOS 8 is the capability to create a backup of your iOS device wirelessly, and have the related backup files stored online ("in the cloud"). To use this iCloud Backup feature, your iOS mobile device must be connected to the Internet via Wi-Fi. Your primary computer is not needed. Thus, the backup can be created from anywhere, and you can later restore your device from anywhere a Wi-Fi Internet connection is present.

When activated, your iOS mobile device automatically creates a backup to iCloud once per day. For this to happen, your iPhone or iPad also must be connected to an external power source. However, at any time, you can manually create a backup of your device to iCloud from within Settings. This can be done when your device is running on battery.

Follow these steps to activate and use the iCloud Backup feature on an iPhone or iPad:

1. Connect your device to the Internet via a Wi-Fi connection.

2. From the Home screen, launch Settings.

3. Tap on the iCloud option.

4. Scroll down and tap on the Backup option.

5. Turn on the virtual switch that's associated with the iCloud Backup option.

6. A new Back Up Now option appears near the bottom of the Backup screen (as shown in Figure 5.8). Tap on it to begin creating a backup of your iOS mobile device.

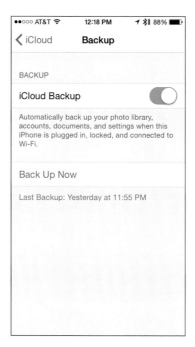

**FIGURE 5.8**

*Manage and launch the iCloud Backup feature from the Backup screen, accessible from within the Settings app.*

> **TIP** The first time you use the iCloud Backup feature to create a wireless backup of your iOS device, the process could take up to an hour (or longer), depending on how much data you have stored on your device. After the backup process begins, a progress meter is displayed at the bottom of the Backup screen within Settings.
>
> In the future, the iCloud Backup process takes place once per day, automatically, when your iOS device is not otherwise in use. These backups save all newly created or revised files and data only, so subsequent iCloud Backup procedures are much quicker.
>
> At the bottom of the Backup screen within Settings, the time and date of the last backup is displayed. If the backup process could not be completed, such as if the device could not connect to the Internet, an error message displays.
>
> At any time, it's possible to manually create an updated backup via iCloud by tapping on the Back Up Now icon displayed on the Backup screen.

The purpose of creating and maintaining a backup of your device is so that you have a copy of all your apps, data, files, content, and personalized settings stored if something goes wrong with your device. If and when you need to access the backup to restore your device using iCloud, when prompted, choose the Restore from iCloud option.

Likewise, if your iPhone or iPad gets lost or stolen and is ultimately replaced, you can restore the content from your old device onto the new one.

> **TIP** To be able to restore your iOS mobile device completely from an iCloud Backup, you also need to turn on and be syncing app compatible apps. Turn on these app-specific features from the iCloud Control Panel screen, which is accessible by launching Settings and tapping on the iCloud option.

# FAMILY SHARING ALLOWS FOR THE SHARING OF PURCHASED CONTENT

Thanks to iCloud's new Family Sharing feature, up to six people can share some or all of their content purchases, while each person retains his or her own private iCloud account. At the same time, a separate Family folder is set up within the

Photos app that enables participating family members to share selected photos within that album but keep all of their other photos private.

> **NOTE** When you set up Family Sharing, a separate Family calendar is automatically created in each participant's Calendar app. This calendar is shared with other family members, while all other Calendar-related data remains private.

To set up a Family Sharing account, one adult in the family needs to turn on this feature, and then invite up to five other family members. To do this, launch Settings, tap on the iCloud option, and then tap on the Family option (shown in Figure 5.9).

**FIGURE 5.9**

*iOS 8 walks you through the Family Sharing setup process from within Settings.*

As you can see from Figure 5.10, you must choose one iCloud account that's associated with a credit card, from which all purchases will be paid from this point forward.

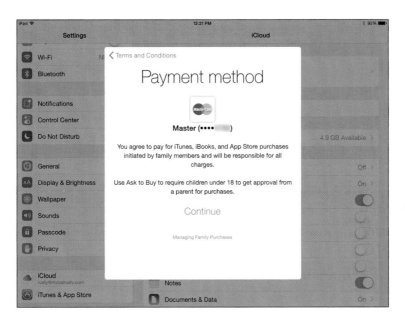

**FIGURE 5.10**

*One of the adults in the family must set up Family Sharing and select one credit or debit card to be used for all subsequent content and in-app purchases.*

One feature of Family Sharing is the ability for family members to share their whereabouts with each other via the Find My Friends app (which is available from the App Store). As you're setting up Family Sharing, you can activate this feature by tapping on the Share Your Location option (shown in Figure 5.11).

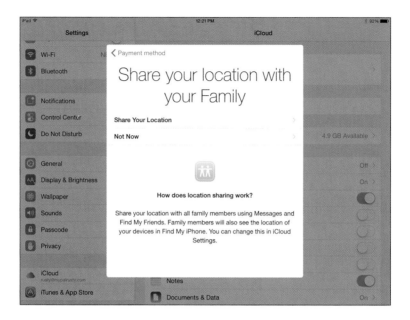

**FIGURE 5.11**

*When setting up Family Sharing, choose whether to turn on the Share Your Location feature from this setup screen.*

Then, from the Family submenu screen (shown in Figure 5.12), tap on the Add Family Member option and enter the name or email address for each family member that will participate. Then select a single Shared Payment Method that can be used to purchase content via this account in the future. Parents can now approve their kids' spending for online content and in-app purchases.

**FIGURE 5.12**

*From the Family submenu screen within Settings, add family members (up to five additional people) and edit your Shared Payment Method.*

As soon as this feature is set up and the family members respond to the email invitation to participate, each person's music, TV shows, movies, eBooks, and compatible apps become available to everyone else. However, it's possible for family members to keep selected content purchases and/or photos private.

> 📝 **NOTE** It's a good idea for parents to set up the Family Sharing feature for their kids and create a separate Apple ID account for each child that the parent maintains control over. To do this, launch Settings, tap on the iCloud option, tap on the Family option, and then tap on the Create an Apple ID for a Child option.

> ✅ **TIP** Before a family member accepts a Family Sharing invitation, his iOS mobile device (or Mac) must already be signed into his personal iCloud account.

When everyone is active with Family Sharing, to access each other's previously purchased content, launch the iTunes Store app, iBooks app (to access iBookstore), or the App Store app (to access apps), and tap on the Purchased option. Select a family member from the displayed menu. The purchased content already acquired by that family member is displayed and becomes downloadable by others. All new purchases are considered acquired by the primary account used to manage the Family Sharing option.

> **✓ TIP**   If you're a parent, turn on the Ask To Buy option when setting up the Family Sharing feature. Then, anytime a child (under age 18) who is linked to the account wants to make a content purchase, the parent receives a text message asking them to approve the purchase. This approval is also required when a child wants to acquire free content.

> **✓ TIP**   As a parent, if you want to hide purchased content from a child, such as an R-rated movie, launch iTunes from your computer and access the iTunes Store. Then, from the Quick Links menu, click on the Purchased icon, and choose the type of content (music, TV shows, or movies, for example) that you want to hide. When you see a listing of purchased content, hover the mouse over the specific content you want to hide from Family Sharing and click on the "X" icon that's associated with these items.

In addition to the other Family Sharing features, events can be created and shared with an automatically created Family calendar in the Calendar app. Any participating family member can create an event with the Calendar app, like they normally would, and choose the Family calendar in the Calendar option in the New Event screen.

To view the Family calendar from the Calendar app, tap on the Calendars option displayed near the bottom center of the screen, and then tap on the Family option to select the Family calendar for viewing (shown in Figure 5.13).

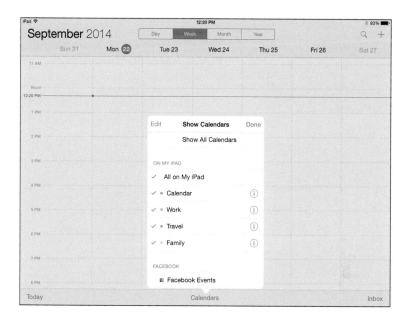

**FIGURE 5.13**

*Choose the Family calendar that's automatically created when Family Sharing is turned on to create, manage, and view family-oriented scheduling events. All your Family Sharing participants can view this shared calendar.*

All of the events displayed in yellow within the sample calendar shown in Figure 5.14 are from the Family calendar, while the other colored events represent additional calendars this iPad Air user maintains in the Calendar app. These other calendars related to Work, Personal, and Travel.

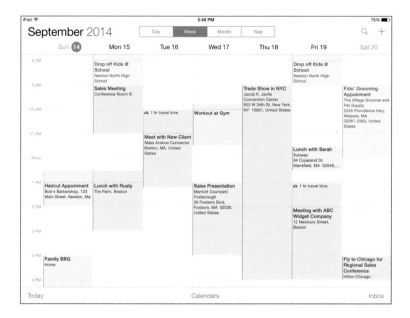

**FIGURE 5.14**

*Using the Week view of the Calendar app on an iPad Air, the events included in the Family calendar are displayed in yellow. As you can see, the Calendar app enables you to view multiple calendars simultaneously.*

Any participating member can add or delete events from the Family calendar; however, any other calendars that are being managed by each person's Calendar app remain separate and private.

> **NOTE** Just like the Family calendar that's accessible by all participating family members, a Family list is also created automatically in the Reminders app. This allows for a centralized list to be accessed and viewed by all participating family members, while at the same time, all other lists stored in each person's Reminders app are kept private.

> **NOTE** Using the Find My Friends app, it's possible to deactivate the Share My Location feature and block family members from viewing your current location. This cannot be done from a child's Apple ID/iCloud account if the account was set up as a "Child Account."

Like all of iCloud's features and functions, what's possible with Family Sharing will evolve over time.

## iCLOUD: MANY USES, ONE STORAGE SPACE

Keep in mind that you are not required to use all of iCloud's various features. You can turn on only those features you believe are beneficial to you, based on how you typically use your iPhone and/or iPad, and what content, data, and information you want to synchronize or back up to your iCloud account.

## IN THIS CHAPTER

- Use the Maps app to obtain turn-by-turn directions between two locations
- Find and display any address, landmark, point-of-interest, or business on a map
- Discover how the Maps app works in conjunction with other iOS apps and features

6

# NAVIGATING WITH THE MAPS APP

In its ongoing quest to provide a highly functional and extremely accurate navigation app, Apple has once again tweaked the Maps app with the release of iOS 8. For example, when you zoom in or out as you're viewing a map on the screen, a graphical map scale is displayed in the upper-left corner to help you more accurately visually gauge distances.

The Maps app continues to require Internet access to function. Although the app works with a Wi-Fi connection, if you plan to use the app's turn-by-turn directions feature, you must use a cellular data connection (which uses up some of your monthly wireless data allocation with each use) because you'll be in motion and will quickly leave the wireless signal radius of any Wi-Fi hotspot.

That being said, a Wi-Fi connection can be used to pre-load driving directions prior to your departure. If your route changes, however, your iOS mobile device will not be able to help if it cannot connect to the Internet.

Using the Maps feature with Siri (which is very convenient) requires even more cellular data usage.

**TIP** To get the most use out of the Maps app, the main Location Services feature in your iPhone or iPad (as well as Location Services for the Maps app) must be turned on. To do this, launch Settings, tap on the Privacy option, and then tap on Location Services. From the Location Services menu screen, turn on the virtual switch displayed near the top of the screen (associated with Location Services). Then, scroll down and tap on the Maps option. Be sure that the While Using option is selected.

**CAUTION** Just as when using any GPS device, do not rely 100 percent on the turn-by-turn directions you're given. Pay attention as you're driving and use common sense. If the Maps app tells you to drive down a one-way street or drive along a closed road, for example, ignore those directions and seek out an alternative route. Don't become one of those people who literally drives into a lake or over a cliff because their GPS told them to. Yes, this does happen.

## GET THE MOST FROM USING THE MAPS APP'S FEATURES

In addition to providing detailed maps, the Maps app is capable of displaying useful information with each map, including real-time, color-coded traffic conditions showing traffic jams and construction, which can be graphically overlaid onto maps. Plus, when you look up a business, restaurant, point of interest, or landmark, the Maps app seamlessly integrates with Yelp! to display detailed information about specific locations.

The Yelp! information screens for each location are interactive, so if you're using an iPhone and tap on a phone number, you can initiate a call to that business or restaurant. Likewise, if you tap on a website URL (on either an iPhone or iPad), Safari launches and the applicable website automatically loads and displays.

**TIP** To enhance the capabilities of the Yelp! integration, download and install the optional (and free) Yelp! app from the App Store. Without the Yelp! app, when appropriate, the Maps app transfers you to the Yelp! website.

> **NOTE** Yelp! is a crowd-sourced online database that contains more than 61 million reviews related to local businesses, stores, restaurants, hotels, tourist attractions, and points of interest. Reviews are created by everyday people who share their experiences, thoughts, and photos. Beyond user-provided reviews, Yelp! also offers details about many businesses and restaurants, often including menus.

Although Maps offers a lot of functionality packed into a standalone app, it's also designed to work with many other apps. For example, as you're viewing an entry in the Contacts app, when you tap on an address, the Maps app launches and displays that address on a map. You can then quickly obtain detailed directions to that location from your current location or from any address you select.

> **TIP** Anytime you receive a text message or view a Calendar event that has an address included with it, iOS 8 automatically determines you're looking at an address and turns it into an active link. Tap on this link to launch the Maps app and view the address or obtain directions to or from that address.

Plus, you can utilize many features built in to the Maps app using voice commands and requests thanks to Siri. For example, regardless of what you're doing on the iPhone or iPad, it's possible to activate Siri and say, "How do I get home from here?" or "Where is the closest gas station?" and then have the Maps app provide you with the directions and map you need.

> **TIP** When you're viewing a map using the Maps app, tap on the My Location icon (which looks like a northeast-pointing arrow) displayed near the bottom-left corner of the screen to pinpoint and display your exact location on the map. Your location is displayed using a pulsating blue dot (shown in Figure 6.1).

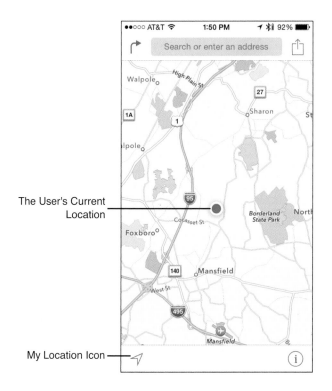

The User's Current Location

My Location Icon

**FIGURE 6.1**

*Tap on the My Location icon (near the lower-left corner of the screen) to pinpoint and display your exact location on a map using a pulsating blue dot.*

## OVERVIEW OF THE MAPS APP'S SCREEN

The main screen of the iOS 8 edition of the Maps app can now display a tiny compass in the upper-right corner of a map, as well as a map scale in the top-left corner of a map. The compass displays automatically when North isn't toward the top of the screen. The map scale appears if you're scrolling around a map using your finger or zooming in or out.

Displayed near the top-left corner of the screen is the Directions option. On the iPhone, this looks like a curved arrow that's pointing to the right. On the iPad, the option actually says "Directions."

> **NOTE** If you're relying on public transportation to get around a popular city, such as Manhattan, Boston, London, or Paris, download an app specifically designed for that public transportation system. To find one, tap the new Apps tab that appears when a route between two locations is provided, or use the Search option in the App Store. For example, enter the search phrase "London Tube Map" to find a variety of interactive apps to help you navigate your way around London's subway/train system.

Use the Search field located at the top center of the Maps screen to find and map out any address. You can enter a complete address (house/building number, street, city, state) or provide less specific information, such as just a city, state, or country. Enter United States to see a map of the entire country. Enter California to view a map of the state.

You also have the option of entering Los Angeles, California, to view a more detailed map of the city, or you can enter a specific street address located within Los Angeles to view it on a detailed map that shows specific streets (and street names).

This Search field is also used to find businesses, restaurants, points of interest, landmarks, and tourist destinations. When the Maps app finds the location you're looking for, you can zoom in or zoom out manually on that map to see more or less detail. Plus, you can change the Map view and switch between the Standard, Hybrid, Satellite, 3D, and/or Flyover views.

> **TIP** In the Search field, enter the name of any contact that has an entry stored in the Contacts app to find and display an address for that contact. The Maps app searches the contents of your iOS device (including the Contacts app), followed by utilizing a web-based search, if applicable.

Anytime a specific location is identified on the map, such as results of a search, those results are displayed using a virtual red push-pin. Tap on a push-pin to view more details about that location and to access a separate Location screen (iPhone) or window (iPad).

Continuously displayed near the bottom-left corner of the main Maps screen is the My Location icon (it looks like a northeast-pointing arrow). At anytime a map is displayed, tap on this icon to locate and display (or update) your current location on the map. This feature is useful if you look up another destination and then want to quickly see where you're located in comparison to that other location. However, when you're using the Maps app for turn-by-turn directions, your iPhone/iPad keeps track of your location in real time and displays this on the map as you're in motion.

As you're viewing a map, tap on the Info icon that's displayed at the bottom-right corner of the screen. A pop-up menu appears that gives you the option to instantly switch between a Standard, Hybrid, or Satellite map view. To do this, tap on the appropriate view that's displayed at the top of this menu (shown in Figure 6.2).

**FIGURE 6.2**

*Tap on the Info icon to reveal this pop-up menu. From here, you can customize how the current map is being displayed.*

Additional options on this pop-up Info menu enable you to Drop A Pin, Show 3D Map, Report A Problem, and/or Show Traffic.

As you're viewing a map, the main Maps app screen includes a Share icon (iPhone) or option (iPad) that's displayed in the top-right corner of the screen. Tap on this Share icon/option to reveal a Share menu (shown in Figure 6.3), from which you can share location details with others, add the location to the Maps app's Favorites list, or print the current map (using an AirPrint-compatible printer).

**FIGURE 6.3**
*The Share menu that's built in to the Maps app enables you to share your location with others via AirDrop, text message, or email.*

> **TIP** The newly redesigned Share menu includes an Add to Favorites button. Tap on this to save the currently viewed location as a Maps bookmark for later reference.

> **WHAT'S NEW** To access your Favorites menu within the Maps app, tap on the Search field that's located in the top center of the screen. Displayed immediately below the Recents heading is the Favorites option. Tap on this to reveal your list of manually saved Favorites locations. When this list is visible, tap any item to reopen the map of that location.

Displayed along the bottom of the Favorites menu are three tabs, labeled Favorites, Recents, and Contacts (shown in Figure 6.4). Tapping on the Favorites tab reveals an interactive list of manually saved Favorites locations that you have bookmarked. Tap on any listing view to reopen a map of that location. Tap on the Edit button to edit, delete, or reorder this list, or swipe your finger from right to left across a listing to delete it.

**FIGURE 6.4**
*The Favorites list can display your saved Favorites locations, your search history, or your Contacts list.*

Tap on the Recents tab to view a list of recently searched or viewed locations. To clear this list, tap on the Clear button displayed near the top-left corner of the screen.

When you tap on the Contacts tab, the All Contacts listing is displayed. This shows a comprehensive list of all entries stored in your Contacts database. All Contacts listings that are displayed in bold, black type have one or more addresses associated with them.

Whether you're looking at the Favorites, Recents, or All Contacts list, tap on one of the listings to view that location on a map. It's then possible to obtain detailed directions to or from that location.

# VIEW A MAP FROM MULTIPLE PERSPECTIVES

As you're viewing a map on the screen, place one finger on the screen and drag it around to move the map around. To rotate the map, place two fingers (slightly separated) on the screen, and rotate your fingers clockwise or counterclockwise.

Use a reverse-pinch finger gesture to zoom in or a pinch finger gesture to zoom out. If you're using the Satellite map view, you can zoom in very close, and then drag your finger around the map to take a bird's-eye tour of the area that's displayed in 3D. This feature works better with a high-speed Wi-Fi Internet connection. In some cases, instead of a 3D view, the Maps app offers a more detailed Flyover view.

# THE UPDATED MAPS APP'S INFO SCREEN

The Info icon is displayed near the bottom-right corner of the main Maps screen. When you tap on this circular "i" icon, a window pops up that enables you to quickly switch between the Standard, Hybrid, or Satellite map view. Simply tap on one of the labeled tabs that are displayed near the top of this window (refer to Figure 6.2).

From the Info window, you can also drop a virtual pin on any location that's displayed on the currently viewed map and show or hide color-coded traffic details on the map.

## THE DROP A PIN OPTION

When you tap on the Drop A Pin option, the full Maps screen returns. Tap anywhere on that map to place a virtual push-pin. The new push-pin is displayed in purple instead of red. After you place a push-pin, it's possible to view detailed information about that particular location, including its exact address. You can then tap on the displayed Info icon to view a location menu that offers a handful of menu options, including Directions To Here, Directions From Here, Create New Contact, Add To Existing Contact, Remove Pin, Add Bookmark, or Report a Problem (shown in Figure 6.5).

**FIGURE 6.5**

*Tap on the purple push-pin you place on a map to reveal a more detailed Info screen pertaining to that location. This window includes a menu as well.*

> **TIP** Tap on the Share icon to access the app's Share menu to share the pinned location with others or add it to your Favorites list.

## THE SHOW/HIDE TRAFFIC OPTION

Regardless of which map view you're looking at, you can have color-coded real-time traffic information superimposed on the map. This feature can help you avoid traffic jams and construction and enables you to seek an alternative route before you get stuck in the traffic.

> **NOTE** Mild traffic is showcased using yellow, while heavy traffic is depicted in red. When construction is being done on a roadway, separate construction icons (in yellow or red) are displayed on the map.

> ☑️ **TIP** The Show Traffic feature works much better when you're viewing a zoomed-in version of a map that shows a lot of street-level detail. Figure 6.6 shows heavy traffic conditions (a dashed red line) along N. Highland Ave. in Hollywood, California, near the famous TCL Chinese Theatre.

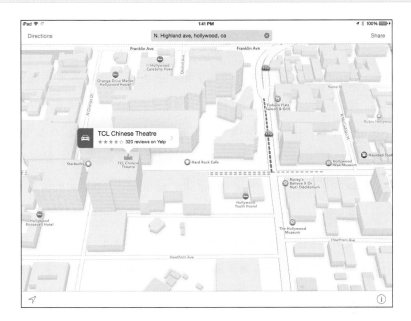

**FIGURE 6.6**

*A red line along a roadway indicates heavy traffic when you have the Show Traffic feature turned on in the Maps app.*

## THE STANDARD, HYBRID, AND SATELLITE TABS

Displayed along the top of the Maps Info window are the three map view command tabs: Standard, Hybrid, and Satellite. The Standard map view (shown in Figure 6.7) displays a traditional-looking, multicolored map on the screen. Street names and other important information are labeled and displayed on the map.

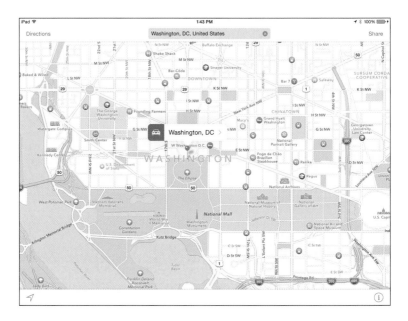

**FIGURE 6.7**

*The Standard map view shows a traditional, multicolored map with street names and other points of interest listed on it.*

The Satellite view uses high-resolution and extremely detailed satellite imagery to show maps from an overhead view, while the Hybrid map view (shown in Figure 6.8) showcases the same satellite imagery but overlays and displays street names and other important information, similar to the information you'd see using the Standard view.

**FIGURE 6.8**

*The Hybrid map view shows street names and other details superimposed over a satellite image.*

> ☑ **TIP**   Anytime you're viewing a map, you can switch between map views.
> Then from the main Maps screen, tap on the My Location icon to display your exact
> location on the map. To switch between a 2D and 3D map view, tap on the Show
> 2D/3D Map option that's displayed as part of the Info menu (refer to Figure 6.2).

> ☑ **TIP**   When you look up any business using the Maps app, if you then
> view the location of the business with the Satellite or Hybrid view, you can
> often determine the best place to park nearby. Consider dropping a pin on that
> location, and then using turn-by-turn directions to get you to that spot. There are
> also third-party apps, like Parker, that can help you find a parking spot or paid
> parking lot within a major city.

# OBTAIN TURN-BY-TURN DIRECTIONS BETWEEN TWO LOCATIONS

The turn-by-turn directions feature of the Maps app is not only easy to use, it's also extremely useful. Begin using this feature from the main Maps app screen. Tap on the Directions icon located at the top-left corner of the screen.

The Start and End fields, as well as the reverse directions icon and recently displayed location results (if applicable), are shown within a pop-up window (see Figure 6.9).

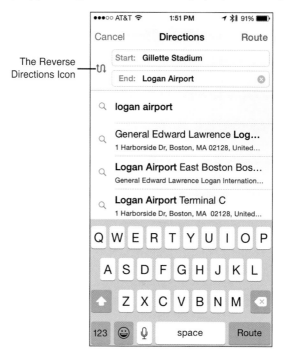

The Reverse Directions Icon

**FIGURE 6.9**

*Fill in the Start and End fields to obtain detailed, turn-by-turn directions between any two locations that you choose.*

In the Start field, the default option is your current location; however, to change this, tap on the field and enter any starting address. Then tap on the End field and enter any ending address.

> **TIP** Displayed below the Start and End field are recent locations you've utilized within the Maps app. Scroll up or down this list using your finger, or tap on any entry to use it as your Start or End location.

> **TIP** In the Start and End field, you can enter a contact entry's name, a full address, a city and state, just a state, or just a country. You can use two-letter state abbreviations, and you don't have to worry about using upper- and lowercase letters. For example, you can type "New York, NY," "new york, ny," or "New York, New York," and get the same result. This goes for contacts or business names as well.

When the Start and End fields have been filled in, tap on the Route option that's displayed near the top-right corner of the window. There's also a Route button on the virtual keyboard.

A route overview map (shown in Figure 6.10) is displayed. The green push-pin represents your starting location and the red-push pin represents your ending location.

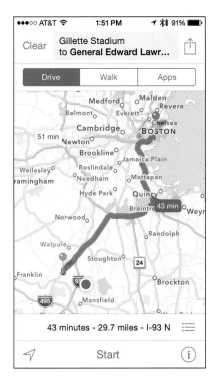

**FIGURE 6.10**

*A sample route overview map shows your start and end location on one map, plus up to three possible driving routes to get there.*

At the top of this route overview map are three command tabs, labeled Drive, Walk, and Apps. To obtain driving directions, tap on the Drive tab. For walking directions, tap on the Walk tab. If you want to use public transportation, tap on the Apps tab, and the Maps app refers you to related apps available from the App Store that can be used to better navigate around the area using public transportation.

If you select driving directions, the Maps app displays between one and three possible routes between the start and end locations.

The primary route is outlined on the route overview map with a dark blue line. One or two alternative routes may be outlined with light blue lines. Associated with each route is an approximate travel time.

> **NOTE** If the route requires you to take toll roads or a ferry service, for example, a warning message appears just below the Drive, Walk, and Apps tabs on the route overview screen.

> **TIP** Turn on the Show Traffic option to display current traffic conditions along the three routes, and then choose the one with the least congestion or construction. Tap on any of the route lines to select your route. The route highlighted with the dark blue line is the default (recommended) route.

When you're ready to begin your journey, tap on the Start option that's displayed near the bottom center of the screen. You're then given real-time turn-by-turn directions. Just like when using a standalone GPS device, a voice guides you through each turn, while also displaying related information on the main map screen (shown in Figure 6.11).

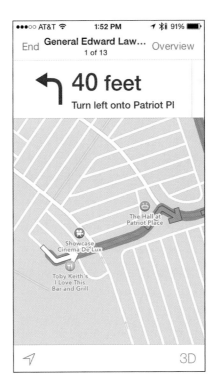

**FIGURE 6.11**

*The Maps app shows detailed turn-by-turn directions on the map screen and speaks to you as you're driving.*

While the turn-by-turn directions are being displayed, the Standard map view is used. Your ETA, as well as how much time is left in your trip and the distance from your destination are displayed along the top the screen. At anytime, tap the Overview option to return to the route overview map, or tap the End option to exit out of the turn-by-turn directions feature and return to the main Maps screen. When available, you can also now tap on the 3D view option. Look for the 3D icon to be displayed in the bottom-right corner of the screen when applicable.

Follow the voice and onscreen prompts until you reach your destination. If you press the Home button, you can return to the Home screen and launch another app while the Maps feature is still running, and then return to the turn-by-turn directions by tapping on the blue bar that says Touch To Return To Navigation. It's displayed near the top-right corner of the screen. This also works when you launch another app via the multitasking bar.

> ## ✓ TIP
> To view text-based directions to your destination, enter a Start and End location using the Directions feature of the Maps app, but before tapping Start to obtain the directions, tap on the Listing icon, which can be found just above the Info icon when viewing the route overview screen. Also, the List Steps option appears if you tap on the screen during the navigation process.
>
> Use your finger to scroll up or down on this list, or tap on one of the individual directions to jump to the map that shows that step.

## LOOK UP CONTACT ENTRIES, BUSINESSES, RESTAURANTS, LANDMARKS, AND POINTS OF INTEREST

One of the other primary uses of the Maps app is to find and display addresses, contacts, businesses, points of interest, or landmarks on a map screen. To do this, from the main Maps screen, simply type what you're looking for into the Search field. In Figure 6.12, Seattle Space Needle was entered into the search field.

**FIGURE 6.12**

*The Seattle Space Needle in Seattle, Washington, is shown here using the hybrid and 3D map view.*

> **TIP** If you're looking for businesses or services in your immediate area, tap on the My Location icon first, so the iPhone or iPad pinpoints your location, and then enter what you're searching for. No city or state needs to be entered. If you don't tap on the My Location icon first, you must enter what you're looking for, followed by the city, a comma, and the state, to find local search results. Otherwise, the Maps app defaults to the last search location.
>
> If the business or service is considered a major point of interest, such as the Seattle Space Needle, Disney World, or O'Hare Airport, you do not need to include the city or state in the Search field.

## USE THE INTERACTIVE LOCATION SCREENS TO FIND MORE INFORMATION

Once search results are displayed on the map in the form of virtual push-pins, tap on any push-pin to view an information banner for a location on a map. In Figure 6.13, a search for Apple Store locations in Los Angeles was performed and displayed on the map.

**FIGURE 6.13**

*The results of a search for Apple Stores in the Los Angeles area appear as red virtual push-pins on this hybrid view map.*

Tap on one push-pin, and then tap the left side of the information banner to obtain "quick" turn-by-turn directions from your current location. Or, tap on the Info icon on the right side of the listing to view an interactive Location screen.

A separate and informative Location screen (shown in Figure 6.14) displays details about that search result using details from the Maps app, the Internet, and from Yelp!. This information includes the phone number, address, website URL, and other information for that search result. The information displayed depends on whether it's a business, restaurant, point of interest, or tourist attraction.

**FIGURE 6.14**

*A detailed Location screen combines location information with details about that location obtained from Yelp!. Information about the Apple Store at The Grove in Los Angeles is shown here.*

**TIP** When looking at multiple search results on a map (refer to Figure 6.13), tap on the List Results option to view a text-based interactive listing of the search results.

As you scroll down on the Location screen, you'll see a Directions To Here and Directions From Here option. Tap on either of these to obtain directions to or from your current location to the address listed on the screen.

Tap on the More Info On Yelp! option to launch the Yelp! app or visit the Yelp! website to view more detailed information about that location.

Create New Contact, Add To Existing Contact, and Report A Problem options are also available by scrolling down in the Location window.

> **TIP** Yelp! relies on individual users like you for its reviews, photos, and information. From the location information screen within Maps, it's possible to add your own photo related to a location, Check-In at that location, or Write a Review of that location (which might be a restaurant, business, or point of interest).

Displayed next to the Reviews From Yelp option is a See More> option. Tap on it to view all the individual reviews that others have published on Yelp! that are related to the selected location. For example, you can use these reviews to help you decide where to dine or determine which mechanic to use at a local service station if your car needs repair.

Another potentially useful feature offered within each location window is a Popular Apps Nearby listing. This showcases a handful of optional third-party apps that are relevant to that specific area. From this listing, you might find apps from local stores, malls, tourist attractions, or media outlets, for example.

> **TIP** If you look up information about a restaurant, the Location screen features Yelp!-related information, including the type of food served, the menu price range (using dollar sign symbols), the hours of operation, and potentially a website link that enables you to view the restaurant's menu. You can also determine whether the restaurant delivers or accepts reservations.
>
> If reservations are accepted, use the optional Open Table app to make reservations online. Activate Siri and say, "Make a reservation for [insert number of people] for [insert day and time]," or initiate a call from an iPhone to the restaurant by tapping on the phone number field.

## THE MAPS APP'S FLYOVER VIEW

In the iOS 8 edition of the Maps app, the 3D map view and the Flyover view that were featured in iOS 7 have been integrated together. The Flyover map view is offered for many major cities, although it doesn't really serve a navigation purpose. This feature, however, can be used to help you get acquainted with the layout of a city and enable you to take a virtual tour of its skyline from your iPhone or iPad.

When it's available, the 3D option that's normally displayed as a map view option is replaced with the Flyover icon (which looks like a building). Tap on it to switch to a stunning Flyover map view.

## MAPS QUICK TIPS

- To customize several settings related to the Maps app, launch Settings and tap on the Maps option. From the Maps menu screen, it's possible to decide whether to show distances in miles or kilometers, plus automatically have the iPhone/iPad translate map labels into English.

- As you're viewing a map, it's almost always possible to zoom in or out using either a reverse-pinch or pinch figure gesture or a double-tap on an area of the map.

- After tapping the Directions option to obtain directions between two addresses, a Reverse icon is displayed to the immediate left of the Start and End. Tap it to switch the addresses you have in the Start and End fields to obtain reverse directions.

- As the Maps app is giving you real-time turn-by-turn directions, tap on the Overview option to switch back to the route overview map. Or tap on the screen to view the List Steps option and see a text-based turn-by-turn directions listing. Tap the Resume option to exit out of this view.

- When using your iPhone or iPad with the Maps app, the iOS mobile device accesses the Internet extensively. This drains the device's battery faster. If you use this feature from your car often, consider investing in a car charger that plugs into your car's 12-volt jack. This way, your iPhone/iPad's battery remains charged (and can recharge) while it's being used.

- Using the Maps app for turn-by-turn directions via a cellular data Internet connection requires a significant amount of wireless data usage. Using this feature can quickly deplete your monthly wireless data allocation unless you're subscribed to an unlimited wireless service plan. Also, if you're using international roaming to access the Internet from abroad, using Maps with a cellular data connection can get very expensive.

- When viewing a map, a compass appears near the upper-right corner of the screen when the map is not oriented with North at the top of the screen. When you tap on the My Location icon, the Map is displayed using a north-facing orientation. If you double-tap on the My Location icon, the map orientates itself in the direction you're traveling.

- Use Siri to quickly find addresses in your Contacts database or to locate a business or point of interest, and then plug in that information to the Maps app without any manual data entry required.

▦ When using almost any other app on your iPhone or iPad, anytime an address is listed, if that address is underlined (meaning that iOS 8 has converted it into a hyperlink), you can tap on that address to launch the Maps app and view the location on a detailed map. At that point, you can use any of the Maps app's features to get directions to that location or learn more about that location.

**iOS 8 WHAT'S NEW** If you are a business operator who wants to customize your company's listing in the Maps app to attract new customers or allow Maps users to find and learn more about your business, visit https://mapsconnect. apple.com. Sign in to Apple's Maps Connect website using your Apple ID, and follow the onscreen prompts up create or update a business listing. In a week or so, the information will be verified and become accessible to anyone using the Maps app from their iOS mobile device or Mac.

## IN THIS CHAPTER

- Learn to use the Facebook and Twitter functionality that's integrated into iOS 8
- Discover how to use the official Facebook and Twitter app
- Discover other online social networking apps for services like YouTube, SnapChat, LinkedIn, Instagram, and Vine

7

# MAKE THE MOST OF ONLINE SOCIAL NETWORKING APPS

One of the reasons why online social networking services have become so incredibly popular around the world, allowing them to change the way people stay in touch and communicate with each other, is because access to these services is incredibly easy.

Available for free from the App Store are official apps from all of the major social networks that enable you to fully manage your online account, stay in touch with your online friends, and share photos, videos, or other content while you're on the go.

Meanwhile, iOS 8 has Facebook, Twitter, Flickr, and Vimeo integration built in to several of the preinstalled apps. This means you can quickly create and publish app-specific content without actually launching a social networking app.

> **✓ TIP** Almost any iPhone or iPad app that has a Share button now enables you to share app-specific information and publish it on Facebook and/or Twitter from within the app you're using.

To begin using any of the popular online social networking services from your iPhone or iPad, you first must set up a free account with that service. This can be done either by visiting the service's main website (such as www.facebook.com or www.twitter.com) on your primary computer or using Safari on your mobile device, or by clicking on the new account setup-related option in the official iOS mobile app for that service. Figure 7.1 shows the opening screen for the official Facebook app. From here, either sign in using your existing email and password related to your Facebook account, or tap on the Sign Up For Facebook option displayed near the bottom center of the screen.

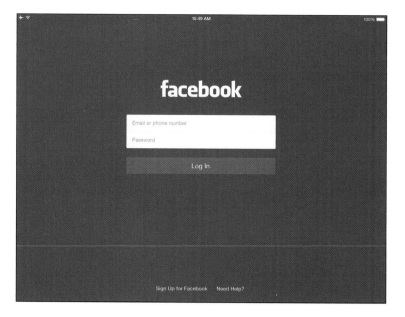

**FIGURE 7.1**

*The opening screen of the Facebook app enables you to set up a new account by tapping on the Sign Up For Facebook button.*

After you've set up an account, enter your username and password in the social networking app on your iPhone or iPad.

! **CAUTION** Many of the online social networking apps automatically tap in to the Location Services function of your iPhone or iPad and publish your location anytime you create a new posting to that service (or upload a new photo or video). To prevent this and protect your privacy, do not grant permission for the online social networking app to access your mobile device's Location Services as you're first setting it up.

Anytime thereafter, it's possible to customize privacy-related settings for many apps by launching Settings and tapping on the Privacy option. Turn on or off the virtual switch associated with Facebook, Twitter, and other displayed online social networking apps (shown in Figure 7.2). Some services, such as Instagram, enable you to add your location to a posting, but only if you want to.

Many people opt to leave Location Services turned on, but as they're using a social networking service from their mobile device, they pay attention to when this feature is going to be utilized and opt to include or leave out their location when creating a new post or uploading content.

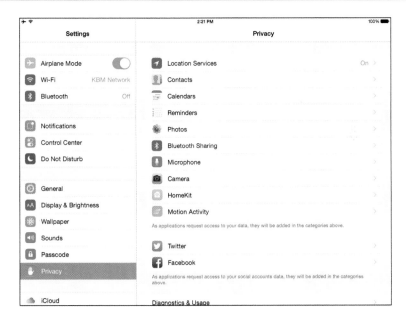

**FIGURE 7.2**

*From the Privacy menu in Settings, you can determine whether Facebook and Twitter can automatically share your exact location whenever you publish content to that service.*

> **TIP** The Facebook service, as well as the Facebook app, offers its own Privacy Settings menu that you should access and customize based on your level of comfort sharing information as you begin using this service. Tap on the menu icon and select the Privacy Shortcuts option or the Settings option to do this.

# FACEBOOK, TWITTER, FLICKR, AND VIMEO INTEGRATION IS BUILT IN TO iOS 8

If you already have a Facebook, Twitter, Flickr, or Vimeo account, you must set up the iOS 8 integration functionality for each of these services separately, plus download and install the official app for each of these services on which you're active.

Setting up account integration with iOS 8 (and many of the apps that come pre-installed on your iOS mobile device) must be done only once per account on each of your iOS mobile devices.

> **NOTE** This integration allows options for the compatible online social networking services to be displayed as part of the Share menu of many apps, including Photos.
>
> If you don't turn on integration with a service, these options will not be accessible from the Share menu of the apps you use.

To set up this integration for each service, follow these steps:

1. Launch Settings from the Home screen.
2. Scroll down to the Twitter, Facebook, Flickr, or Vimeo option that's displayed as part of the main Settings menu. Tap on the app you want to configure.
3. Tap on the Username and Password option and enter the appropriate information (shown in Figure 7.3).
4. Tap on the Sign In option.
5. If you haven't already done so, tap on the Install button displayed next to the app logo to download and install the official app. Once the app is downloaded, you must sign in to the service from the app, and once again supply your account username and password (this time, while using the app).

**FIGURE 7.3**

*Add your existing Twitter account information to the Twitter submenu within Settings, and then tap Sign In to log in to your account. This enables iOS 8 and many apps to include a Share via Twitter option as part of the app's Share menu.*

6. When the app is installed, if applicable, tap on the Settings option below the app icon on the service-specific menu within Settings to customize specific features of the online social networking app.

7. Near the bottom of the service-specific menu within Settings, under the heading Allow These Apps To Use Your Account, turn on or off the virtual switches associated with specific apps. Your Calendar and Contacts apps can synch with your Facebook account if you allow them.

8. When applicable, tap on the Update Contacts button that's also displayed on the service-specific menu within Settings. This enables your iPhone or iPad to access your online account and compare your online friends with the entries you already have in the Contacts app. When appropriate, the Contacts app pulls additional information from services such as Facebook and adds details to each Contacts entry. For example, when you do this for the Facebook app, Contacts adds Profile pictures, birthdays, and other information listed on the Facebook profile to your Contacts entry.

> **✓ TIP**   If you manage multiple Twitter accounts, repeat steps 1–4 for each account after selecting the Twitter option from the main Settings menu. Later, you can select from which account you publish new content as you use the Tweet command from within the Share menu of various apps.

From the Share menu of many apps (shown in Figure 7.4), you can now publish new content directly to your compatible online social networking account. However, if you want to fully manage your account and interact directly with your online friends, you must download and install the official app for each other service on which you're active. Find these apps by performing a search in the App Store or looking in the Social Networking category.

**FIGURE 7.4**

*After you turn on Facebook, Twitter, Flickr, or Vimeo integration, options for publishing content to these services appear in the Share menu of many compatible apps, including Photos.*

# MANAGE YOUR FACEBOOK ACCOUNT USING THE OFFICIAL FACEBOOK APP

The official Facebook app offers much of the same functionality for managing your Facebook account as using the web browser on your primary computer to access www.facebook.com. However, the Facebook app is custom designed to fully utilize the iPhone or iPad's touchscreen and format content for the screen size of the iOS mobile device you're using.

> ✅ **TIP** On the iPad, more content is displayed when you use the official Facebook app in landscape mode.

> ✅ **TIP** Facebook frequently updates its official app. One of the major changes made in Fall 2014 was that Facebook separated the online messaging service from the official app, requiring users to download both the Facebook app and Facebook Messenger to fully utilize the service's popular chatting feature.

Available by tapping the More icon found near the bottom of the official Facebook app on the iPhone, or in the top-left corner of the app's screen on the iPad, is the Menu icon, as well as the Friend Request, Messenger, and Notifications icons.

Tap on the Menu icon to access the Facebook app's main menu. From here (on the iPad), you can access your own Wall, read your news feed (which includes the status updates from your online friends), see a listing of events you've been invited to, manage your friends, and see which of your friends are close to your current location (based on their last check-in). On the iPhone, tap on the News Feed command icon that's displayed in the bottom-left corner of the screen to read your News Feed.

From this main menu, a handful of other options for managing all aspects of your Facebook account are available. Meanwhile, near the top of the screen when viewing the News Feed screen, you'll see the Status, Photo, and Check-In options.

# PARTICIPATE IN CHATS USING THE FACEBOOK MESSENGER APP

To participate in a real-time text or audio-based chat with one of your Facebook friends, you now must use the Facebook Messenger app, which you can launch from the Home screen or from within the Facebook app by tapping on the Messenger icon in the app (iPhone), or by tapping on the Facebook friend's name that's displayed on the right side of the screen in landscape mode (iPad). As of Fall 2014, the Facebook app does continue to display the names and online status/availability of your online friends on the screen.

When viewing your friends list in the official Facebook app, a green dot displayed to the right of an online friend's name indicates that person is currently online and able to chat. A cell phone icon to the right of his name indicates he's accessing Facebook from his mobile phone. If a time, such as 4m, for four minutes, appears with the phone icon, this tells you the last time they accessed Facebook from their mobile phone.

After tapping on a Facebook friend's name to initiate or return to a chat, the Facebook Messenger app automatically launches and a chat window is displayed (shown in Figure 7.5). Text bubbles down the left side indicate what your friend types, while the text bubbles down the right side show what you've typed.

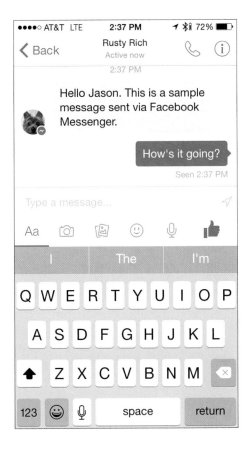

**FIGURE 7.5**

*Participate in real-time text or audio-based chats with your Facebook friends via the Facebook Messenger app, which works on its own or with the official Facebook app.*

**TIP** To initiate an Internet-based audio call with someone else via the Facebook Messenger app (shown in Figure 7.6), tap on the phone icon that's displayed near the top of the screen when engaged in a text message–based conversion with someone.

**FIGURE 7.6**

*In addition to sending/receiving text messages, video clips, audio clips and emoticons, Facebook Messenger enables you to participate in Skype-like voice calls via the Internet with your Facebook friends.*

To enter a new message, tap on the empty field to make the virtual keyboard appear, and type your message. To attach a photo/video clip to the message, tap on the photo icon, or to take a photo/video clip using your iPhone or iPad's camera, tap on the camera icon. If you want to include an emoticon in the form of a Facebook sticker into your message, tap on the smiley face icon. Tap on the microphone icon to record and send an audio message. After you've composed your message, tap the Send button to send it to the other person.

## READ YOUR NEWS FEED USING THE FACEBOOK APP

From the Facebook app's main menu, tap on the News Feed option to discover what your friends are up to. When the News Feed screen is displayed, along the top of the screen, tap the Status option to update your own status. To upload photos to your Facebook account and share them online, tap on the Photo option. The Check-In option enables you to share your current location and details about the activity you're currently engaged in.

Scroll down a bit to read your current News Feed. The postings are displayed in reverse chronological order, with the most recent or most recently commented-upon posts listed first. Just below the poster's name is the time they posted it and their location. Along the bottom of each posting are three icons. Tap Like to "Like" the post. If you want to add a comment related to the update, tap the Comment icon. If you want to share the post with your friends on your own Facebook Wall, tap the Share icon.

> **✓ TIP** If you're active on several online social networking services, be mindful of the permissions you grant to these apps. Many of them are now designed to work together and share information. So, if you post a new tweet on your Twitter account, it can automatically appear on Facebook as a Status Update. The same is true for Instagram and Facebook, for example. You can customize how these various services interact and what information they share by visiting their main websites (such as www.facebook.com or www.twitter.com) and logging in to your account.

# MANAGE YOUR TWITTER ACCOUNT(S) USING THE OFFICIAL TWITTER APP

The official Twitter app enables you to manage one or more Twitter accounts from your iPhone or iPad. Using the app, it's possible to compose and publish new tweets, access your Twitter feed and see what the people you're following are up to, manage your account's followers, send private messages to other Twitter users, and discover content that's of interest to you using the Discover feature with keyword (hashtag) searches and/or tracking what's currently trending on Twitter.

When composing a tweet with the official Twitter app (shown in Figure 7.7), or by selecting the Twitter option from the Share menu of any compatible app, the Compose Tweet screen (iPhone) or window (iPad) is displayed. Use the virtual keyboard or the Dictation feature to compose an outgoing tweet to publish to your Twitter feed. It's also possible to use Siri to compose and publish content to either Facebook or Twitter using voice commands.

**FIGURE 7.7**
*Manage all aspects of your Twitter account, which include composing and sending tweets using the official Twitter app.*

A tweet can be up to 140 characters in length. Aside from text, you can also attach a photo that's taken using the iPhone or iPad's built-in camera (or a photo that's already stored on your mobile device), include a website URL, or add your exact location to the tweet.

> **TIP** As you're composing a tweet, a character counter is displayed in the Compose Tweet screen/window. Keep in mind that when you attach a photo, website URL, or your location to the tweet, this utilizes some of the 140 characters you have available.

To find and follow your real-life friends who are already active on Twitter, launch the Twitter app, tap on the Add Friends icon, and then use the Find People, Categories, or other Find Friends tools that are built in to the app. For example, if you tap on the Find Friends button, the app searches through your Contacts database and matches up email addresses in your Contacts entries with active Twitter members and enables you to follow those people by tapping on a Follow button that appears next to each Search result.

One nice feature of the official Twitter app is that you can manage multiple accounts and quickly switch between them. As you're composing a tweet, if you have multiple accounts, simply tap on your Twitter username in the Compose Tweet screen/window, and you can choose from which of your accounts you want to send the tweet.

You can create or update your personal profile at any time from within the Twitter app. To do this, launch the app, tap on the Me option, and then tap on the gear-shaped icon. From the menu that appears, tap on Edit Profile. You can then change your profile photo, Twitter feed header, your name, the optional website URL you associate with your account, and your short (one-sentence) bio or description. Tap the Save button to save your changes.

> **⌇ NOTE**  Visit the App Store to discover dozens of additional third-party apps that enable you to easily manage one or more Twitter accounts. Many of these third-party apps, such as Twitterific, TweetCaster, or Tweetbot, are paid apps that offer extra functionality that's not found in the official Twitter app.

# DISCOVER THE OFFICIAL APPS FOR OTHER POPULAR ONLINE SOCIAL NETWORKING SERVICES

Official (free) apps from virtually all the popular online social networking services are available from the App Store. You can also find some third-party (paid) apps that offer a different mix of features and functions for managing one or more online social networking accounts.

## THE YOUTUBE APP

As an online-based video sharing service, YouTube offers millions of hours worth of free videos you can watch on demand. The official YouTube app enables you to enjoy the service's content from anywhere your iOS mobile device has an Internet connection.

If you want to access your YouTube account, watch YouTube videos, or upload your own YouTube videos from an iPhone or iPad, the easiest way to do this is using the official YouTube app. Alternatively, you can visit www.youtube.com from the Safari web browser.

The interface for the YouTube app is pretty straightforward. Tap the menu icon displayed near the top-left corner of the screen to sign in to the YouTube service using your established username and password, and then tap the Settings option to customize how the app functions.

> **TIP** When you sign in to the YouTube service from within the app, the YouTube app's main menu adds a My Subscriptions heading. Below it are details about all of the YouTube Channels to which you subscribe. Tap on any of these listings to quickly find the latest videos from your favorite YouTubers.

Displayed under the From YouTube heading of the main menu, tap on the category for videos you're interested in viewing. From the main YouTube screen, tap on the Search icon, and then within the Search field, enter any keyword to quickly find videos you might be interested in related to a certain topic.

> **TIP** Tap on the microphone icon to the right of the Search field to access Google's own voice-recognition feature that works with the YouTube app.

When you tap on a video listing, what's displayed on the screen (shown in Figure 7.8) is similar to what you'd see when accessing YouTube from your primary computer. This includes a video window in which the YouTube video plays. Tap on the video window to access onscreen controls to play or pause the video, view the time slider, and tap the Full Screen mode icon or the AirPlay icon.

**FIGURE 7.8**

*The official YouTube app enables you to watch unlimited videos for free or manage a YouTube Channel and publish your own videos to share them with others.*

Tap on a video's About tab to view details about the YouTube channel on which the video was published and details about the video itself. You can utilize Like, Dislike, and Share icons, as well as a Subscribe button and Suggested Videos related to the one you're watching.

> **NOTE** Videos you watch using the YouTube app are streamed to your mobile device. These videos are not, however, saved on your device. To avoid quickly using up your monthly cellular wireless data allocation, if applicable, opt to use this app with a Wi-Fi Internet connection.

## THE VINE APP

Compared to YouTube or Vimeo, Vine is a relatively new social networking service that enables everyday people to upload and publish videos. These videos, however, can be only 7 seconds long. Think of this service as a cross between YouTube and Twitter. The official Vine app enables you to access your Vine account, upload and publish videos from your mobile device, or watch the videos that have been published by your online friends or other Vine users.

The main menu of this app offers Home, Explore, Activity, and Profile options. To shoot and upload a video using the video camera and microphone built in to the iPhone or iPad, tap the movie camera icon displayed near the top-right corner of the screen.

To view videos from your online friends, tap the Home option and then scroll down. As you watch each video, tap on the Smiley Face icon to "like" a video, the Comment icon to write and publish a public comment, or the Share icon to share someone else's Vine video with your online friends. Tap the More icon to reveal a submenu which offers options that enable you to Report This Post, Share This Post, or Cancel. You can also read the comments related to a video that have been posted by other people.

 **WHAT'S NEW** Like many other social networking services, Vine has introduced a direct messaging feature that enables you to privately communicate with individual people. Tap on the Messages icon that's displayed in the top-right corner of the screen to access this functionality.

## THE INSTAGRAM APP

Instagram is a social networking service that enables users to create and share an ongoing stream of individual photos. Each photo can include a caption, keywords, and your location. What's cool about Instagram is that instead of using the Camera app to snap pictures, you can use the Instagram app and then use its photo editing tools to quickly add a special effects filter and border. Unlike other photo sharing services, Instagram crops images into a square shape (shown in Figure 7.9).

**FIGURE 7.9**

*Snap or select a photo, crop it, and then add a special effects filter and/or border before publishing it on Instagram.*

Instagram offers a fun and easy way to share with others moments of your life, in the form of snapshots taken using the camera that's built in to your iOS mobile device (shown in Figure 7.10).

**FIGURE 7.10**

*Instagram users can share individual photos and manage their online account using the official Instagram app.*

**TIP** To view photos posted by strangers, tap on the Explore icon displayed near the bottom of the screen. Then, simply scroll down. You can also use the Search Users and Hashtags feature to quickly find and view images with specific keywords associated with them.

## DISCOVER THE SNAPCHAT ALTERNATIVE

Particularly among kids and teens, SnapChat has become a popular messaging app primarily because this service automatically deletes text, video, and audio messages just seconds after they've been viewed by the recipient. The SnapChat app, iOS mobile device, and the SnapChat service do not keep a transcript of private messages between users.

> ☑ **TIP**  The "self destructing message" function found in SnapChat has proven so popular that it is now offered as an optional feature in the iOS 8 version of the Messages app when audio or video messages are sent and received.

## THE LINKEDIN APP

If you're an entrepreneur, business professional, or small business operator, LinkedIn is the online social networking service designed for you. Use the service to pinpoint and attract new customers, interact with vendors, seek out expert advice, find employment opportunities, and share information with your online network and/or the service's 313 million members.

The official LinkedIn app enables you to access your online account from anywhere using your iOS mobile device. A separate version of the app is available for the iPhone and iPad. Using the core LinkedIn service is free; however, various subscriptions are available as in-app purchases ($9.99 to $99.00 per month) that offer access to premium content and features.

> 📱 **WHAT'S NEW**  Just as many preinstalled apps enable you to share app-specific content to Facebook, Twitter, and iCloud from the Share menu built in to the app, thanks to iOS 8, third-party app developers are being given tools to incorporate new ways to share content from within their apps. As a result, in the near future, we'll be seeing more apps offering integration with social networking services and cloud-based services via their Share menus.

## BECOME A BLOGGER AND START BLOGGING FROM YOUR iPHONE OR iPAD

Although becoming active on Facebook, Twitter, or any of the other popular online social networking services is a form of blogging, if you're interested in launching your own more traditional blog, and then being able to update it with new content while on the go, your iPhone or iPad can be used for "mobile blogging" as well.

Many of the most popular blog hosting services, including Wordpress.com, Wordpress.org, Blogger.com, and Tumblr, have their own proprietary apps that enable you to create engaging content using text, photos, and video clips.

What's great about blogging is that you can fully customize your content and you're not constrained by having to stick to a particular format or length for each entry. Whether you're creating and managing a personal blog to be shared with close friends and family or you operate a blog on behalf of your business, the official WordPress and Blogger apps, for example, enable you to create content, manage your account, and track traffic to your blog from virtually anywhere.

**(iOS 8) WHAT'S NEW** As this book was being written, a new social networking service called Ello was preparing to launch. This service combines features from Twitter, Tumblr, and other competing sites to create a unique tool for communicating and sharing information with online friends.

What is unique about Ello is that it does not track your online activities, you are not bombarded with marketing messages (sponsored posts), and the service displays no ads whatsoever. Ello is being called the "anti-Facebook" for this reason.

To learn more, visit www.ello.co, or search for the official Ello app in the App Store when it becomes available.

8

# SHOOT, EDIT, AND SHARE PHOTOS AND VIDEOS

People love taking photos, and thanks to the two digital cameras built in to all of the iPhone and iPad models released within the past few years, plus improvements made to the Camera and Photos apps in iOS 8, it has never been easier or more fun to shoot, edit, view, print, and share your digital images or video clips.

The iPhone 5s, iPhone 6, and iPhone 6 Plus all offer an 8-megapixel iSight rear-facing camera, along with the enhanced Camera and Photos apps that come preinstalled with iOS 8. Thus, it's possible to take crystal-clear photos and create large and vibrant full-color prints from your digital image files, or share those images using options offered by the Photos app's Share menu.

**iOS 8 WHAT'S NEW** The iPhone 6 and iPhone 6 Plus also incorporate other technology into the camera, including what Apple calls Focus Pixels, making the camera capable of capturing even more vibrant and clear images than what's possible using other iPhone or iPad models.

**TIP** By tapping on the Share icon in the Photo app, you can easily share your images in several ways. It's possible to attach up to five photos to an outgoing email message from within Photos, attach preselected photos to a text/instant message, tweet a photo to your Twitter followers, upload photos directly to your Facebook account, upload photos to your Flickr account, or use the AirDrop feature to wirelessly share photos with newer model Macs, iPhone, iPad, or iPod touch devices that are in close proximity to you.

It also continues to be possible to sync your images with your primary computer via iTunes Sync or share your digital images with all your computers and iOS devices using iCloud.

**iOS 8 WHAT'S NEW** At the same time Apple released iOS 8, it introduced iCloud's Family Sharing feature, which enables up to six family members to share photos and create a central online-based Album. With Family Sharing, each family member retains their own private iCloud account, but can simultaneously have certain content shared between their accounts.

In early 2015, Apple has announced it will be updating the iCloud service to include iCloud Photo Library, which will replace iCloud's My Photo Stream and Shared Photo Stream features and make it easier to back up, sync, and share your photos via the iCloud service.

# SOME CAMERA APP FEATURES ARE AVAILABLE ON ONLY CERTAIN iPHONE AND iPAD MODELS

The Camera app continues to be one of the core apps that come preinstalled with the iOS 8 operating system. The same version of the Camera app is installed on all iOS mobile devices. However, based on which iPhone or iPad model you're using, some of the features and functions of the Camera app might not be available to you. Features such as the ability to shoot slow motion video at up to 240 frames per second, for example, require a lot of extra processing power from the iPhone or iPad's main processor chip. Thus, only devices that run using Apple's A8 processor can utilize all of the Camera app's built-in features.

In addition, iOS 8 introduces several Camera features to the iPad that were previously available only on iPhones, such as the ability to shoot Pano (panoramic) images. However, some older iPads still lack various Camera app features and functions.

That being said, if you're using any iPhone or iPad model released within the past two years, you can take awesome photos using the Camera app. The Camera and Photos apps also continue to work with many third-party apps, so you can use specialized editing tools or share your photos online in a variety of ways.

# THE CAMERA AND PHOTOS APPS ARE CHOCK FULL OF NEW FEATURES

**iOS 8 WHAT'S NEW** New to iOS 8 is a feature that enables you to hide photos from "public" view on your device. To do this, as you're viewing a photo (or a thumbnail for a photo), hold your finger on the image for one or two seconds. The Copy and Hide tabs appear. Tap on the Hide tab. When you hide a photo, it will not appear in the Moments, Collections, or Years view in the Photos app, but it will still appear in Albums.

When it comes to taking, viewing, editing, and sharing pictures using your iPhone or iPad, the Camera and Photos apps each offer powerful new features. For example, on the iPhone 5s, iPhone 6, and iPhone 6 Plus, you now have access to a Timer and Time-Lapse shooting feature, in addition to the app's other shooting modes.

**iOS 8 WHAT'S NEW** If you enjoy capturing HD video using your iPhone or iPad, the iOS 8 version of the Camera app enables the iPhone 6 and iPhone 6 Plus to capture 1080p HD video at either 30 or 60 frames per second. (The iPhone 5s can capture 1080p HD video at 30 frames per second.)

# METHODS FOR LOADING DIGITAL IMAGES INTO YOUR iPHONE OR iPAD

Before you can view, edit, print, and share your favorite digital images, you first must either shoot them using the Camera app or transfer the images into your iOS device.

> **NOTE** Facebook, Twitter, Instagram, and other third-party apps enable you to access and use your iPhone or iPad's built-in cameras without using the Camera app. It's also possible for these apps to access the Camera app's image folders, such as the Camera Roll folder or the Recently Added folder (depending on which version of iOS 8 you are using), where newly shot images are stored.

Aside from shooting images using one of your iOS device's built-in cameras, there are several ways to import photos and then store them in the Photos app:

- Use the iTunes sync process with the iPhoto or Photos app running on a Mac. By linking your iPhone or iPad with your Mac (via the supplied USB cable), you can transfer photos or entire albums.

- Load photos from your My Photo Stream or Shared Photo Stream. Learn how to work with these iCloud features later in this chapter. These features will be replaced in early 2015 with the iCloud Photo Library feature, which will also work seamlessly with the Photos app and your existing iCloud account.

- Receive and save photos sent via email. When a photo is embedded in an email, hold your finger on it for a second or two until a menu appears, giving you the option to save the image (in the Camera Roll folder of the Photos app) or copy it to your device's virtual clipboard (after which you can paste it into another app). This feature, along with other Share options, is shown using the Mail app in Figure 8.1.

**FIGURE 8.1**

*If you receive a digital photo attached to an incoming email, you can save the image in the Camera Roll folder by holding your finger on the image thumbnail (in the email), and then tapping on the Save Image option when it appears.*

> **TIP**  If multiple images are attached or embedded within an incoming email, from the Mail app, when you use your finger and hold it on one of the images, a Save [number] Images option is displayed in addition to the Save Image option (refer to Figure 8.1). Use the Save [number] Images option to save all the photos in the email at once to your Camera Roll folder in the Photos app.

- Receive and save photos sent via text/instant message or Twitter. Tap on the image you receive using the Messages app, and then tap on the Save command.

- Save images directly from a website as you're surfing the Web. Hold your finger on the image you're viewing in a website. If it's not copy-protected, after a second or two a menu appears, enabling you to save the image or copy it to your device's virtual clipboard (after which you can paste it into another app). Tap on the Save Image or Copy options, respectively.

- Accept images sent to your iPhone or iPad wirelessly via AirDrop (shown in Figure 8.2). For this feature to work, AirDrop must be turned on, which can be done from the Control Center. Launch Control Center, tap on the AirDrop option, and then select Contacts Only or Everyone. When someone attempts to wirelessly send you one or more images, follow the onscreen prompts to download and store the images in the Camera Roll folder of the Photos app.

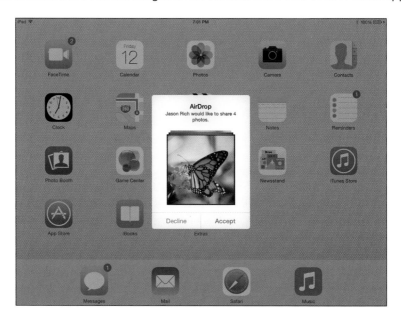

**FIGURE 8.2**

*When someone sends an image via AirDrop to your iPhone or iPad, a pop-up window with an image thumbnail, along with an Accept and Decline button, is displayed.*

■ Use the optional Camera Connection Kit ($29, available from Apple Stores or Apple.com) to load images from your digital camera or its memory card directly into your iPhone or iPad.

> **NOTE** When you use the Save Image command, the image is stored in the Camera Roll album of the Photos app. You can then view, edit, enhance, print, or share it.

## THE REDESIGNED CAMERA APP

The Camera app that comes preinstalled with iOS 8 has been enhanced with new features, yet it still remains very easy to use if you want to snap a photo or shoot video. There are a variety of ways you can launch the Camera app to begin shooting photos or video quickly.

## WAYS TO LAUNCH THE CAMERA APP

There are three easy ways to launch the Camera app, including:

- From the Home screen, tap on the Camera app icon.
- From the Lock screen, place your finger on the camera icon that's displayed in the bottom-right corner of the screen, and then swipe your finger upward.
- Tap on the Camera app icon that's displayed in the Control Center.

## HOW TO SHOOT PHOTOS OR VIDEO WITH THE CAMERA APP

The main camera viewfinder screen appears as soon as you launch the Camera app on an iPhone, iPod touch, or iPad. Figure 8.3 shows the main Camera app screen on an iPhone, while Figure 8.4 shows the same screen on an iPad. The main area of the screen serves as your camera's viewfinder. In other words, what you see on the screen is what you'll photograph or capture on video.

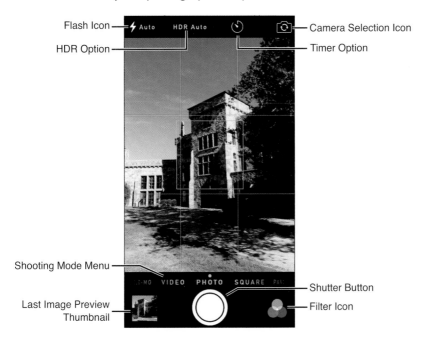

**FIGURE 8.3**

*From the Camera app's main screen (shown here on the iPhone 5s), you can snap digital photos or shoot video.*

Camera
Selection Icon

Timer Icon
HDR Mode Icon

Autofocus Sensor
Box

Shutter Button

Shooting
Mode Menu

Last Image
Preview Thumbnail

**FIGURE 8.4**

*The Camera app looks slightly different on an iPad but offers much of the same functionality.*

On the iPhone (if you're using an iPhone 5s, iPhone 6, or iPhone 6 Plus), along the bottom of the screen are several command icons and options. When using the Camera app with the iPad, all command icons and options are displayed along the right margin of the screen.

> **NOTE** If you're using an older iPhone or iPad model, such as an iPhone 4s, iPhone 5, or iPad 3, some of the features and functions discussed in this chapter are not available to you.

Tap on the thumbnail image of the last photo or video clip you shot in the lower-left corner to view it and use some of the Photo app's viewing and editing functions.

At the bottom center of the screen on the iPhone is the camera's round shutter button. Tap on this to snap a photo or to start and stop the video recording process. In Video mode, the shutter button icon transforms from a bright red circle into a red square (pause button) when you tap on it to begin shooting a video clip.

The shooting mode options—Time-Lapse, Slow-Mo, Video, Photo, Square, and Pano—appear just above the shutter button. Use your finger to manually scroll left or right to select your shooting mode, which will be highlighted in yellow.

The new Time-Lapse feature (shown in Figure 8.5) enables you to set up your iPhone or iPad and set the Camera app to automatically snap one photo periodically (the time interval is dynamically set by the iOS device) until you manually turn off this function. This feature works best if you mount the iOS mobile device on a tripod or use it with a stand. It's great for capturing changes that happen in a single scene over time, such as a sunrise or sunset. The content created when using the Time Lapse feature is stored in the Photos app as a video, not as a series of photos.

**FIGURE 8.5**

*Turn on the Time Lapse feature, and then tap the Shutter button to begin automatically taking photos over time. Notice that a timer graphic now surrounds the Shutter button.*

The Slo-Mo option enables you to shoot high-action video but play it back in slow motion. The iPhone 6 and iPhone 6 Plus, which uses Apple's A8 processor chip, enable you to capture slow-motion video at up to 240 frames per second, as opposed to 120 frames per second using the iPhone 5s and some iPad models. This shooting mode is ideal if you're shooting a fast-moving subject or a high-action activity.

Video is used to shoot 1080p HD-quality video using your iPhone or iPad. Depending on which device you're using, you can shoot at 30 or 60 frames per second. Keep in mind that your iPhone or iPad is ideal for shooting relatively short video clips. These HD video files take up a tremendous amount of storage space, so if you want to shoot long home videos, consider using a dedicated video camera.

Photo is used to snap regular digital (still) images. Square automatically pre-crops images as you're shooting to be compatible with services such as Instagram. You wind up with square images.

Pano launches the Camera app's panoramic mode for shooting vast landscapes, skylines, or large groups of people (shown in Figure 8.6).

**FIGURE 8.6**

*The Pano (panoramic) shooting mode is ideal for shooting images of vast landscapes, large groups of people, or very wide areas (shown here).*

The latest iPhone and iPad models each have two built-in cameras—one in the front, and one on the back of the device. The front-facing camera makes it easier to snap photos of yourself or participate in video calls (via FaceTime or Skype).

The rear-facing camera (which enables you to take higher-resolution photos or video) enables you to photograph whatever is in front of you. Tap on the camera-shaped icon located in the upper-right corner of the screen to switch between cameras.

☑ **TIP**  Unless you're taking a "selfie," which is a photo of yourself, use the rear-facing camera if possible. This is a much higher-resolution camera. Using it will enable you to shoot more detailed, vibrant, and higher-quality images or video.

🔍 **MORE INFO**  The HDR mode in the Camera app stands for High Dynamic Range. It can be used with the rear-facing camera only. When turned on, this feature captures the available light differently, and can help you compensate for a photo that would otherwise be over- or underexposed.

When you take a photo with HDR mode turned on, the iPhone or iPad actually captures several separate images simultaneously, and then automatically blends them into a single image in a fraction of a second. By doing this, it's possible to capture more depth and contrast, plus make better use of available lighting. The result is often a more detailed and vibrant photo.

You can decide whether the original photo and the HDR mode version of a photo are both saved in the Camera Roll folder, or if just the HDR version of the image is saved. To make this adjustment, launch Settings, tap on the Photos & Camera option, and then set the virtual switch that's associated with the Keep Normal Photo option.

Depending on which iPhone or iPad model you're using, you might have access to HDR Auto mode. This allows the camera to decide whether a photo benefits from this feature. Turning on HDR Auto mode takes some of the guesswork out of picture taking and often results in better-quality images.

The HDR button is displayed near the top center of the Camera app screen on the iPhone, or just above the Shutter button on the iPad. Tap it to toggle the HDR mode when taking photos.

On the latest iPhone models are three HDR-related options: On, Off, or Auto. If HDR Auto is available on your iOS mobile device (shown in Figure 8.7), it enables you to consistently capture the most vibrant photos in a wide range of lighting situations.

**FIGURE 8.7**

*On the latest iPhone models, you can set HDR mode On, Off, or to Auto mode by tapping on the option at the top of the screen. On older iPhone and most iPad models, only the On or Off options are available.*

On the iPhone, the flash icon is in the upper-left corner of the main Camera screen. It controls whether the iPhone automatically uses the built-in flash when needed as you're shooting photos or video with the rear-facing camera. Tap the icon, then tap the On, Off, or Auto option to toggle this feature.

On some newer iPhone models, an Auto option is also offered. This enables the smartphone to analyze the available light for you and determine whether the flash is needed. Keep in mind that even in low-light situations, you can often achieve better results if you shoot photos using the HDR shooting mode, as opposed to using the flash.

The iPhone 5s, iPhone 6, and iPhone 6 Plus utilize what Apple calls a True Tone flash. This is really two flashes that work together and emit light in different colors, allowing the Camera app to analyze the available light in a shooting situation and enhance it, while keeping the natural colors within a photo. The True Tone flash automatically reduces the red-eye effect when taking pictures of people and can often reduce or eliminate unwanted shadows within photos.

> **(iOS 8) WHAT'S NEW** In addition to the Time-Lapse option, the Camera app now offers a Timer option. To turn this on, tap on the Timer icon, and then set the timer for 3 or 10 seconds. This determines how long the Camera app waits between the time you press the Shutter button and when an image is actually taken and saved. This feature is available on most iPhone and iPad models.

## TAKE ADVANTAGE OF THE NEW AUTOFOCUS AND EXPOSURE CONTROL OPTIONS

As you're looking at the Camera app's viewfinder and framing your shot, you can force the app to focus in on your intended subject by tapping on the screen directly over where your subject appears.

When you do this, the Autofocus Sensor box appears in the viewfinder, and the Camera app then focuses in on your subject. If you're shooting people, the Camera app automatically identifies each person's face within a photo and focuses in on those faces.

> **(iOS 8) WHAT'S NEW** In addition to the Autofocus Sensor, depending on which iOS mobile device you're using, a new manual Exposure Control slider might also be displayed. It looks like a sun-shaped icon that's displayed to the immediate right of the Autofocus Sensor.
>
> When this Exposure Control slider is displayed (shown in Figure 8.8), place your finger on the sun-shaped icon and slide it upward to downward to manually adjust the exposure before snapping the photo.

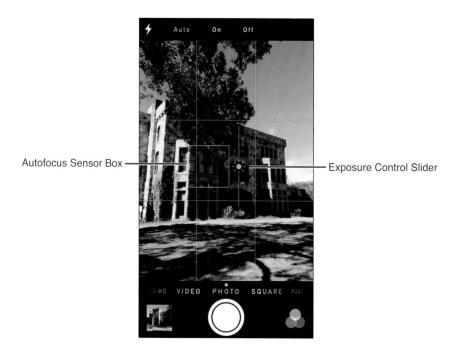

**FIGURE 8.8**

*Instead of tapping in various places in the viewfinder to adjust the exposure, the iOS 8 version of the Camera app now offers an Exposure Control slider.*

## HOW TO SNAP A PHOTO

Snapping a single digital photo using the Camera app is simple. Follow these steps:

1.  Launch the Camera app.
2.  Make sure the shooting mode is set to Photo or Square.
3.  Choose which of your device's two cameras you want to use by tapping on the camera selection icon.
4.  Compose your image by holding up your device and pointing it at your subject.
5.  If desired, set the Timer feature.
6.  To add a special effect to the image as you're shooting, tap on the Filter icon and then select one of the eight displayed filters by tapping on its preview image (shown in Figure 8.9). The filter thumbnail serves as the shutter button for snapping a photo when you tap on it. Filters are not available on all iOS mobile devices. However, if your iPhone or iPad does support filters,

the iOS 8 edition of the Camera app can take advantage of third-party filters in addition to the special effect filters that come bundled with the app.

**FIGURE 8.9**

*As you're shooting a photo, you can choose one of the eight image filters and add an effect, such as Mono, Fade, or Chrome. Choose None to shoot without using a filter. You can also add a filter later when editing a photo using the Photos app.*

7. Select the main subject of your photo, such as a person or an object. Tap your finger on the screen where your subject appears in the viewfinder. An autofocus sensor box appears on the screen at the location you tap. Where this box is positioned is what the camera focuses on (as opposed to something in the foreground, background, or next to your intended subject).

8. If necessary, use the new Exposure Control slider to manually adjust the exposure just before snapping a photo. Keep in mind that using the Photos app, you can later adjust or correct a variety of problematic issues within a photo, including its exposure, contrast, saturation, color, and shadows. These are new editing tools built in to the iOS 8 edition of the Photos app.

> **✓ TIP**  As you're holding your iPhone or iPad to snap a photo or shoot video, be sure your fingers don't accidentally block the camera lens that's being utilized. On the more recent iPhone models, next to the rear-facing camera lens is a tiny flash. Keep your fingers clear of this as well.

> **✎ NOTE**  If you're taking a group photo (up to 10 people), the Camera app detects this, and multiple autofocus sensors appear on all of your subjects' faces.

> **✓ TIP**  On the iPhone 5s, iPhone 6, or iPhone 6 Plus, to use the Burst shooting mode, simply press and hold down the shutter button in the Camera app. You can capture at least 10 images per second. You can later delete the images you don't need but choose the shot that best depicts a specific instant. Images shot using the Burst shooting mode are stored in an album called Bursts. This shooting mode is ideal for photographing a fast-moving subject.

9. If you want to use the Camera app's zoom feature, use a pinch motion on the screen. A zoom slider (shown in Figure 8.10) appears near the bottom of the screen. Use your finger to move the dot in the slider to the right to zoom in, or to the left to zoom out on your subject. Alternatively, you can use a pinch or reverse-pinch finger gesture to manage the zoom feature while shooting.

10. On the iPhone, tap on the Flash icon in the top-left corner of the screen. You have three flash-related options. When turned on, the flash activates for every picture you take. When turned off, the flash does not activate at all, regardless of the lighting conditions. When you select Auto, the Camera app activates the flash when it deems additional light is needed. If you have HDR (Auto) mode turned on, this overrides the flash, and the flash does not work.

11. When you have your image framed in the viewfinder, tap on the shutter button to snap the photo. Or tap the Volume Up (+) or Volume Down (-) button on the side of your iPhone/iPad.

12. The photo is saved in the Camera Roll album of Photos. You can now shoot another photo or view the photo using the Photos app.

**FIGURE 8.10**

*As you're framing an image, you can zoom in (or out) on your subject using the onscreen zoom slider. Use a pinch finger gesture on the screen to make this slider appear, and then move the slider to the right or left to increase or decrease the zoom level.*

> **NOTE**  If you've taken a Panoramic shot, used the Burst shooting mode, shot a video, or shot a slow-motion video, in addition to saving your photo or video in the Photo app's Camera Roll album, it's also stored in the Bursts, Videos, or Panoramas album, respectively.

## HOW TO SHOOT A PANORAMIC PHOTO

To take advantage of the panoramic shooting mode to snap a photo of a landscape, city skyline (shown in Figure 8.11), or a large group of people, follow these steps:

**FIGURE 8.11**

*The Panorama shooting mode is ideal for capturing vast landscapes, city skylines, or large group photos.*

1. Launch the Camera app.

2. Swipe on the shooting modes to select the Pano shooting mode.

3. Position your iPhone or iPad's viewfinder to the extreme left of your wide-angle shot. (When using the Pano shooting mode, you must hold the smartphone or tablet upright, in portrait mode).

> ☑ **TIP**  If you tap on the large arrow icon in the viewfinder, you can switch the panning direction from right to left, instead of left to right as you're capturing a panoramic shot.

4. Tap the shutter button icon, and then slowly and steadily move your iPhone or iPad from left to right (refer to Figure 8.6). If you go too fast, a message appears on the screen telling you to slow down.

5. The panorama slider moves from left to right as you capture your image. You can tap the shutter button again when you're finished, or continue moving the iOS device to the right until the entire length of the image has been captured.

6. The panoramic photo is saved in the Panoramas folder of the Photos app. You can then view, edit, or share it from within Photos.

> ☑ **TIP**  When viewing a panoramic photo, hold your iPhone or iPad in landscape mode; however, when shooting a panoramic shot, hold it in portrait mode.

# HOW TO SHOOT 1080P HD VIDEO

From the Camera app, you can easily shoot video. Follow these basic steps for shooting video on your iPhone or iPad:

1.  Launch the Camera app.

2.  Swipe on the shooting modes to select the Video shooting mode option. (If you want to shoot slow-motion video, select the Slo-Mo option, if it's offered by your iOS mobile device.)

3.  Tap the camera selection icon to choose which camera you want to use. You can switch between the front- and the rear-facing camera at any time; however, the front-facing camera does not enable you to shoot 1080p video. You can, however, shoot lower-resolution, 720p HD video using this camera.

4.  If applicable, tap on the Flash icon that's displayed near the top-left corner of the screen (iPhone) to turn on the flash and use it as a continuous light source while filming video.

5.  Hold your iPhone or iPad up to the subject you want to capture on video. Set up your shot by looking at what's displayed on the screen.

6.  In the viewfinder, tap on your intended subject to make the autofocus sensor appear. If necessary, and if your device supports this feature, you can also manually adjust the Exposure Control using the displayed slider.

7.  When you're ready to start shooting video, tap on the shutter button. The red dot turns into a red square. This indicates you're now filming. Your iPhone or iPad captures whatever images you see on the screen, as well as any sound in the area.

8.  As you're filming video, notice a timer displayed on the screen (shown in Figure 8.12). Your only limit to how much video you can shoot is based on the amount of available memory in your iOS device and how long the battery lasts. However, this app is designed more for shooting short video clips, not full-length home movies.

**FIGURE 8.12**

*When shooting video on your iPhone or iPad, make sure the timer (displayed at the top center of the screen) is counting up. This indicates you're actually recording.*

9.   As you're filming, tap anywhere on the screen to focus in on your subject using the app's built-in autofocus sensor.

10.  To stop filming, tap again on the shutter button. Your video footage is saved. You can now view, edit, and share it from within the Photos app or a video app, such as iMovie.

> **TIP**   Although the Photos app enables you to trim your video clips as well as view and share the videos, if you want to edit your videos, plus add titles and special effects, you should use Apple's feature-packed iMovie app, which is available from the App Store. For more information about iMovie, visit www.apple.com/apps/imovie.

☑ **TIP** Depending on which iPhone or iPad model you're using, at the same time you're shooting video, you might discover a second, circular (white) Shutter button displayed to the left of the primary Shutter button (refer to Figure 8.12). When available, this second Shutter button can be used to snap high-resolution digital images at the same time you're shooting HD video.

# TIPS FOR SHOOTING EYE-CATCHING PHOTOS

Even though you're using a smartphone or tablet to shoot photos, as opposed to a full-featured, digital SLR or point-and-shoot digital camera, you can still use basic photo composition and framing techniques to snap professional-quality images.

To generate the best possible in-focus, well-lit, and nicely framed images, follow these basic shooting strategies (many of which also apply when shooting video):

- Pay attention to your primary light source. As a general rule, the light source (such as the sun) should be behind you (the photographer) and shining evenly onto your subject. When light from your light source shines directly into your camera's lens (in this case, your iPhone or iPad), you wind up with unwanted glares or an overexposed image.

- As you look at the viewfinder screen, pay attention to shadows. Unwanted shadows can be caused by the sun or by an artificial light source. Make sure shadows aren't covering your subject(s).

☑ **TIP** Shooting indoors using the flash can generate unwanted shadows. Try to keep your subject at least two or three feet away from a wall or backdrop to reduce shadows, and don't get too close to your subject.

- When you're using the flash, red-eye often becomes a problem. To prevent this, try to shine more light on your subject and not rely on the flash. Or step farther away from your subject physically, but use the zoom feature to move in closer.

> **✓ TIP** Like any camera, the flash built in to your iPhone has an optimal range that generates the best lighting results, generally between 3 and 10 feet from your intended subject. If you're too close to your subject when using the flash, the photo comes out overexposed. If you're too far away, the photo might turn out underexposed. You can compensate by moving closer or farther away from your subject, and then use the zoom feature when necessary.

> **✎ NOTE** When you use the digital zoom built in to the Camera app, a photo's image quality is reduced the further you zoom in. It also becomes even more essential to hold the iPhone steady as you're taking pictures when you use the zoom feature.

- As you get ready to tap the shutter icon and snap a photo, hold your iOS device perfectly still. Even the slightest movement could result in a blurry image, especially in low-light situations. Try using the Volume Up or Volume Down button as your Shutter button instead of the on-screen button to help you keep the iPhone/iPad steady.

- If you're shooting in poor light, take advantage of the iPhone's HDR On or HDR Auto feature.

> **✓ TIP** As you're looking at your primary subject through the "viewfinder" (the iPhone or iPad's screen when using the Camera app), tap on the intended subject on the screen once to set the Autofocus.
>
> To activate the Auto Exposure Lock, press and hold your finger on the screen for a second or two. A yellow square appears on the screen over your subject. This informs the iPhone or iPad about what you want your primary subject to be, and ensures the best possible focus and available lighting utilization.
>
> If needed, take advantage of the manual new Exposure Control slider to adjust the shot's exposure as you're shooting.
>
> One benefit to using the Auto Exposure Lock is that it remains set until it's manually changed, so you can take a handful of photos in succession, without having to refocus on your subject. To turn off the Auto Exposure Lock, tap on the viewfinder screen again.

# HOW TO USE THE RULE OF THIRDS WHEN SHOOTING

It's a common mistake for amateur photographers to point the camera at the subject head-on, center the subject in the frame, and snap a photo. The result is always a generic-looking image, even if it's well-lit and in perfect focus. Instead, as you look at the viewfinder screen to compose or frame your image, utilize the Rule of Thirds. This is a shooting strategy used by professional photographers, but it's very easy to take advantage of, and the results will be impressive.

Imagine a tic-tac-toe grid being superimposed on your camera's viewfinder. To make the grid appear in the Camera app's viewfinder, launch the Settings app, select the Photos & Camera option, and then turn on the virtual switch associated with the Grid option (shown in Figure 8.13). The center box in the tic-tac-toe grid corresponds to the center of the image you're about to shoot as you look at the viewfinder screen.

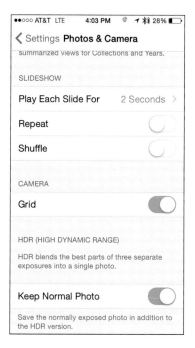

**FIGURE 8.13**

*To turn on the Grid, launch Settings, tap on the Photos & Camera option, and then turn on the virtual switch associated with the Grid feature.*

Instead of framing your subject in this center box, reframe the image so your subject is positioned along one of the horizontal or vertical lines of the grid, or so that the main focal point of the image is positioned at one of the grid's intersection points.

> **☑ TIP**  As you're shooting, instead of holding the camera head-on, directly facing your subject, try shooting from a different perspective, such as from slightly above, below, or to the side of your subject. You can also shoot from a slight diagonal perspective. This enables you to create more visually interesting images.

Using the Rule of Thirds when framing your images takes a bit of practice, but if you use this shooting technique consistently and correctly, the quality of your images vastly improves. Of course, you also want to take into account lighting, as well as what's in the foreground, in the background, and to the sides of your main subject. And be sure to tap your creativity when choosing your shooting angle or perspective for each shot.

> **☑ TIP**  When you're shooting a subject in motion, capture the subject moving into the frame, as opposed to moving out of it, while also taking into account the Rule of Thirds.

> **🔍 MORE INFO**  To expand the capabilities of the iPhone or iPad's Camera app, consider investing in the optional OlloClip 4-in-1 lens or the OlloClip Telephoto + Circular Polarizing Filter Lens. These small and lightweight accessories, which are sold separately, clip onto the iPhone or iPad over the built-in camera's lens. For more information, visit www.olloclip.com.

## USING THE PHOTOS APP TO VIEW, EDIT, ENHANCE, PRINT, AND SHARE PHOTOS AND VIDEOS

Use the Photos app to view images stored on your iOS device or in your iCloud account. The iOS 8 version of the Photos app includes a robust selection of photo editing and image enhancement tools.

> **✓ TIP** Images in the Photos app are auto-sorted based on when or where they were shot. Years displays thumbnails of all images shot within a particular year and includes details about where those images were shot (shown in Figure 8.14). Collections break down a Years grouping to display images based on when and where they were shot. Moments enable you to display thumbnails of images within a Collection that represent one location or date.
>
> As you're viewing thumbnails in the Moments view, tap on one of them to view a single image. Or, at the bottom of the screen, tap on Photos, Shared, or Albums to view a different set of images stored on your mobile device.

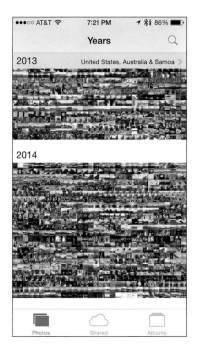

**FIGURE 8.14**

*From the Photos app, you can view tiny thumbnails of all images shot within a particular year. Tap on any thumbnail to view the image in full-screen mode.*

On the iPhone, the functionality of the Photos app is almost identical to the iPad version; however, the appearance of some of the screens and the position of certain command icons and menus differs due to the size of each device's screen.

To exit out of the Moments or Collections thumbnail view, use the options displayed at the top-left corner of the screen. From the Years view, tap on a collection (within the main area of the screen) or tap on the Photos, Shared, or Albums icon that's displayed along the bottom of the screen.

When viewing Moments, each group of photos that are shot at the same place and in the same time frame are automatically grouped together into an event.

As you're viewing these events, tap on the Share button associated with it to quickly share all images in that event, or select and share specific images from it via AirDrop, Messages, or iCloud. Tap on the Select option at the top-right corner of the screen to choose one or more events or thumbnails. Once selected, tap either the Share or Trash icon in the top-left corner of the screen to manage those images.

## VIEW AN IMAGE IN FULL-SCREEN MODE

When viewing thumbnails of your images, tap on any single image thumbnail to view a larger version of it. On the iPhone, the Edit icon is displayed in the upper-right corner of the screen, the Share icon is displayed in the lower-left corner of the screen, and the Trash icon is displayed near the lower-right corner of the screen. The new Favorites icon is displayed at the bottom center of the screen (shown in Figure 8.15).

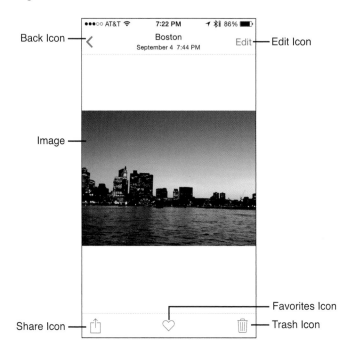

**FIGURE 8.15**

*The Edit, Share, Favorites, and Trash icons are displayed when viewing a single image on your iPhone or iPad's screen.*

On the iPad, the Favorites and Edit icons are displayed in the top-right corner of the screen. The Share icon can be found in the lower-left corner of the screen, and the Trash icon is positioned in the bottom-right corner of the screen. Along the bottom-center of the screen are thumbnails for all of the images stored in the Album/folder you're currently accessing.

**WHAT'S NEW** By tapping on the Favorites icon that's associated with each image, you can group those Favorite images separately, and then opt to view or share only Favorite images.

As you're viewing a photo, tap on it to hide or show the Edit, share, Favorites, and Trash icons, which automatically appear and then disappear after a few seconds when you first open a photo. Tap on the Edit icon to reveal the Photo app's new image editing options (shown in Figure 8.16).

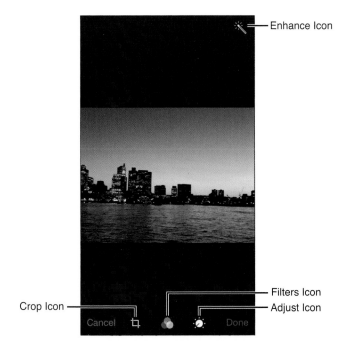

**FIGURE 8.16**

*After tapping the Edit icon, the command icons you use to ultimately edit and enhance that image are displayed.*

To exit the single-image view and return to the multi-image thumbnail view, tap anywhere on the screen to make the command icons appear, then tap on the left-pointing arrow-shaped icon displayed in the upper-left corner of the screen.

## EDITING VIDEOS

When you tap on the thumbnail for a video clip, you have the option of playing that clip in the Photos app. Or you can tap anywhere on the screen (except for the Play icon in the center of the screen) to access the video trimming (editing) feature, as well as the Share icon and the trash can icon (used to delete the video clip from your iOS device).

To trim a video clip, look at the filmstrip display of the clip located at the top of the screen, and move the left or right editing tabs accordingly to define the portion of the clip you want to edit.

The box around the filmstrip display turns yellow, and the Trim command icon appears on the right side of the screen. Before tapping on Trim, tap on the Play icon to preview your newly edited video clip.

If it's okay, tap on the Trim icon to save your changes. Two additional command icons will appear, labeled Trim Original and Save As New Clip. Trim Original alters the original video clip and replaces the file, whereas the Save As New Clip option creates a separate file and keeps a copy of the original clip.

## COMMANDS FOR EDITING PHOTOS

When you tap on the Edit icon while viewing a single image, several command icons are displayed along the bottom of the screen (refer to Figure 8.16). These icons provide the tools for quickly editing and enhancing your image. These command options are displayed as graphic icons and include the following.

## ENHANCE

On the iPhone, this icon is displayed in the upper-right corner of the screen. On the iPad, it's displayed to the left of the Crop icon (or above it, if you're holding the tablet in landscape mode). Enhance offers a one-touch editing tool that automatically adjusts aspects of a photo, like its contrast, exposure, and color, to make the image look better and make colors appear more vibrant. This feature can be turned on or off and is not manually adjustable.

# CROP

Shown in Figure 8.17, use the Crop tool to manually adjust the cropping of the image by dragging one of the corners of the white frame horizontally, vertically, or at a diagonal). The Crop tool also now enables you to straighten a photo and readjust its angle by placing your finger on the straightening dial and moving it up or down. Tap on the Image Rotation icon to rotate the image 90 degrees.

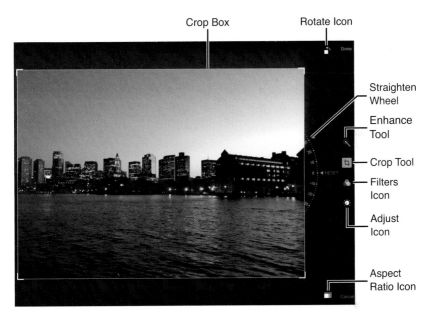

**FIGURE 8.17**
*Tap on the Crop icon to access tools for cropping, straightening, and/or rotating an image. (Shown here on the iPad Air.)*

> **TIP** After using any of the Crop-related tools, be sure to tap Done to save your changes. Alternatively, tap Cancel to exit out of this option without saving your changes. On the iPhone, when you activate the Crop tool, an image rotation slider is also displayed. This tool enables you to straighten photos, for example.

> **☑ TIP** As you're cropping an image, tap on the Aspect icon to select an aspect ratio, such as Original, Square, 3:2, 5:3, 4:3, 5:4, 7:5, or 16:9. Unless you need the image in a specific size, choose the Original option and then use the crop edges to adjust your image. Selecting an aspect ratio forces the basic dimensions to stay intact as you crop the image. This enables you to make accurately formatted prints later, without throwing off the image dimensions.

## FILTERS

The Photos app offers a handful of preinstalled special effect filters. After tapping on the Filters icon, select the filter you want to apply to your image with a single on-screen tap. A preview of the altered image is displayed. To save the changes, tap Done. To discard the changes, tap Cancel or tap on another filter.

> **(iOS 8) WHAT'S NEW** In addition to the filters that come preinstalled with the Photos app, third-party developers can now create optional filters you can use with the Photos app.

## ADJUST

The Photos app now enables you to edit or enhance many different aspects of a photo. Begin by tapping on the Adjust icon. Then, from the Adjust submenu, tap on the Light, Color, or B&W option. Each one of these options reveals another submenu, which offers a variety of editing tools.

### THE LIGHT TOOLS

When you tap on the Light Tool, a slider appears on the bottom of the screen (iPhone) or right side of the screen (iPad) that enables you to manually increase or decrease the overall lighting effect within the image being viewed (shown in Figure 8.18).

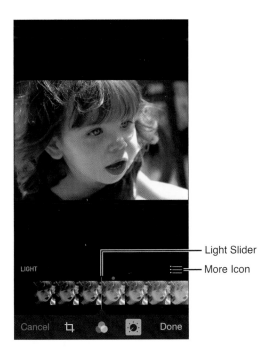

**FIGURE 8.18**

*It's possible to use a slider to manually adjust the master Light tool. (Shown on the iPhone 5s.)*

When you tap on the More icon (after tapping on the Light option), another submenu with options for Exposure, Highlights, Shadows, Brightness, Contrast, and Black Point is displayed (shown in Figure 8.19).

Tap on any of these options to reveal a separate slider you can use to manually adjust that option. Keep in mind that you can mix and match the use of these options to create truly customized visual effects.

Additional Light-Related Adjustment Tools

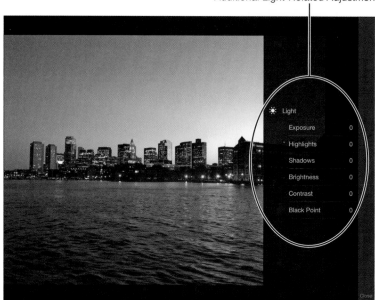

**FIGURE 8.19**

*Tap on the More icon to reveal additional light-related editing and image enhancement tools.*

## THE COLOR TOOLS

When you tap on the Color icon, a master Color slider is displayed. Use your finger to manually adjust this feature. Tap on the More icon to reveal additional Color-related options, including Saturation, Contrast, and Cast. Each of these tools (shown in Figure 8.20) has its own slider that you can manually adjust. Again, after making a change, be sure to tap on the Done option to save your edits. Alternatively, tap Cancel/Close to exit out of the selected editing tool without making any changes.

**FIGURE 8.20**

*After tapping on the Color icon, tap the More icon to access tools for adjusting the Saturation, Contrast, and Cast within a photo. Shown here is the Saturation slider on the iPad Air.*

## THE B&W TOOLS

Tap on the B&W icon to instantly convert a full-color image into black and white. It's then possible to manually adjust the black, white, and grayscale colors using the B&W slider that's displayed.

By tapping on the More icon after selecting the B&W editing tool, additional submenu options enable you to manually adjust the image's Intensity, Neutrals, Tone, and Grain, which all relate directly to the black-and-white effect (shown in Figure 8.21).

**FIGURE 8.21**

*Not only can you convert a full-color photo into black and white, you can then fully customize the black-and-white effect using a series of sliders related to the Intensity, Neutrals, Tone, and Grain tools.*

After making a change, tap Done to save your edits or Cancel/Close to exit out of the selected editing tool without making any changes.

## RED-EYE REMOVAL

If you used the flash to snap a photo of a person, and the red-eye effect occurs, you can automatically remove this effect by tapping on the Red-Eye Removal icon. This icon appears only when a photo was taken using the iOS mobile device's built-in flash.

## PRINTING PHOTOS

iOS 8 is fully compatible with Apple's AirPrint feature, so if you have a photo printer set up to work wirelessly with your iOS device, you can create photo prints from your digital images using the Print command in the Photos app. Follow these steps to print an image:

1. Launch the Photos app from the Home screen.

2. From the main View Images screen, tap on any thumbnail to view an image

in full-screen mode. You might need to open an album first by tapping on the Album's thumbnail if you have the Albums viewing option selected.

3. Tap on the full-screen version of the image to make the various command icons appear.

4. Tap on the Share icon.

5. From the Share menu, select the Print option.

6. When the Printer Options submenu appears, select your printer, determine how many copies of the print you'd like to create, and then tap on the Print icon.

> ⌕ **MORE INFO** To print wirelessly from your iOS device using the AirPrint feature, you must have a compatible printer. To learn more about AirPrint, and to configure your printer for wireless printing from your iPhone or iPad, visit http://support.apple.com/kb/HT4356.

## THIRD-PARTY APPS FOR ORDERING PRINTS FROM YOUR IMAGES

If you want to order professional quality prints of photos directly from your iPhone or iPad and have them shipped to your door within a few days, you can use one of several apps (such as FreePrints) that are available from the App Store.

The free KickSend app determines your current location and tells you which one-hour photo labs are in close proximity. You can then upload your photos to that lab directly from your iPhone or iPad, and within 30 to 60 minutes, pick up your prints at the selected location. KickSend is easy to use and works with participating Walgreen's, CVS Pharmacy, Target, and Wal-Mart locations.

The free Shutterfly app also enables you to order prints directly from your iOS mobile device, plus it gives you the option to create custom photo gifts, such as coffee mugs, mouse pads, iPhone cases, T-shirts, and other products that showcase your images. Enlargements can also be ordered, as can canvas prints and other types of wall art that showcase your favorite photos.

> **☑ TIP**  When emailing a photo to a lab (or someone who will be printing them on their home photo printer), to achieve the best possible prints, send the images in Full Size mode from your iOS device. To do this, after filling in the Email field and tapping Send, tap on the Actual Size button on the iPhone when the image quality menu appears. On the iPad, tap on the Images option that's displayed to the right of the Front field, and then when the Image Size options appear, tap on the Actual Size tab.

## SHARING PHOTOS AND VIDEOS

The iOS 8 version of the Photos app offers a new and expanded Share menu (shown in Figure 8.22). After you have selected one or more images, tap the Share icon to access the Share menu.

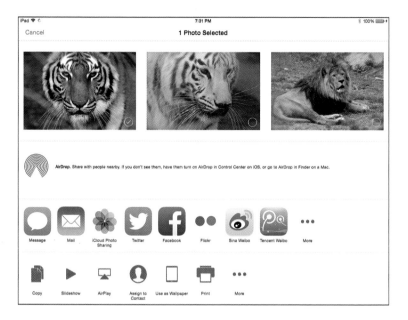

**FIGURE 8.22**

*The Share menu offered by the iOS 8 version of the Photos app has been expanded.*

## SEND IMAGES WIRELESSLY VIA AIRDROP

If you're within close proximity to another Mac, iPhone, or iPad and the other computer or iOS mobile device also has the AirDrop feature turned on, you can wirelessly send images from within the Photos app using the AirDrop feature. This feature becomes active only when others nearby can receive an AirDrop transmission.

> ## NOTE
> AirDrop works only with some of the newer iOS mobile devices. Likewise, a Mac must be running the latest version of the OS X Yosemite operating system to wirelessly transfer photos.

## SEND IMAGES VIA TEXT/INSTANT MESSAGE

Tap this option to send images via the Messages app. When the New Message window appears, fill in the To field with the recipient's cell phone number or iMessage account username. Tap the plus-sign icon to send the same message to multiple recipients.

You can optionally add text to the photo(s) that are attached to the message. To add more images to the outgoing message, tap on the Camera icon. When you're ready, tap the Send option to send the photos and message.

## EMAIL UP TO FIVE IMAGES AT A TIME

From either the iPhone or iPad, when looking at thumbnails for images in an Album, tap on the Edit button to select between one and five images, and then tap on the Share icon.

Select the Mail option and fill in the To field when prompted. If you want, edit the Subject field and/or add text to the body of the email, and then tap the Send button.

When viewing a single image, tap on the Share button, select Mail, fill in the To field, and edit the Subject. If you want, add text to the body of the message, and then tap the Send button.

## TWEET A PHOTO TO YOUR TWITTER FOLLOWERS

To tweet a photo, after tapping the Share icon while viewing a single photo in full-screen mode, select the Tweet option. Compose your tweet message (which will already have the selected image attached), and then tap the Send icon.

It's also possible to tweet photos from the official Twitter app or from a third-party Twitter-related app, such as Twitterific (available from the App Store).

## PUBLISH PHOTOS ON FACEBOOK

To publish one or more photos to Facebook with an optional text-based status update, tap the Facebook button in the Share menu. From the Facebook window, tap the Album option to choose an existing Facebook Photos Album to which the image should be added.

Next, tap the Location option to publish the location where the image was shot on Facebook along with the photo. Tap on the Audience option to decide who can view the image(s) on Facebook. Your options include Public, Friends, Friends Except Acquaintances, Only Me, Close Friends, or people within a specific Facebook group you've created.

To the left of the photo thumbnail, use the virtual keyboard to enter a caption for the image(s) you're about to upload, and then tap the Post option (displayed at the top-right corner of the Facebook window) to publish the photos.

> **TIP**   An alternative to using the Photos app to publish photos to Facebook is to use the official Facebook app. This gives you additional options, such as the ability to tag photos with the names of the people who appear in them. Plus, the Facebook app enables you to add special-effect filters to images before uploading them.

## UPLOAD IMAGES TO FLICKR

Flickr is an online-based photo sharing service and photo lab operated by Yahoo!. To upload selected images to your existing Flickr account, select the images from within the Photos app, tap the Share icon, and then tap the Flickr option. You then can choose an album to which your selected images are uploaded.

It's also possible to use the official Flickr app to upload and manage your account from your iPhone or iPad.

## COPY AN IMAGE TO ANOTHER APP

From within the Photos app, you can store a photo in your iOS device's virtual clipboard and then paste that photo into another compatible app. To copy a photo into your device's virtual clipboard, follow these steps:

1. From within the Photos app, select a single photo and view it in full-screen mode.

2. Tap on the image to make the command icons appear.

3. Tap on the Share icon.

4. Tap on the Copy option. The photo is stored in the virtual clipboard.

5. Launch a compatible app and hold your finger down on the screen to use the Paste option and paste your photo from the clipboard into the active app.

## CREATE A SLIDESHOW

To create and display an animated slideshow featuring selected images, launch Photos and select a group of images. Next, tap the Share icon and choose the Slideshow option.

From the Slideshow Options screen, choose to display the image on the iPhone (or iPad) or via Apple TV. Select your Transition effect from the menu and decide whether you want music to accompany the presentation. By turning on the virtual switch associated with Play Music, you can choose music that's stored in the Music app of your iOS mobile device. To begin the Slideshow, tap on the Start Slideshow option.

## SHOW IMAGE ON A TELEVISION VIA AIRPLAY

Instead of viewing an image in full-screen mode on your iPhone or iPad, tap the AirPlay icon and select Apple TV to wirelessly transmit the image to your HD television set. To use this feature with an HD TV, you need the optional Apple TV device. To use the feature with a Mac, be sure AirPlay on your Mac is turned on.

## SAVE THE IMAGE TO YOUR CAMERA ROLL FOLDER

If you're viewing images stored in your Photo Stream or a Shared Photo Stream (or your iCloud Photo Library, once this option is introduced in early 2015), tap on the Save To Camera Roll option (which appears only when it's available) to store the image in the Camera Roll folder of the Photos app.

## ASSIGN IMAGE TO CONTACT

To link an image stored in the Photos app to a specific contact in the Contacts app, follow these steps:

1. From within the Photos app, select a single photo and view it in full-screen mode.

2. Tap on the image to make the various command icons appear.

3. Tap on the Share icon.

4. Tap on the Assign to Contact option.

5. An All Contacts window is displayed. Scroll through the listing, or use the Search field to find the specific entry with which you want to associate the photo.

6. Tap on that person's or company's name from the All Contacts listing.

7. When the Choose Photo window opens, use your finger to move or scale the image. What you see in the box is what will be saved.

8. Tap on the Use icon to save the photo and link it to the selected contact.

9. When you launch Contacts and access that person's entry, the photo you selected appears in the entry.

### USE AS WALLPAPER

As you're viewing a photo, you can assign it to be the wallpaper image used on your Home screen or Lock screen by tapping on the Share icon and then choosing the Use As Wallpaper option. When the image is previewed on the screen, tap on the Set button. From the Set Lock Screen, Set Home Screen, or Set Both menu, choose where you want the selected image displayed.

## DELETING PHOTOS STORED ON YOUR iOS DEVICE

To delete one image at a time as you're viewing them in full-screen mode, simply tap on the Trash icon displayed on the screen.

To select and delete multiple images at once as you're looking at thumbnails, tap on the Select button. Tap on each thumbnail that represents an image you want to delete. A checkmark icon appears within each image thumbnail indicating that the image has been selected. Tap on the Trash icon to delete the selected images.

## iCLOUD INTEGRATION WITH THE PHOTOS APP

The Photos app integrates seamlessly with Apple's iCloud service. When iOS 8 was introduced, the iCloud service continued to enable users to create a single My Photo Stream to back up and sync up to 1,000 of the most recent images shot or stored in an iPhone, iPad, or Mac. When it came to sharing images with others in the form of online galleries or albums, iCloud offered the Shared Photo Stream feature.

Slated to be introduced in early 2015, Apple is replacing the My Photo Stream and Shared Photo Stream features with the iCloud Photo Library. Once introduced, iCloud Photo Library will enable you to store your entire digital photo library online. You'll be able to sync that library with all of your Macs, PCs, and iOS mobile devices that are linked to the same iCloud account.

Within your iCloud Photo Library, you will be able to create multiple Albums to better organize your images. Then, using the Photos app, you can manage your library and select individual images, groups of images, or entire albums to share with selected people. Only the photos or albums you choose to share with specific people will become accessible by those people. All of your other images stored in iCloud Photo Library will remain accessible only to you.

## THE PHOTOS APP SUPPORTS iCLOUD'S FAMILY SHARING

One aspect of iCloud's new Family Sharing is what Apple refers to as the Family Album. One single Family album becomes accessible by up to six family members, who can then freely add, edit, delete, and share images stored within that single album. Everyone's other image albums remain private and separate from the Family album.

When you turn on the Family Sharing feature within iCloud, the Family Album is automatically created. To learn more about this iCloud feature, refer to Chapter 5, "Ways to Use iCloud's Latest Features with Your iPhone and/or iPad," or visit Apple's website (www.apple.com/icloud/family-sharing).

# MAKE AND RECEIVE CALLS WITH AN iPHONE

Although your iPhone is capable of handling a wide range of tasks, one of its core purposes is to serve as a feature-packed cell phone. Your iPhone makes and receives voice calls using a cellular network that's operated by the service provider you selected when the phone was activated. The Phone app that comes preinstalled on your iPhone offers a vast selection of calling features that make it easy to stay in touch with people.

 **WHAT'S NEW** Thanks to the new Handoff feature, it's now possible to answer an incoming call that's made to your iPhone using your iPad or Mac. Plus, depending on your cellular service provider, it might also be possible to initiate calls via the Internet from a Wi-Fi hotspot using your service provider's Voice Over LTE network and iOS 8's new Call Over Wi-Fi feature. Several major U.S.-based service providers will be introducing compatibility with this feature in 2015. These features are explained later in this chapter.

> **✓ TIP**  If you're an iPad user, you can also make and receive Voice-over-IP (Internet-based) phone calls using Skype or a similar app. These calls can be made to or received from any landline or cell phone. You can participate in Skype-to-Skype calls for free. In addition to voice-over-IP calls, Skype can be used for free video calls with Mac, PC, iOS mobile device, Android, or Windows mobile device users. Using FaceTime for video calls works only with other Mac or iOS mobile device users.
>
> Skype is also ideal for saving money when you're making international calls from the United States, or to avoid hefty international roaming charges when you're calling home to the United States when traveling overseas.
>
> Yet another Internet calling option is to use FaceTime for audio or video calls, or to use the audio calling feature now offered by Facebook Messenger to initiate calls with your Facebook friends.

After you set up and activate your new iPhone with a cellular service provider and choose a calling plan, it's capable of receiving incoming calls and enables you to make outgoing calls using the Phone app.

In the United States, a growing number of popular cellular service providers now offer iPhone compatibility. When you purchase an iPhone, you must decide in advance which wireless service provider to sign up with (a two-year service agreement with a hefty early termination fee is typically involved). You can, however, purchase an "unlocked" iPhone with no service contract, and then pay a month-to-month fee for service. This requires you to pay an unsubsidized price for the iPhone (starting around $549 for a 16GB iPhone 5s), and then pay between $35 and $70 per month for voice, data, and text services.

Choose a wireless service provider that offers the best coverage in your area, the most competitively priced calling plan based on your needs, and the extra features you want or need. When looking at coverage area maps for various service providers, if you have an iPhone 5s, iPhone 6, or iPhone 6 Plus, focus on 4G LTE coverage, as opposed to 3G or plain 4G service.

Not all wireless service providers enable iPhone users to talk and surf the Web at the same time. Likewise, some offer better international roaming coverage than others, while some are more generous when it comes to monthly wireless data allocation.

Keep in mind that the iPhone hardware is slightly different based on which wireless service provider you choose, so you typically can't switch providers after you've acquired the iPhone.

> ☑ TIP  For your iPhone to make or receive calls, it must be turned on and *not* in Airplane mode. Unless you're using the new Call over Wi-Fi function (which not all cellular service providers support), a decent cellular service signal, which is displayed in the upper-left corner of the screen in the form of dots, is also a necessity. The more dots you see (up to five), the stronger the cellular signal (which is based on your proximity to the closest cell towers). For more on Airplane mode, see Chapter 1, "Tips and Tricks for Customizing Settings."

# ANSWERING AN INCOMING CALL

Regardless of what you're doing on your iPhone, when an incoming call is received, everything else is put on hold and the Phone app launches, unless the iPhone is turned off, in Airplane mode, or the Do Not Disturb feature is turned on, in which case incoming calls automatically go to voicemail.

To control the volume of the ringer, press the Volume Up or Volume Down buttons on the side of your iPhone; or to turn off the ringer (which causes the phone to vibrate when an incoming call is received), turn on the Mute button on the side of the iPhone.

> ☑ TIP  While your iPhone is still ringing, to silence the ringer and send the incoming call to voicemail after a 5- to 10-second delay, press the Power button or Volume Up or Volume Down button once. To send the incoming call immediately to voicemail, double tap on the Power button or tap the Decline option displayed on the screen.
>
> You also can silence the iPhone's ringer by switching on the Mute button (located on the side of the iPhone, above the Volume Up button). Your phone vibrates instead of ringing when an incoming call is received.
>
> To control the Vibrate feature, launch Settings, tap on the Sounds option, turn on the virtual switch that's associated with Vibrate On Ring and/or Vibrate On Silent, and then tap on the Ringtone option that's found under the Sounds and Vibration Patterns heading to select a custom vibration pattern when incoming calls are received.
>
> Yet another way to be left alone is to put your phone in Do Not Disturb mode. This can be done automatically at certain predetermined times, or manually whenever you want to be left alone. To do this, access Control Center and tap on the Do Not Disturb icon.

There are several ways to answer an incoming call. If you're doing something else on your iPhone and it starts to ring, the caller ID for the incoming caller appears, along with a green-and-white Accept button and a red-and-white Decline icon (as shown in Figure 9.1). Tap the Accept button to answer the call. If you tap Decline or wait too long to answer, the call automatically goes to voicemail.

**FIGURE 9.1**

*Your iPhone notifies you when an incoming call is received. You can then answer or decline the call.*

If you're using your iPhone with EarPods, ear buds, or a headset with a built-in microphone, you can answer an incoming call by pressing the Accept button on the headset.

> **TIP** When you receive an incoming call, displayed above the Decline and Accept buttons (or the Slide To Answer slider on the Lock screen) are two other options (refer to Figure 9.1) labeled Remind Me and Message.
>
> When you tap on Message, a menu containing four prewritten text messages, along with a Custom button, is displayed. Tap on one of the message buttons to send that message to the caller via text/instant message. Or tap on the Custom button to type a custom message to send to that caller. The incoming call is also transferred to voicemail.

To customize the prewritten messages available from the Message option, launch Settings, tap on the Phone option, and then tap on the Respond with Text option. Displayed on the Respond with Text menu screen are three customizable fields, under the heading, "Can't Talk Right Now." Tap on one of these fields to replace one of the default messages with your own.

The other option for managing incoming calls is the Remind Me option. When you tap on this button, the incoming call is sent to voicemail, but you can quickly set a reminder (and alarm) for yourself to call that person back in one hour, when you leave your current location, or when you get home. For these last two options to function, Locations Services related to the Phone app must be turned on from within Settings.

If the iPhone is in Sleep mode when an incoming call is received, unlock the phone by swiping your finger from left to right on the Slide to Answer slider, which automatically takes the phone out of Sleep mode, unlocks it, and answers the incoming call (shown in Figure 9.2).

**FIGURE 9.2**

*When an incoming call is received while the phone is in Sleep mode, you need to unlock the phone to automatically answer it.*

> **NOTE** Answering the phone using an optional Bluetooth headset automatically unlocks the phone if it's in Sleep mode.

> **TIP** If you're too busy to answer an incoming call on your iPhone, you can let the call go to voicemail or set up call forwarding so that the incoming call automatically gets rerouted to another phone number, such as your home or office number. To set up call forwarding and turn this function on or off as needed, launch Settings, and then tap on the Phone option.
>
> From the Phone menu in Settings, you can view your iPhone's phone number, set up and turn on call forwarding, turn on or off call waiting, and decide whether you want your iPhone's number to be displayed on someone's caller ID when you initiate a call.
>
> Also from Settings, you have the option of enabling the International Assist feature, which makes initiating international calls much less confusing.

> **TIP** From the Phone submenu within Settings, if you turn on the virtual switch associated with Contact Photos in Favorites option, photos of the people on that list (if available) are displayed along with their name. For this feature to work, you must have the person's photo stored in their entry in your Contacts database or they must be a Facebook friend (and you must have Facebook integration turned on).

After you answer an incoming call, you have a few options. You can hold the iPhone up to your ear and start talking, or you can tap the Speaker icon to use your iPhone as a speakerphone. You can also use the phone with a wired or wireless Bluetooth headset, which offers hands-free operation. The headset option is ideal when you're driving, plus it offers privacy (versus using the iPhone's speakerphone option).

> **CAUTION** If you're driving, choose a headset that covers only one ear, or use the Speaker option for hands-free operation. Refrain from holding the phone up to your ear or covering both ears with a headset. (See the section, "A Few Thoughts About Wireless Headsets," for headset considerations.) Make sure you're familiar with state and local laws in your area related to the use of cell phones while driving.

When using a Bluetooth headset, you don't need to hold the phone up to your ear to carry on a conversation. If you're using a headset, tap on the headset's answer button when you receive an incoming call to answer it. There's no need to do anything on your iPhone.

One other option, when you're in a compatible car (or in a vehicle equipped with an iPhone Hands-Free Kit), is to take advantage of the vehicle's CarPlay or Hands-Free compatibility. This enables your phone to link to your vehicle and use the in-dash infotainment system to make and receive calls, utilizing your vehicle's built-in microphone and stereo system speakers to interact with the other party. The call is still handled by your iPhone, but the iPhone is operated hands-free (and eyes-free).

## USE iOS 8'S NEW HANDOFF FEATURE TO ANSWER INCOMING iPHONE CALLS ON YOUR iPAD OR MAC

One easy-to-use new feature apps is called Handoff. When activated, as long as your iPhone is within wireless proximity to your iPad or Mac (they can typically be up to 33 feet apart), it's possible to answer an incoming call that's made to your iPhone from your iPad (shown in Figure 9.3) or Mac.

**FIGURE 9.3**

*When an iPhone and iPad are linked to the same iCloud account and have the Handoff option turned on, it's possible to answer an incoming call on the iPad from up to 33 feet away from the smartphone.*

> **NOTE** All Macs and iOS mobile devices that are set up to work with Handoff and iOS 8's other Continuity features must also be linked to the same iCloud account. Keep in mind that some older iPhones and iPads do not support the Handoff feature.

To set up this feature, launch Settings, tap on the General option, and then tap on the Handoff & Suggested Apps option. From the Handoff & Suggested Apps submenu, turn on the virtual switch that's associated with the Handoff option.

Next, repeat this process on your iPad. If you have a Mac that's running the OS X Yosemite operating system, turn on the Handoff feature from within System Preferences.

When the feature is turned on, your iPhone automatically maintains a wireless link to your iPad and/or Mac. When an incoming call is received, all connected devices ring, Caller ID information is displayed, and you can Accept or Decline the call from any connected device.

On the iPad or Mac, the tablet or computer acts like a speakerphone by taking advantage of the built-in microphone and speaker(s). You can also pair a Bluetooth wireless headset to your iPad and/or Mac.

To initiate a call from your iPad or Mac via your iPhone and the Handoff feature, tap on any displayed phone number from within the Contacts, Calendar, or Safari apps (on your iPad or Mac) to initiate a call to that number using the computer or tablet you're currently working with.

## MANAGING THE DO NOT DISTURB FEATURE

To activate and customize the Do Not Disturb feature, launch Settings and tap on the Do Not Disturb option. To later enable or disable this feature, access the Control Center and tap on the crescent moon–shaped icon (shown in Figure 9.4).

Do Not Disturb Icon

**FIGURE 9.4**

*Accessing the Do Not Disturb feature can easily be done from Control Center.*

When turned on, a moon icon is displayed on the iPhone's or iPad's status bar, and all calls and alerts are silenced (shown in Figure 9.5).

Do Not Disturb Icon

**FIGURE 9.5**

*Determine whether the Do Not Disturb feature is turned on by looking for the moon-shaped icon in the upper-right corner of the iPhone's screen.*

This feature can be turned on or off at anytime, or you can schedule specific times you want Do Not Disturb to be activated, such as between 11:00 p.m. and 7:00 a.m. on weekdays. From the Do Not Disturb menu in Settings (shown in Figure 9.6), you can also determine whether certain callers are allowed to reach you when the phone is in Do Not Disturb mode.

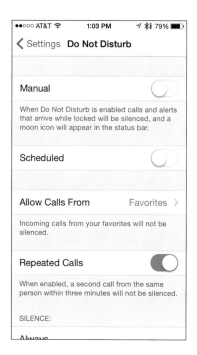

**FIGURE 9.6**

*From the Do Not Disturb menu screen in Settings, be sure to customize this feature so it best meets your needs and schedule, based on when you want to be left alone.*

Keep in mind that when your iPhone is turned off, all incoming calls are forwarded directly to voicemail, and it is not possible to initiate an outgoing call. Likewise, incoming text messages, FaceTime calls, and other communications from the outside world are not accepted when an iPhone is turned off, in Do Not Disturb mode, or in Airplane mode. Instead, notifications for these missed messages are displayed in Notification Center (depending on how you set up Notification Center), within their respective apps, and potentially on the Lock screen when you turn on the device or turn off Airplane mode.

## MANAGE CALLS IN PROGRESS FROM THE CALL IN PROGRESS SCREEN

As soon as you answer an incoming call, the Phone app's display changes to the Call In Progress screen. This screen contains several command icons: Mute, Keypad, Speaker, Add Call, FaceTime, Contacts, and End. The caller's information and a call timer are displayed at the top of the screen.

**NOTE** When you receive an incoming call, if the caller ID for that caller matches up with a contact stored in the Contacts app, that person's name, which number the call is from (Home, Work, Mobile, and so on), and the caller's photo (if you have a photo of that person linked to the contact) are displayed.

If there's no match in your Contacts database, the regular Caller ID data is displayed, which can include the person's name, phone number, and the city and state from which the call is originating. You might also receive calls labeled Private or Unknown.

**TIP** It's possible to block incoming calls from specific phone numbers. To block a caller, you must first create a new contact in the Contacts app for the person or company you want to block. Then, tap on the Blocked option in the Phone menu of the Settings app (shown in Figure 9.7), followed by the Add New option. Choose a phone number from your Contacts database. Until you manually remove that contact from your Blocked list, no calls, texts, or FaceTime calls will be accepted from that number.

**FIGURE 9.7**

*Customize features of the Phone app from within Settings, like the ability to block certain incoming calls.*

Here's a summary of the command icons available to you from the Call In Progress screen during a phone conversation:

- **Mute**—Tap on this icon to turn off your iPhone's microphone. You can still hear what's being said to you, but the person you're speaking with cannot hear you. When you're ready to be heard again, turn off the Mute feature by tapping on this icon again.

- **Keypad**—Replace the current menu screen with the numeric telephone keypad. This is necessary for navigating your way through voicemail trees (for example, when you're told to press 1 for English, press 2 to speak with an operator, press 3 to track an order, and so on).

- **Speaker (or Audio Source)**—Tap the Speaker icon to switch from Handset mode (in which you hold the iPhone up to your ear to have a phone conversation) to Speaker mode, which turns your iPhone into a speakerphone. If you're using your iPhone with a headset, a third Headset option is listed, and this menu feature is labeled Audio Source as opposed to Speaker.

- **Add Call (+)**—During a conversation with someone, you can initiate a conference call and bring a third party into the conversation by tapping on Add Call, as described later in this chapter.

- **FaceTime**—If the person to whom you're talking is also using an iPhone, and both devices have access to an Internet connection, tap on the FaceTime icon to switch from a traditional phone call to a real-time video call using the FaceTime app. This is a free service.

> **TIP** In addition to being able to launch FaceTime from the Phone app and switch from a normal call to a video call, you can also use the separate FaceTime app to initiate a video call from your iPhone.

- **Contacts**—While you're conversing on the phone, you can access your Contacts database and look up someone's information by tapping on this option.

- **End**—Tap on the large red-and-white End button or tap the end call button on your headset, if applicable, to terminate the call.

> ☑ TIP  Your phone conversation can continue while you're using other apps. Depending on your wireless service provider, you might even be able to participate in a phone conversation and surf the Web at the same time. To launch another app, press the Home button and tap on its app icon from the Home screen. Or to access the app switcher, double-tap on the Home button, and then tap on any app icon that appears.
>
> When you view the Home screen while still on the phone, a green-and-white banner shows, "Touch to return to call," along with a call timer. Tap on this green bar to return to the Phone app.

## RESPOND TO A CALL WAITING SIGNAL WHILE ON THE PHONE

As you're chatting it up on the phone, if someone else tries to call you, you hear a call waiting tone, and a related message appears on your iPhone's screen. You can control the Call Waiting feature from the Settings app.

When a second call comes in, the caller ID information of the new caller is displayed on the screen, along with several command icons and buttons (shown in Figure 9.8). These commands are End & Accept, Send To Voicemail, or Hold & Accept.

If you place the first call on hold and answer the new incoming call, you have the opportunity to merge the two calls and create a conference call or switch between the two calls and speak with each person individually (while the other is on hold).

> ☑ TIP  When the call waiting signal goes off on your iPhone, typically only you hear it. Thus, the person you're speaking with on the other end of the line does not know you've received another call. So before tapping the End & Accept or Hold & Accept button, be sure to tell the person you were originally speaking with what's going on.

While engaged in a conference call on your iPhone, the names of the people with whom you're engaged in a call are displayed along the top of the screen, along with an Info icon. Tap on the circular "i" icon to the right of this information to reveal a new screen that enables you to manage any of the parties involved with the conference call.

**FIGURE 9.8**

*When you're on a call and you simultaneously receive another incoming call, in addition to hearing the Call Waiting signal, you're given several onscreen options.*

While you're engaged in a three-way call (with two other parties), you can tap on the Add Call option again to add more parties to the conference call.

On the secondary Conference Call Info screen, associated with each name/Caller ID number is an End button and a Private button. Tap on End to disconnect that party, or tap Private to speak with just that party privately and place the other party (or parties) on hold. You can then reestablish the conference call by tapping on the Back button to return to the previous Conference Call screen, and then tap on the Merge Calls icon again.

## MAKING CALLS FROM YOUR iPHONE

There are several ways to initiate a phone call from your iPhone; however, you typically must first launch the Phone app. Then, you can do the following:

- Dial a number manually using the keypad.
- Access a listing from your Contacts database (from within the Phone app), choose a number, and dial it.

- Use Siri (which is explained in Chapter 2, "Using Siri, Dictation, and CarPlay to Interact with Your Mobile Device"). This can be done anytime, regardless of what app is running on your iPhone or whether you're looking at the Home screen.

- Redial a number from the Phone app's Recents call log.

- Select and dial a phone number from the Phone app's Favorites list.

- Dial a number displayed in another compatible app or iOS 8 feature, such as Maps, Messages, Mail, Safari, Contacts, or the Notification Center window. When you tap on a displayed phone number, it dials that number and initiates a call using the Phone app.

## MANUAL DIALING

To initiate a call by manually dialing a phone number, follow these steps:

1. Launch the Phone app from the Home screen.

2. Tap on the Keypad icon displayed at the bottom of the screen.

3. Using the numeric phone keypad, dial the number you want to reach, including the area code. If you're making an international call, include the country code as well.

4. If you make a mistake when entering a digit, tap the small "X" icon that's displayed near the top-right corner of the screen.

> **TIP** As you're manually entering a phone number, if you want to create a Contacts entry for it, tap on the "+" icon that's displayed in the top-left corner of the screen, and then tap on the Create New Contact or Add To Existing Contact option.

5. When the phone number is entered and displayed at the top of the screen, tap the green-and-white Call button to initiate the call.

6. The display on the iPhone changes to display a "Calling" message until the call connects, at which time the Call Menu screen is displayed.

> **NOTE** As you enter a phone number using the keypad, if that number is already stored in your Contacts database (in the Contacts app), the person's name automatically displays at the top of the screen, just below the phone number you entered.

You can also use the Cut, Copy, and Paste features of iOS 8 to copy a phone number displayed in another app, and then paste it into the phone number field on the Keypad screen. Or, if you tap on a phone number that's displayed in the Contacts app or while surfing the Web using Safari, for example, the Phone app automatically launches and a call to that number is initiated.

## DIALING FROM A CONTACTS ENTRY IN THE PHONE APP

From within the Phone app, it's possible to look up any phone number stored in your personal contacts database that's associated with the Contacts app. The Phone and Contacts apps work nicely together on your iPhone. To use this feature, follow these steps:

1. Launch the Phone app from the Home screen.

2. Tap on the Contacts icon displayed at the bottom of the screen.

3. An alphabetized listing of the contacts stored in the Contacts app is displayed. At the top of the screen is a blank Search field. Using your finger, either scroll through the alphabetized list of contacts or use the iPhone's virtual keyboard to find a stored listing.

4. Tap on any listing to view its complete Contacts entry. This might include multiple phone numbers, such as Home, Work, and Mobile. Then tap on the phone number you want to dial.

5. The display on the iPhone changes. A "Calling" message is displayed until the call connects, at which time the Call Menu screen is displayed.

## USE SIRI TO INITIATE CALLS

After you have added entries into your Contacts database using the Contacts app, you can use Siri to dial someone's phone number by speaking into the iPhone. For example, activate Siri and say, "Call John Doe at work." More information about using Siri with the Phone app can be found in Chapter 2.

## REESTABLISH CONTACT FROM THE APP SWITCHER'S RECENTS LISTING

Regardless of what you're doing on your iPhone (or iPad), when you press the Home button twice, the app switcher screen appears. One new feature in iOS 8 is that above the listing of apps currently running on your iOS mobile device is now a Recents heading.

Below this heading are profile photos and the names of the people you've recently had contact with via the Phone (iPhone), FaceTime (iPhone/iPad), or Messages (iPhone/iPad) apps. Tap on a profile photo, and then tap the appropriate command icon to quickly call or message that person.

## USE iOS 8'S NEW CALL OVER WI-FI CALLING FEATURE

Typically, when you initiate a call from your iPhone 5c, iPhone 5s, iPhone 6, or iPhone 6 Plus, your smartphone connects to the cellular network you've subscribed to, such as AT&T Wireless, Verizon Wireless, Sprint, or T-Mobile. Thanks to iOS 8's new Call over Wi-Fi feature, if you're not in a good cellular network coverage area but your compatible iPhone is within a Wi-Fi hotspot, a call can be made to any landline or other cellphone via the Internet.

For iPhone 6 and iPhone 6 Plus users, once a Wi-Fi call is initiated, if you leave the Wi-Fi hotspot, your call is automatically transferred to the cellular network's Voice Over LTE feature, if your cellular service supports this option. Likewise, if you're using the Voice Over LTE feature and a Wi-Fi signal becomes available, the call is seamlessly transferred to the Wi-Fi network; otherwise, the call is dropped if the Wi-Fi signal is lost.

If available, to manually initiate calls using the Call over Wi-Fi feature, as opposed to a cellular network, launch Settings, tap on the Phone option, and then turn on the virtual switch that's associated with the Wi-Fi Calling option.

> **NOTE** When Apple introduced Call Over Wi-Fi in September 2014, T-Mobile was the only cellular service provider in the United States supporting it. Starting sometime in 2015, AT&T Wireless, Verizon Wireless, and other service providers have announced support for this feature.

## MANAGING YOUR VOICEMAIL

Your unique iPhone phone number comes with voicemail, which enables people to leave you messages if you're not able to speak with them when they call.

Just as with any voicemail service, you can record your outgoing message, play back missed messages from your iPhone, or call your iPhone's voicemail service and listen to your calls from another phone.

# RECORD YOUR OUTGOING MESSAGE

To record your outgoing voicemail message, which is what people hear when they call your iPhone and you don't answer, follow these steps. Or you can have a computer-generated voice instruct callers to leave a message.

1. Launch the Phone app from the Home screen.

2. Tap on the Voicemail icon, displayed in the lower-right corner of the screen.

3. In the upper-left corner of the Voicemail screen, tap on the Greeting option.

4. From the Greeting screen (shown in Figure 9.9), tap on the Default option to skip recording a message and have a computer voice use a generic message. Or tap on the Custom option to record your own outgoing voicemail message.

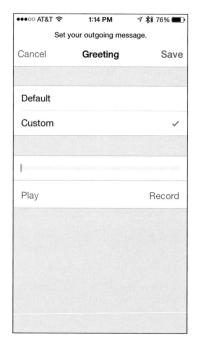

**FIGURE 9.9**

*The Greeting screen in the Phone app. From here, you can record an outgoing greeting.*

5. After you tap the Custom option, tap on the Record option that's also displayed on the Greeting screen. Hold the phone up to your mouth and begin recording your message.

6. When you're finished recording, tap on the Stop option. You can now play back your message by tapping on the Play option, or tap on the Save option to save your message and activate it.

# HOW TO PLAY AND DELETE VOICEMAIL MESSAGES

It's possible to listen to voicemail messages either from your iPhone or by calling your iPhone's voicemail from another phone.

## LISTEN TO VOICEMAIL FROM YOUR iPHONE

From your iPhone, to listen to and then save or delete an incoming voicemail message, follow these steps:

1. Launch the Phone app from the Home screen.
2. Tap on the Voicemail icon that's displayed in the bottom-right corner of the screen.
3. Under the Voicemail heading seen at the top of the screen is a listing of missed voicemail messages. Tap on a message to highlight it.

> **NOTE**  When you see a blue dot to the left of a voicemail message listing, this indicates it's a new, unheard message. After you listen to the message, the blue dot disappears. When you tap on the message to listen to it, the blue dot changes into a Pause/Play icon.

4. After a message is highlighted, tap on the small play/pause icon. The message begins playing. It might, however, take a few seconds for the message to load. A brief pause should be expected.
5. Near the bottom of the voicemail listing is a slider that depicts the length of the message, along with Call Back and Delete options. As your message plays, the thin blue line on the timer slider moves to the right. You can listen to parts of the message again by moving this slider around with your finger.
6. When you're finished listening to the message, you can leave the listing alone (which keeps the message saved on your phone) or tap the Delete option to erase it. You also have the option of calling back the person who left the message by tapping on the Call Back option.
7. To exit the voicemail options, tap on any of the other command icons displayed at the bottom of the Phone app's screen, or press the Home button on your iPhone.

> **☑ TIP**  You might find it easier to listen to your voicemail messages via speaker phone, by first tapping on the Speaker or Audio option that's displayed below the timer slider.

> **☑ TIP**  If you accidentally delete an important voicemail, don't panic. From the voicemail screen, scroll to the very bottom of your voicemail message list and tap on the Deleted Messages icon. Tap on a message to highlight it, and then tap on the Undelete icon.

## LISTEN TO YOUR iPHONE'S VOICEMAIL FROM ANOTHER PHONE

You also have the option of using another phone to call your iPhone's voicemail service and listen to the messages that were left. Follow these steps:

1. From any other phone besides your iPhone (including a landline or another cellphone), dial your iPhone's phone number.

2. When your iPhone's voicemail picks up, press the * key on the phone from which you're calling.

3. When prompted by the computer voice, enter the numeric password that's associated with your voicemail.

> **☑ TIP**  To set or change your voicemail password, launch the Settings app and tap on the Phone option. From the Phone menu in Settings, scroll down to the Change Voicemail Password option and tap on it. When the Password screen appears, use the keypad to create a password. To change a password, first enter your current password, tap Done, and then enter a new voicemail password.

4. Follow the voice prompts to listen to or delete your messages.

5. As you're listening to your messages, you can press certain keys to manage specific functions. These options vary based on your cellular service provider, but might include the following:

   - Press 1 to play back your messages.
   - Press 5 to hear details about a message, including the incoming phone number and the time/date it was recorded, as well as the message length.

- Press 7 to delete the current message.
- Press 9 to save the message.
- Press # to skip the current message.
- Press 0 for more options.

6. Hang up when you're finished listening to your voicemail messages.

## CREATE AND USE A FAVORITES LIST

From within the Phone app, you can create a Favorites list, which is a customized list of your most frequently dialed contacts. To access this list, launch the Phone app, and then tap on the Favorites icon that's displayed in the bottom-left corner of the screen.

To add a contact to the Favorites list, tap on the plus-sign (+) icon that you see in the upper-right corner of the screen. Select any listing from your Contacts database and tap on it. When the complete listing for that entry appears, tap on the specific phone number you want listed in your Favorites list. The newly created Favorites listing appears at the end of your Favorites list.

> **TIP** Each favorites entry can have one name and one phone number associated with it, so if a Contact entry has multiple phone numbers listed, choose one. If you want quick access to someone's home, work, and mobile numbers from your Favorites list, create three separate entries for that person.
>
> When you create the entry in Favorites, the type of phone number (Home, Work, Mobile, iPhone, and so on) is displayed to the right of the person's name. A Favorites listing can also relate to someone's FaceTime identifier (their iPhone number, Apple ID, or the email address they used to set up their FaceTime account).

To edit the contacts already listed in your Favorites list, tap on the Edit option in the upper-left corner of the screen. After tapping Edit, change the order of your Favorites list by holding your finger on the rightmost icon next to a listing, and then dragging it upward or downward to the desired location. Or delete a listing by tapping on the red-and-white negative-sign icon displayed to the left of a listing. When you're finished making changes, tap on the Done icon that's displayed in the upper-left corner of the screen.

> **TIP** As you're viewing your Favorites list, tap on the Info ('i') icon, shown to the right of each listing. This enables you to view that person's entire entry from within your Contacts database.

To dial a phone number listed in your Favorites list, simply tap on its listing. The Phone app automatically dials the number and initiates a call.

## ACCESSING YOUR RECENTS CALL LOG

The Phone app automatically keeps track of all incoming and outgoing calls. To access this detailed call log, launch the Phone app from the Home screen, and then tap on the Recents icon displayed at the bottom of the screen.

At the top of the Recents screen are two command tabs, labeled All and Missed, along with an Edit option. Tap on the All tab to view a detailed listing of all incoming and outgoing calls, displayed in reverse-chronological order. Missed incoming calls are displayed in red. Tap on the Missed tab to see a listing of calls you didn't answer. Tap on the Edit option to delete specific calls from this listing, or tap on the Info ("i") icon to view more details about that caller, including their recent call history with you.

> **TIP** Missed calls are also displayed in the Notification Center window on your iPhone or as an icon badge or alert on your Home screen, depending on how you set up Notifications for the Phone app in the Settings app. To customize the Notifications options for the Phone app, launch Settings from the Home screen and tap on the Notifications option. From the Notifications screen in Settings, tap on the Phone option. You can adjust how your iPhone alerts you to missed calls by personalizing the options on this Phone screen.

Each listing in the Recents call log displays the name of the person you spoke with (based on data from your Contacts database or the Caller ID feature) or their phone number. If it's someone from your Contacts database, information about which phone number (home, work, mobile, or such) the caller used appears below the name.

If the same person called you, or you called that person, multiple times in a row, a number in parentheses indicates how many calls were made to or from that person. This is displayed to the right of the name or phone number.

On the right side of the screen, with each Recents listing, is the time the call was made or received. To view the Contacts entry related to that person, tap on the right-pointing blue-and-white arrow icon associated with the listing. At the top of a contact's entry screen are details about the call itself, including its time and date, whether it was an incoming or outgoing call, and its duration.

To call someone back who is listed in the Recents list, tap anywhere on that listing except for on the blue-and-white arrow icon.

# DO YOU TALK TOO MUCH? KEEPING TRACK OF USAGE

Some iPhone voice plans come with a predetermined number of talk minutes per month. Some plans offer unlimited night and weekend calling, but calls made or received during the day count against your monthly minute allocation.

**! CAUTION** Contact your wireless service provider (or read your service agreement carefully) to determine the time period that's considered prime daytime, versus night or weekend, because it varies greatly. Unlimited night and weekend calling does not start until 9:00 p.m. with some wireless service providers. If you have a truly unlimited calling plan, however, this is not a concern.

If your plan does have a monthly allocation for talk minutes, if you go over your monthly minute allocation, you will be charged a hefty surcharge for each additional minute used.

**TIP** Each wireless service provider that supports the iPhone offers a free app for managing your wireless service account. It's available from the App Store. Use it to manage all aspects of your account, pay your monthly bill, and view your voice, data, and text-messaging use at any time. You can also set the alert option in the app to remind you each month when the bill is due for payment.

# CUSTOMIZING RINGTONES

Thanks to the iTunes Store, you can purchase and download custom ringtones for your iPhone. You can use one ringtone as your generic ringtone for all incoming calls, or you can assign specific ringtones to individual people.

> **✓ TIP**   iOS 8 comes with more than two dozen preinstalled ringtones. To shop for ringtones, launch Settings, select Sounds, and from the Sounds menu screen, tap on the Ringtone option. Tap on the Store option that's displayed near the top-right corner of the Ringtone menu screen (within Settings).
>
> When you purchase and download a new ringtone, it becomes available on your iPhone's internal ringtones list. Most ringtones from the iTunes Store cost $1.29 each.
>
> Using the iTunes software on a PC or Mac, or using a specialized app, such as Ringtone Maker, Ringtone Wizard, or Ringtone Pro, it's also possible to create your own ringtones using music or audio from your iTunes library.

To choose a default ringtone for all your incoming calls, launch Settings and select the Sounds option. From the Sounds menu screen, scroll down to the Ringtone option and tap on it. A complete listing of ringtones stored on your iPhone is displayed.

## CUSTOM RINGTONES FOR SPECIFIC CONTACTS

To assign a custom ringtone to a specific person so that you hear it when that person calls your iPhone, follow these steps:

1. Launch the Contacts app from the iPhone's Home screen.
2. From the All Contacts screen, find the specific contact with whom you want to link a custom ringtone. You can scroll through the listing or use the Search field to find a contact.
3. When the contact is selected and you're looking at that Contacts entry, tap the Edit option that's displayed in the upper-right corner of the screen.
4. From the Info screen that displays that contact entry's data, scroll down to the Ringtone field and tap on it (shown in Figure 9.10).

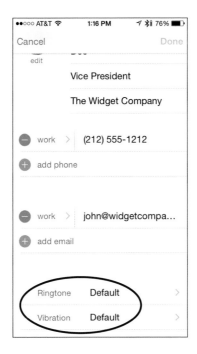

**FIGURE 9.10**

*It's possible to choose a custom ringtone from each entry in the Contacts app.*

5. When the Ringtone screen appears, select a specific ringtone from the list that you want to assign to the contact and tap on it. You can choose a specific song (purchased from iTunes) or ringer sound that reminds you of that person.

6. Tap on the Done icon to save your selection and return to the contact's Info screen.

7. When that contact calls you, you will hear the ringtone you just linked to that contact (as opposed to the default ringtone).

**iOS 8 WHAT'S NEW** Also from a Contact's entry screen in the Contacts app, it's now possible to choose a special vibration pattern for the phone when that person calls. To do this, tap on the Vibration option and choose a vibration pattern from the Vibration menu (shown in Figure 9.11), or scroll to the bottom of this screen and tap on the Create New Vibration option to create a custom vibration pattern for that contact.

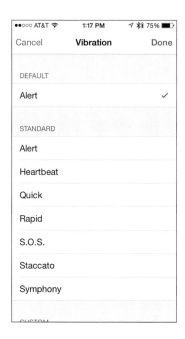

**FIGURE 9.11**

*In addition to choosing a custom ringtone for specific contacts, it's possible to assign custom vibration patterns to these people.*

# MORE INFORMATION ABOUT BLUETOOTH WIRELESS HEADSETS

Many states have outlawed using a cellphone while driving unless you have a wireless headset or hands-free feature on your phone. Although the speakerphone feature of your iPhone counts as a hands-free feature, to ensure the best possible call quality while you're driving, invest in a wireless Bluetooth headset.

Not only can you use a wireless Bluetooth headset while driving, but you can keep it on your person throughout the day and use it whenever you make or receive calls using your iPhone. This enables you to keep your hands free while you're talking or to easily access other apps or iPhone features during a phone conversation. If you invest in only one accessory for your iPhone, and you plan to use the iPhone to make and receive phone calls, a wireless Bluetooth headset is a worthwhile investment (although a good-quality iPhone case is also highly recommended).

Bluetooth wireless headsets are priced as low as $20 but can cost as much as $200. If you want to ensure the highest-quality phone conversations possible, so that people can hear you and you can hear them, even if there's background noise present, invest in a good-quality Bluetooth wireless headset that includes a noise-canceling microphone and a good-quality speaker. Plus, choose a headset that's comfortable to wear and has a long battery life.

10

# IMPROVE YOUR HEALTH AND AUTOMATE YOUR HOME USING YOUR iOS MOBILE DEVICE

One of the things that's built in to every iPhone and iPad model running iOS 8 is potential. In other words, what your smartphone or tablet is or will soon be capable of is limited only by the imaginations of app developers and your willingness to embrace cutting-edge new ways to utilize this technology in your everyday life.

Built in to iOS 8 are a vast assortment of tools available to app developers that now make it easier to create cutting-edge apps related to health, fitness, and home automation. As third-party developers begin to utilize these tools, and equipment manufacturers build iPhone compatibility and integration into their products, what will soon be possible using your smartphone or tablet are things that just a few years ago were only featured in science fiction novels, movies, and comic books.

> **NOTE** Home automation refers to your ability to control other equipment in your home from your iPhone, such as the lights, a television set and cable box/DVR, door locks, thermostat, burglar alarm, security monitors, and even some major appliances.

# DISCOVER THE NEW iPHONE-SPECIFIC HEALTH APP

Among all the other app icons displayed on your iPhone's Home screen is a new app called Health. On its own, the Health app can't do much. However, for people who are fitness, health, and/or nutrition conscious, the Health app works as a "dashboard" with a growing number of other workout and fitness, diet, and lifestyle apps, and it can help you monitor and analyze your daily activity, food intake, and sleep patterns.

Beyond just working with other apps, the Health app is designed to integrate and communicate with optional equipment, such as the Apple Watch, as well as a vast selection of other fitness and medical devices, ranging from heart-rate monitors to workout machines, digital scales, and various types of sleep and blood sugar monitors. The Health app is designed to gather information from these sources and help you track your progress and share this data with appropriate professionals, when applicable.

The Health app comes preinstalled with iOS 8; however, as of Fall 2014, the potential of what this app will be able to do when used with other apps and equipment has barely been tapped. Apple is working closely with hospitals and medical equipment companies, fitness companies (including Nike), as well as many app developers to begin creating health, fitness, and diet tools for the iPhone that will make it easier for anyone to lead a healthier lifestyle.

What's nice about the Health app is that it's fully customizable. You determine what data it collects or what you enter into it, and then you determine how that data is used and whether it can be shared. If you ultimately choose to share certain information in the app, such as your fitness or workout progress with a personal trainer, you can still keep other medical data private.

> **TIP** To discover what apps are designed to work with Health, visit the App Store, tap on the Explore icon that's displayed near the bottom of the screen, and then tap on the Health & Fitness or Medical options.

# START USING THE HEALTH APP RIGHT AWAY

Without allowing your iPhone to communicate with other optional fitness or medical equipment, the Health app's capabilities are limited to being a secure personal database for medical, diet, and health-related information that you manually enter into the app, or that can be imported from other apps installed on your iPhone.

To get started using the Health app, launch it from the Home screen. By default, the Dashboard screen is displayed. This is where collected data from optional apps and equipment is displayed in one centralized place. Using this data, you can easily track your health, fitness, diet and/or sleep patterns. Tap on the Day, Week, Month, or Year tabs that are displayed along the top of the screen to sort and display this information, if applicable.

> **NOTE** If you're not using the Health app with other apps or optional equipment, a Dashboard Empty message is displayed near the center of the screen.

Displayed along the bottom of the screen are four command icons, labeled Dashboard, Health Data, Sources, and Medical ID. Tap on the Health Data icon to access a menu of categories related to the types of data the Health app is capable of collecting, tracking, analyzing, and sharing. As you can see from Figure 10.1, options include Body Measurements, Fitness, Me, Nutrition, Results, Sleep, and Vitals.

Tap on any of these options, and you can manually enter relevant data. For example, tap on the Me option to enter your Birthdate, Biological Sex, and Blood Type. Tap on Nutrition to manually track your intake of specific food types or the nutritional aspects of the food you eat. For example, from the Nutrition menu, tap on Caffeine, and then each time you consume a caffeinated beverage, tap on the Add Data Point option (shown in Figure 10.2).

From the Add Data screen, the time and date are automatically recorded (however, you can tap on these fields to override them), and then you're prompted to enter your consumption amount. As you do this over time, you can tap on the Day, Week, Month, or Year tabs displayed at the top of the Caffeine screen, for example, to display how much caffeine you consume and what times of day you're most apt to consume it. As you tap on each tab, this information is also displayed in chart form on the screen.

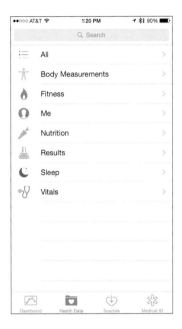

**FIGURE 10.1**

This is the main Health Data menu that's displayed when you tap on the Health Data icon.

**FIGURE 10.2**

You can manually track your intake of various types of foods or other nutrition-related information using the Health Data option built in to the Health app.

> **☑ TIP** As you're tracking specific types of nutritional intake data, whether it's caffeine, fiber, iron, potassium, sodium, sugar, or total fat, for example, turn on the virtual switch associated with the Show On Dashboard option (refer to Figure 10.2) to display this particular information on the app's main Dashboard.
>
> Tap on the Share Data option to specify exactly which apps and outside sources you're willing to share this particular data with.

When it comes to selecting which apps and optional equipment you want to utilize with the Health app, this is controlled by tapping on the Sources icon. From here, you control which apps and equipment can transmit data to or retrieve data from the Health app. If no optional apps or equipment are being used, the word None is displayed under the Apps heading.

## EVERY iPHONE USER SHOULD UTILIZE THE HEALTH APP'S MEDICAL ID FEATURE

Whether or not you're using any additional apps or equipment, you can utilize the Medical ID tool that's built in to the Health app. This is basically a digital summary of vital medical information that you can make available to doctors, paramedics, or medical personnel in case of an emergency.

To use the Medical ID component of the Health app, tap on the Medical ID icon (in the lower-right corner of the screen). From the Medical ID welcome screen, tap on the Create Medical ID option, and then tap on each field to manually enter medical information about yourself (shown in Figure 10.3).

Here, you can list your medical conditions, emergency contacts, primary care physician, your birthday (age), height, weight, blood type, and whether you want to be an organ donor. For easy identification, you can also include a photo of yourself in the app.

> **☑ TIP** After filling in these fields with your personal data, it's possible to later edit it by tapping on the Edit icon that's displayed in the top-right corner of the screen.
>
> At the top of this Medical ID Edit Screen is a virtual switch associated with the Show When Locked option. Turn on this option if you want a doctor or emergency medical professional to be able to access your Medical ID information from your locked iPhone, without knowing its passcode.

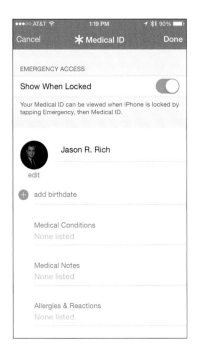

**FIGURE 10.3**

*By filling in the Medical ID component of the Health app with your personal data, it can later be accessed by medical professionals in an emergency situation.*

> **TIP** Tap on the Medical ID Edit option to reveal additional fields that you can manually fill in. The more information you include, the more helpful it could be to doctors in an emergency situation. For example, be sure to fill in the Medical Notes and Allergies & Reactions fields, as well as the Medications field with an up-to-date listing of medications you take.

## FITNESS TRACKERS CAN ALSO COMMUNICATE WITH THE HEALTH APP

In addition to the Apple Watch being designed to work seamlessly with the Health app on the iPhone to gather fitness-related data and transmit it wirelessly and in real time, several third-party fitness trackers are available. For example, there's the popular Nike+ FuelBand SE (www.nike.com/FuelBand); several products from Fitbit (www.fitbit.com), including the Fitbit Flex, Fitbit Ultra, Tory Burch ring, and the Metal Fret Pendant; and Jawbone's Up24 fitness and sleep tracker bracelet (https://jawbone.com/up). Each of these products works with a proprietary iPhone app as well as the Health app.

> **NOTE** Many of the third-party fitness tracker accessories offer similar fitness-related functionality to what the Apple Watch offers, but these devices are typically priced at less than $150.00, compared to the starting price of Apple Watch, which is $349.00.

Other companies offer more high-tech medical devices that work with the iPhone (and Health app). For example, there's the iBGStar Glucose Meter (www.ibgstar.us), iPhoneECG Electrocardiogram from AliveCor (www.alivecor.com), and the Withings Blood Pressure Monitor (www.withings.com/us/blood-pressure-monitor.html).

# HOME AUTOMATION IS EASY USING YOUR iPHONE/iPAD

Built in to iOS 8 are tools that Apple refers to as HomeKit. As an iPhone or iPad user, this is not something you have direct access to, because they're tools designed for use by app developers and companies that manufacture home automation-related products that can be controlled wirelessly using an iPhone or iPad.

In the last few years, dozens of companies have released cutting-edge products related to home automation that are affordable and extremely easy to use. Some of the most successful home automation products released thus far include the Philips Hue Lighting System (www.meethue.com), NEST thermostat (www.nest.com), and the Kevo Kwikset automated door lock (www.kwikset.com).

In addition, every major home security company, including ADT (www.adt.com) and Xfinity Home Security (www.comcast.com/home-security.html), has introduced complete systems that can be remotely controlled from an iPhone. These systems enable you to control the burglar alarms, smoke detectors, door locks, lights, and the garage door opener, for example.

There are also many inexpensive do-it-yourself home security and monitoring tools that don't require an ongoing monthly fee. For example, for about $100.00, you can purchase a wireless camera that can be used for home security (or as a baby/pet monitor). It can be plugged in anywhere in your home, and then will transmit live video and sound directly to your iPhone, which you can view from anywhere in the world. For these cameras to work, an in-home wireless network is required, plus your iPhone requires Internet access.

Most cable and satellite TV companies and DVR (digital video recorder) makers, including TiVo, have also developed proprietary apps that allow iPhone (or iPad) users to remotely program and control their home theater system from virtually anywhere, and in some cases, stream content that's saved on a DVR directly to an iPhone or iPad's screen for remote viewing.

Meanwhile, a company called Belkin (www.belkin.com) has been a pioneer in the iPhone/iPad home automation arena. This company offers a lineup of WeMo products that include the WeMo Insight Switch electrical outlet and WeMo Light Switch.

The Insight Switch plugs into any existing electrical outlet, and then using a special app, enables users to remotely turn on or off what's plugged into that outlet using their iPhone or iPad, while the WeMo Light Switch replaces any traditional light switch with one that can also be remotely controlled from a smartphone or tablet.

Belkin has also introduced the WeMo LED Starter Kit to compete with Philips Hue Lighting System and provide consumers with an easy to way install and use programmable LED lights within a home or office. Plus, the company has given Crock-Pot cooking a high-tech twist with the Crock-Pot Smart Slow Cooker with WeMo, which allows for this Crock-Pot to be remotely programmed and controlled from anywhere using an iPhone or iPad.

In the near future, more categories of home automation products will be made available. One of the more interesting categories are smart appliances, such as refrigerators, washers, and dryers, that will be controllable from an iOS mobile device. Imagine being at a supermarket, tapping on your iPhone's screen, and being able to determine whether you need to add milk to your shopping list based on what's currently in your fridge.

Thanks to Apple's HomeKit tools that app developers are now working with, home automation apps will become compatible with Siri, so they'll accept voice commands and requests to remotely control various products and devices from an iPhone or iPad.

Plus, security features that utilize the TouchID sensor that's built in to the Home button of the iOS mobile devices could be used in addition to passwords to keep unauthorized people from remotely accessing or controlling various home automation products being used in your home.

How these HomeKit tools will be implemented by the various home automation companies and app developers is yet to be seen. However, Apple has developed these tools to enhance security-related tasks associated with home automation, and at the same time, has issued some strict guidelines in terms of how these technologies can be used to provide home automation services without infringing on a consumer's privacy.

11

# SEND AND RECEIVE EMAILS, TEXTS, AND INSTANT MESSAGES WITH THE MAIL AND MESSAGES APPS

If you're someone who's constantly on the go, being able to send and receive emails from virtually anywhere there's a cellular or Wi-Fi Internet connection enables you to stay in touch, stay informed, and be productive from wherever you happen to be. Managing one or more email accounts from an iPhone or iPad is more practical than ever, thanks to the improvements made to the Mail app that comes preinstalled with iOS 8.

The Mail app offers a comprehensive set of tools, features, and functions to help you compose, send, receive, and organize emails from one or more existing accounts. From your iPhone or iPad, you can simultaneously manage your personal and work-related email accounts, as well as the free email account that's provided when you set up an iCloud account.

Before you can begin using the Mail app, it's necessary to set up your existing email accounts from within Settings.

> **NOTE** If you don't yet have an email account, there are several ways to get one. You can sign up for a free Apple iCloud account, which includes an email account. In addition, Google offers free Gmail accounts (http://mail.google.com), and Yahoo! offers free Yahoo! Mail accounts (http://features.mail.yahoo.com), both of which are fully compatible with your iOS device's Mail app.

## HOW TO ADD EMAIL ACCOUNTS TO THE MAIL APP

Use the Add Account tool available within Settings to initially set up your iOS device to work with your existing email account(s). This process works with virtually all email accounts, including Yahoo! Mail, Google Gmail, AOL Mail, iCloud Mail, Microsoft Exchange, and other email accounts established using industry-standard POP3 and IMAP email services.

If you have an email account through your employer that doesn't initially work using the setup procedure outlined in this chapter, contact your company's IT department or Apple's technical support for assistance.

> **NOTE** The process for setting up an existing email account to use with your iPhone or iPad and the Mail app needs to be done only once per account.

Follow these steps to set up your iOS device to work with each of your existing email accounts:

1. From the Home screen, launch Settings.
2. Tap on the Mail, Contacts, Calendars option.
3. When the Mail, Contacts, Calendars menu appears, tap on the Add Account option displayed near the top of the screen, below the Accounts heading.
4. From the Add Account screen, select the type of email account you have. Your options include iCloud, Microsoft Exchange, Google Gmail, Yahoo! Mail, AOL Mail, Microsoft Outlook.com, and Other (shown in Figure 11.1). Tap on the appropriate option. If you have a POP3 or IMAP-compatible email account that doesn't otherwise fall into one of the provided email types, tap on the Other option, and follow the onscreen prompts.

**FIGURE 11.1**
*Choose the type of email account you'd like to add by tapping on the appropriate menu option.*

If you have an existing Yahoo! email account, for example, tap on the Yahoo!
icon. When the Yahoo! account setup screen appears (shown in Figure 11.2),
use the iPhone or iPad's virtual keyboard to enter your account name, email
address, password, and a description for the account.

> **☑ TIP** As you're adding an email account from within Settings, the
> account name should be your full name or whatever you want to appear in the
> From field of outgoing emails. You can opt to use just your first name, a family
> name (such as "The Anderson Family"), or a nickname, based on what you want
> to share with the recipients of your emails. The Description can be anything that
> helps you personally differentiate that account from your other accounts, such
> as Home email, Work email, or Yahoo! email. It is something that you see only on
> your device.

**FIGURE 11.2**

*If you're setting up a Yahoo! Mail account, tap on the Yahoo! option, and then fill in your account information.*

5. Tap on the Next button located in the upper-right corner of the window. Your iOS device connects to the email account's server and confirms the account details you've entered. The word Verifying appears on the screen.

6. After the account has been verified, a new window with options is displayed. They're probably labeled Mail, Contacts, Calendars, Reminders, and Notes, although depending on the type of email account you're setting up, not all of these options might be available. They're used to determine what additional app-specific data can be linked with the Mail account, such as your Contacts database, the schedule from your Calendar app, your to-do list from the Reminders app, or your notes from the Notes app.

> **❗ CAUTION**  If you're already syncing app-specific data for Contacts, Calendar, Reminders, and/or Notes with iCloud, do not also sync them with Yahoo!, Google, or a Microsoft Exchange–compatible account, or you could wind up with duplicate records or entries in each app. Likewise, if you're already syncing your app-specific data with Google, don't also sync this information using iCloud.

7. Tap on the Save button located in the upper-right corner of this window. An Adding Account message is briefly displayed, and details about the email account you just set up are added to your iOS device and become immediately accessible via the Mail app.

8. If you have another existing email account to set up, from the Mail, Contacts, Calendars screen in the Settings app, tap on the Add Account option again, and repeat the preceding procedure. Otherwise, exit the Settings app and launch the Mail app from the Home screen.

Depending on the type of email account you're setting up, the information for which you're prompted varies slightly. For example, to set up an existing Microsoft Exchange email account, the prompts you need to fill in during the email setup procedure include Email Address, Domain, Username, Password, and a Description for the account. To set up an existing iCloud email account, you only need to enter your existing Apple ID and password.

> **TIP** If you plan to set up a POP3 or IMAP email account, in addition to your existing email address and password, you are prompted to enter your host name [mail.example.com] and outgoing mail server information [smtp.example.com]. Obtain this information from your email account provider or the IT department at your company before attempting to set up this type of account on your iPhone or iPad.

After the account is set up, it is listed in Settings under the Accounts heading when you tap on the Mail, Contacts, Calendars option.

> **TIP** When you purchase a new iOS device, it comes with free technical support from AppleCare for 90 days. If you purchased AppleCare+ with your iOS device, you have access to free technical support from Apple for two years. This includes the ability to make an in-person appointment with an Apple Genius at any Apple Store and have someone set up your email accounts on your iPhone or iPad for you.
>
> To schedule a free appointment, visit www.apple.com/retail/geniusbar. Or call Apple's toll-free technical support phone number and have someone talk you through the email setup process. Call 800-APL-CARE (275-2273).

# HOW TO CUSTOMIZE MAIL OPTIONS FROM SETTINGS

To customize options available in the Mail app, launch Settings and select the Mail, Contacts, Calendars option. On the Mail, Contacts, Calendars screen (shown in Figure 11.3) are a handful of customizable features pertaining to how your iOS device handles your email accounts.

**FIGURE 11.3**

*From Settings, you can customize a handful of settings relating to the Mail app.*

**TIP** It's possible to customize each email account separately. This includes how your iOS device displays new incoming email details in the Notification Center window, as well as how alerts or banners are utilized for each account. To set this up for each account, launch Settings, tap on Notifications, select the Mail option, and then one at a time, tap on the listing for each of your email accounts. There's also a separate listing for VIP, which enables you to set separate alerts for important incoming emails from people on your VIP list.

At the top of the Mail, Contacts, Calendars screen within Settings is a listing of the individual email accounts you have already linked with the Mail app. Below this is the Fetch New Data option. Use this to determine how often your iOS device automatically accesses the Internet to check for and download new incoming email messages from each email account's server.

**TIP** From the Fetch New Data screen, you can enable or disable the Push feature. When turned on, your iPhone or iPad automatically accesses and displays new incoming emails as they arrive on your email account's server. When the Push feature is turned off, you can select how often you want to check for new emails. Your options include Every 15 Minutes, Every 30 Minutes, Hourly, or Manually. You can customize this setting separately for each of your email accounts.

The benefit of using the Fetch feature set to Manually is that you can greatly reduce the amount of wireless data usage you utilize. This is important if you have a monthly cellular data allocation through your wireless service provider. If you have an account that offers unlimited wireless data or you utilize a Wi-Fi connection, this is not a concern.

By scrolling down on the Mail, Contacts, Calendars menu screen, you see the Mail heading. Below this heading is a handful of customizable options relating to how the Mail app manages your email accounts and email messages:

- **Preview**—As you look at your Inbox (or any mailbox) using the Mail app, you can determine how much of each email message's body text is visible from the mailbox summary screen, in addition to the From, Date/Time, and Subject. You can choose None or between one and five lines of the email message.

**TIP** The Preview option also impacts the email-related notifications that appear in the Notification Center if you assign it to continuously monitor the Mail app. You can adjust this in Settings by tapping on the Notifications option under the main Settings menu.

- **Show To/Cc Label**—Decide whether to view the To and Cc fields when viewing the preview screen for emails.
- **Swipe Options**—This new iOS 8 feature enables you to manage the Inbox of your email accounts. Now, as you're looking at the previews of each message

in your inbox, you can swipe from left to right or right to left across each message listing to access menu options (shown in Figure 11.4).

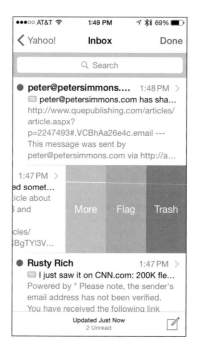

**FIGURE 11.4**

*iOS 8 gives you access to commonly used commands for managing incoming messages by swiping your finger across a message listing.*

**WHAT'S NEW** By tapping on Swipe Options in the Mail, Contacts, Calendars submenu, you can determine which email management–related commands become available to you when you swipe left to right or right to left across a message listing when viewing an Inbox.

When you swipe from left to right, it's possible to choose whether the Mark As Read, Archive or Flag command is made available. If you select the None option, the left to right swipe feature is disabled.

When you swipe right to left, you can choose whether the Mark As Read or Flag command becomes available in addition to the Trash and More options (which are default options).

Choose the email message commands you most often use to organize your incoming messages so you can access them faster (refer to Figure 11.4).

- **Flag Style**—When you flag an email as important, the Flag style determines whether the Mail app displays a flag-shaped icon or a colored dot next to the flagged email message.

- **Ask Before Deleting**—This option serves as a safety net to ensure that you don't accidentally delete an important email message from your iOS device. When this feature is turned on, you're asked to confirm your message deletion request before an email message is actually deleted. By default, you cannot delete email messages stored on your email account's server. When you delete a message from the Mail app, it is deleted from your iPhone or iPad but is still accessible from other devices. On your iOS device, it might also appear in the Trash folder that's related to that email account, depending on how it is set up.

- **Load Remote Images**—When an email message has a photo or graphic embedded in it, this option determines whether the image is automatically downloaded and displayed with the email message. You can opt to refrain from automatically loading graphics with email messages to reduce the amount of data transferred to your iPhone or iPad (which is a consideration if you're connected to the Internet via a cellular data network). You still have the option to tap on the placeholder icon in the email message to manually download the images in a specific message.

> **NOTE** In addition to reducing your cellular data usage, disabling the Load Remote Images option can help you cut down on the amount of spam (unsolicited emails) you receive, because remote image loading can be tracked by the senders of spam and used to verify valid email addresses.
>
> However, when turned off, displaying images embedded within an email requires an additional step on your part, because you now must tap the image icon to load the image if you want to view it.

- **Organize by Thread**—This feature enables you to review messages in reverse chronological order if a single message turns into a back-and-forth email conversation in which multiple parties keep hitting Reply to respond to messages with the same subject. When turned on, this makes keeping track of email conversations much easier, especially if you're managing several email accounts on your iPhone or iPad. If it's turned off, messages in your Inbox are displayed in reverse chronological order as they're received, not grouped by subject.

- **Always Bcc Myself**—When this feature is turned on, a copy of every outgoing email is sent to your Inbox. Typically, all outgoing messages automatically get saved in a Sent folder that's related to that account. If your email account type does not enable you to access sent emails from another computer or device, using the Bcc Myself option compensates for this. When you send an email message from your iPhone/iPad, using this feature also ensures that the message becomes accessible from your primary computer.

- **Mark Addresses**—By tapping on this option, you can enter a portion of an email address, and then be alerted each time an email is received that meets that search criteria. For example, if you do business with many people who work at Widget.com, in the Mark Address field, if you store "widget.com," anyone with an email address ending with widget.com, such as johndoe@widget.com, sales@widget.com, or janedoe@wideget.com is automatically flagged in your Inbox to get your attention. This feature is particularly useful if you're using an iPhone in a corporate environment.

- **Increase Quote Level**—When turned on, anytime you reply to a message or forward a message, the contents of that original email appear indented, making it easier to differentiate between the message you add and the original message being replied to or forwarded. This option impacts message formatting, not actual content.

- **Signature**—For every outgoing email that you compose, you can automatically add an email signature. The default signature is "Sent from my iPhone" or "Sent from my iPad." However, by tapping on this option within Settings, you can create customized signatures for each email account. A signature might include your name, mailing address, email address, phone number(s), and so forth.

- **Default Account**—If you're using the Mail app to manage multiple email accounts, when you reply to a message or forward a message, it is always sent from the email account to which the message was originally sent. However, if you tap on the Compose New Email icon to create a new email from scratch, the email account from which the message is sent is whichever you have set up as the Mail app's default account. If you wish to change this account for a specific email, simply tap on the From field as you're composing a new email and select one of your other accounts.

# TIPS FOR VIEWING YOUR INCOMING EMAIL

When you launch the Mail app on your iPhone or iPad, the Inbox for your various email accounts is displayed. You can opt to display incoming messages for a single email account, or display the incoming messages from all of your email accounts by selecting the All Inboxes option.

Even though Mail enables you to simultaneously view incoming emails from multiple accounts within a single listing, behind the scenes, the app automatically keeps your incoming and outgoing emails, and your various email accounts, separate. So if you opt to read and respond to an email from your work-related Inbox, for example, that response is automatically sent out from your work-related email account and saved in the Sent Folder for that account.

> **TIP** The Mail app is fully compatible with Siri. Be sure to refer to Chapter 2, "Using Siri, Dictation, and CarPlay to Interact with Your Mobile Device," for more information.

Viewing all the Inboxes for all of your accounts simultaneously makes it faster to review your incoming emails, without having to manually switch between email accounts.

If you have multiple email accounts being managed from your iOS device, to view all of your Inboxes simultaneously, or to switch between Inboxes, follow these steps:

1. Launch the Mail app.

2. The Inbox you last looked at is probably displayed. If only one email account is set up to work with your iPhone, the last email you viewed is displayed.

3. Tap on the left-pointing, arrow-shaped Mailboxes option displayed in the upper-left corner of the screen to select which Inbox you want to view. If you're looking at a particular account's Inbox, the arrow-shaped option is labeled Back.

4. From the menu that appears, the first option displayed is All Inboxes. Tap on this to view a single listing of all incoming emails. Or tap on any single email account that's listed on the Mailboxes screen.

> ☑ **TIP**   Tap on the VIP mailbox listing to view only emails from your various inboxes that have been received from people you've added to your VIP List. When you tap on the VIP option, these emails are displayed in a single list, although it is comprised of VIP messages from all the accounts you're managing on your iPhone or iPad.
>
> Below the VIP listing under the Inboxes heading is a Flagged listing. This enables you to view a separate mailbox comprised of only emails you've previously flagged as being important. Again, this is a comprehensive list from all the accounts you're managing on your iPhone or iPad. The Mail app keeps the messages sorted behind the scenes, based on which account each is associated with.

# COMPOSING AN EMAIL MESSAGE

In the Mail app, you can easily compose an email from scratch and send it to one or more recipients. To compose a new email, tap on the Compose icon. On an iPhone, the Compose icon can be found in the lower-right corner of the screen in the Mail app. On an iPad, the Compose icon is displayed in the upper-right corner of the screen.

> ✎ **NOTE**   The Compose icon looks like a square with a pencil on it.

When you tap on the Compose icon, a blank New Message email message template appears on the iPhone or iPad's screen. On the iPhone, a New Message screen is displayed. On the iPad, a New Message pop-up window appears. Using the virtual keyboard, fill in the To, Cc, Bcc, and/or Subject fields (as shown in Figure 11.5). You must fill in the To field with a valid email address for at least one recipient. The other fields are optional.

You can send the same email to multiple recipients by either adding multiple email addresses to the To field, or by adding additional email addresses to the Cc and/or Bcc fields.

If you're managing one email account from your iOS device, the From field is automatically filled in with your email address. However, if you're managing multiple email addresses from the iPhone or iPad, tap on the From field to select which email address you want to send the message from if you don't want to use the default account.

**FIGURE 11.5**

*Tap on the Compose icon to create an email from scratch and send it from your iOS device.*

**TIP** As you fill in the To field when composing an email, the Mail app automatically accesses your Contacts database and matches up entries. This can save you time because you don't have to manually enter email addresses. If you know that the person you're sending an email to already has an entry including their email address in your Contacts database, you can type that person's name in the To field.

The Mail app also remembers email addresses from people not in your Contacts database, but whom you've corresponded with through email via the app. When you begin manually entering an email address, the Mail app offers suggestions. Either select a suggestion or continue typing.

Next, tap on the Subject field and use the virtual keyboard to enter the subject for your message. As you do this, the subject appears at the very top center of the Compose window (replacing the New Message heading).

> **TIP**  When using almost any app with a Share menu, to compose and send an email that contains app-specific content without first launching the Mail app, tap on the Share icon, and then select Mail.
>
> A New Message screen appears with the related app-specific content already attached to that outgoing email message. Use the virtual keyboard to compose your email, and then tap on the Send icon. The email message is sent and you are returned to the app you were using.

To begin creating the main body of the outgoing email message, tap in the main body area of the message template on the screen, and begin using the virtual keyboard (or the external keyboard you're using with your iPhone or iPad) to compose your message. You also have the option of tapping on the Dictation key and then dictating your message using iOS 8's Dictation feature.

> **! CAUTION**  If you have the Auto-Capitalization, Auto-Correction, and/or Check Spelling feature(s) turned on, as you type, the iPhone or iPad automatically corrects anything that it perceives as a typo or misspelled word. Be very careful when using these features because they are notorious for plugging the wrong word into a sentence. Especially if you're creating important business documents and emails, make sure you proofread whatever you type on your iPhone or iPad carefully before sending it. Typically, these features are helpful, but they do have quirks that can lead to embarrassing and unprofessional mistakes.
>
> To control the Auto-Capitalization, Auto-Correction, and Check Spelling features, launch the Settings app, tap on the General option, select the Keyboard option, and then turn on or off the virtual switch that's associated for each option that's displayed in the Keyboard menu screen.

> **(iOS 8) WHAT'S NEW**  When turned on, iOS 8's QuickType feature monitors what you're typing, in real time, anticipates what you're about to type (based on the context of what you're typing), and suggests appropriate words or phrases. This feature can speed up and improve the accuracy of your typing. The QuickType suggestions are displayed as tabs just above the virtual keyboard (shown in Figure 11.6). Tap on a suggestion tab to select that word and insert it into your message. Then continue typing.

QuickType Suggestion Tabs

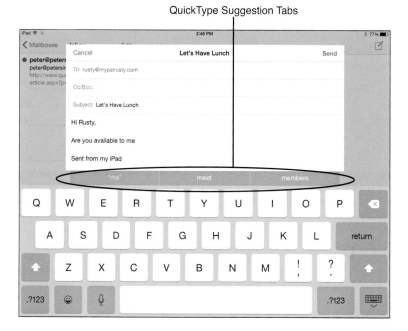

**FIGURE 11.6**

*iOS 8's QuickType features works nicely when composing emails using the Mail app.*

The signature you set up from within Settings for the selected From account is automatically displayed at the bottom of each newly composed message. You can return to Settings to turn off the Signature feature, or change the signature that appears. A signature can also be edited or added manually directly from the Compose screen as you create or edit each message.

When your email is fully written and ready to be sent, tap on Send in the upper-right corner of the Compose window. In a few seconds, the message is sent from your iOS device, assuming that it is connected to the Internet. A copy of the message appears in your Sent or Outbox folder.

As a message is being sent, a "Sending" notification appears near the bottom of the Mail app's screen.

> **NOTE** The Mail app enables you to format your outgoing email messages and include **bold**, *italic*, and/or underlined text (as well as combinations, like ***bold-italic*** text).

To format text in an email message you're composing, type the text as you normally would using the virtual keyboard. After the text appears in your email, hold your finger on a word to make the Select, Select All, Paste, Insert Photo or Video, and Quote Level command tabs appear above that word.

Tap on Select, and then use your finger to move the blue dots that appear to highlight the text you want to modify. When the appropriate text is highlighted in blue, tap the right-pointing arrow that appears above the text (next to the Cut, Copy, and Paste commands), and then tap on the **B**/<u>U</u> option. A new menu appears above the highlighted text with three options, labeled Bold, Italics, and Underline. Tap on one or more of these tabs to alter the highlighted text. On the iPad, all options are listed and no scrolling is required.

## INSERT A PHOTO OR VIDEO INTO YOUR OUTGOING EMAIL

As you're composing an outgoing email, to insert a photo or video clip that's stored on your iPhone or iPad into that email, place and hold your finger anywhere in the body of the email where you want to embed the photo or video.

> **NOTE** On the iPhone, tap on the right-pointing arrow displayed to the right of the Select, Select All, and Paste commands to access the Insert Photo or Video option.

When the Insert Photo or Video tab is displayed, tap on it. The Photos screen (iPhone) or window (iPad) appears. Select the photo you want to insert into the email by selecting an album and then tapping on an image or video thumbnail. The photo/video you selected is previewed in the Choose Photo window. Tap on the Use button to insert the photo or video into your email.

You can repeat this process to include multiple images within an email (up to five), keeping in mind that the overall file size associated with the outgoing email is often limited by your email service.

> **TIP** When you insert a photo into an outgoing email on the iPad, to the right of the Cc/Bcc, From: field a new option that says Images: [file size] is displayed. To alter the image file size (and by default, the resolution) of the attached photo(s), tap on the Images option. Under the From field, an Image Size option appears. To the right of this option are four command tabs: Small, Medium, Large, and Actual Size. Each is accompanied by the file size of the image(s) you're sending. Tap on one of these options.

# USING SELECT, SELECT ALL, CUT, COPY, AND PASTE

The iOS operating system offers Select, Select All, Cut, Copy, and Paste commands, which are accessible from many iPhone or iPad apps, including Mail. Using these commands, you can quickly copy and paste content from one portion of an app to another, or from one app into another app, whether it's a paragraph of text, a phone number, or a photo.

To use these commands, use your finger to hold down on any word or graphic element on the screen for one or two seconds, until the Select and Select All tabs appear above that content. To select a single word or select what content you want to copy or cut, tap on the Select tab. Or to select all the content on the screen, tap the Select All tab.

After text (or a graphic element, such as a photo) is selected, tap on the Cut tab to delete that selected content from the screen (if this option is available in the app you're using), or tap the Copy tab to save the highlighted content in your iPhone or iPad's virtual clipboard.

Now, move to where you want to paste that saved content. This can be in the same email or document, for example, or in another app altogether. Choose the location on the screen where you want to paste the content, and hold your finger on that location for two or three seconds. When the Paste tab appears, tap on it. The content you just copied is pasted into that location.

> **✓ TIP**  In the Mail app, as you use the Select, Select All, Cut, Copy, and Paste commands, notice a Quote Level option that appears on the menu above the highlighted text or content you select. Tap on this to increase or decrease the indent of that content, which impacts how it's formatted on the screen.

# HOW TO SAVE AN UNSENT DRAFT OF AN EMAIL MESSAGE

If you want to save a draft of an email without sending it, as you're composing the email message, tap on the Cancel button that appears in the upper-left corner of the Compose message window. Two command buttons appear: Delete Draft and Save Draft. To save the unsent draft, tap on Save Draft.

You can return to it later to modify and/or send it. To do this, from the main Inbox screen in Mail, tap on the left-pointing Mailboxes icon that looks like an arrow displayed at the upper-left corner of the screen. From the Mailboxes screen, scroll down to the Accounts heading and tap on the listing for the email account from which the email draft was composed.

When you see a list of folders related to that email account, tap on the Drafts folder. Tap on the appropriate listing to open that email message. You can now edit the message or send it.

## TIPS FOR READING EMAIL

After you launch the Mail app, you can access the Inbox for one or more of your existing email accounts, compose new emails, or manage your email accounts. Just like the Inbox on your main computer's email software, the Inbox of the Mail app (shown in Figure 11.7 on an iPhone, and Figure 11.8 on an iPad) displays your incoming emails.

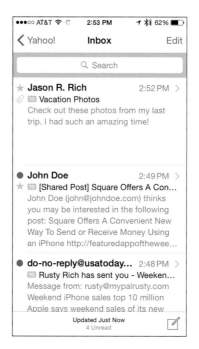

**FIGURE 11.7**

*The Inbox screen of the Mail app displays a listing of your incoming emails on the iPhone 5s.*

**FIGURE 11.8**

*On the iPad, the Inbox provides a listing of your incoming emails.*

> **TIP**  As you're looking at the inbox for any of your email accounts (or the All Inboxes mailbox), to the left of each email message preview you might see a tiny graphic icon (refer to Figure 11.8). A blue dot represents a new and unread email (or an email that has been marked as unread). A solid blue star represents a new and unread email from someone on your VIP list, while a gray star icon represents a read email from someone on your VIP list.
>
> An orange flag-shaped icon displayed to the left of an email preview means that you have manually flagged that message (or message thread) as urgent. Instead of a flag icon, a blue dot with an orange circle can be displayed indicating a message is urgent and unread. Just an orange dot will appear after it's read. You can choose between a flag or a dot icon from Settings.
>
> A curved, left-pointing arrow icon means that you have read and replied to that message, while a right-pointing arrow icon means you've read and have forwarded that message to one or more people.
>
> If no tiny icon appears to the left of an email preview listing, this means the message has been read and is simply stored in that inbox (or mailbox).

> **NOTE** If you're using the Mail app on an iPad while holding the tablet in portrait mode, to open the Inbox sidebar, tap on the left-pointing arrow icon that's displayed in the top-left corner of the screen. It's accompanied by an option that says Mailboxes or Back.

## THE MAIL APP'S INBOX

When you're viewing your Inbox(es), a list of the individual emails is displayed. Based on the customizations you make from the Settings app that pertain to the Mail app, the Sender, Subject, Date/Time, and up to five lines of the message's body text can be displayed for each incoming message listing.

On the iPhone, when viewing your Inbox and the listing of incoming (new) email messages, tap on any message listing to read that message in its entirety. When you do this, a new message screen appears. At the bottom of this screen is a series of command icons for managing that email.

On the iPad, the email message that's highlighted in gray on the left side of the screen is the one that's currently being displayed, in its entirety, on the right side of the screen. Tap on any email listing on the left side of the screen to view the entire message on the right side of the screen. Icons at the top of the screen are used for managing that email.

At the top of the Inbox message listing are two command icons, labeled Mailboxes (or the name of the mailbox you're viewing) and Edit.

Just below the Inbox's heading is a Search field. You might need to swipe your finger downward along the Inbox to reveal it. Tap on this Search field to make the virtual keyboard appear, enabling you to enter a search phrase and quickly find a particular email message. You can search the content of the Mail app using any keyword, a sender's name, or an email subject, for example.

### THE EDIT BUTTON

Located on top of a mailbox's message listing (to the right of its heading) is a command button labeled Edit. When you tap on this button, you can quickly select multiple messages from a mailbox, such as your inbox, to delete or move to another mailbox (or folder) (as shown in Figure 11.9).

**TIP** After tapping the Edit button, you can manually select one or more message listings to move or delete, or tap on the Mark All option to select all the messages in that Inbox. You can then Flag or Mark As Read/Unread all of the selected messages.

**TIP** If you tap on the Mark button that's displayed to the right of the Trash and Move buttons, you can then flag them or mark one or more emails as read or unread at the same time. You can also move selected messages to your Junk folder. Mark option replaces the Mark All option in this situation.

After you tap the Edit button, an empty circle icon appears to the left of each email message preview listing. To move or delete one or more messages from the current mailbox's listing (which could be your Inbox, VIP, Archive, or Junk mailbox), tap on the empty circle icon for that message. A blue-and-white check mark fills the empty circle icon when you do this, and the Trash and Move command icons displayed at the bottom of the screen become active. For some types of email accounts, a Delete All button is also displayed, enabling you to select and delete all messages within that mailbox at the same time.

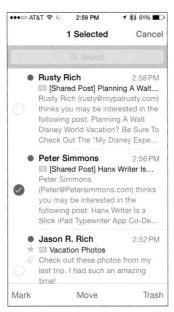

**FIGURE 11.9**

*Tap the Edit button to manage your incoming messages, delete them in quantity, or move them to the Junk folder.*

After you've selected one or more messages, tap the Trash button to quickly delete one or more messages simultaneously from the mailbox (which sends them to the Trash folder), or tap the Move button, and then select to which folder you want to move those email messages.

To exit this option without doing anything, tap on the Cancel button displayed at the top of the Inbox listing, to the right of the Inbox heading.

## HOW TO DELETE INDIVIDUAL INCOMING MESSAGES

On your iPhone or iPad, as you're looking at the listing of messages in your Inbox (or any mailbox), you can also delete individual messages, one at a time. Swipe your finger from right to left over a message listing. Tap on the red-and-white Trash button that appears on the right side of that email message listing (refer to Figure 11.4) to delete the message.

New to iOS 8 are additional (and customizable) command options that are displayed when you swipe from right to left across a message listing. By default, the Trash and More options are offered.

Tap on More to access a new pop-up menu (shown in Figure 11.10) that offers the Reply, Forward, Flag, Mark As Read, Move To Junk, Move Message, and Notify Me options.

**FIGURE 11.10**

*After swiping from right to left across a message listing in your Inbox, tap on the More option to reveal this menu.*

> **TIP** Another way to delete a message from your Inbox, or any mailbox, is to tap on a message listing to view that message, and then tap on the Trash icon. On the iPhone, the Trash icon is displayed at the bottom center of the screen. On the iPad, it's displayed near the upper-right corner of the screen.

## HOW TO VIEW YOUR EMAILS

When a single email message is selected from the Inbox listing, that message is displayed in its entirety. At the top of the message, see the From, To, Cc/Bcc (if applicable), Subject, and the Date/Time it was sent.

In the upper-right corner of the email message is a blue Hide command. If you tap on this, some of the message header information will no longer be displayed. To make this information reappear, tap on the More option.

As you're reading an email, tap on the flag icon to flag that message and mark it as urgent, or mark the email as unread. These options appear within a pop-up menu. When you flag a message, an orange flag (or an orange dot) becomes associated with that message, which is displayed in the message itself (to the right of the date and time), and in the inbox (mailbox) in which the message is stored. Plus, from your Inboxes menu, if you tap on the Flagged option, you can view a separate mailbox that contains only flagged (urgent) messages.

## TAKE ADVANTAGE OF THE MAIL APP'S VIP LIST FEATURE

In addition to flagging individual messages as important, you can have the Mail app automatically highlight all emails sent from particular senders, such as your boss, important clients, close friends, or family members. Once you add a sender to your VIP List, all of their incoming emails are marked with a star-shaped icon instead of a blue dot icon that represents a regular, new incoming email.

To add someone to your VIP List, as you're reading an email from that person, tap on the From field (their name/email address). A Sender screen (iPhone) or window (iPad) appears. At the bottom of this window, tap on the Add To VIP button. This adds and keeps that sender on your custom VIP list until you manually remove them.

To later remove someone from your VIP list, read any of their email messages and again tap on the From field. When the Sender window appears, tap on the Remove From VIP button (which has replaced the Add To VIP button).

☑ **TIP** From the Mailboxes menu, you can also tap on the VIP listing to view a special mailbox that displays only incoming emails from people on your VIP list. Using the VIP List feature helps you quickly differentiate important emails from spam and less important incoming emails that don't necessarily require your immediate attention.

## HOW TO DEAL WITH INCOMING EMAIL MESSAGE ATTACHMENTS

The Mail app enables you to access certain types of attachment files that accompany an incoming email message. Dozens of different file formats are compatible with the Mail app. As you add third-party apps that support other file formats, they become recognized by the Mail app. This includes files related to text, photos, audio clips, video clips, PDFs, and eBooks, as well as iWork and Microsoft Office documents and files.

To open an attached file using another app, in the incoming email message, tap and hold down the attachment icon for one to three seconds. If the attachment is compatible with an app that's installed on your iPhone or iPad, you're given the option to transfer the file to that app or directly open or access the file using that app.

If an incoming email message contains an attachment that is not compatible or accessible from your iOS device, you can't open or access it. In this case,  you must access this content from your primary computer.

## ORGANIZE EMAIL MESSAGES IN FOLDERS

Email messages can easily be moved into another folder, enabling you to better organize your emails. Here's how to do this:

1. From the Inbox listing, tap the Edit button that's located above the Inbox listing. Or, if you're viewing an email message, swipe your finger from right to left across the message listing.

2. Tap the Move option. A menu that offers various folders and options available for that email account are displayed (shown in Figure 11.11).

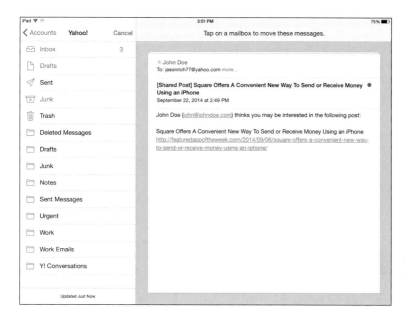

**FIGURE 11.11**

*To move an email message between folders, tap on the Move Message option, and then tap on the name of the folder to which you want to move the message.*

3. Tap on the Move Message option, and then tap on the mailbox folder to which you want to move the message. The email message is moved to the folder you select.

**WHAT'S NEW** The Move option is also available by swiping from right to left across a message listing from your inbox, and then tapping on the More option. (Refer to Figure 11.4.)

**TIP** As you're managing incoming and outgoing emails, the Mail app uses the default mailboxes that are already associated with that email account, such as Inbox, Drafts, Sent, Trash, and Junk. For some accounts, you are limited to only these default mailboxes. However, for many types of email accounts, you can create additional mailboxes and then move messages into those mailboxes to organize them.

To create a custom mailbox (assuming that your account allows for this feature), from the Inbox, tap on the Mailboxes icon. When the Mailboxes screen appears, under the Accounts heading, tap on the account for which you want to create a mailbox. A listing of the existing mailboxes for that account is displayed.

Tap on the Edit button at the top of the screen. Then, tap on the New Mailbox icon that appears at the bottom of the screen. Enter the name of the mailbox you want to create, and then tap on the Save button. Your new mailbox is now displayed with that email account. The process works the same on the iPhone and iPad, but the position of the icons varies slightly.

## FORWARDING, PRINTING, AND REPLYING TO MESSAGES

From the Mail app, you can forward an incoming message to someone else, reply to the message, or print the email by tapping on the left-pointing, curved-arrow icon that's displayed when you're viewing an email. On an iPhone, the curved-arrow icon is displayed at the bottom of the screen. On an iPad, it can be found in the upper-right corner of the main Inbox screen (next to the Trash icon).

When you tap on this icon, as you're reading any email message, a menu offers the following three options: Reply, Forward, and Print. If the message you're viewing has more than one recipient, an additional option, Reply All, appears.

To reply to the message you're reading, tap on the Reply icon. An email message template appears on the screen that already contains the content of the message you're replying to. Refer to the "Composing an Email Message" section for details on how to write and send an email message from the Mail app.

To forward the email you're reading to another recipient, tap on the Forward icon. If an attachment is associated with the email, you're asked, "Include attachments from original email?" with two options displayed on the screen, Include and Don't Include. Tap on the appropriate response.

When you opt to forward an email, a new message template appears on the screen. However, the content of the message you're forwarding appears in the body of the email message. Start the message-forwarding process by filling in the To field. You can also modify the Subject field (or leave the message's original subject), and then add to the body of the email message with your own text. This text appears above the forwarded message's content.

> **TIP** To forward an email to multiple recipients, enter each person's email address in the To field of the outgoing message, separating each address with a comma (,), or tap on the plus icon (+) that appears to the right of the To field to add more recipients.

When you're ready to forward the message, tap on the blue-and-white Send button that appears, or tap the Cancel button to abort the message-forwarding process.

If you have an AirPrint-compatible printer set up to work with your iOS device, you can tap the Print icon that appears when you tap the left-pointing curved-arrow icon as you're reading an email.

## MAIL APP QUICK TIPS

- To refresh your Inbox, swipe your finger downward on the inbox screen (iPhone) or column (iPad).

- As you're reading email, if the text is difficult to see, you can automatically increase the size of all text displayed in the Mail, Contacts, Calendar, Messages, and Notes apps by adjusting the Accessibility option within Settings. To make this font size adjustment, launch Settings. Select the General option, and then tap on the Accessibility option. From the Accessibility menu screen, tap on the Large Text option.

- As you're reading emails, all of the touchscreen finger motions you've learned work on the section of the iOS device's screen that's displaying the actual email messages. You can scroll up or down and/or zoom in or out.

> **(iOS 8) WHAT'S NEW** Another new Mail-related feature added to iOS 8 is called Notify Me…. As you're reading an email, tap on the flag icon and then select the Notify Me… option to activate this feature for the message you're reading. Then, when you receive a response from anyone that's related to this email thread, you are automatically notified.

# COMMUNICATE EFFECTIVELY WITH THE MESSAGES APP

Text messaging was designed to make quick communications between two or more people faster and easier. Today, "texting" has become a preferred and highly efficient form of communication.

In addition to sending and receiving text-based messages, the Messages app supports the sending and receiving of photos, video messages and video clips, emoticons, and audio messages.

> **NOTE**    Using short text-based messages and a special "language" composed of abbreviated terminology, such as LOL (meaning "laugh out loud") or BRB (meaning "be right back"), people of all ages have begun to rely on text messaging and instant messaging as a convenient way to communicate (as shown in Figure 11.12).

**FIGURE 11.12**

*Text messaging is done using the Messages app. Text-based conversations are formatted to be easy to read and follow.*

> **NOTE** On the iPad, if the person you're communicating with via the Messages app has an entry in your Contacts app database, and that entry contains their photo, it is displayed in the Messages app; otherwise, the person's initials are displayed by default if their entry contains no photo. Or, if there's no Contacts entry at all for the person, a generic head graphic is used. On the older iPhones, only the person's name or phone number is displayed.

Most iPhone service plans have three components: voice, data, and text messaging. When you sign up with a wireless service, you can choose a paid text-messaging plan that allows for the sending or receiving of a predetermined number of text messages per month or pay extra for an unlimited text-messaging plan. If your plan has no text messaging component, you are charged for every text message you send or receive. These days, most shared family plans come with unlimited text messaging, however.

There are different types of text messages. There are text-only messages (SMS, or Short Message Service), as well as text messages that can contain a photo or video clip (MMS or Multimedia Messaging Service). These messages can be sent to one or more people simultaneously.

> **WHAT'S NEW** The Messages app now supports audio and video messages when used to communicate with other iMessage users. Instead of typing a message, use the app's audio recording interface to record a short audio message and then send it to one or more recipients. Alternatively, it's possible to record and send a short video message using one of the cameras that are built in to your iPhone or iPad. How to do this is explained shortly.

On the iPhone, the process of composing, reading, sending, and receiving text, audio, or video messages is done using the Messages app. The Messages app can be used with your cellular service provider's text messaging service and/or Apple's own iMessage service.

📝 **NOTE** iMessage is a free text-messaging service operated by Apple that utilizes the Internet and allows iOS mobile device and Mac users to communicate with other iOS device and Mac users, as long as the devices have access to the Internet. This means you can send an iMessage even if you are connected to the Internet via Wi-Fi, unlike an SMS or MMS text message, which requires a cellular network connection.

💬 **WHAT'S NEW** Thanks to iOS 8's Handoff option, if someone sends your iPhone a text message, the Messages app that's running on your iPhone can now automatically forward the message to your iPad or Mac. Thus, you can send and receive messages via your iPhone's cellular network from any of your Macs or iOS mobile devices that are linked to the same iCloud account as long as your iPhone is within about 33 feet proximity to the iPad and/or Mac.

💬 **WHAT'S NEW** From Settings, you can now set up the Messages app to store all of your text messages forever, or save internal storage space in your mobile device by adjusting the Keep Messages option to 30 Days or 1 Year. To do this, launch Settings, tap on the Messages option, and then tap on the Keep Message option.

## GET STARTED USING THE MESSAGES APP WITH APPLE'S iMESSAGE SERVICE

Whether your iPhone or iPad is connected to the Internet via a Wi-Fi or cellular data connection, using iMessage with the Messages app that comes preinstalled on your device, you can communicate via instant messages with other Mac and iOS mobile device users.

Unlike the text-messaging services available through wireless service providers, Apple's iMessage service is free of charge, and it allows for an unlimited number of text messages to be sent and received. (When using iMessage via a Cellular data connection, this uses some of your monthly data allocation, if applicable.)

The service also taps into your iPhone or iPad's other functions and allows for the easy sharing of photos, videos, locations, and contacts; plus, it works seamlessly with Notification Center.

iMessage enables you to participate in text-based, real-time conversations. When someone is actively typing a message to you during a conversation on iMessage, a bubble with three periods in it appears. You can view and respond to the message a fraction of a second after it is sent.

## SET UP A FREE iMESSAGE ACCOUNT

Because traditional text messaging is tied to a cell phone, which has a unique phone number, there is no need to have a separate username or account name when using the text-messaging feature through your cellular service provider. If you know someone's cell phone number, you can send a text message to that person from your cell phone (and vice versa). However, because iMessage is web-based, before using this service, you must set up a free iMessage account.

The first time you launch the Messages app to use it with the iMessage service, you're instructed to set up a free account using your existing Apple ID. Or, instead of using your Apple ID, tap on the Create New Account option to create an account that's linked to another existing email address.

**NOTE** iPhone users can associate their cell phone numbers with their iMessage accounts to send and receive text messages using this service. However, an Apple ID or existing email address can be used as well.

To do this, you must complete the information requested from the New Account screen. When the requested New Account information is entered, tap on the Done icon in the upper-right corner of the New Account window. Keep in mind that if you simply enter your existing Apple ID/iCloud account information to set up your iMessage account, and then tap on the Sign In icon, the initial process for establishing an iMessage account is quick.

**TIP** Just as when you're using FaceTime, the unique Apple ID, email address, and/or iPhone phone number you use to set up your iMessage account is how people find you and are able to communicate with you.

So if you want someone to be able to send you messages via iMessage, that person must know the iPhone phone number, Apple ID, or email address you have set up to work with the iMessage account. Likewise, to send someone a text message via iMessage, you need to know the iPhone phone number, Apple ID, or email address the recipient used to set up his or her iMessage account.

> **📝 NOTE**    When you send a text message, it is represented as a blue text bubble (shown earlier in Figure 11.12), if you're using the iMessage service. If you're using your cellular service provider's texting service, your text bubbles are displayed in green.

## PROS AND CONS OF USING iMESSAGE

The biggest benefits to using iMessage over other text-messaging services are that it's free and that you can send/receive an unlimited number of messages. The Messages app itself also nicely integrates with other features, functions, and apps on your iPhone or iPad.

If you're away from your iPhone or iPad when an incoming text message arrives, don't worry. The Notification Center app can continuously monitor the Messages app and inform you of any missed messages in the Notification Center window.

Another convenient feature of iMessage is that you can begin a text-message–based conversation using your iPhone, for example, and switch to using your iPad or Mac to continue that conversation. This, however, is now possible with all types of text messaging via the Messages app if you turn on iOS 8's Handoff feature.

Keep in mind, to initiate a new conversation with someone, you must know their cell phone number, Apple ID, or the email address they used to set up their iMessage account. However, after you know this, sending and receiving text messages with that person becomes a straightforward process. You can store the person's account information in your Contacts database (which links to the Messages app).

## TIPS AND TRICKS FOR USING THE MESSAGES APP

The Messages app on the iPhone has two main screens: a summary of conversations labeled Messages, and an actual conversation screen labeled at the top of the screen using the name of the person(s) with whom you're conversing. Both of these screens have a handful of icon-based commands that give you access to the app's features and functions.

On the iPad, the Messages screen is divided into two main sections. On the left is a listing of your previous conversations. When Messages is running, the right side of the iPad screen is the active conversation window. From here, you can initiate a new conversation or respond to incoming messages, one at a time.

# CREATE AND SEND A TEXT MESSAGE

The first time you launch Messages on the iPad, the New Message screen is visible, the cursor flashes on the To field, and the virtual keyboard is displayed. If you have contact information stored in the Contacts app, as soon as you start typing in the To field, Messages attempts to match up existing contacts with the name, cell phone number, or email address you're currently typing. When the intended recipient's name appears, tap on it.

> **TIP** To initiate a conversation with someone else, tap on the New Message icon that appears in the upper-right corner of the Messages screen on the iPhone or next to the Messages heading on the upper-left side of the iPad's screen.

To quickly search your Contacts database to find one or more recipients for your text messages, you can also tap on the blue-and-white plus icon in the To field as you're composing a new message. A scrollable list of all contacts stored in Contacts displays, along with a Search field you can use to search your contacts database from within the Messages app.

> **TIP** If you're using an iPhone, to use your cellular service provider's SMS text-messaging service to send a message to another cell phone user, enter the recipient's cell phone number in the To field of a new message. This applies if the person doesn't have an entry in your Contacts database.
>
> If you're using an iPhone or iPad to send a message to another iOS mobile device or Mac user via iMessage, in the To field, enter the recipient's Apple ID or the email address the user has linked with his iMessage account. If the person is using an iPhone, his iMessage account might be associated with his iPhone's phone number, based on how he initially set up the account.
>
> In your Contacts database, you can create a separate field for someone's iMessage username, or when viewing the person's Contacts listing, simply tap on the appropriate contact information based on how you want to send the text message.

After filling in the To field with one or more recipients, if you have the Subject feature turned on in Settings, tap on the optional Subject field to create a subject for your text message, and then tap on the blank field located to the left of the Send icon to begin typing your text message. On the iPhone, a blank field for the body of your text message is available, displayed to the left of the Send icon.

If you're sending only text in your message, enter the text and then tap on the Send icon. Or to attach a photo or video clip to your outgoing text message, tap on the camera icon displayed to the left of the field where you're typing the text message.

> ☑ **TIP**  When you tap on the camera icon as you're composing a text message, two command options are displayed. Tap on the Take Photo or Video option to launch the Camera app from within Messages, and quickly snap a photo or shoot a video clip using your iPhone or iPad's built-in camera.
>
> If you already have the photo or video clip stored on your phone or tablet that you want to share, tap on the Choose Existing option to launch the Photos app in Messages, and then tap on the thumbnail for the photo or video clip you want to attach to the message.

## RECORD AND SEND AN AUDIO MESSAGE

New to iOS 8 is the ability to record and send short audio messages via the Messages app (when you're using the iMessage service). To do this, launch Messages, select the person you want to send the message to, and then press and hold your finger on the microphone icon that's displayed to the right of the compose message field. This begins the recording process. Simply start speaking into your iPhone or iPad (shown in Figure 11.13).

When you're finished recording, lift your finger from the microphone icon. You can delete the audio message by now tapping on the "X" icon, or send your audio message to the intended recipient by tapping on the up-arrow icon or swiping your finger upward.

Using the Message app, it's also possible to receive an incoming audio message. Instead of text being displayed, an audio message icon is displayed. Tap on it to play the message.

**FIGURE 11.13**

*Press and hold your finger on the microphone icon in the Messages app to record a short audio message.*

> **TIP** From within Settings, you can set up the Messages app to automatically delete audio messages after 2 minutes, or keep them forever (or until you manually delete them). Storing audio messages requires additional internal storage space in your iPhone or iPad. To adjust this setting, launch Settings, tap the Messages option, and then from under the Audio Messages heading, tap on the Expire option.
>
> It's also possible to set up the Messages app with the Raise To Listen feature. When turned on, if you receive an incoming audio message, it automatically plays when you pick up the iPhone and hold it up to your ear.

## RECORD AND SEND A VIDEO MESSAGE

In addition to text and audio, the Message app enables you to record and send short video messages using the camera built in to your iPhone or iPad. Again, this feature only works when utilizing the iMessage service.

To record a video clip from within the Messages app, launch the app, choose a recipient, and then tap on the camera icon that's displayed to the left of the text message composition field.

Select the Take Photo or Video option. When a modified version of the Camera app is displayed (shown in Figure 11.14), select the Video shooting mode and record your video. Alternatively, you can select the Photo shooting mode, snap a photo, and send that image to the intended recipient.

**FIGURE 11.14**

*Tap on the Camera icon to access a scaled-down version of the Camera app (shown here), or press and hold the camera icon to quickly shoot a video message or snap a photo and send it via the Messages app.*

When someone sends you an incoming video message, tap on the message icon to play it. From within Settings, it's possible to set up the Message app to automatically delete incoming video messages 2 minutes after they've been viewed. This enables you to conserve internal storage space on the device. Alternatively, you can select the Never option to store incoming video messages until you manually delete them.

To do this, launch Settings, tap on the Messages option, and then tap on the Expire option that's found under the Video Messages heading. Tap on either the After 2 Minutes or Never option.

> **NOTE** Audio and video messages can only be received by iPhone, iPad, and iPod touch users who are using the iOS 8 version of the Messages app or by Mac users running the OS X Yosemite version of Messages.

## PARTICIPATING IN A TEXT-MESSAGE CONVERSATION

As soon as you tap Send to initiate a new message conversation and send an initial text, audio, photo, or video message, the New Message window transforms into a conversation window, with the recipient's name displayed at the top center. Displayed on the right side of the conversation window are the messages you've sent. The responses from the person you're conversing with are left-justified and displayed in a different color on the screen with text bubbles.

As the text-message–based conversation continues and eventually scrolls off the screen, use your finger to swipe upward or downward to view what's already been said.

> **TIP** Whenever there's a pause between the sending of a message and the receipt of a response, the Messages app automatically inserts the date and time in the center of the screen so that you can later easily track the time period during which each conversation took place. This is particularly helpful if there are long gaps and the conversation did not take place in real time.

To delete or forward part of a text message, press and hold down that section of the message. A Copy and More option is displayed. Copy enables you to transfer the selected content to your device's virtual clipboard and then copy it elsewhere. The More option enables you to select more of the text message conversation and then delete or forward it by tapping on the trashcan or Forward icon.

> **TIP** From the Messages conversation screen on an iPad, tap on the Contact icon displayed in the upper-right corner of the conversation window to view the complete Contacts database entry for the person with whom you're conversing.

To delete entire conversations in the Messages app, press and hold one section of the message conversation, and then tap on the More option. Next, tap on the Delete All option to delete the entire conversation. Or from the Messages screen, which lists the individual conversations you've had or are engaged in, swipe your finger across a listing from right to left, and then tap on the Delete option.

## RESPONDING TO AN INCOMING MESSAGE

Depending on how you set up the Messages app in Settings, you can be notified of an incoming message in a number of ways. Notification of a new text message can be set to appear in the Notification Center window. Or, if the Messages app is already running, a new message alert is heard and a new message listing appears on the Messages screen (iPhone) or under the Messages heading on the left side of the iPad screen. If you already have the conversation screen open and a new message from that person you're conversing with is received, that message appears on the conversation screen.

**TIP** When a new message arrives, a blue dot appears to the left of the new message's listing (under the Messages heading on the iPad or on the Messages screen on the iPhone). The blue dot indicates it's a new, unread message.

To read the incoming message and enter into the conversation window and respond, tap on the incoming message listing. If you're looking at the listing in the Notification Center window, for example, and you tap on it, the Messages app launches and the appropriate conversation window automatically opens.

After reading the incoming text message, use the virtual keyboard to type your response in the blank message field, and then tap the Send icon to send the response message.

## RELAUNCH OR REVIEW PAST CONVERSATIONS

From the Messages screen on the iPhone, or from the left side of the screen on the iPad when the Messages app is running, you can view a listing of all saved conversations. Each listing displays the person's name, the date and time of the last message sent or received, and a summary of the last message sent or received. Tap on any of the listings to relaunch that conversation in the Conversation window. You can either reread the entire conversation or continue the conversation by sending a message to that person.

> **☑ TIP** By tapping on one listing at a time, you can participate in multiple conversations at once.
>
> On the iPhone, to exit the conversation screen you're currently viewing, tap on the left-pointing arrow icon that's displayed in the upper-left corner of the screen, labeled Messages.
>
> On the iPad, tap on one of the other listings under the Messages heading on the left side of the screen.

From the Messages screen on the iPhone (or the Messages listing on the iPad that's displayed on the left side of the screen), tap on the Edit icon, and then tap on the red-and-white icon that's displayed next to a conversation to quickly delete the entire conversation.

## PARTICIPATING IN A GROUP CONVERSATION

While previous versions of the Messages app have allowed you to participate in group conversations, prior to iOS 8, it was not possible to manage those conversations. Now, if you get into a group messaging conversation and it becomes too active and annoying, it's possible to opt out of the discussion.

To do this, from the conversation screen, tap on the Details option, and then turn on the Do Not Disturb feature. Turn off this virtual switch if you want to rejoin the conversation later.

To exit out of the conversation altogether, tap on the Details option and select the Leave This Conversation option.

Also from the Details screen, you can add new people to the group conversation by tapping on the Add Contact option.

## SHARE MORE INFORMATION FROM THE DETAILS SCREEN DURING A CONVERSATION VIA THE MESSAGES APP

During the conversation, if you want to share your exact location with the other participant(s), tap on the Details option, and then tap on the Send My Current Location option to send a map that depicts your current location. However, if you move from that location, the information is not updated.

If you want to make your whereabouts known to the conversation's participant(s) on an ongoing basis, tap on the Share My Location option, and then choose the Share for One Hour, Share Until End of Day, or Share Indefinitely option by tapping on it.

Because sending and receiving photos and video clips as part of a Messages conversation has become popular, the Messages app now enables users to quickly see a thumbnail summary of all photos or video clips sent or received during each conversation. This eliminates the need to scroll upward on the screen to "rewind" a conversation to re-view a photo or video clip. To view the thumbnail summary, tap on the Details option and then scroll toward the bottom of the Details screen. Tap on any thumbnail to view a larger version of it. Press and hold your finger on the image to copy it into iOS 8's virtual clipboard to paste it into another app or conversation in the Messages app.

## CUSTOMIZE THE MESSAGES APP

In Settings, you can customize several settings related to the Messages app. To do this, launch Settings from the Home screen, and then tap on the Messages option that's displayed in the main Settings menu.

In the Messages setup window, you can turn on or off the iMessage service altogether, plus make adjustments that are relevant to sending and receiving messages from your iOS mobile device. For example, by adjusting the virtual switch associated with the Send Read Receipts option to the on position, your contacts are notified when you've read their messages.

You can also set preferences for using text messages (SMS and MMS messages) versus iMessage.

If you turn on the virtual switch associated with the Character Count option, as you're composing a new message, the number of characters it contains is automatically displayed.

### MESSAGES APP QUICK TIPS

- It's possible to use Siri to dictate and send text messages using your voice. To do this, activate Siri and say something like, "Send text message to Rusty Rich." When Siri says, "What would you like it to say?," speak your message, and then confirm it. When prompted, tell Siri to send the text message you dictated. Siri can also be used to read your newly received text messages, without having to look at or touch the iPhone's screen.

- If you want to block someone who has an entry in your Contacts database from being able to send you a message via the Message app, one way to do this is to launch Settings, tap on the Messages option, tap on the Blocked option, and then tap on the Add New option. Select the Contacts entry for the person or company you want to block. To unblock that person, return to the Blocked submenu screen in Settings and swipe your finger from right to left across the blocked person's name.

- To quickly search for something in any of your Messages app conversations, from the Messages screen that lists the conversations in which you're currently participating, tap on the Search field that's displayed at the top of the screen and enter a name, keyword, or phrase you're looking for. You can also access iOS 8's Spotlight Search feature, which includes the content of the Messages app within searches.

- To temporarily silence all alerts related to the Messages app, activate the Do Not Disturb feature, which can be done from the Control Center or from within Settings. As soon as you turn off this feature, you're alerted to all missed messages.

# 12

# SURF THE WEB MORE EFFICIENTLY USING SAFARI

Chances are, if you know how to use a Mac or PC, you already know how to surf the Web using a browser such as Safari, Microsoft Internet Explorer, Firefox, or Google Chrome on your computer.

The Safari web browser on your iPhone (shown in Figure 12.1) or iPad (shown in Figure 12.2) offers the same basic functionality as the web browser for your desktop or laptop computer, but it's designed to maximize the iPhone or iPad's touchscreen and screen size.

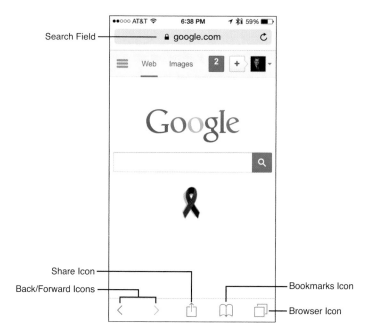

Search Field

Share Icon

Back/Forward Icons

Bookmarks Icon

Browser Icon

**FIGURE 12.1**

*The main screen of the Safari web browser on the iPhone 5s.*

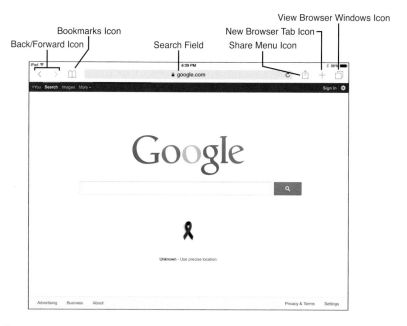

View Browser Windows Icon

Bookmarks Icon

New Browser Tab Icon

Back/Forward Icon

Search Field

Share Menu Icon

**FIGURE 12.2**

*The main screen of the Safari web browser on the iPad.*

With the release of iOS 8, Apple once again enhanced the Safari app, giving it a handful of new features that make web surfing a more enjoyable, secure, potentially more private, and more efficient experience.

Using iOS 8's new "Handoff" function, you can begin surfing the Web using Safari on one of your Macs or iOS mobile devices, and then pick up exactly where you left off on another, as long as all of the equipment is linked to the same iCloud account.

> **TIP** To turn on the Handoff feature, launch Settings, tap on the General option, and then tap on the Handoff & Suggested Apps option. From the Handoff & Suggested Apps submenu, turn on the virtual switch that's associated with the Handoff option. This must be done on each device.

> **WHAT'S NEW** In the iOS 8 edition of Safari, Apple has once again streamlined the interface, and some important command icons are now located in different places. For example, across the top of the Safari screen on an iPhone, you simply see the Search field. Along the bottom of the screen (from left to right) are the Back, Forward, Share, Bookmarks, and Switch Browser Window icons (also referred to as the Tabbed Browser icon).
>
> Displayed across the top of the Safari screen on an iPad (from left to right) are the Back and Forward icons, followed by the Bookmarks icon. The Search field is displayed across the top center of the screen, and to the right of it are the Share, Add Browser Tab, and Switch Browser Window icons.

As you'd expect from your iPhone or iPad, surfing the Web using the Safari app is a highly customizable experience. For example, you can hold your device in Portrait or Landscape mode while surfing.

On most websites, you can also zoom in on or zoom out of specific areas or content, such as a paragraph of text or a photo, using the reverse-pinch finger gesture (to zoom in) or the pinch gesture (to zoom out), or by double-tapping on a specific area of the screen to zoom in or out.

# CUSTOMIZE YOUR WEB SURFING EXPERIENCE

To customize your web surfing experience using Safari, launch Settings, and then tap on the Safari option. The Safari menu screen appears (shown in Figure 12.3) with a handful of customizable options. Here's a summary of what each is used for:

■ **Search Engine**—The smart Search field is used to enter specific website URLs (addresses) and to find what you're looking for on the Web via a search engine, such as Google, Yahoo!, or Bing. This option enables you to select your default (favorite) Internet search engine. So if you select Google as your default, whenever you perform a search using Safari's Search field, the browser automatically accesses Google to obtain your search results.

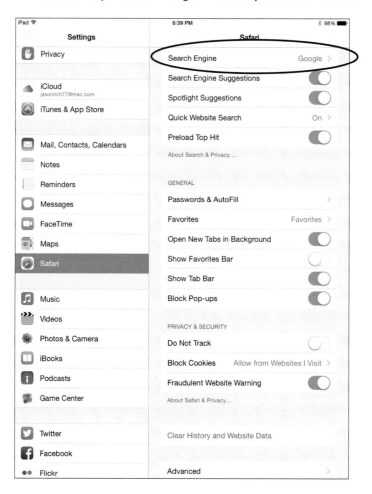

**FIGURE 12.3**

*Customize your web surfing experience when using Safari from within Settings on your iOS device.*

**WHAT'S NEW** New Safari-related Settings options, labeled Search Engine Suggestions, Spotlight Suggestions, Quick Website Search, and Preload Top Hit, are available. Each can be turned on or off.

Search Engine Suggestions, for example, offers additional (related) search term suggestions when you enter a website address or search term in Safari's Search field.

Spotlight Suggestions shows related websites when you perform a search using your iPhone or iPad's Spotlight Search feature. Quick Website search can be used to search a specific website for a specific term. For example, in Safari's search field, enter "Wiki New York" to access the Wikipedia website and display information related to New York.

Turn on the Preload Top Hit option if you want your favorite and most frequented websites to be displayed first when performing a relevant search.

These options determine when website suggestions are offered when using Safari's Search field, Spotlight Search, or other search-related functions.

**TIP** Regardless of which Internet search engine you select to be your default in the Settings app (Google, Yahoo!, Bing, or DuckDuckGo), you can always add the others (or any other search engine) to your Bookmarks or Favorites menu, so that you can access the other search engines directly.

**NOTE** DuckDuckGo.com is a search engine that does not track your web surfing behaviors or activities, so it offers a more private experience. However, you can utilize Safari's newly enhanced Privacy features to prevent your web surfing activities from being tracked.

To do this, from the Safari menu within Settings, turn on the virtual switch that's associated with the Do Not Track option (refer to Figure 12.3).

■ **Passwords & AutoFill**—One of the more tedious aspects of surfing the Web is constantly having to fill in certain types of data fields, such as your name, address, phone number, email address, and website-related passwords.

When turned on, this feature remembers your responses and automatically inserts the data into the appropriate fields. It also pulls information from your own Contacts app entry.

To customize this option and link your personal contact entry to Safari, tap on the Passwords & AutoFill option, turn on the Use Contact Info option, and then tap on My Info to select your own Contacts entry.

You can also set whether Safari remembers names and passwords for specific websites you visit, as well as credit card information that you use to make online purchases. This functionality is part of what Apple calls iCloud Keychain. On the iPhone 6 and iPhone 6 Plus, online payments are now handled using the new Apple Pay feature.

- **Favorites**—This feature serves as a shortcut for accessing websites you frequently visit. As you begin typing a website address or website name into the Search field, Safari accesses your Favorites list and auto-inserts the appropriate website URL. When you tap on the Search field, a screen with icons representing sites in your Favorites list is displayed. Your Favorites list of websites automatically syncs between any Macs and iOS mobile devices that are linked to the same iCloud account.

> **TIP** If you've created custom Bookmark folders when using Safari on your Mac, you can access and manage them from your iOS mobile device. Plus from the Favorite option within Settings, you can make one of these custom folders your default.

- **Open Links (iPhone only)**—Anytime a new web page opens as a result of you tapping on a link, this feature determines whether the new browser window is opened as the new active browser window or whether it opens in the background.
- **Open New Tabs in Background (iPad only)**—Anytime a new web page opens as a result of you tapping on a link, this feature determines whether the new browser window is opened as the new active browser window or whether it opens in the background.
- **Show Favorites Bar (iPad)**—When you turn on the virtual switch associated with this feature in Settings, your Favorites Bar displays across the top of the Safari screen, just below the row of command icons and the Search field. The default setting for this feature is off because it utilizes some of your onscreen real estate.
- **Show Tab Bar (iPad)**—When you turn on the virtual switch associated with this feature in Settings, when multiple browser windows are open in Safari, tabs for each window are displayed along the top of the screen, just below

the row of command icons and the Search field. The default setting for this feature is on.

- **Block Pop-Ups**—When turned on, this feature prevents a website you're visiting from creating and displaying extra windows or opening a bunch of unwanted browser tabs. The default for this option is turned on because this makes for a more enjoyable web surfing experience.

- **Do Not Track**—By default, when you surf the Web using Safari, the web browser remembers all the websites you visit and creates a detailed History list that you can access to quickly revisit websites. By turning on the Do Not Track feature, Safari does not store details about the websites you visit.

- **Block Cookies**—Many websites use cookies to remember who you are and your personalized preferences when you're visiting that site. Cookies contain data that gets saved in your iPhone or iPad and is accessible by the websites you revisit. When this option is turned on, Safari does not accept cookies from websites you visit. Thus, you must reenter site-specific preferences and information each time you visit that site. The Blocked Cookies submenu offers three options: Always (meaning all cookies are blocked), From Third Parties and Advertisers (meaning cookies unrelated to websites you purposely visit are blocked), and Never (meaning no cookies are blocked).

- **Fraudulent Website Warning**—This feature helps prevent you from visiting impostor websites designed to look like real ones, which have been created for the purpose of committing fraud or identity theft. It's not foolproof, but keeping this feature turned on gives you an added level of protection, especially if you use your iOS device for online banking and other financial transactions.

- **Clear History and Website Data**—Using this feature, you can delete the contents of Safari's History folder that stores details about all the websites you have visited. At the same time, cookies (data pertaining to specific websites you've visited) are also deleted.

- **Use Cellular Data**—This option enables your iPhone or iPad to use the cellular data service (as opposed to a Wi-Fi Internet connection) to download Reading List information to your device from your iCloud account so that it can be read offline. Although this feature is convenient, it also utilizes some of your monthly cellular data allocation, which is why an on/off option is associated with it. The option is available on all iPhones, as well as iPads with Cellular + Wi-Fi capabilities.

- **Advanced**—From this submenu, you can view details about website-specific data that Safari has collected. If you choose, you can manually delete this information. You also can enable or disable the JavaScript feature.

# HOW TO USE TABBED BROWSING WITH SAFARI

Safari's main screen contains the various command icons used to navigate the Web. On the iPhone, these icons are displayed along the bottom of the Safari screen, while the smart Search field is displayed along the top of the screen.

If you're using Safari on an iPad, the Title bar displays all of Safari's command icons along the top of the screen. Immediately below the Title bar, if you have the option turned on, your personalized Favorites Bar is displayed. Below the Favorites Bar, the Tabs bar becomes visible if you have more than one web page loaded in Safari at any given time (and you have this featured turned on).

## SWITCHING BETWEEN WEB PAGES ON AN iPHONE

The iPhone version of tabbed browsing involves Safari opening separate browser windows for each active web page. By tapping on the Switch Browser Window icon at the bottom-right corner of the Safari screen, you can quickly switch between open browser windows (shown in Figure 12.4) because only one at a time can be viewed.

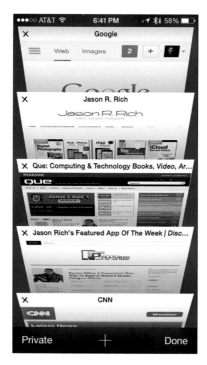

**FIGURE 12.4**

Safari's Switch Browser Window View (also referred to as the Tab View) is shown here on the iPhone 5s. To open a new page, tap on the + option near the bottom center of the screen.

**iOS 8 WHAT'S NEW** If you press down on the + option for a second or two, a Recently Closed Tabs menu screen appears on either the iPhone or iPad. You can easily reopen a previously visited but closed browser window by tapping on one of the items listed in this menu (which is based on your personal web surfing history).

When you're viewing the Switch Browser Window View screen (also referred to as the Tab View), tap on the New Page icon (which looks like a plus sign) to create a new (empty) browser window, and then manually surf to a new website by typing a URL or search term into the unified smart search field, selecting a favorite icon, or selecting a bookmark.

**TIP** When viewing the Switch Browser Window screen in Safari, tap on the Private option to turn on the Private web surfing mode. This prevents Safari from storing details about the websites you visit and syncing this information with your iCloud account. When you're using this privacy feature, the background color of Safari's toolbars change to dark gray.

To switch between active (viewable) browser windows that are open, simply tap on one of the tabs displayed. You can scroll through them using an upward or downward swipe motion with your finger as needed. To rearrange the order of the taps, place your finger on a tab and drag it to a new location. To close a page (tab), tap on its "X" icon.

**iOS 8 WHAT'S NEW** If you have the Handoff feature turned on, scroll down to the bottom of the Switch Browser Window screen on your iPhone to see listings for open browser windows on your Mac(s) or other iOS mobile devices that are linked to the same iCloud account (shown in Figure 12.5). Tap on any of these listings to pick up exactly where you left off on that other device.

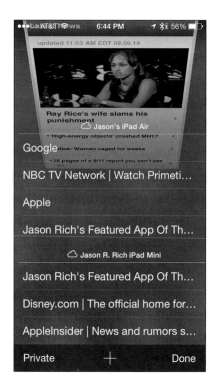

**FIGURE 12.5**

*Use the Handoff feature to access open browser windows on your iPhone that were left open on any of your Macs or other iOS mobile devices that are linked to the same iCloud account.*

Tap the Done button (in the lower-right corner of the screen) to exit the Switch Browser Window screen and return to the main Safari web browser screen. Or tap on one of the web page thumbnails as you scroll through them on the Switch Browser Window screen.

## TABBED BROWSING ON THE iPAD

When you tap on a link in a web page that causes a new web page to automatically open, a new tab in Safari is created and displayed, assuming you have the Open New Tabs in Background option (in Settings) turned off. Tabs are shown in Figure 12.6.

Browser Tabs

**FIGURE 12.6**

*On the iPad, tabs are displayed along the top of the screen. Each tab represents a separate browser window that's open. Thus, by tapping on a tab, you can quickly switch between open browser windows and visit multiple websites simultaneously.*

As you're viewing a web page, you can simultaneously open another web page by tapping on the New Browser Window icon (the + icon that's displayed near the top-right corner of the Safari screen (between the Share and Switch Browser Window icons). When you do this, a new tab is created, and you can visit a new web page without closing the web page you're currently viewing.

Along the Tab bar on the iPad, you can have multiple web pages accessible at once. Instantly switch between web pages simply by tapping on its related tab. The website name is displayed in the tab.

To close a tab, tap on the small x that appears on the left side of that tab.

**iOS 8 WHAT'S NEW** If you have the Handoff option turned on, when surfing the Web using your iPad, tap on the Switch Browser Window icon that's displayed in the top-right corner of the screen to display all the open browser windows on each of your other Macs and/or iOS mobile devices that are linked to the same iCloud account (shown in Figure 12.7). Tap on any of these preview windows or listings to open that browser window on your iPad and pick up exactly where you left off when using the other computer or device.

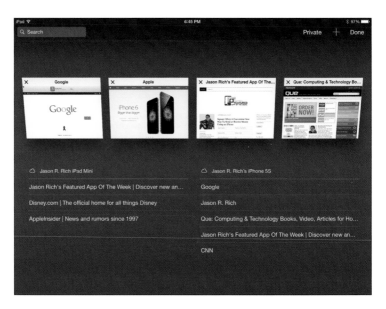

**FIGURE 12.7**
*Access any browser window that was left open on your Mac(s) or other iOS mobile devices when you tap on the Switch Browser Window icon that's displayed in the top-right corner of the Safari screen when using an iPad.*

> **!CAUTION** With the Handoff feature turned on, as you're surfing the Web on your iPhone or iPad, someone can literally follow along and see what web pages you're visiting in real time if they're using Safari on one of your Macs or other iOS mobile devices; that is, if they're signed in using your account. To prevent this, activate Safari's Private Browsing feature and turn off the Handoff feature.

## REMOVE SCREEN CLUTTER WITH SAFARI'S READER OPTION

Not to be confused with Safari's Reading List feature (which is explained shortly), Safari Reader works on the iPhone and iPad and enables you to select a compatible website page; strip out graphic icons, ads, and other unwanted elements that cause onscreen clutter; and then read just the text (and view related photos) from that web page on your iOS device's screen.

The Safari Reader works only with compatible websites, including those published by major daily newspapers and other news organizations. If the feature is available while you're viewing a web page, the Reader icon (as shown in Figure 12.8 and Figure 12.9) is displayed before that web page's URL, on the extreme left side of the Smart Search field.

Reader Icon

**FIGURE 12.8**

*An article from QuePublishing.com, without the Reader feature active.*

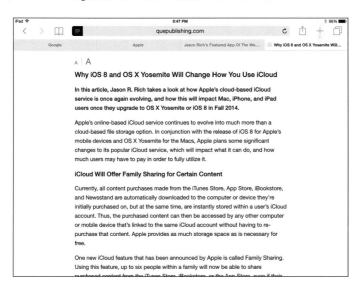

**FIGURE 12.9**

*The same article from QuePublishing.com, but with the Reader feature active.*

When you see the Reader icon displayed, tap on it. An uncluttered screen that contains just the article or text from that web page, along with related photos, is displayed. Use your finger to scroll up or down. Tap on the small or large "A" that's displayed near the top-left corner of a Reader screen to decrease or increase the size of the text, respectively.

Tap the Reader icon a second time to exit the Reader window and return the web page to its normal appearance.

# CREATE AND MANAGE READING LISTS

As you're surfing the Web, you might come across specific web pages, articles, or other information that you want to refer to later. In Safari, you can create a bookmark for that website URL and have it displayed as part of your Bookmarks list or within your Favorites Bar, or you can add it to your Reading List, which is another way to store web page links and content that's of interest to you.

> **NOTE** The Reading List feature downloads entire web pages for offline viewing, as opposed to simply storing website addresses that you can refer to later. Although this feature downloads text and photos associated with a web page, it does not download animated graphics, video, or audio content associated with that page.

To add a website or web-based article to your personalized Reading List for later review, tap on the Share icon, and then tap on the Add to Reading List button displayed as part of Safari's redesigned Share menu.

To later access your Reading List to view any of the stored web pages or articles, tap on the Bookmarks icon, and then tap on the Reading List tab. Figure 12.10 shows an example of a Reading List. The Reading List tab looks like eyeglasses.

Reading List Tab

Bookmark Icon | Reading List Saved Articles and Web Pages

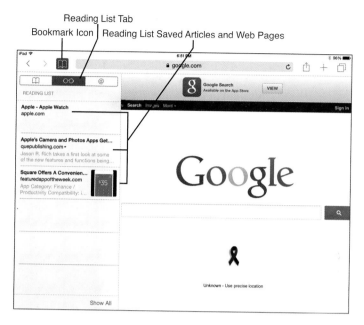

**FIGURE 12.10**

*Creating a Reading List is another way to store links related to specific content on the Web that you want to easily be able to find again and access later.*

> **TIP**  Like your Bookmarks list and Favorites Bar, the items stored in your Reading List can automatically be saved to iCloud and almost instantly made available on any other computer or iOS device that's linked to your iCloud account. See the section, "Create, Manage, and Sync Safari Bookmarks," for details on setting up these features for syncing with your iCloud account, as well as with your Macs and other iOS mobile devices.

## WORKING WITH BOOKMARKS

When you tap on the Bookmarks icon on an iPad, the Bookmarks menu appears along the left side of the screen. It remains visible until you tap the Bookmarks icon again.

On the iPhone, when you tap the Bookmarks icon, the Bookmarks menu is displayed on a new screen in Safari.

At the top of the Bookmarks menu on both the iPhone and iPad are three tabs. The left-most tab (shaped like a book) is the Bookmarks tab. When you tap on it, your saved list of website bookmarks is displayed. The center tab is the Reading List tab. Tap on it to reveal your reading list.

The Shared Links tab (represented by the @ symbol) enables you to see a listing of website links shared with you by your Contacts, as well as subscriptions to RSS feeds or social media accounts (including Twitter). Set this up by tapping on the Subscriptions option that's displayed in the lower-right corner of this menu.

After you tap on the Subscriptions option, you can add compatible social accounts (such as Twitter), or if you're visiting a website or blog that has an RSS feed associated with it, visit that site and then tap on the Add Current Site option to make it a subscribed feed. From the Subscriptions panel that's displayed, you can then delete a subscribed feed by tapping on its corresponding "-" icon.

## OPTIONS FOR SHARING WEB CONTENT IN SAFARI

There are probably times when you're surfing the Web and come across something funny, informative, educational, or just plain bizarre that you want to share with other people, add to your Bookmarks list, or print. The iOS 8 version of Safari makes sharing web links extremely easy, thanks to a handful of available options.

Anytime you're visiting a web page that you want to share with others, tap on the Share icon to reveal a redesigned Share menu (as shown in Figure 12.11).

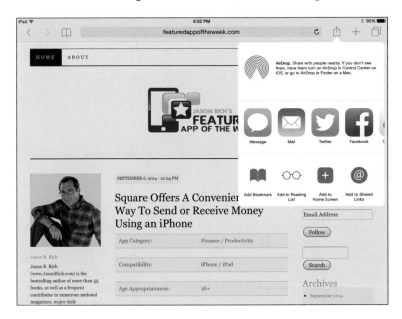

**FIGURE 12.11**

*Safari's Share menu offers a handful of ways to store and share web page content.*

> **NOTE** The options that are available to you from the Share menu vary depending on several factors, including the content you're viewing, as well as whether you have Facebook, Twitter, Vimeo, or Flickr integration set up to work with iOS 8.

On the iPhone, the Share icon is displayed near the bottom center of the Safari screen. On the iPad, the Share icon can be found to the immediate right of the smart search field at the top of the screen.

> **TIP** If you have the AirDrop feature turned on, when you access the Share menu in Safari, an AirDrop option is available. This enables you to wirelessly share content with nearby (compatible) Mac, iPhone, iPad, or iPod touch users. Some older Mac and iOS mobile device models don't offer AirDrop.
>
> To turn on AirDrop, open Control Center and tap on the AirDrop button. Then choose whether you want to communicate wirelessly with Contacts Only or all AirDrop users in your immediate vicinity. If AirDrop is not turned on, this feature does not appear in the Share menu.

The following options are often available from the Share menu, but vary based on the content you're reviewing and how you have integration with some Sharing-related options set up:

- **Message**—Send details about the web page you're currently viewing to one or more other people via text or instant message using the Messages app (without having to leave Safari). Tap on Message, fill in the To field, and then tap the Send button. The website URL is automatically embedded within the text or instant message.

- **Mail**—To share a website URL with others via email, as you're looking at the web page or website you want to share, tap on the Share icon and select the Mail option from the Share menu. In Safari, an outgoing email window appears.

  Simply fill in the To field with the recipient's email address, and tap the Send icon. The website URL automatically is embedded in the body of the email, with the website's heading used as the email's subject. Before sending the email, you can add text to the body of the email message or change the subject.

- **Twitter**—If you have an active Twitter account that's set up for use with iOS 8, tap on the Twitter option from the Share menu to create an outgoing tweet that automatically has the website URL attached.

  When the Twitter window appears, enter your tweet message (up to 140 characters, minus the length of the automatically shortened version of the website URL). Tap the Send icon when the tweet message is composed and ready to share with your Twitter followers.

> **TIP** If you're managing multiple Twitter accounts from your iOS mobile device, in the outgoing tweet window, tap on the From field, and then select from which of your Twitter accounts you want to send the tweet you're composing.

- **Facebook**—Thanks to Facebook integration within iOS 8, when you tap on the Facebook option, you can update your Facebook status and include details about the web page you're currently viewing in Safari.

> **NOTE** Some other social media apps and services, including Pinterest, now enable you to display a share-related option directly within iOS 8's Share menu.

- **Add Bookmark**—Tap on this option to add a bookmark to your personal Bookmarks menu or Favorites Bar that's stored in Safari. You can later access your bookmarks and/or Favorites by tapping on the Bookmark icon. When you store a web page as a Favorite, it is displayed along the Favorites Bar on the top of the iPad's screen. This Favorites Bar is displayed only if you turn on this option in Settings. To do this, launch Settings, tap on the Safari option, and then turn on the virtual switch that's associated with the Show Favorites Bar option.

> **NOTE** When using Safari on the iPhone, you can maintain a Favorites Bar (if you sync this data from a computer or other iOS device); however, to conserve onscreen space, the Favorites Bar is not displayed across the top of the Safari screen like it is on an iPad. Instead, on an iPhone, the Favorites Bar is displayed as an additional Bookmark folder when you tap on the Bookmarks icon.

When you opt to save a bookmark, an Add Bookmark window appears (as shown in Figure 12.12). Here, you can enter a title for the bookmark and decide whether you want to save it as part of your Bookmarks menu or in your Favorites Bar. It's also possible to create separate subfolders in your Bookmarks menu to organize your saved bookmarks.

**FIGURE 12.12**

*You can save a website URL as a bookmark in your Bookmarks menu or to be displayed as part of Safari's Favorites Bar.*

- **Add to Reading List**—Instead of adding a web page URL to your Bookmarks list or Favorites Bar, you can save it in your Reading List for later reference. (It is downloaded to your iPhone or iPad for later viewing, even if no Internet connection is then available.) To access your Reading List, tap on the Bookmarks icon, and then tap on the Reading List tab.

- **Add to Home Screen**—In addition to saving a website URL in the form of a bookmark or in your Reading List, another option is to save it as a Home screen icon. This feature is explained later, in the "Launch Your Favorite Websites Quickly with Home Screen Icons" section.

- **Add to Shared Links**—When applicable, this option enables you to share details about the web page you're viewing with others who access your Shared Links menu.

- **Copy**—Use this command to copy the web page URL you're looking at to the virtual clipboard that's built in to iOS 8. You can then paste that information into another app.

- **Print**—From Safari, you can wirelessly print a website's contents to any AirPrint-compatible printer that's set up to work with your iOS mobile device. To print a web page, tap on the Print command. From the Printer Options screen, select the printer you want to use, and then choose the number of copies you want printed. Tap the Print icon at the bottom of the Print Options window to send the web page document to your printer.

# CREATE, MANAGE, AND SYNC SAFARI BOOKMARKS

Thanks to the fact that Safari is fully integrated with iCloud, if you have an active iCloud account, your iOS device automatically syncs your Bookmarks and related Safari data with your other iOS mobile devices, as well as the compatible web browsers on your primary computer(s).

To activate this iCloud sync feature, launch Settings from the Home Screen, and then tap on the iCloud option. When the iCloud menu screen appears, make sure your iCloud account is listed at the top of the screen, and then make sure the virtual on/off switch associated with the Safari option is turned on. This must be done on each of your iOS mobile devices just once.

Your Bookmarks list, Favorites Bar, open browser windows (tabs), and Safari Reading List are automatically continuously synced with your iCloud account. Thus, when you add a new bookmark while surfing the Web on your iPad, for example, within seconds that same bookmark appears in your Bookmarks list on your iPhone and on Safari that's running on your Mac.

> 📝 **NOTE**   For Windows PC users, if you download the optional iCloud Control Panel for your PC (www.apple.com/icloud/setup/pc.html), you can have your Bookmarks and related web browser data on your PC sync with your iOS mobile device(s) and Mac(s). Simply add a checkmark to the Bookmarks option that's displayed in the iCloud Control Panel. This feature is compatible with the Windows version of the Internet Explorer, Firefox, and Chrome web browsers. When prompted, simply select which web browser you want to sync your Safari bookmarks and data with.

# SYNC USERNAMES AND PASSWORDS USING iCLOUD KEYCHAIN

When the iCloud Keychain feature is turned on (on each of your iOS mobile devices and Macs), anytime you enter a username and password for a website you visit, Safari stores that information and syncs it in your personal iCloud account. Then, anytime you revisit that website on any of your Macs or iOS mobile devices that are linked to the same iCloud account, your username and password for that website are remembered and you're automatically logged in.

> **NOTE** iCloud Keychain also remembers credit card information you use when making online purchases from a website. All usernames, passwords, and credit card details are stored using 256-bit AES encryption to maintain security.

To turn on and begin using iCloud Keychain, launch Settings and tap on the iCloud option. Then, from the iCloud Control Panel, turn on the virtual switch that's associated with the Keychain option. Follow the onscreen prompts that walk you through the feature's built-in security precautions.

Next, return to the main Settings menu and tap on the Safari option. Tap on the Passwords & AutoFill option. From the Passwords & AutoFill menu, turn on the virtual switch associated with the Names and Passwords option if you want iCloud Keychain to remember the usernames and passwords you use to access various websites you visit.

> **NOTE** Most online banking, credit card, and financial websites do not support iCloud Keychain for security purposes. When you visit these websites, Safari might remember your username, but you must manually enter your password each time.

To ensure that Safari stores all of your website-related usernames and passwords, also turn on the virtual switch associated with the Always Allow option. However, when using this feature, it's a good strategy to also activate the Passcode Lock feature of your iOS mobile device to prevent unauthorized people from accessing personal information when using your iPhone or iPad to surf the Web.

If you also want iCloud Keychain to store your credit card details for when you shop online, turn on the virtual switch associated with the Credit Cards option.

Then, tap on the Saved Credit cards option and enter your credit card details. This needs to be done only once.

Using iCloud Keychain, you no longer need to remember the unique usernames and passwords that you associate with each of the websites you frequently visit. Plus, to make your web surfing experience even more secure, you can use the built-in Password Generator feature to create highly secure passwords for you (which the web browser then remembers).

## LAUNCH YOUR FAVORITE WEBSITES QUICKLY WITH HOME SCREEN ICONS

If you regularly visit certain websites, you can create individual bookmarks for them. However, to access those sites, you still must launch Safari from your iPhone or iPad's Home screen, tap on the Bookmarks icon, and then tap on a specific bookmark listing to access the related site.

A time-saving alternative is to create a Home screen icon for each of your favorite websites.

To create a Home Screen icon, surf to one of your favorite websites using Safari. After it loads, tap on the Share icon, and tap on the Add to Home Screen button from the Share menu.

The Add to Home window appears. It displays a thumbnail image of the website you're visiting and enables you to enter the title for the website (which is displayed below the icon on your device's Home screen). Keep the title short. When you've created the title (or if you decide to keep the default title that Safari creates), tap on the Add option in the upper-right corner of the window.

> **NOTE**  When you use the Add to Home feature in Safari, if you're creating a shortcut for a website designed to be compatible with an iPhone or iPad, a special logo or related icon (as opposed to a web page thumbnail) is displayed.

Safari closes, and you are returned to your device's Home screen. Displayed on the Home screen is what looks like a new app icon; however, it's really a link to your favorite website. Tap on this icon to automatically launch Safari from the Home screen and load your web page.

After you create a Home screen icon for a web page, it can be treated like any other app icon. You can move it around on the Home screen, add the icon to a folder, or delete the icon from the Home screen.

# ADDITIONAL NEW FEATURES ADDED TO SAFARI

The following is information about other useful new Safari-related features to improve your web surfing experience.

## SWITCH BETWEEN MOBILE AND DESKTOP VERSIONS OF WEBSITES

When you visit a website from an iOS mobile device, if that website has a specially formatted mobile version available, it's that mobile version you're given access to by default. However, if you want to view the desktop version of a website from your iPhone or iPad, tap on the website's URL that's displayed in the Search field, and then place your finger near the center of the screen and swipe downward.

Next, tap on the Request Desktop Site option (shown in Figure 12.13), and the full version (as opposed to the mobile version) of that website is displayed.

**FIGURE 12.13**
*Switch from a mobile-formatted website to the full version of that website by tapping on the Request Desktop Site option.*

## SCAN CREDIT AND DEBIT CARD INFORMATION USING YOUR iPHONE OR iPAD'S CAMERA

Another new Safari feature is related to using iCloud Keychain to store credit card information when shopping online. When used with iOS 8, instead of manually entering new credit card details, it's now possible to use the iPhone or iPad's built-in camera to scan your debit or credit card(s) and have the information automatically stored in your mobile device.

To add a new credit or debit card to your iCloud Keychain, launch Settings, tap on the Safari option, and then tap on the Password & AutoFill option. Turn on the Credit Cards option, which is displayed as part of the Passwords & AutoFill menu screen. Next, tap on the Saved Credit Cards option.

Tap on the Add Credit Card option on the Credit Cards submenu. When the Add Credit Card window appears, tap on the Use Camera option to scan each of your debit or credit cards. Otherwise, manually fill in the Cardholder, Number, Expires, and Description fields, and tap the Done option.

If you're using a newer iOS mobile device that's compatible with Apple Pay, credit card details for this feature are added the same way, although Apple Pay can import the iCloud Keychain information that pertains to your credit card details.

> **NOTE** Although many improvements have been made to the web surfing capabilities of Safari on the iPhone and iPad, what's still missing is Adobe Flash compatibility. Adobe Flash is a website programming language used to generate many of the slick animations you see on websites. Unfortunately, these animations are not visible when you access a Flash-based website using the iOS version of Safari.
>
> If you want limited Flash compatibility on your iPhone or iPad, try using a third-party web browser app, such as Photon Flash Web Browser for iPhone ($3.99) or Photon Flash Web Browser for iPad ($4.99). Both versions are available from the App Store and offer compatibility with some (but not all) Flash-based content on the Web.

## HOW TO VIEW YOUTUBE VIDEOS

After Google, YouTube has become the world's second most popular search engine. When people want to learn new things or be entertained, they often prefer to watch free videos, as opposed to reading lots of online content.

Most of the videos published on YouTube can be viewed using Safari on your iPhone or iPad. Simply point the web browser to www.YouTube.com, and if applicable, sign in using your YouTube username and password.

However, for a more enjoyable and feature-packed YouTube experience on your iPhone or iPad, be sure to download and install the official (and free) YouTube app that's available from the App Store. This app enables you to search for and view any YouTube videos, manage your YouTube channel subscriptions, and even manage your own YouTube channel.

## IN THIS CHAPTER

- Get acquainted with the Calendar, Contacts, Reminders, and Notes apps
- Discover strategies for staying organized, on time, and productive with your iOS mobile device
- How to keep your app data synced between your iOS mobile devices, computer(s), online apps, and iCloud

# 13

# TIPS FOR USING CALENDAR, CONTACTS, REMINDERS, AND NOTES

Veteran iPhone or iPad users should immediately discover that the Contacts, Calendar, Reminders, and Notes apps that come bundled with iOS 8 have the same core functionality as before, but each has been enhanced with new features to make it even easier to be productive and stay organized in your everyday life.

Getting back to Apple's "continuity" theme for iOS 8, Contacts and Calendar are even more seamlessly integrated with many other apps and iOS 8 operating system functions. As a result, the more personal content and data you add to the Contacts and Calendar apps, for example, the more useful apps like Mail, Safari, Maps, and Messages can be, plus Siri can then assist you with a wider range of tasks by accessing data that's related to the people you know and your schedule.

The Calendar, Contacts, Reminders, and Notes apps continue to be fully compatible with iCloud, which makes synchronizing your app-related data a straightforward

process. Plus, from any computer or mobile device that's connected to the Internet, it's possible to access the online versions of these apps, which are automatically populated with all of your most current app-specific data.

In addition, it's possible to more easily synchronize data with other online-based calendars or contact management apps related to Microsoft Exchange, as well as Google, Yahoo!, or Facebook.

Using your iPhone or iPad's Notifications functionality, Calendar, and Reminders can easily be set up so alerts, alarms, reminders, and notifications related to your schedule and lists are consistently displayed in the Today screen of the Notification Center.

> **NOTE** The features and functions offered by the Calendar, Contacts, Reminders, and Notes apps are virtually identical on all models of the iPhone, iPad, and iPod touch. However, due to varying screen sizes, the location of specific command icons, options, and menus often varies. However, after you get to know how each app function works in general, you can easily switch between these apps on your iPhone, iPad, Mac(s), and/or the iCloud.com website without confusion.

## SYNC APP-SPECIFIC DATA WITH ONLINE-BASED APPS

To sync your Calendar, Contacts, Reminders, and/or Notes data with Yahoo!, Google, or Microsoft Exchange–compatible software, launch Settings and tap on the Mail, Contacts, Calendars option. Under the Accounts heading, tap on Add Account. Choose which type of account you want to sync data with, such as iCloud, Microsoft Exchange, Google, Yahoo!, AOL, or Outlook.com. Tap on the Other option if you use alternate contact management and/or scheduling software that supports the industry-standard LDAP or CardDAV data file format.

When prompted, enter your name, email address, password, and an account description (as well as any other requested information). After your account is verified, a menu screen in Settings related to that account lists app-specific options, such as Mail, Contacts, Calendars, Reminders, and/or Notes. Turn on the virtual switch associated with any or all of these options. Your iPhone or iPad can automatically and continuously sync your app-specific data on your iOS device with your online-based account. So, if you turn on the virtual switch associated with Calendars, for example, your schedule data is continuously synchronized.

To sync scheduling and/or contact-related data with Facebook, launch Settings and tap on the Facebook option. When prompted, enter your Facebook username and password. Then, near the bottom of the Facebook menu screen in Settings, turn on the virtual switch that's associated with Calendars and/or Contacts.

Periodically tap on the Update All Contacts option as you add new online Facebook friends. Calendar and/or contacts data is imported from Facebook and incorporated into your Calendar and/or Contacts apps. This includes profile pictures of your online friends who also have an entry in your Contacts database.

# SYNC APP-SPECIFIC DATA WITH ICLOUD

The Calendar, Contacts, Reminders, and Notes apps work seamlessly when syncing data between your iOS mobile devices, Mac(s), and PC(s) that are linked to the same iCloud account. To set up this feature, launch Settings, tap on the iCloud option, and then turn on the virtual switches associated with Contacts, Calendars, Reminders, and/or Notes. This needs to be done only once, but it must be done separately on each device or computer that's linked to the same iCloud account.

> **NOTE**  By setting up app-specific data syncing for Contacts, Calendar, Notes, and Reminders via iCloud, your data automatically gets imported into the online version of these apps that are available via iCloud.com (www.iCloud.com). So, when you sign in to iCloud.com using your Apple ID and password, and then launch the online version of Contacts, Calendar, Notes, or Reminders, all of your current app-specific data is available to you. This can be done from any computer or mobile device that's connected to the Internet, even if that computer or device is not normally linked to your iCloud account.

# GET ACQUAINTED WITH THE CALENDAR APP

With its multiple viewing options for keeping track of the scheduling information stored in it, the Calendar app is a highly customizable scheduling tool. In the Calendar app, any appointment, meeting, activity, or entry that you create and store within the app is referred to as an *event*.

Because the Calendar app can manage and display multiple color-coded calendars at once, when you create a new event, you can choose which calendar it is stored in. For example, you can maintain separate calendars for Work, Personal, Family, Travel, and/or for whatever organization you volunteer for and allocate time to.

From within Calendar, you can also share some or all of your schedule information with colleagues and maintain several separate, color-coded calendars to keep personal and work-related responsibilities, as well as individual projects, listed separately, while still being able to view them on the same screen.

**(iOS 8) WHAT'S NEW** One new iCloud feature that's compatible with the Calendar app is Family Sharing. When you turn on this feature, a separate color-coded calendar labeled Family is created in the Calendar app. This calendar can be accessed by up to five other family members. Thus, your teens can add details about their after-school activities, sports practices, or drama rehearsals, while weekend family events can be viewed for all to see. Plus, everyone can keep tabs on upcoming vacation dates.

While the Family calendar data is viewable by anyone with Family Sharing access, events stored within other calendars remain private, or viewable only by people whom you invite to see the information.

More information about setting up iCloud's Family Sharing feature can be found in Chapter 5, "Ways To Use iCloud's Latest Features with Your iPhone and/or iPad."

## CONTROLLING THE CALENDAR VIEW

Launch Calendar from your iOS device's Home screen, and then choose in which viewing perspective you'd like to view your schedule data. Regardless of which view you're using, tap on the Today option to immediately jump to the current date on the calendar. The current date is always highlighted with a red dot.

On the iPad, switching between Calendar views is as easy as tapping on the Day, Week, Month, or Year tab displayed in the top center of the Calendar app screen.

On the iPhone and iPad, the Calendar app opens on the last view option that you were using previously. However, on the iPhone, you also have access to a detailed Day, Week, Month, or Year view, as well as a new Listing view, which works with the Month or Day view.

**(iOS 8) WHAT'S NEW** On the iPhone, the most obvious new feature in the Calendar app is the Listing icon. When the Month calendar view is selected, tap on this icon (which appears near the top-right corner of the screen) to display a list of events for the day you select. This information gets displayed below the month view of the calendar (shown in Figure 13.1).

When you select the Day view in the Calendar app, the Listing icon shows you all your appointments, hour-by-hour, in a scrollable format that also enables you to quickly see your schedule for the previous or upcoming days, in addition to the currently selected day.

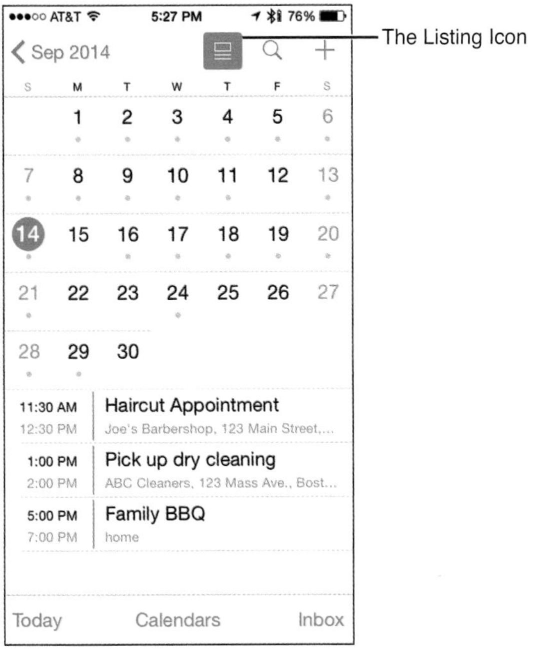

**FIGURE 13.1**

*The new Listing icon in the Calendar app provides yet another way to format and view your schedule on the iPhone's screen.*

The Year view shows mini calendars for the entire year (shown in Figure 13.2). To switch from the Year view to the Month view (shown in Figure 13.3), tap on any month in the Year view.

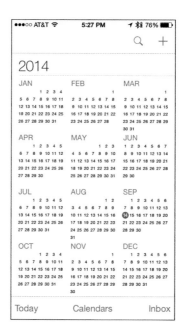

**FIGURE 13.2**

Shown here is the Calendar app's Year view on the iPhone 5s.

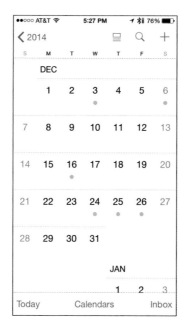

**FIGURE 13.3**

Shown here is the Calendar app's Month view on the iPhone 5s.

From the Month view, switch to the Week view by rotating your iPhone from portrait to landscape mode. In other words, hold your smartphone sideways.

Also from the Month view, to switch to the Day view (shown in Figure 13.4 on the iPhone), tap on a day that's displayed in the calendar. From the Month view, any day that displays a gray dot in it has event details associated with it.

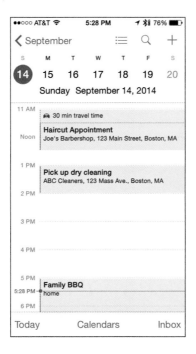

**FIGURE 13.4**

*Shown here is the Calendar app's Day view on the iPhone 5s.*

> **TIP** On the iPhone, from the Month or Day view, tap on the new Listing icon to view a more detailed scrollable listing for the selected day's events.

The Year, Month, Week, and Day views in the iPhone version of the Calendar app are switchable in a hierarchical order. If you're in the Day view, for example, you can switch back to the Month view by tapping on the Back icon (which looks like a left-pointing arrow). It's displayed in the top-left corner of the screen.

Whether you're using the Calendar app on an iPhone or iPad, your Calendar view options include the following.

## THE CALENDAR APP'S DAY VIEW

This view displays your events individually, based on the time each event is scheduled for. When using the iPad version of the app, this information is displayed on a split screen. On the left is an hour-by-hour summary of your day, and on the right is a synopsis of the events for that day. This is shown in Figure 13.5 on the iPad Air.

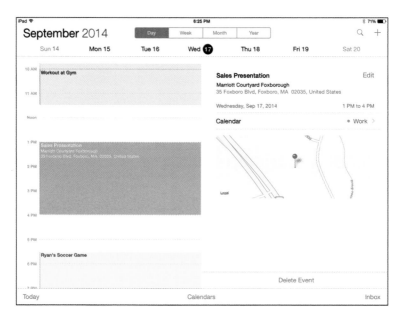

**FIGURE 13.5**

*The Day view of the Calendar app lets you see your schedule broken down one day at a time, in one-hour increments. (Shown here on the iPad Air.)*

**NOTE** On the iPhone, the Day view displays a week's worth of calendar dates near the top of the screen. Below that, the selected date is displayed, followed by an hour-by-hour rundown of your events.

On the iPad, the Day display is split into two sections. The selected date, along with a week's worth of calendar dates, is displayed at the top of the screen, followed by a summary listing of appointments and/or events displayed on the left side of the screen. Details about one selected appointment or event are displayed on the right side of the screen by tapping on it.

Use the Day view of the Calendar app to see a detailed outline of scheduled events for a single day. Swipe your finger to scroll up or down to see an hour-by-hour summary of that day's schedule.

Swipe right or left along the week's worth of calendar days to see upcoming or past dates, and to view another day's schedule. Tap on a specific day to switch to that date's day view.

> **TIP** To quickly find an event, tap on the Search icon, and then enter any relevant text to help you find the item you're looking for that's stored in the Calendar app. You can enter a date, time, name, business, meeting location, or other pertinent information. Tap on a search result to view that event listing in detail in the Calendar app.
>
> You can also use Siri to quickly find an upcoming event. Activate Siri and say, "When is my next appointment with [name]?", "When am I meeting with [name]?", or "What does my schedule look like for [date]?".

> **TIP** Another fast way to find upcoming event information in the Calendar app is to access the Spotlight Search feature from the Home screen. When viewing the Home screen, place your finger near the center of the screen and swipe downward. In the Search field that appears, enter any keyword, phrase, or date to quickly find a specific event that's stored in the Calendar app.

## THE CALENDAR APP'S WEEK VIEW

This view uses a grid format to display the days of the week along the top of the screen and time intervals along the left side of the screen (shown in Figure 13.6 on the iPad Air). With it, you have an overview of all events scheduled during a particular week (Sunday through Saturday).

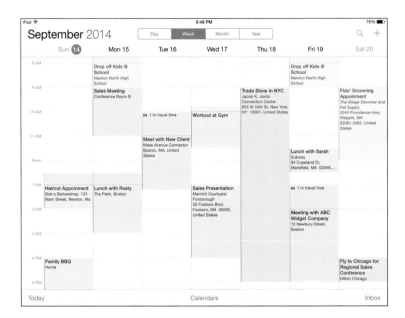

**FIGURE 13.6**

*The Calendar app's Week view shown here on the iPad Air.*

Scroll along the dates displayed near the top of the screen to quickly view your schedule for past or future weeks.

> ☑ **TIP**   To fine-tune this or any other Calendar app view, tap on the Calendars option that's displayed near the bottom center of the screen. A listing of the separate color-coded calendars that the Calendar app is managing is displayed. Tap on a listing to add or remove it from the Calendar view you're looking at.
>
> When you remove a calendar from the calendar view, this does not delete any data; it simply hides the events that are stored in that particular calendar from the display.

## THE CALENDAR APP'S MONTH VIEW

This view enables you to see a month's worth of events at a time. On the iPhone, tap any single day to immediately switch to the Day view and review a detailed summary of events slated for that day. From the Month view, use your finger to scroll up or down to look at past or future months. On the iPad, use the Day, Week, Month, or Year tabs, located at the top of the screen to switch Calendar views.

## THE CALENDAR APP'S YEAR VIEW

This Year view enables you to look at 12 mini calendars (with minimal detail displayed). For example, use this view to block out vacation days, travel days, and so on, and get a comprehensive view of your overall annual schedule.

> **TIP** Tap on the Inbox option, displayed near the bottom-right corner of the screen, to view invites for events from other people that you might want to import into one of your calendars.

# HOW TO ENTER A NEW EVENT INTO THE CALENDAR APP

Regardless of which calendar view you're using, follow these steps to enter a new event:

1. Tap the New Event icon (which looks like a plus sign) in the upper-right corner of the screen. This causes a New Event window to be displayed (shown in Figure 13.7 on the iPad Air).

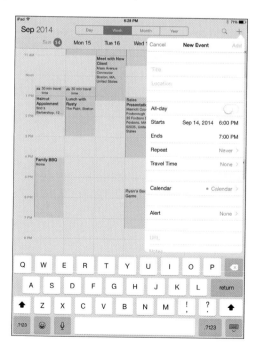

**FIGURE 13.7**

*Add a new event to the Calendar app from the New Event screen (iPhone) or window (iPad).*

2. The first field in the New Event window is labeled Title. Using the virtual keyboard, enter a heading for the event, such as "Ryan's Soccer Practice," "Call Email," or "Mandatory Sales Meeting at Work."

3. If a location is associated with the event, tap the Location field that's located below the Title field, and then use the virtual keyboard to enter an address or a location. Entering information into the Location field is optional. You can be as detailed as you want when entering information into this field.

[📝 NOTE Many of the fields within the New Event screen (iPhone) or window (iPad) are optional. In other words, you may only fill in the fields that are relevant to the new event you're creating. However, the more information you include, the more useful Maps, Siri, and Spotlight Search will be later when you want to refer to event information.

4. If the appointment will last for the entire day, tap the All-Day virtual switch, moving it from the off to the on position. Otherwise, to set the time and date for the new event to begin and end, tap the Starts field.

5. Use the scrolling Date, Hour, Minute, and AM/PM dials to select the start time for your event.

6. After entering the start time, scroll down and tap on the Ends option, and again use the scrolling Date, Hour, Minute, and AM/PM dials to select the end time for your event.

[📝 NOTE If the new event you're creating repeats every day, every week, every two weeks, every month, or every year, tap the Repeat option, and choose the appropriate time interval. The default for this option is Never, meaning that it is a nonrepeating, one-time-only event.

7. One new feature in the Calendar app that's available when creating a new event is called Travel Time. Tap on this field, and then turn on the virtual switch that's associated with the Travel Time option. You can then add between 5 minutes and 2 hours of travel time to that event by tapping on one of the listed options. So, if this event turns out to be one hour away from your previous event scheduled on the same day, one hour's worth of travel time can be added to your schedule.

8.  If you're managing several calendars within the Calendar app, as you create each new event, tap on the Calendar option to select in which calendar the new event will be placed. The default calendar is called Home, but you can change this from within Settings.

9.  To invite other people to the event, tap on the Invitees option and, when prompted, fill in the To field with the invitees' names or email addresses. Use their name if they already have a contact entry in the Contacts app; otherwise, enter an email address for each person separated by a comma. The people you add as invitees are sent an email allowing them to respond to the invite. The Calendar app keeps track of RSVPs for event attendees and displays this information in the app. This option becomes available only for certain calendar times, like if you're syncing data with Microsoft Exchange, Google, or iCloud.

10. To set an audible alarm for the event, tap the Alert option. The Event Alert window temporarily replaces the Add Event screen (iPhone)/window (iPad). In the Event Alert window, tap on the option for how much advance notice you want before the scheduled event. Your options include None, At Time of Event, 5 minutes, 15 minutes, 30 minutes, 1 hour, 2 hours, 1 day, 2 days, or 1 week before. Once you tap a selection, you are returned to the Add Event screen/window.

> **TIP** After you've added an alert, a Second Alert option displays in the Add Event screen/window. If you want to add a secondary alarm to this event, tap the Second Alert option, and when the Event Alert window reappears, tap on the interval when you want the second alarm to sound. This is useful if you want to be reminded of an appointment or deadline several hours (or days) before it's scheduled to occur, and then again several minutes before, for example.

11. Tap on the Show As option to classify how you want an event to appear within your calendar. The default option is Busy. This is information others can see if you opt to share specific calendars with other people.

12. Tap on the URL field to add a website address that's associated with the event.

13. Tap on the Notes field to add text-based notes you want to associate with the new event. It's also possible to paste content from other apps into the Notes field.

14. Tap the Done option to save the event. Tap the Cancel icon to exit without saving any new information.

NOTE As soon as you create a new event, that information syncs with your iCloud account and all other computers and/or mobile devices that you have linked to that account. If you have the Calendar app set up to sync with another scheduling app or online service, your new data syncs with that app.

This near instant data synchronization also applies if you delete an event.

TIP Although not directly related to the Calendar app, when you're away from home, if you access Notification Center, in addition to the weather forecast and your day's events (based on data from the Calendar app), a message telling you how long it will take you to get home from your current location is now displayed as part of the Today screen (shown in Figure 13.8).

**FIGURE 13.8**

*The Today screen in Notification Center offers information about your day's events, a weather forecast, and how far away from home you are, based on your current location.*

# USE SIRI TO ENTER NEW EVENTS INTO THE CALENDAR APP

Instead of manually entering event information into your iPhone or iPad using the virtual keyboard, or importing/syncing scheduling data from another computer or device, you always have the option to use Siri. Refer to Chapter 2, "Using Siri, Dictation, and CarPlay to Interact with Your Mobile Device," for more information.

> **TIP** Using Siri, say something like, "When is my next appointment with [name]?" You can also say, "Show me my schedule for Wednesday," or ask, "What's on my calendar for July 7?" to quickly find an event. If you enter information into the Location field as you're creating events, you can later ask Siri, "Where is my next meeting?"

# VIEWING INDIVIDUAL APPOINTMENT DETAILS

From any view in the Calendar app, tap an individual event to display the details related to that item.

When you tap on a single event listing, a new screen/window opens (shown in Figure 13.9). Tap the Edit icon in the upper-right corner to modify any aspect of the event listing, such as its title, location, start/end time, alert, invitees, or notes.

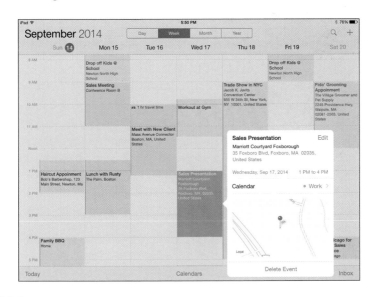

**FIGURE 13.9**

*Detailed information about each event stored within the Calendar app can easily be viewed (shown here on the iPad Air).*

## HOW TO DELETE AN EVENT FROM THE CALENDAR APP

To delete an event entry entirely, tap the red-and-white Delete Event option at the bottom of the Edit window. Or when you're finished making changes to an event entry, tap on the Done option in the upper-right corner of the window.

> **TIP** The Calendar app works with several other apps, including Contacts and Notification Center. For example, in Contacts, you can enter someone's birthday into an entry, and that information can automatically be displayed in the Calendar app.
>
> To display birthday listings in Calendar, tap the Calendars button displayed near the bottom center of the screen in the Calendar app, and then tap on the Birthdays option to add a check mark to that selection. All recurring birthdays stored in Contacts appear in Calendar.
>
> There are also two options related to the Facebook app that enable you to display all the birthdays for your online Facebook friends and/or all Facebook Events related to your account in the Calendar app. This can be found under the Facebook heading of the Show Calendars screen/window.

## QUICKLY FIND APPOINTMENT OR EVENT DETAILS

In addition to viewing the various calendar views offered within the Calendar app, use the in-app Search or Spotlight Search options to find individual events.

The in-app Search button can be found near the top-right corner of the Calendar app screen. Use the virtual keyboard to enter any keyword or phrase associated with the event you're looking for.

Without first launching the Calendar app, from the iPhone's or iPad's Home screen, access the Spotlight Search option (assuming you have not manually disabled this function in Settings). In the Search field that appears, enter a keyword, search phrase, or date associated with an event. When a list of relevant items is displayed, tap the event you want to view. This launches the Calendar app and displays that specific event.

## CUSTOMIZING THE CALENDAR APP

There are many ways to customize the Calendar app beyond choosing between the various calendar views. For example, you can set audible alerts and/or use onscreen alerts and banners to remind you of events. You can also display Calendar-related information in the Notification Center and/or Lock Screen.

> **TIP** To customize the audio alert generated by the Calendar app, launch the Settings app, and then select the Sounds option. Tap on the Calendar Alerts option and choose a sound from the menu. Choose the None option from the Calendar Alerts menu to set up Calendar so it never plays audible alerts or alarms.

From the Mail, Contacts, Calendars submenu within Settings, under the Calendars heading, determine how far back in your schedule you want to sync appointment data between your primary computer and your iOS device(s). Your options include Events 2 Weeks Back, Events 1 Month Back, Events 3 Months Back, Events 6 Months Back, and All Events. All Events is the default option.

Tap on the Time Zone Override option, and then turn on the virtual switch associated with this feature, if you want the Calendar app to always show event date and times in a selected time zone, regardless of which alternate time zone you've traveled to. After you turn on the virtual switch associated with this feature, tap on the Time Zone option to select a time zone.

## USE THE CONTACTS APP TO KEEP TRACK OF PEOPLE YOU KNOW

The art of networking is all about meeting new people, staying in contact with them, making referrals and connections for others, and tapping the knowledge, experience, or expertise of the people you know to help you achieve your personal or career-related goals.

In addition to the contacts you establish and maintain within your network, your personal contacts database might include people you work with, customers, clients, family members, people from your community with whom you interact (doctors, hair stylist, barber, dry cleaners, and so on), your real-world friends, and your online friends from Facebook, for example.

> **NOTE** Contacts is a powerful and customizable contact management database that works with several other apps that also came preinstalled on your iPhone or iPad, including Mail, Calendar, Safari, FaceTime, and Maps, as well as optional apps, like the official Facebook and Twitter apps. It's also fully compatible with iOS 8 functions such as Siri and Spotlight Search.

# YOU DETERMINE WHAT INFORMATION YOU ADD TO EACH CONTENT ENTRY

Chances are, the same contacts database that you rely on at your office or on your personal computer at home can be synced with your iPhone or iPad and made available to you using the Contacts app.

Of course, Contacts can also be used as a standalone app, enabling you to enter new contact entries as you meet new people and need to keep track of details about them using your iOS mobile device(s).

The information you maintain in your Contacts database is highly customizable, which means you can keep track of only the information you want or need. For example, in each contact entry, you can store a vast amount of information about a person or company, including the following:

- First and last name
- Name prefix (Mr., Mrs., Dr., and so on)
- Name suffix (Jr., Sr., Ph.D., Esq., and so on)
- Phonetic first, middle, and last name
- Nickname
- Job title
- Department
- Company
- Multiple phone numbers (work, home, cell, and so on)
- Multiple email addresses (work, personal, and so on)
- Multiple mailing addresses (work, home, and so on)
- Multiple web page addresses (URLs)
- Facebook, Twitter, Skype, Instant Messenger, or other online social networking site usernames
- Birthday
- Important Date (such as a recurring anniversary)
- Related Names (other people associated with the person, such as their spouse, children, secretary, and assistant)

**NOTE** To include some of these fields in a Contacts entry, you must use the Add Field option and select the field type from the submenu.

You can also customize your contacts database to include additional information, such as each contact's photo, as well as detailed and freeform notes related to a contact.

When you're using the Contacts app, your entire contacts database is instantly searchable using data from any field within the database, so even if you have a database containing thousands of entries, you can find the person or company you're looking for in a matter of seconds, using a wide range of search criteria.

## THE CONTACTS APP WORKS SEAMLESSLY WITH OTHER APPS

After your contacts database has been populated with entries, Contacts works with many other apps on your iPhone and/or iPad. Here are just a few popular examples:

- When you compose a new email message in Mail, you can begin typing someone's full name or email address in the To field. If that person's contact information is already stored in Contacts, the relevant email address automatically displays in the email's To field.

- If you're planning a trip to visit a contact, you can pull up someone's address from your Contacts database and obtain driving directions to the person's home or work location using the Maps app.

- If you include each person's birthday in your Contacts database, that information can automatically be displayed in the Calendar app to remind you in advance to send a card.

- As you're creating each Contacts entry, you can include a photo of that person—by either activating the Camera app from the Contacts app to snap a photo or using a photo that's stored in the Photos app—and link it with the entry. You also can insert photos of Facebook friends into the app automatically. See the section called, "How to Add a Photo to a Contacts Entry," later in this chapter.

- When using FaceTime, you can create a Favorites list of people you engage in video calls with often, compiled from entries in your Contacts database.

- From the Messages app, you can access your Contacts database when filling in the To field as you compose new text messages to be sent via iMessage, text message, or instant message.

- If you're active on Facebook or Twitter, you have the option of adding each contact's Facebook username or Twitter username to their Contacts entry. When you turn on the Facebook feature, the Contacts app automatically downloads each entry's Facebook profile picture and inserts it into your Contacts database.

When you first launch the Contacts app, its related database is empty. However, you can create and build your database in two ways:

- You can sync the Contacts app with your primary contact management application on your computer, network, or online (cloud)-based service, such as iCloud.
- You can manually enter contact information directly into the app.

As you begin using this app and come to rely on it, it's possible to enter new contact information or edit entries either on your iOS mobile device or using your primary contact management application, and keep all the information synchronized, regardless of where the entry was created or modified.

## WHO DO YOU KNOW? HOW TO VIEW YOUR CONTACTS

From the iPhone or iPad's Home screen, tap the Contacts app to launch it.

On the iPhone, the All Contacts screen displays an alphabetical listing of all entries in your Contacts database. Along the right side of the screen are alphabetic tabs, and a Search field is located near the top of the screen.

**NOTE** If you've used the Contacts app previously and it has been running in the background, the last contact entry you viewed will be displayed when you relaunch the app.

On the iPad, in the middle of the screen are alphabetic tabs. The All Contacts heading is near the upper-left corner of the screen. Below it is a Search field. After you have added entries in your contacts database, they are listed alphabetically on the left side of the screen, below the Search field (as shown in Figure 13.10).

**TIP** If you tap the Search field, you can quickly find a particular entry by entering any keyword associated with an entry, such as a first or last name, city, state, job title, or company name. Any content in your Contacts database is searchable from this Search field.

You can also tap a letter tab on the screen to see all entries "filed" under that letter by a contact's last name, first name, or company name, depending on how you set up the Contacts app in the Settings app's Mail, Contacts, Calendars option.

**FIGURE 13.10**

*On the iPad Air, the All Contacts listing and individual listings are shown on the left and right side of the screen, respectively. On the iPhone, this information is divided into two separate screens.*

On the iPhone, to see the complete listing for a particular entry, tap on its listing from the All Contacts screen. A new screen shows the specific contact's information (shown in Figure 13.11).

On the iPad, to see the complete listing for a particular entry, tap on it from the All Contacts display on the left side of the screen. That entry's complete contents are then displayed on the right side of the screen.

If you're using Siri, you can quickly find and display any contact in your Contacts database by activating Siri and saying, "Find [name] within Contacts."

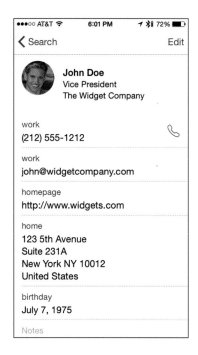

**FIGURE 13.11**

*A sample contact entry from the Contacts app displayed on the iPhone 5s.*

## MEET SOMEONE NEW? CREATE A NEW CONTACTS ENTRY

To create a new Contacts entry, tap the New Contact icon (which looks like a plus sign). On the iPhone, it's displayed in the upper-right corner of the All Contacts screen. On the iPad, the New Contact icon can be found near the top center of the Contacts app's screen.

After tapping on the New Contact icon, the New Contact screen appears.

> **NOTE** As you're creating each Contacts entry, you can fill in whichever fields you want. You can always edit a contact entry to include additional information later.

In the New Contact screen (iPhone) or window (iPad) are several empty fields related to the entry, starting with the First Name field (shown in Figure 13.12).

**FIGURE 13.12**

*Shown here on the iPad Air, from this New Contact screen, you can create a new contact and include as much information pertaining to that person or company as you want.*

Some fields, including Phone, Email, and Mailing Address, enable you to input multiple listings, one at a time. So you can include someone's home phone, work phone, and mobile phone (iPhone) numbers in the entry. Likewise, you can include multiple email addresses, and/or a home address and work address for an individual.

One of the available fields is Add Related Name. Use this field to add the names of your contact's mother, father, parent, brother, sister, child, friend, spouse, partner, assistant, manager, or other. You can also add your own titles for the Related People field.

> **TIP** You can change the label associated with certain fields (which are displayed in blue) by tapping the field label itself. This reveals a Label menu, offering selectable options for that field. For example, the Label options for the Add Phone field include Home, Work, iPhone, Mobile, Main, Home Fax, Work Fax, Pager, and Other. At the bottom of this Label window, tap the Add Custom Label option to create your own label if none of the listed options applies.
>
> Tap the label title of your choice. A check mark appears next to it, and you are returned to the New Contact screen/window.

At the bottom of the New Contact screen is an Add Field option. Tap it to reveal a menu containing a handful of additional fields you can add to individual Contacts entries as applicable, such as a middle name, job title, and nickname.

If there's a field displayed that you don't want to utilize or display, simply leave it blank as you're creating or editing a Contacts entry.

Each time you add a new mailing address to a contact's entry from within the New Contact screen/window, the Address field expands to include a Street, City, State, ZIP, and Country field.

After you have filled in all the fields for a particular entry, tap the Done option, which is displayed in the upper-right corner of the New Contact screen/window. Your new entry gets saved and added to your contacts database, and is synced with your other computers and/or mobile devices.

## HOW TO ADD A PHOTO TO A CONTACTS ENTRY

To the immediate left of the First Name field is a circle that says Add Photo. When you tap this field, a submenu with two options—Take Photo and Choose Photo— is displayed. If the entry already has a photo associated with it, Edit Photo and Delete Photo options are also displayed.

Tap Take Photo to launch the Camera app from within the Contacts app and snap a photo to be linked to the Contacts entry you're creating. Alternatively, tap on the Choose Photo option. In this case, the Photos app launches so that you can choose any digital image that's currently stored on your iOS mobile device. When you tap the photo of your choice, a Choose a Photo window displays on the Contacts screen, enabling you to move and scale the image with your finger.

> **TIP**  As you're previewing the image (shown in Figure 13.13), use a pinch or reverse-pinch finger motion to zoom in or out, and then hold your finger down on the image and reposition it within the frame.

After cropping or adjusting the photo selected, tap the Use icon displayed in the upper-right corner of the Choose Photo window to link the photo with that contact's entry.

**FIGURE 13.13**

*Linking a photo with someone's Contacts entry enables you to visually identify the person as you're reviewing your contacts.*

> **TIP** If you use an iPhone, or FaceTime on your iPhone or iPad, from the Ringtone option in the New Contact window/screen, it's possible to select the specific ringtone you will hear each time that particular contact calls you. Your iPhone or iPad has many preinstalled ringtones. From the iTunes Store, you can purchase and download thousands of additional ringtones, many of which are clips from popular songs, movies, or TV shows.

## EDITING OR DELETING AN ENTRY

To edit a contact, tap on its listing from the All Contacts screen to display the contact details, then tap on the Edit option that's displayed in the upper-right corner of the screen. Tap any field to modify it using the virtual keyboard. Delete a field by tapping on the red-and-white minus sign icon associated with it, and then tap the Delete button that appears to the right of the entry.

You can also add new fields in an entry by tapping any of the green-and-white plus sign icons and then choosing the type of field you want to add.

When you're finished editing a Contacts entry, again tap the Done option.

> **☑ TIP**  To delete an entire entry from your Contacts database, as you're editing a contact entry and looking at the Contact window/screen for that entry, scroll down to the bottom of it and tap the Delete Contact option that's displayed in red.
>
> Keep in mind that if you have your Contacts database syncing with iCloud or another contacts database, the contact you delete is removed from all your computers and devices that are connected to the Internet within seconds. There is no "undo" option.

## SHARING CONTACT ENTRIES

From the main All Contacts screen, tap on the contact listing you want to share. When the contact's entry is displayed, scroll down toward the bottom of the entry until you see the Share Contact option. Tap it. You can then choose to share the contact's details with someone else via AirDrop, text/instant message (via the Message app), or email (via the Mail app).

If you choose Mail, an outgoing email message form displays on your iPhone or iPad's screen. Fill in the To field with the person or people you want to share the contact info with. The default subject of the email is Contact. However, you can tap this field and modify it using the virtual keyboard.

If you choose Message, an instant/text message screen (iPhone) or window (iPad) is displayed, enabling you to fill in the To field with the names or text/instant message usernames or mobile phone numbers for the people with whom you want to share the information.

The entire Contacts entry you selected (stored in .vcf format) is already embedded in the outgoing email or text/instant message. When you've filled in all the necessary fields, tap the blue-and-white Send icon. Upon doing this, you are returned to the Contacts app.

The recipient(s) quickly receives your email or message. When he/she clicks on the email's attachment (the contact entry you sent), it can automatically be imported into their contact management application as a new entry, such as in the Contacts app on their Mac, iPhone, or iPad.

## CONTACTS APP QUICK TIPS

▦ If someone shares a Contacts entry with you via email, when you're viewing the incoming email on your iPhone or iPad, tap the email's attachment. The Contacts entry that was emailed is displayed in a window. At the bottom of this window, as the recipient of the contact's information, tap the Create New Contact or Add to Existing Contact option to incorporate this information into your Contacts database.

▦ To add a contact entry to your Phone or FaceTime app's Favorites list, when you're viewing any single contact, scroll downward. Tap the Add to Favorites button, and then choose a phone number or FaceTime address that's associated with that contact to feature within your Favorites list.

▦ As you're creating or editing a contact entry, in the Notes field, you can enter as much information pertaining to that contact as you want using freeform text. It's also possible to paste content from another app into this field using the iOS's Select, Copy, and Paste commands, and using the multitasking capabilities of your iPhone or iPad to quickly switch between apps.

▦ If you use Contacts on your Mac and Contacts on your iPhone and/or iPad, syncing your contacts is most easily done using iCloud, as long as all of the computers and mobile devices are linked to the same iCloud account. In Settings on the iOS device, select the iCloud option, and then turn on the virtual switch associated with Contacts that's part of the iCloud submenu. Be sure to do this on each of your iOS mobile devices. On each of your Macs, launch System Preferences, click on the iCloud icon, and then add a checkmark to the Contacts checkbox.

▦ When creating or editing contacts, it's extremely important to associate the correct labels with phone numbers, email addresses, and address data. For each phone number you add to a contact's entry, for example, it can include a Home, Work, Mobile, iPhone, or Other label (among others). For many of the functions of iOS 8 that utilize data from your Contacts database to work correctly (including Siri), it's important that you properly label content you add to each Contacts entry.

# ORGANIZE YOUR LIFE WITH THE NOTES AND REMINDERS APPS

Instead of using sticky notes or cocktail napkins to jot notes to yourself, the Notes app is ideal for note taking, keeping track of ideas, and managing text-based information that does not require the full functionality of a word processor. Using the Reminders app, you can easily manage multiple to-do lists simultaneously and add alarms and deadlines to individual to-do items. Plus, you can be reminded of responsibilities, tasks, or objectives exactly when you need this information based on your geographic location or a predetermined time and date.

The Reminders app works nicely with Siri, Notification Center, and iCloud, which makes synchronizing your app-related data a straightforward process.

On the iPad, all information relevant to a specific app or function is typically displayed on a single screen. On the iPhone, however, that same information is often split up and displayed on several separate screens.

## USE REMINDERS TO MANAGE YOUR TO-DO LISTS

On its surface, Reminders is a straightforward to-do list manager. However, it offers a plethora of interesting and useful features.

**NOTE** Reminders is just one option for managing to-do lists on your iPhone or iPad. If you use the Search feature in the App Store (with the keyword "to-do list"), you'll discover many more apps created by third parties that can be used for this purpose. Many of these apps offer a different set of features and functions than what's offered by the Reminders app.

For starters, you can create as many separate to-do lists as you need to properly manage your personal and professional life or various projects for which you're responsible.

**TIP** Reminders enables you to color code to-do lists. Tap on the Edit button displayed to the right of a list's title, and then tap on the Color option. Seven different colors are displayed. Tap on your selection. The list title is displayed in the selected color.

Because your iPhone has Location Services (GPS) capabilities, it always knows exactly where it is. Thus, you can create items within your to-do lists and associate one or more of them with an alarm that alerts you when you arrive at or depart from a particular geographic location, such as your home, office, or a particular store.

For example, you can have your morning to-do list or call list automatically display on your iPhone's screen when you arrive at work, if you associate just one item on that list with a location-based alarm. Likewise, if you use Reminders to maintain a list of office supplies you need to purchase at Staples or OfficeMax, you can have it pop up on the screen when you arrive at your local office supply superstore.

In addition, you can have a reminder alarm set to warn you of an upcoming deadline. This can be displayed on your iPhone or iPad's screen in the Notification Center or as separate alerts or banners, depending on how you have the Reminders app set up to work with your device.

As you're setting up an alarm, if you want it to repeat every day, every week, every two weeks, every month, or every year, tap on the Repeat option and make your selection. By default, the Never option is selected, meaning the alarm does not repeat.

> **☑ TIP**   Just as you do for other apps, to set up Reminders to work with Notification Center and/or display onscreen alerts or banners, launch Settings, tap on the Notifications option, and then tap on the listing for the Reminders app. You can then customize the settings on the Reminders menu screen within Settings.

## KEEP UP TO DATE WITH REMINDERS

When you launch Reminders for the first time on the iPad, the control center for this app appears on the left side of the screen. On the right side of the screen is a simulated sheet of lined paper.

Tap on the Add List option in the bottom-left corner of the screen to create a new list from scratch. However, if you've already been using the Reminder app on another iOS mobile device or Mac that's linked to the same iCloud account, all of your lists synchronize with the iPhone or iPad you're currently using.

When you create a new list from scratch, it is displayed on the right side of the screen using the temporary heading New List. Enter a title for the new list, and then associate a color with it. Tap on the Done option when you're ready to begin populating the list with items (as shown in Figure 13.14), or repeat this process to create another list.

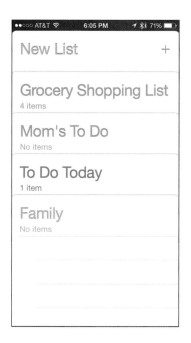

**FIGURE 13.14**

*Using Reminders, it's possible to create and manage one or more to-do lists. Each list can have as many separate items as you wish.*

On the iPhone, to create a new list from scratch as you're looking at a list, tap the list name to bring up a master list screen. The New List (+) option is displayed at the top of this screen. Tap on this option, and then type the name of the list and associate a color with it (shown in Figure 13.15). Tap on the Done option. You can then begin populating the list with items or repeat this process to create another list.

When viewing a list, tap on an empty line of the simulated sheet of paper to add an item. The virtual keyboard appears. Enter the item to be added to your to-do list. Next, tap on the Return key on the keyboard to enter another item, or tap on the Details icon (the blue *i* with a circle around it) to the right of the newly added item to associate an alarm, priority, and/or notes with it.

When you're finished adding new list items, tap on the Done option.

To set a date-specific alarm on either the iPhone or iPad, turn the virtual switch associated with Remind Me On a Day to the on position, and then tap on the date and time line that appears below it to set the date and time for the alert.

**FIGURE 13.15**

*To create a new list, tap on the New List (+) option displayed near the top of the Reminders screen on the iPhone. Then name your list and start adding items, one at a time.*

On the iPhone only, you can set a location-based alarm for that item. To set an alarm based on a location, enter the Details screen, and then turn on the virtual switch associated with the Remind Me At A Location option. Select a location or enter an address, and then decide whether you want to be alerted when you arrive or when you leave that destination by tapping on the When I Arrive… or When I Leave… tab. On the iPad, you can set an alarm only based on a date and time.

> **TIP** You have the option to set a priority with each to-do list item (shown in Figure 13.16). Your priority options include None, Low (!), Medium (!!), and High (!!!).
>
> Although setting a priority for a list item displays that item with one, two, or three exclamations points to signify its importance, adjusting an item's priority does not automatically change its location within the list. You must manually rearrange the order of items on a list.
>
> To do this, while looking at a list, tap on the Edit button. Then place your finger on the Move icon (three horizontal lines) that's associated with the list item you want to move and drag it up or down to the desired location within the list. Tap the Done button to save your changes.

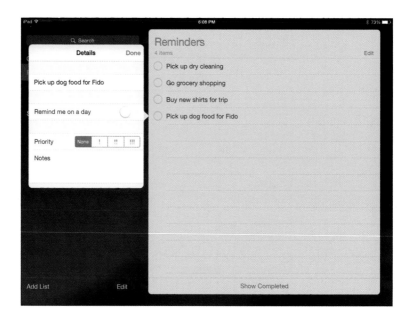

**FIGURE 13.16**

*As you're populating a list, tap on the "i" icon to reveal the Details window (shown here on the iPad Air). From here, you can add a Priority to an item on your list.*

Different alarms can be associated with each item in each of your to-do lists. You also have the option to create a to-do list item but not associate any type of alert or alarm with it.

When an alarm is generated for a to-do list item, a notification can automatically appear in your iOS device's Notification Center, assuming that you have this feature turned on.

**TIP** One additional feature of the Reminders app is that you can display a separate to-do list associated with each day on the calendar. When you use the Remind Me On A Day option, a date becomes associated with that item. Then, to review upcoming items related to a particular day using an iPhone, access the Search field from the main menu of lists stored within the app. Displayed to the right is an Alarm Clock icon. Tap on this to display scheduled items for the current day.

On the iPad, tap on the Scheduled option on the left side of the screen.

> ✓ **TIP**    At the bottom of every to-do list on the iPad is a new Show Completed option. Tap this to display all items originally added to the list you're viewing that have since been moved to the Completed list.

To delete an item from a to-do list, swipe your finger from right to left across the item. A More button and a Delete button are displayed. Tap on Delete to confirm your selection, or tap on the More button to reveal the Details window.

As soon as you make changes to a to-do list item, if you have iCloud functionality turned on for the Reminders app and have access to the Internet, your additions, edits, or deletions sync with iCloud.

## HOW TO DELETE AN ENTIRE TO-DO LIST

If you want to delete an entire list, enter the list and click on the Edit button, and then click on Delete List at the bottom of the screen. A warning pops up asking to confirm the deletion.

On the iPad, you can also locate the list you want to delete from the column on the left, and swipe your finger from right to left across it. When the Delete button appears, tap on it. You also have the option of tapping the Edit button, and then tapping on the negative sign icon that's associated with the list you want to erase. In Edit mode, you can also change the order of your lists by placing your finger on the icon that looks like three horizontal lines that's associated with a list, and dragging it up or down.

To exit Edit mode, tap on the Done option.

> ✎ **NOTE**    If you also use a Mac, it comes with the Reminders and Notes apps preinstalled. These are fully compatible with, and work just like, the iPhone editions of these apps. Online versions of the Contacts, Calendar, Reminders, and Notes apps are also available to you via www.iCloud.com.

## PERFORM BASIC TEXT EDITING AND NOTE TAKING WITH THE NOTES APP

While the Reminders app enables you to maintain to-do lists, the Notes app serves as a basic text editor that enables you to create, edit, view, and manage notes.

> **NOTE** The Notes app offers very basic formatting functionality. If you need the features and functions of a full-featured word processor, you should use Pages, Microsoft Word, or another word processing app on your iPhone or iPad. Notes is designed for basic note taking, not word processing.

> **TIP** An even more robust note taking app for the iPad is available for free from Microsoft. It's called OneNote and is compatible with other versions of Microsoft's OneNote that run on a PC or Mac.

Just like Reminders, the Notes app comes preinstalled with iOS 8. In addition, a similar Notes app comes preinstalled on the Mac, so if you set up this app to work with iCloud, all of your notes remain synced on all of your computers and/or iOS mobile devices that are linked to the same iCloud account.

On the iPhone, the Notes app has two main screens—one that lists each of your note titles and serves as a menu for accessing them, and a second for actually creating and viewing each note on a virtual yellow lined notepad (shown in Figure 13.17).

**FIGURE 13.17**

*From the note editing screen on the iPhone, you can create, edit, or view individual notes.*

On the iPad, if you hold the device horizontally, the listing of notes is displayed on the left side of the screen, while the right side of the screen displays the individual notes (shown in Figure 13.18).

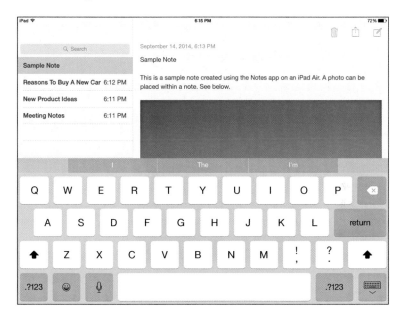

**FIGURE 13.18**
*The iPad displays all aspects of the Notes app on a single screen.*

To create a new note, tap on the New option (iPhone) or the Compose icon (iPad) that's displayed near the top-right corner of the screen. Begin typing your note using the virtual keyboard, or activate the Dictation function.

**NOTE**   By default, the first line of text you enter into a new note becomes that note's title. This is what is displayed on the Notes listing screen/column.

When you're finished typing, dictating, or editing a note on the iPad, you may exit out of the app or select a different note, and your work is saved automatically.

On the iPhone, when you're finished typing or viewing a note, tap on the Done option. You can also use the Trash or Share options displayed in the top-right corner of the iPad and bottom of the iPhone screens.

Tap on the trash can icon to delete a note you're currently viewing.

**WHAT'S NEW** The most obvious new feature that's built in to the Notes app is integration with iOS 8's QuickType feature. As you're typing, displayed above the virtual keyboard are suggestions for words or phrases you're currently typing. Using this feature can speed up your text entry, plus improve your typing accuracy.

**NOTE** The Notes app has been integrated with the iPhone's or iPad's Dictation feature, so you don't have to manually type notes into the app. Instead, you can use your voice to dictate each note. Tap on the Microphone icon displayed within the virtual keyboard to activate the Dictation feature, and then begin speaking. Tap on the Microphone icon again when you're finished speaking. This feature works only when your iOS mobile device has Internet access.

The main Notes list enables you to see the titles for each note that's stored in the app. To delete a note from this screen, swipe your finger from right to left across the note's title. Confirm your decision by tapping on the Delete button. To open and view a note, tap on its listing.

**WHAT'S NEW** Another new iOS 8 feature offered by the Notes app is the ability to insert photos directly into your notes. To do this, as you're creating or editing a note, press and hold your finger down on the screen for two to three seconds, in the location where you want to insert the photo. When the Insert Photo tab appears, tap on it, and then select a photo that's stored in the Photos app on your iPhone or iPad. It is not possible, however, to resize the image after it's placed within a note.

**CAUTION** If you have Notes set up to sync with iCloud and your other iOS mobile devices and/or Mac(s), as soon as you delete or change a note, those changes are reflected almost immediately on iCloud and on your other computers and/or iOS mobile devices that are linked to the same account. There is no "undo" option.

Tap on the Share icon to send the note to one or more recipients via AirDrop, Mail, or the Messages app. You can also print or copy a note by tapping on the appropriate option displayed in the Share menu. When you use the copy command, the note's content gets saved in your iPhone or iPad's virtual clipboard so you can then paste the contents of the note into another app. It's also now possible to share Notes via Twitter or Facebook via the app's Share menu.

As you're creating or viewing a note, press and hold your finger on any word to make the Cut, Copy, Replace, BIU (bold, italics, underline), Define, and Insert Photo options appear (shown in Figure 13.19).

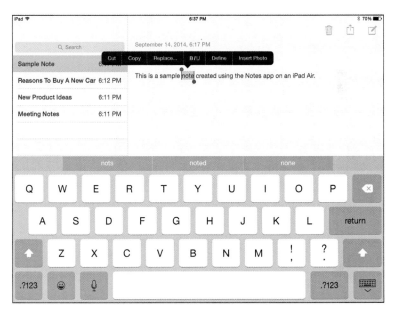

**FIGURE 13.19**

*Hold your finger on a word, and then highlight that work to access the Cut, Copy, Replace, BIU (bold, italics, underline), Define, and Insert Photo options.*

Tap on Define to look up the definition of the selected work. A pop-up window displaying the definition appears.

The Notes app's functionality is relatively basic and straightforward. However, this app comes in particularly handy to jot down ideas or memos without having to worry about formatting text (as you would when using a word processing app). To help keep you organized, the time and date you create each note is automatically saved with the note itself.

## QUICK TIPS FOR NOTES

- The Notes app enables you to set up separate accounts, within which you can store multiple notes. On the iPhone, to create or manage accounts, from the main Notes screen, tap on the Accounts option. To view all notes stored in all accounts, tap on the All Notes option. On the iPad, tap on the Accounts option displayed near the top-left corner of the screen to create or manage accounts, which are then listed on the left side of the screen.

- Anytime you include a phone number, address, date/time, website URL, or email address within a note, it becomes an active link. Tap on it to initiate a call (iPhone) or text message (iPhone or iPad) to that number or to add a contact to the Contacts app. Likewise, when an address is listed, tap on its link to launch the Maps app and view that address on a detailed map. Or when a website URL is included in a note, tap on it to launch Safari and visit that website.

- If there are sentences or phrases that you use often within your notes, set up keyboard shortcuts for them to reduce the amount of typing that's necessary. To do this, launch Settings, tap on General, select the Keyboard option, and then tap on Shortcuts.

(iOS 8) **WHAT'S NEW**   For iPad users, an alternative to acquiring an optional and external keyboard to use instead of the virtual keyboard is to attach the Touchfire keyboard overlay over your iPad's virtual keyboard (shown in Figure 13.20).

The keyboard overlay is made from a flexible and see-through silicone rubber material that fits over the virtual keyboard and gives the keys a more tactile feel. For some people, this accessory makes it faster and more accurate when touch typing using the virtual keyboard.

A version of the Touchfire keyboard overlay is available for each iPad model, including the iPad Air and iPad mini. Visit www.touchfire.com for more information.

**FIGURE 13.20**

*The optional Touchfire keyboard overlay fits over the virtual keyboard on any iPad or iPad mini, and gives the keys a more three-dimensional, tactile feel as you're typing.*

▇ When using the Dictation function with the Notes app, you can speak for up to 30 seconds at a time, allow the iPhone or iPad to translate what you've said into text and insert that text into your note, and then repeat the process as needed. Edit your text using the virtual keyboard.

▇ To save time entering text into the Notes app, don't forget you can also use Siri. Regardless of what you're doing on the iPhone or iPad, simply activate Siri and begin by saying the word "Note" or "Create Note." For example, say, "Create note: Gather old clothing to donate on Saturday."

▇ It's possible to sync your Notes with Outlook running on a PC. To do this, be sure to download the iCloud Control Panel software for Windows from Apple's website, and then turn on the syncing feature associated with the Notes app. Notes can also be synced if you use Outlook on a Mac or Microsoft's OWA app on the iPad.

▇ When you set up your iPhone or iPad to support alternative keyboard layouts, you can incorporate these alternative characters or emojis into your notes with ease. As you're typing, tap on the globe-shaped alternative keyboard key on the virtual keyboard, and then select the emoji or character you want to include in your note. To load an alternative keyboard layout, first launch Settings, tap on the General option, and then tap on the Keyboard option. From the Keyboards submenu, tap on the Keyboards option, and then tap on the Add New Keyboard… option. Select an alternative keyboard layout from the menu, such as Emoji.

14

# GET ACQUAINTED WITH THE MUSIC, VIDEOS, AND iTUNES STORE APPS

What do eight-track tapes, vinyl records, cassettes, and CDs have in common? These are all outdated methods for storing music that have been replaced by digital music players, such as Apple's iPods. The music in your personal library can now be kept in a purely digital format, transferred via the Internet, shared with family members, and listened to on a digital music player.

iOS 8 comes with the Music app preinstalled. This app serves as a full-featured digital music player, enabling you to play music and audiobooks. However, before playing your music or audio content, you first must load digital music files into your iPhone or iPad. There are several ways to do this, including the following:

- Purchase digital music directly from the iTunes Store (using the iTunes Store app) on your iPhone or iPad. An Internet connection is required. Your purchases are billed to the credit or debit card that's linked to your Apple ID.

**WHAT'S NEW** When you activate the iCloud Family Sharing feature, you can share some or all of your iTunes Store digital content purchases with up to five other family members. You decide what content gets shared and have the option of keeping some of your content private, so it's only available through your iCloud account on all of your own iOS mobile devices and Macs. Family Sharing only needs to be set up once. See Chapter 5, "Ways to Use iCloud's Latest Features with Your iPhone and/or iPad."

- You can purchase music using the iTunes software on your primary computer (used to connect to the iTunes Store), and then transfer content purchases and downloads to your iPhone or iPad using the iTunes Sync process or through iCloud.

- You can "rip" music from traditional CDs and convert it to a digital format using your primary computer, and then transfer the digital music files to your iOS device. For this, the free iTunes software on your computer, or other third-party software, is required.

- You can upgrade your iCloud account by adding the optional iTunes Match service, for $24.99 per year, and access your entire digital music library via iCloud, whether that music was purchased from the iTunes Store, ripped from your own CDs, or purchased/downloaded from another source. To learn more about iTunes Match, visit www.apple.com/itunes/itunes-match.

- You can shop for and download music from another source besides the iTunes Store, load that music into your primary computer, convert it to the proper format, and then transfer it to your iPhone or iPad using the iTunes Sync process, or use a specialized app to experience that content.

**NOTE** The Apple iTunes Store offers the world's largest collection of digital music that's available for purchase and download. This includes all the latest hits and new music from the biggest bands and recording artists, as well as up-and-coming and unsigned artists/bands. You can also find classic songs and oldies from all music genres.

The Music app is used for playing digital music and audiobooks. If you want to watch videos, TV show episodes, or movies that you've purchased and/or downloaded from the iTunes Store, use the Videos app, which also comes preinstalled with iOS 8.

**TIP** Instead of storing music on your iOS mobile device, you also have the option to stream music via the Internet. One way to do this is using iTunes Radio, an online-based streaming music service that enables you to listen to music for free via the Music app when your mobile device has Internet access. This service is similar to Pandora. Learn more about it later in this chapter.

**iOS 8 WHAT'S NEW** In addition to enabling you to stream music, iTunes Radio has begun offering streaming from news/talk radio stations, including National Public Radio (NPR).

To experience the free podcasts available from the iTunes Store, use Apple's own Podcasts app (which now comes preinstalled with iOS 8). To access a vast collection of educational and personal enrichment content available from the Apple, also for free, take advantage of the under-hyped iTunes U service. To do this, you need to download and install the free iTunes U app from the App Store.

**NOTE** When you stream content from the Internet, it gets transferred from the Internet directly to your iOS device. However, your iPhone or iPad does not save streamed content, just as your standalone television set doesn't record the shows you watch (unless you have a DVR or another recording device hooked up to it).

Streaming content from the Internet requires a specialized app, which is provided by the source of the content. Later in this chapter, you'll discover which apps to use to access specific on-demand television programming, movies, videos, radio stations, and other content that gets streamed (not downloaded) to your iPhone or iPad.

**TIP** If you're planning a trip where Internet access is not assured, plan to purchase and download several TV shows or movies, and store them on your iPhone or iPad to keep yourself entertained. Even if the airplane offers Wi-Fi, streaming audio or video services, such as Netflix, HuluPlus, and iTunes Radio, are typically disabled.

Without using an external battery pack, your iPhone or iPad should give you around 10 hours of battery life, during which you can watch videos (TV shows or movies) you've previously downloaded.

# TIPS FOR USING THE MUSIC APP

The Music app displays the music in your digital music library that's currently stored on your device (as shown in Figure 14.1 on the iPad). It enables you to play one song at a time, listen to entire albums, or create personalized playlists that can provide hours' worth of music listening without having to tinker with the app.

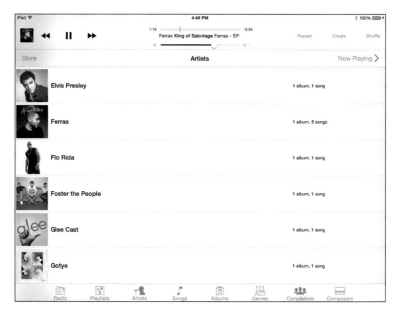

**FIGURE 14.1**

*Shown here is the main Artists screen of the Music app (on the iPad). On the iPhone, the same features and functionality are available from the Music app, but the menu layout is different due to the smartphone's smaller screen size.*

If you have the Music app set up to work with iCloud, all the music you've purchased from the iTunes Store (in addition to what's stored on your iOS device) is displayed. Songs that are accessible to you for download via iCloud have an iCloud icon displayed next to their listings. Tap on the iCloud icon to download the song (or album) and store it on your iPhone or iPad.

☑ **TIP**   To initially set up the Music and iTunes Store apps to work with iCloud, launch Settings and tap on the iTunes & App Store option. Near the top of the iTunes & App Store submenu, enter your Apple ID and password. This needs to be done only once.

✐ **NOTE**   When you download music (or other iTunes Store content) to your iPhone or iPad, you are using storage space that could otherwise be used to hold more apps, photos, or other types of data, but your purchased content is then accessible at anytime, without the need for a continuous Internet connection.

☑ **TIP**   The Music app works nicely with Siri. Use your voice to command Siri to play music from a specific artist, a specific playlist, or to play a specific song, just by speaking its title. This applies to music stored on your iPhone or iPad.

For example, if you want to hear "Shake It Off" from Taylor Swift, and it's stored on your iOS device, activate Siri and say, "Play Shake It Off." Or to play a Maroon 5 song, say "Play a song from Maroon 5." It's also possible to use Siri to pause, restart, skip, or shuffle your music.

Thanks to iOS 8's multitasking capabilities, you can play music from the Music app while using other apps on your iPhone or iPad. When music is playing, you can even place your iOS device into Sleep mode, and the music continues playing unless you pause it first.

☑ **TIP**   In addition to controlling your music from the Music app, similar controls are offered from the Lock screen (while music is playing) or from the Control Center. To access Control Center, swipe your finger upward from the bottom of the screen. Using these Music app controls, it's easy to play, pause, fast forward, or review the last song, playlist, or album (or audiobook) that was loaded into the Music app (as shown in Figure 14.2). These controls also work with iTunes Radio, as well as other apps that are capable of playing in the background, such as the Podcast player, Pandora, or Spotify.

To access Control Center from the Lock screen, it's necessary to turn on this feature. To do this, launch Settings, tap on Control Center, and then turn on the virtual switch associated with the Access on Lock Screen option.

**FIGURE 14.2**

*Access the Music app controls from the iPhone or iPad's Control Center. From here, it's possible to play, pause, fast forward, rewind, move between music tracks, and adjust the volume.*

It's also possible to control the Music app from the controls found on the cord of the Apple EarPods or Apple's original ear buds, as well as on some other optional corded headphones.

**iOS 8 WHAT'S NEW** When the Apple Watch is released in 2015, it can be used to remotely control the music that's stored in your iPhone. This includes streaming iTunes Radio via your iPhone's Internet connection. You'll be able to store and play back music in the Apple Watch, as well.

To fully manage your digital music library, create playlists, and play songs or albums using the Music app, launch the app from the Home screen. Displayed along the bottom of the screen are various icons for selecting music-related options.

> **NOTE** From Settings, it's possible to customize some of the Music app–related options available to you. To do this, launch Settings, and then select the Music option. In addition to turning on or off the iTunes Match service (if you've subscribed to it), you can tinker with the EQ (to adjust how the audio sounds) or impose a maximum volume limit when listening to music (shown in Figure 14.3).
>
> If you want your iPhone or iPad to download music from iTunes and/or iCloud only when you're connected to the Internet using a Wi-Fi connection (as opposed to a cellular data connection, which uses up some of your monthly wireless data allocation), from Settings, select the iTunes & App Stores option. Then, adjust the virtual on/off switch associated with the Use Cellular Data option, and turn off this feature. When you do this, iCloud and iTunes Match functionality are disabled in the Music app unless a Wi-Fi connection is present.

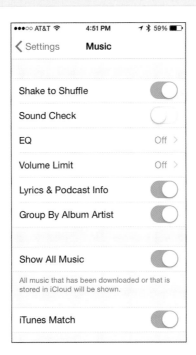

**FIGURE 14.3**
*You can adjust Music app–related options from within Settings (shown here on the iPhone 5s).*

☑ **TIP** Quickly find any song stored on your iPhone or iPad by using a keyword search. After launching the Music app, place your finger near the center of the screen and swipe downward to access the app's Search field. Then, enter a song title (or a portion of a title), an artist's name, an album title, or any other keyword that's relevant to your music to find specific music content stored in your iOS device.

Enter your keyword or search phrase, and then tap the Search key on the keyboard to see the results. Tap on the search result of your choice to select a specific song, album, or artist.

You can also use the Spotlight Search feature from the Home screen to locate music or any purchased content that's stored in your iOS mobile device.

## MUSIC APP CONTROLS ON THE iPHONE

When you launch the Music app on your iPhone, you can then tap on the Radio, Playlists, Artists, Songs, or More icons that are displayed along the bottom of the screen. The default selection is Radio, which gives you access to the free iTunes Radio service.

After tapping on the Playlist, Artists, or Songs icons, the Store option is displayed in the upper-left corner of the screen. Tap on it to launch the iTunes Store app via the Internet and shop for new music.

Here's more information about how to use the Music app's five command icons (shown in Figure 14.4):

- ▪ **Radio**—Access the online-based iTunes Radio streaming music service and listen to music for free. A continuous Internet connection is required.

- ▪ **Playlists**—Create and manage personalized playlists in the Music app. A playlist is a "digital mix tape" that you manually compile from music that's in your digital music library. You can choose the songs, as well as the song order.

☑ **NOTE** An iCloud icon displayed to the right of a song listing (see Figure 14.4) indicates that you own the music but it's not currently stored in your device. Tap the iCloud icon to download it from your iCloud account. By tapping on the title, if you have a continuous Internet connection available, you can also stream that music directly from your iCloud account by tapping on its title or cover artwork (as opposed to the iCloud icon).

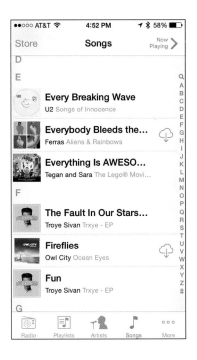

**FIGURE 14.4**

*When you tap on the Songs icon at the bottom of the Music app, you'll see an alphabetized listing of songs you own.*

- **Artists**—View an alphabetized listing of all recording artists and music groups whose music you own. Tap on an artist's name or graphic to view the albums or individual songs you own from that artist, music group, or band.

- **Songs**—View a complete alphabetical listing of all songs stored in your iOS device, sorted by song title.

**TIP**   If you rotate your iPhone to view the Music app in landscape mode, you can browse through your music by viewing album cover artwork using the Cover Flow menu (shown in Figure 14.5). Swipe your finger across the screen to view album artwork. Tap on the album cover to view the songs you own from that album, and then tap on a song listing to play it.

**FIGURE 14.5**

*The Cover Flow menu on the iPhone enables you to scroll through the music you own on your iPhone.*

- ■ **More**—View a listing of songs stored in your iPhone or iPad sorted by Albums, Compilations, Composers, or Genres.

> ☑ TIP   You can change the menu buttons that are displayed along the bottom of the Music app's screen on the iPhone. To do this, launch the Music app, tap on the More button, and then tap on the Edit button at the top-left corner of the screen.
>
> From the Configure screen that's displayed, one at a time, drag one of the command buttons shown at the top of the screen to the desired location along the menu bar that the Music app displays along the bottom of the screen. As you do this, keep in mind that the More button remains constant. Tap the Done option when you're finished.

## CREATE A MUSIC APP PLAYLIST

Playlists are personalized collections of songs that you can group together and then play at any time. Each playlist is given its own title and can include as many songs from your personal music collection as you wish.

You can create separate playlists for working out, to enjoy while you drive, to listen to when you're depressed, or to dance to when you feel like cutting loose. Unless you fill up the device's storage capacity, there is no limit to the number of separate playlists you can create and store on your iOS device. If you have your iOS mobile device set up to sync with your iCloud account, your Playlists sync with your other iOS mobile devices and Macs automatically.

Here's how to create a playlist:

> **TIP** When listening to a playlist, you can play the songs in order, or have the Music app randomize the song order (using the Shuffle command). A playlist can also be put into an infinite loop, so it continuously plays until you press Pause. This can also be done when listening to an album or other grouping of songs.

1. Launch the Music app, and tap on the Playlist button at the bottom of the screen.

2. To create a new playlist, tap on the New Playlist… (+) option displayed near the top of the screen.

3. Enter your own title for your new playlist, such as Workout Music or Favorite Songs, and tap the Save option.

4. From the Playlists menu screen, tap on your newly created Playlist (which currently has no contents). Then, tap on the Songs icon at the bottom of the screen.

5. When the Songs screen appears, one at a time, tap on the red-and-white plus sign icon that's associated with each song that you want to add to your Playlist, as shown in Figure 14.6. All songs currently stored on your device (or available to you from iCloud) are listed in the Songs screen. Tap the Done option to save your selections.

After you finish creating your playlist, it automatically appears on your screen (shown in Figure 14.7). The name of your new playlist displays near the top of the screen with the songs it contains listed below.

Use the Edit, Clear, or Delete buttons below the playlist title to manage or modify your newly created playlist. Tap the Edit button to delete individual songs from the playlist or change the order of the songs, as shown in Figure 14.8. To delete a song, tap on the negative sign icon. To move a song, place your finger on the Move icon displayed to the right of a song's title (it looks like three horizontal lines) and drag it up or down to reposition that song in the playlist's order. Tap the Done button when you're finished editing your playlist.

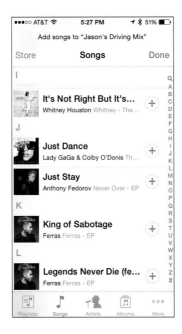

**FIGURE 14.6**

*Choose the songs you want to add to your playlist by tapping the + icon (on the right) to add each song.*

**FIGURE 14.7**

*A sample playlist screen shown here on the iPhone 5s.*

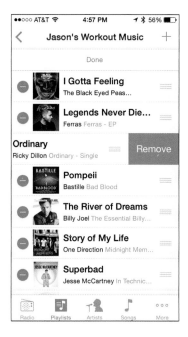

**FIGURE 14.8**

*The Playlist screen of the Music app enables you to play, edit, or manage a selected playlist. It's shown here in Edit mode. From here, you can delete songs or arrange them.*

Tap the Clear button to keep the master playlist file but remove all the songs from it. Or tap the Delete button to delete the playlist altogether from your iOS device (and your iCloud account).

> **NOTE** If you notice an iCloud icon displayed at the bottom of the playlist, this means one or more of the songs you've selected is stored on your iCloud account but not on your iPhone or iPad. Tap the iCloud icon to download that music from your iCloud account and add it to your playlist. Because you own the music, you are not charged to download it again.

To listen to your newly created playlist, return to the main Playlist screen by tapping on the Playlists button at the bottom of the screen (if you're not already there), and tap on the playlist title of your choice. Next, tap on a song from that playlist and begin listening. To start the playlist from the beginning, tap on the first song listed. Tap on the Shuffle option to continue playing the playlist in a random order.

# FIND YOUR WAY AROUND THE NOW PLAYING SCREEN

The Music app's Now Playing screen on the iPhone (shown in Figure 14.9) shows what song is currently playing. You'll also see commands to play or pause the music and rewind or fast forward. A volume slider, for adjusting the music's volume, is also displayed.

**FIGURE 14.9**
*Use the command icons on the Now Playing screen to control the current song or move to the previous/next track.*

> **TIP** As you're viewing the Now Playing screen, tap on the song's title to replace the title listing with the app's song rating system. Tap on between one and five stars to rate the song. You can later sort songs based on the rating you've given them.

If you press and hold the rewind or fast forward icon, you can move backward or advance within the song that's currently playing. However, if you tap on one of these two icons, you jump to the previous track or advance to the next track in your playlist, respectively.

Displayed along the top of the screen is a left-pointing arrow icon that enables you to return to the previous screen you were viewing. In the upper-right corner of the screen is an icon that enables you to view a text-based listing that includes additional information about the song or album that's playing. This screen also shows what other music you own from that same band or artist.

Album- or artist-related artwork is displayed in the center of the Now Playing screen and, below that, the song's title that's currently playing is displayed, along with the artist's name and the album name with which the song is associated. (Refer to Figure 14.9 to see an example of the Now Playing screen on the iPhone.)

Just above the song title information is the song's time slider. Use your finger to move this slider right to advance within the song, or left to move back in the song manually. On the left of this slider, a timer shows how much of the song you've already listened to. On the right side of the slider is a timer that shows how much of the song is remaining.

If you are listening to a playlist, displayed along the bottom of the Now Playing screen are three additional options: Repeat Playlist, Create, and Shuffle. Repeat Playlist enables music in that Playlist to keep repeating until it's manually paused. Use the Create option to create a new Playlist from scratch. Tap on the right-most shuffle icon to shuffle the order of the songs in the playlist or album you're listening to.

If available, the AirPlay icon can also be seen on this screen. It enables you to stream your music from your iOS mobile device to your home theater system or television speakers (via Apple TV), AirPlay-compatible external audio speakers, or Bluetooth-compatible (wireless) headphones.

When music is playing, you can control the volume from the onscreen volume slider, using the Volume Up or Volume Down buttons on the side of your iOS device, or using the controls found on the cord of your Apple earbuds or Apple EarPods.

Also while music is playing, you can exit out of the Now Playing screen and access other areas of the Music app, use another app altogether (thanks to the multitasking feature of your iPhone or iPad), or place your device into Sleep mode and continue listening to the music.

## MUSIC APP CONTROLS ON iPAD

When you launch Music on your iPad and then tap on the Playlist, Artists, Songs, Albums, Genres, Compilations, or Composers icon (shown in Figure 14.10), the Store option appears near the top-left corner of the screen. Tap it to access the iTunes Store via the Internet to shop for new music using the iTunes app.

**FIGURE 14.10**
*This is what the Music app looks like on the iPad when the Albums button (located near the bottom center of the screen) is selected.*

> **TIP** Have you ever been listening to the radio, watching TV, or riding in an elevator and want to know the name of a song that's playing so you can purchase it? Well, there's an app for that. Download the free Shazam app from the App Store. When you hear a song you want to identify, launch the app. It "listens" to what's playing, and then identifies the song for you, complete with its title and artist. It then launches the iTunes Store app, giving you the option to purchase the song. This is one of the most popular, free iPhone/iPad apps of all time. Another similar app is called SoundHound.

On the iPad, displayed near the bottom of the screen are eight command buttons labeled Radio, Playlists, Artists, Songs, Albums, Genres, Compilations, and Composers. These command buttons function just like on the iPhone, as described earlier in this chapter. Tap on a listing to access the music controls and begin playing a song.

When the music controls are displayed, near the upper-left corner are the Rewind, Play/Pause, and Track Forward icons. Near the top center of the screen, the song's time slider, song title, artist information, and volume slider are displayed. Look near the top-right corner of the screen to find the Repeat and Shuffle All options.

Move the volume slider to the right to increase the volume or to the left to decrease it. You can also use the volume control buttons on the side of your iPad for this purpose, or, if applicable, the volume control buttons on the cord of your headset. If available, the AirPlay icon is displayed on the Music app screen, as well.

# MORE MUSIC APP FEATURES

After music is playing on your iPhone or iPad, you can exit the Music app and use your iOS device for other purposes. The music keeps playing. It automatically pauses, however, if you receive an incoming call on your iPhone or an incoming FaceTime call on your iPhone or iPad.

After you purchase a song from iTunes, it gets downloaded to the computer or device from which it was purchased, and is also instantly made available, at no extra charge, to all of your other Macs, PCs, and iOS devices via iCloud.

As you're looking at a song listing or album graphic in the Music app (after tapping on the Songs, Artists, or Albums button), you can delete that content from your iOS device to free up storage space. If it's a song listing, swipe your finger across that listing, from right to left. When the Delete button appears (as shown in Figure 14.11), tap on it.

**FIGURE 14.11**

*You can delete one song at a time from your iOS device by swiping your finger from right to left across the listing, and then tapping on the Delete button.*

Keep in mind that when you delete a song or album from your iOS mobile device, that music remains in your iTunes library (and stored on iCloud), so you can re-download it (or stream it) at anytime, as long as your iPhone or iPad has Internet access.

> **TIP**  After you've downloaded one or more singles (individual songs) from an artist or band's album, you can later purchase the rest of the album and get credit for the eligible song(s) you've already purchased by tapping on the Complete My Album option as you're shopping for music from the iTunes Store.
>
> To use the Complete My Album feature, launch the iTunes Store app, tap on the Music icon (displayed at the bottom of the screen), and then access the listing for the Album you want to purchase. You can use the Search field to find the album quickly. If you already own songs from that album, the Price icon automatically displays a prorated price, and it has a Complete My Album label next to it. The prorated price is based on how many songs you already own from the album.

Apple wants you to shop for your music from the iTunes Store for obvious reasons; however, you do have other options. From your primary computer, you can shop for music from other sources, import the music files into the iTunes software, and then perform an iTunes Sync. Or you can upgrade to the iTunes Match service and gain access to your entire digital music library via iCloud.

Some other sources for legally buying and downloading music include the Amazon MP3 music store (www.amazonmp3.com), Napster (www.napster.com), eMusic (www.eMusic.com), and Rhapsody (www.rhapsody.com).

## STREAM MUSIC TO YOUR iPHONE OR iPAD USING iTUNES RADIO

While the iTunes Store enables you to purchase and then download music, Apple's iTunes Radio service enables you to stream music from the Internet to your iOS mobile device (or Apple Watch) and listen to it as you would listen to a traditional radio station. However, instead of being beamed over radio waves, iTunes Radio programming is sent from the Internet to your mobile device and played using the Music app.

iTunes Radio is a free way to hear new music from popular and up-and-coming artists, listen to songs from your favorite artists that you don't own, or enjoy a selection of songs from a specific music genre or era (such as the 70s or 80s).

iTunes Radio programming does include some commercials (unless you're an iTunes Match subscriber, in which case the programming is commercial free); however, it is fully customizable. You can choose your favorite artists, bands, music genres, or eras, and then hear music that's custom programmed to your liking. As you're listening to a station, you can also pause and then resume the music at anytime.

As long as your mobile device has Internet access (Wi-Fi is preferred), you can control and stream iTunes Radio from the Music app by tapping on the Radio icon that's displayed at the bottom of the app screen.

> **TIP**  When listening to iTunes Radio, if you hear a song you like and want to buy and immediately download it from the iTunes Store, tap on the price icon displayed near the top-right corner of the screen.

The first time you use iTunes Radio, you're given the options to Learn More or Start Listening. Tap Start Listening to get started with iTunes Radio (shown in Figure 14.12), then choose from one of the hundreds of pre-created stations, or tap on the Add a Station icon to create your own custom station from scratch.

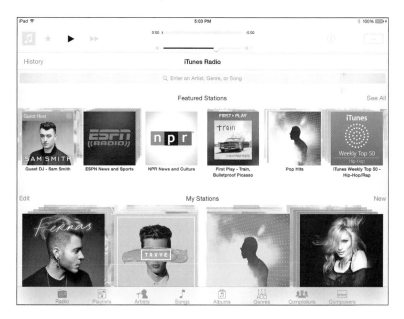

**FIGURE 14.12**

*From the main iTunes Radio screen, select a Featured Station or create your own.*

After selecting or creating a station, the music controls are displayed near the top of the screen. These include a Play/Pause icon as well as a Fast Forward icon. Instead of a Rewind icon, however, there's a star-shaped Favorite icon. When you hear a song you like, tap on this icon. A submenu appears with three options: Play More Like This, Never Play This Song, and Add To iTunes Wish List.

By tapping on the Play More Like This option, iTunes Radio learns about your music preferences over time and fine tunes the custom programming it offers so that the songs played are always to your liking.

If a song does play that you don't like, tap on the Fast Forward icon to skip to the next song on the station's playlist. There's also a Never Play This Song option, which prevents it from being added to future programming you listen to.

> ☑ **TIP**   As music is playing via iTunes Radio, tap on the Info icon (a lowercase "i" in a circle) to display more information about the artist or band, purchase their song or album, or create a new custom iTunes Radio station based around that artist, group, song, or music genre.

In addition to iTunes Radio, there are several other popular streaming music services with their own proprietary apps for the iPhone and iPad. For example, there's Pandora, iHeartRadio, and Spotify. Many traditional radio stations, as well as NPR and Sirius/XM Satellite Radio, also have their own apps that enable you to stream live and on-demand audio programming from the Internet to your mobile device. Some of these other services either charge to hear ad-free programming or have a subscription fee associated with them.

## USE THE VIDEOS APP TO WATCH TV SHOWS, MOVIES, AND MORE

After you purchase and download TV show episodes, movies, or music videos from the iTunes Store, that video-based content can be enjoyed on your iPhone and/or iPad using the Videos app. It can also be viewed on your primary computer using the iTunes software and shared between devices via iCloud. If you have Apple TV, you can also stream videos to your home theater system.

After you've downloaded or transferred iTunes Store video content to your iPhone or iPad, it is accessible from the Videos app. When you launch the Videos app on your iPhone or iPad, you'll see multiple tabs on the screen, based on the types of video content stored on your device (as shown in Figure 14.13). These tabs are labeled TV Shows, Rentals, Movies, and/or Music Videos. On the iPhone, they're displayed near the bottom of the screen, whereas on the iPad, they're displayed near the top center.

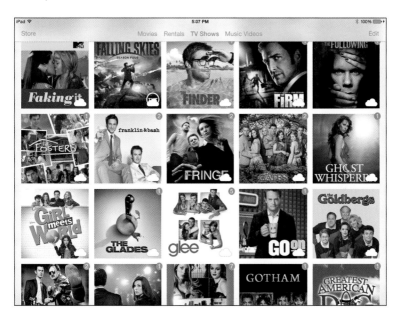

**FIGURE 14.13**

*The Videos app shows what video content you have stored on your device. Content is categorized based on whether it's a TV show episode, movie, movie rental, or music video. Here, the TV Shows tab (near the top center of the screen) is selected.*

> **NOTE** If you have movies rented from iTunes, as opposed to movies you own stored on your iOS device, a tab labeled Rentals is displayed in addition to or instead of a tab labeled Movies. Movie rentals can be viewed only on the device on which they were rented, and cannot be transferred from one iOS mobile device to another. You can, however, use AirPlay to play rented movies from your iPhone or iPad on an HD TV that's equipped with Apple TV.

When you tap on the TV Shows, Movies, Rentals, or Music Videos tab, thumbnail graphics representing that video content is displayed. To begin playing a video, tap on its thumbnail graphic.

If an iCloud icon appears in the thumbnail graphic, it means you own that content but it is not currently stored on your mobile device. By tapping on the iCloud icon, you can automatically download that video content from your iCloud account to the device you're using.

> **TIP** When looking at the graphic thumbnails for TV shows you own, the number displayed in a blue circle near the top-right corner indicates how many episodes of that particular TV series you own. Tap on the thumbnail to see a listing of specific episodes and then view them.

To delete video content from your iPhone, access the listing for that particular TV show episode, movie, or music video, and then swipe your finger from right to left across the listing. Tap the Delete button to confirm your decision.

On the iPad, to delete movies, tap on the Edit button near the top-right corner of the screen, and then tap on the "X" icon that appears on the movie thumbnail listing(s) you want to delete. You can use this same method to delete TV show episodes or entire seasons.

After you delete iTunes Store–purchased content from your iPhone or iPad, you can always re-download it from your iCloud account for free.

To shop for additional video content from the iTunes Store while using the Videos app, tap on the Store button displayed in the upper-left corner of the screen.

To play a video, tap on a thumbnail representing the video that you want to watch. If you've downloaded a TV show, for example, a new screen appears listing all episodes from that TV series currently stored on your iOS device (as shown in Figure 14.14). Tap on the episode of your choice to begin playing it. You can also tap on the Play icon.

> **NOTE** In Figure 14.14, to the right of some episode listings is a round Downloading icon. This indicates the episode is currently downloading from iCloud to the iOS mobile device.
>
> The iCloud icon that's displayed to the right of some episode listings indicates that episode is owned but not currently stored on the iPad that's being used. It can, however, be downloaded from iCloud at anytime by tapping on this icon.

For music videos or movies, a similar information screen pertaining to that content is displayed. Tap on the Play icon to begin watching your movie or music video.

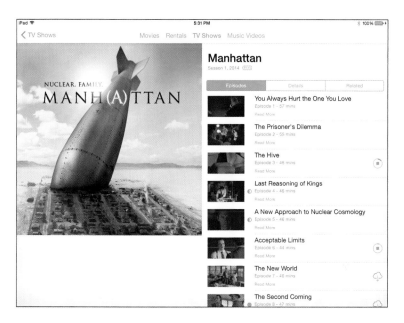

**FIGURE 14.14**

*Multiple episodes of the same TV series are grouped together for easy access and viewing.*

**TIP** When playing video content, you can hold your iPhone or iPad in either portrait or landscape mode. However, the video window is significantly larger if you position your iOS mobile device sideways and use landscape mode.

If applicable based on the video content you're watching, you can instantly switch between full-screen mode and letterbox mode as your onscreen viewing option by tapping the icon displayed in the upper-right corner of the screen.

While video content is playing on your iPhone or iPad, it displays in full-screen mode. Tap anywhere on the screen to reveal the onscreen command icons used for controlling the video as you're watching it. These controls are identical on the iPhone and iPad (shown in Figure 14.15). When a video is playing, these controls disappear from the screen automatically after a few seconds. Tap anywhere on the screen to make them reappear.

**FIGURE 14.15**
*The onscreen icons for controlling the video you're watching on your iOS device.*

**iOS 8 WHAT'S NEW** If you're watching a purchased movie acquired from the iTunes Store, below the Play, Rewind, and Fast Forward controls you might discover tabs that enable you to access movie-related "extras" that would otherwise be made available as part of the DVD or Blu-Ray version of the movie. Tap on any of these tabs to access the bonus content, which are movie-specific.

Along the top center of the screen is a time slider. On either end of this slider are timers. To the left is a timer that displays how much of the video you've already watched. On the right of the slider is a timer that displays how much time in the video remains. Tap on the Done button in the upper-left corner of the screen to exit the video you're watching.

**TIP** To manually fast-forward or rewind while watching a video, place your finger on the dot icon that appears on the timer slider. Move it to the right to advance within the video, or move it to the left to rewind within the video.

Near the bottom center of the screen as you're watching video content are the Rewind and Fast Forward icons. Tap on the Rewind icon to move back by scene or chapter, or tap the Fast Forward icon to advance to the next scene or chapter in the video (just as you would while watching a DVD). Press and hold the Rewind or Fast Forward icon to rewind or fast forward while viewing the onscreen content. You can rewind or advance by a few seconds at a time.

Tap the Play icon to play the video. When the video is playing, the Play icon transforms into a Pause icon, used to pause the video.

> **NOTE** If you pause a video and then exit the Videos app, you can pick up exactly where you left off watching the video when you relaunch the Videos app. This information is automatically saved.

To the left of these three icons is the volume control slider. Use it to manually adjust the volume of the audio. You can also use the volume control buttons located on the side of your iPhone or iPad or, if applicable, the volume control buttons on the cord of your headset (such as the Apple EarPods).

Located near the lower-right corner of the screen while a video is playing (when the controls are visible) are the Captions and AirPlay icons. Tap on the Captions icon to adjust captions and/or switch between audio languages, if the video content you're watching supports these features. If not available, the text-bubble icon is not visible.

Tap on the AirPlay option to stream the video from your mobile device to your television set or home theater system when using an Apple TV. If you have Bluetooth- or AirPlay-compatible speakers, you can stream just the audio from a TV show or movie, for example, to external speakers or wireless headphones.

> **NOTE** You must use Wi-Fi to stream video from your iOS mobile device to your HD television via Apple TV. Both the iOS mobile device and Apple TV must be linked to the same wireless network.

☑ TIP   From the iTunes Store, it's possible to purchase TV show episodes (or entire seasons from your favorite series), as well as full-length movies. In addition, you can rent certain movies.

When you rent a move from the iTunes Store, it remains on your device for 30 days before it automatically deletes itself, whether or not the content has been viewed. However, after you press Play in the Videos app and begin watching rented content, you have access to that video for only 24 hours before it deletes itself. During that 24-hour period, you can watch and rewatch the movie as often as you'd like.

The first time you tap Play to watch a rented movie, you're prompted to confirm your choice. This starts the 24-hour clock and allows the rented movie to begin playing.

Unlike movies you purchase from iTunes (that you can load into all of your computers and/or iOS mobile devices that are linked to the same Apple ID account), rented movies can be stored on only one computer, Apple TV, or iOS mobile device at a time. You can, however, transfer unwatched rented movies between devices.

# USE THE iTUNES STORE APP TO ACQUIRE NEW MUSIC, TV SHOWS, MOVIES, AND MORE

The iTunes Store app comes preinstalled with iOS 8 and is used to acquire music, movies, TV shows, audiobooks, and ringtones.

To utilize this app (shown in Figure 14.16), your iOS mobile device will need Internet access. For smaller-sized files, such as songs, albums, or ringtones, a cellular data connection can be used. However, for larger-sized files, such as TV show episodes and movies, you must use a Wi-Fi Internet connection.

📝 NOTE   You can access the iTunes Store using the iTunes Store app by launching it from the Home screen or directly from the Music or Videos app by tapping on the Store button.

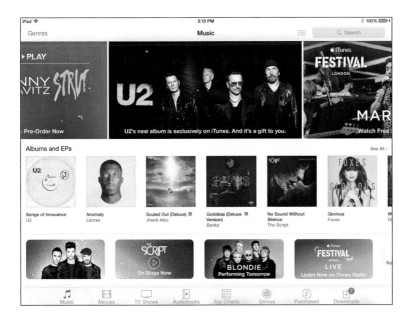

**FIGURE 14.16**

*The iTunes Store app is used to purchase content and acquire free music and videos.*

On the iPhone, displayed along the bottom of the iTunes Store screen are five command icons: Music, Movies, TV Shows, Search, and More. Tap on the More icon to access Audiobooks, Ringtones, Genius, and Purchased options.

On the iPad, seven command icons are displayed along the bottom of the screen, which left to right are labeled Music, Movies, TV Shows, Audiobooks, Top Charts, Genius, and Purchased. The Search field is displayed in the top-right corner of the screen.

To shop for music (or acquire free music), tap on the Music icon. Likewise, to purchase or rent movies, tap on the Movies icon. For TV shows (either individual episodes or entire seasons of a series), tap on the TV Shows icon. Use the Search feature to quickly find audio or video content using keywords.

> **TIP**  After you tap on the More icon on the iPhone, tap Purchased to view all past purchases from the iTunes Store. As content is downloading, you can view the progress of that download by tapping on the Purchased icon.

Just like when using the App Store to acquire new apps for your mobile device, when you make a purchase from the iTunes Store, all charges are automatically billed to the credit or debit card you have linked with your Apple ID or offset against any credit your account might have from redeemed gift cards.

> **TIP** You can redeem an iTunes Gift Card and add the credit to the Apple ID account used for making online purchases from the iTunes Store, App Store, iBookstore, or Newsstand. When you select the Redeem option, it's now possible to scan the physical gift card using the camera that's built in to your iOS mobile device so you don't have to manually type the long redemption code.

When you make a purchase from your iPhone or iPad, it immediately gets downloaded to that mobile device and, at the same time, gets stored in your iCloud account. The online storage space required for purchased iTunes Store content is provided free of charge, and does not count against the 5GB of free online storage space your iCloud account comes with.

The same content can then be downloaded and experienced on your other Macs and iOS mobile devices that are linked to the same iCloud account. It's also possible to share this content with up to five other family members if you have iCloud's Family Sharing featured turned on.

> **TIP** The iTunes Store offers a Complete My Season feature for TV show seasons. If you purchase one or more single episodes of a TV series (from a specific season), you can later return to the iTunes Store and purchase the rest of the episodes from that season at a reduced price (based on how many episodes from that season you already own). This feature works just like the Complete My Album feature but relates to TV shows.

> **NOTE** If you're interested in purchasing and listening to audiobooks on your iOS mobile device, thousands of titles are available from the iTunes Store and can be played using the Music app. However, the Audible.com service also offers a vast and ever-growing audiobook library. Audiobook titles can be purchased online and enjoyed using the free Audible app that's available from the App Store.

# QUICKLY FIND TV EPISODES YOU WANT TO PURCHASE ON iTUNES

When shopping for TV show episodes to purchase and watch using the iTunes Store app, tap on the TV shows button that's displayed near the bottom of the screen. Shows are displayed by series name. The search results display the TV show by season number and by available episodes.

Tap on the TV series artwork icon that's associated with the season from which you want to purchase episodes to reveal a listing of individual episodes from that season, in chronological order, based on original airdate. The most recently aired episodes are toward the bottom of the list, so scroll down.

At the top of the screen, you also have the option of purchasing the entire season at a discounted rate, plus choosing between high definition (HD) or standard definition (SD) video quality. The HD version of TV shows utilize much larger file sizes and take up much more internal storage space within your device, but they look much better when you watch them.

To save money, purchase an entire season of your favorite show's current season. This is called a Season Pass. Then, when a new episode airs each week and becomes available from the iTunes Store (about 24 hours later), it can be downloaded to your iOS device and made available to you via iCloud using a Wi-Fi Internet connection. You'll also receive a weekly email, plus Notification Center alerts from Apple telling you when each new episode in your Season Pass is available.

When you shop for TV episodes from the iTunes Store (via the iTunes app), those files get downloaded and stored on your iPhone or iPad. They're commercial free and available to watch whenever you wish. They're also permanently accessible via your iCloud account to be downloaded to any computer, iOS device, or Apple TV device that's linked to the same iCloud account. Once an episode is download to your iPhone or iPad, an Internet connection is no longer needed to watch it.

> **TIP** Each week, the iTunes Store offers free episodes of featured TV shows. To discover which episodes are being offered, launch the iTunes Store app, tap on the TV Shows icon, scroll down to the bottom of the screen, and under the TV Shows Quick Links heading, tap on Free TV Episodes. Then, from the Free TV Episodes screen, look under the Free Full-Length Episodes heading to see what's currently available. You can often find the pilot episode for new shows being offered for a limited time before or just after its television debut.

> **📝 NOTE**  Keep in mind that, without commercials, a one-hour program appears in the iTunes Store (and in the Videos app) as being between 42 and 44 minutes long, while a half-hour program appears as between 21 and 24 minutes long.

# STREAMING VIDEO ON YOUR iOS MOBILE DEVICE

To stream video content to your iPhone or iPad from the Internet, you must use a specialized app, based on where the content is originating from on the Internet.

Whenever you're streaming video content from the Internet, you can pause the video at any time. Depending on the app, you also can exit the app partway through a video and resume watching it from where you left off when you relaunch the app later.

> **❗ CAUTION**  The capability to stream content from the Internet and experience it on your iPhone or iPad gives you on-demand access to a wide range of programming; however, streaming audio or video content requires a tremendous amount of data to be transferred to your iOS device. Therefore, if you use a cellular data connection, your monthly wireless data allocation can quickly get used up. So, when you're streaming Internet content, it's best to use a Wi-Fi connection.
>
> Not only does a Wi-Fi connection often allow data to be transferred to your iPhone or iPad at faster speeds, there's also no limit as to how much data you can send or receive. Plus, when streaming video content, you can often view it at a higher resolution using a Wi-Fi connection.

The following sections describe some of the popular apps for streaming TV shows, movies, and other video content directly from the Internet.

Keep in mind that many cable television service providers (such as Xfinity/Comcast and Time Warner) and satellite TV service providers, as well as individual television networks (ABC, NBC, CBS, The CW, USA Network, Lifetime, SyFy, and so on), and even specific TV shows, often have their own proprietary apps available for streaming content from the Internet directly to your iPhone and/or iPad.

> ## NOTE
> Some premium cable networks, including HBO, Showtime, Starz, and Cinemax, have their own proprietary apps that can be used to stream on-demand content. These apps are HBO Go, Showtime Anytime, Starz Play, and MaxGo, respectively.
>
> To gain full access to these free apps, sign in using a username and password provided by your cable or satellite TV provider. You must already subscribe to the premium channel as part of your cable or satellite TV service. In some cases, a limited programming selection can be streamed if you're not a paid subscriber.

There are also paid streaming services, such as Netflix and HuluPlus, that offer vast libraries of TV shows and movies available for streaming. These services charge a flat monthly fee to stream as much programming as you want to your computer(s) and mobile device(s).

When you stream TV episodes from the Internet using a specialized app, this programming does not get stored on your iOS device and is available only when your iPhone or iPad has a constant connection to the Internet while you're watching that content. In many cases, a Wi-Fi connection is required.

> ## NOTE
> As a general rule, free streamed programming from a television network app (from ABC, NBC, or CBS, for example) includes commercials. Programming from a premium cable network that you're already paying for through your cable TV service (such as HBO or Showtime) is commercial free, as are streamed TV shows or movies accessed through a paid service, such as Netflix or HuluPlus. When you purchase TV show episodes from the iTunes Store, they are always commercial free.

> ## CAUTION
> Most of the streaming video apps for the iPhone and iPad work only in the United States. If you try to access HBO Go from abroad, for example, the app will not work.

## HULUPLUS

Full-length and commercial-free episodes from thousands of current and classic TV series (as well as an ever-growing library of movies) are available on your iOS device using the HuluPlus app. However, although the app itself is free, the HuluPlus service requires you to pay a flat monthly subscription fee ($7.99) to access and view content.

HuluPlus members can access season passes to current TV shows airing on ABC, FOX, and NBC, for example, or pick and choose from thousands of episodes from classic TV series. A Wi-Fi connection is recommended, although the app does work with a 3G or 4G cellular Internet connection.

The HuluPlus app enables you to pause programs and resume them later, plus create a queue of shows to watch on your tablet.

> **MORE INFO**   Visit www.hulu.com/plus to subscribe to the HuluPlus service and browse available programming.

## XFINITY TV AND TWC TV

If Xfinity (Comcast) is your cable TV provider, use this app to watch a wide range of free, on-demand programming, including TV shows and movies.

The free TWC TV app from Time Warner Cable offers similar functionality. If you subscribe to another cable TV or satellite TV service, check the App Store to see whether a similar app is available.

> **TIP**   One benefit to the Xfinity app is that you can download and save certain programs to your mobile device so you can watch that content later, without an Internet connection.

## NETFLIX

Netflix is a subscription-based service that enables you to watch thousands of movies and TV show episodes via the Internet on your Internet-enabled television, on your computer screen, from a video game console (such as Xbox 360, Xbox One, PlayStation 3, or PlayStation 4), using Apple TV, using a DVR (such as TiVo), or directly on your iPhone or iPad (when you use the free Netflix app). The subscription fee for Netflix is a flat $7.99 per month for unlimited access.

You can watch as much streaming content as you'd like per month from any compatible computer or iOS mobile device. Simply browse the Netflix Instant

Watch library, and tap on the Play button when you find the movie or TV show episode you want to watch. You can also create and manage an Instant Queue, which is a personalized listing of shows or movies from Netflix that you'd like to watch in the future or that you consider a Favorite.

# YOUTUBE

The official YouTube app (free) is available for the iPhone and iPad from the App Store. This app enables you to watch unlimited streaming videos produced and uploaded by everyday people, companies, television networks, and other organizations. In addition to millions of entertaining videos and video blogs, YouTube features free educational content and how-to videos. All YouTube content is free of charge to watch. Some of it is advertiser supported, however.

**TIP** In addition to streaming videos, TV shows, and movies to watch on your iPhone or iPad, you can stream audio programming from AM, FM, and satellite-based radio stations and radio networks, as well as Internet-based radio stations. Some of the apps available for doing this include Pandora Radio, TuneIn Radio Pro, Spotify, iHeartRadio, and SiriusXM. A monthly fee applies to stream SiriusXM programming.

**NOTE** Using specialized apps from TV networks and cable channels, in addition to watching on-demand programming of shows that have already aired, in some cases it's becoming possible to stream live television programming as well. This is now possible using the CNN app, for example.

15

# CUSTOMIZE YOUR READING EXPERIENCE WITH iBOOKS AND NEWSSTAND

When it comes to reading eBooks, Apple has a solution to meet every person's reading habits and taste. Thanks to Apple's own iBooks app, eBooks can easily be read on any iOS mobile device (or Mac).

 **WHAT'S NEW** For the first time, the iBooks app comes preinstalled with iOS 8. It's no longer an optional app that needs to be downloaded and installed separately from the App Store.

If you have a Mac, iPhone, and/or an iPad, you can use iCloud to sync your eBook library and related bookmarks between computers and iOS mobile devices (that are linked to the same iCloud account) automatically, so your books, even if you've acquired hundreds of them, are available to you

regardless of which Mac or iOS mobile device you're using. It's also now possible to use iCloud's Family Sharing to share eBook titles among your family members.

Anything having to do with shopping for, downloading, installing, and then reading eBooks on your iPhone or iPad is done using the iBooks app.

> **TIP** You also have the option to download and use other third-party eBook reading apps with your iOS mobile device. These apps, which include the Amazon Kindle and Barnes & Noble Nook apps, are discussed later in this chapter.

iBooks has two main purposes. First, it's used to access Apple's online-based iBookstore. From iBookstore, you can browse an ever-growing collection of eBook titles (including traditional book titles from bestselling authors and major publishers that have been adapted into eBook form). Although some eBooks are free, most must be paid for.

> **TIP** As with purchases from the iTunes Store, App Store, or Newsstand, eBook purchases made from iBookstore get charged to the credit or debit card associated with your Apple ID. iBookstore and Newsstand purchases can also be paid for using prepaid iTunes gift cards.

The iBooks app is used to transform your smartphone or tablet into an eBook reader, which accurately reproduces the appearance of each page of a printed book on your device's screen, regardless of the device's screen size. So reading an eBook is just like reading a traditional book in terms of the appearance of text, photos, or graphics that would otherwise appear on a printed page.

One advantage to reading an eBook, as opposed to a traditionally printed book, is that the iBooks app enables you to customize the appearance of a book's pages. For example, you can select a font that is appealing to your eyes, choose a font size that's comfortable to read, and even change the background color of the screen to a Sepia or Night theme, which some people find less taxing on their eyes.

iBooks offers many features that make reading eBooks on your iOS device a pleasure. For example, when you stop reading and exit the iBooks app (by pressing the Home button), the app automatically saves the page you're on using a virtual bookmark, and then later reopens to that page when the iBooks app is restarted. It can also sync your bookmarks and eBook library with iCloud and your other Macs and iOS mobile devices automatically.

> 📝 **NOTE** Thanks to iCloud, you can begin reading a book on one Mac or iOS mobile device, and then pick up exactly where you left off on another, simply by opening the iBooks app. You are allowed to install copies of your eBooks on all computers and devices that are linked to the same iCloud account, so you do not have to purchase the same eBook multiple times.

## CUSTOMIZE iBOOKS SETTINGS

To customize settings related to iBooks, launch Settings and tap on the iBooks option (shown in Figure 15.1). You can turn on or off Full Justification and/or Auto-Hyphenation, as well as the Both Margins Advance feature (which, when turned on, enables you to tap the left or right margin of the screen to turn a page, instead of using a horizontal finger swipe).

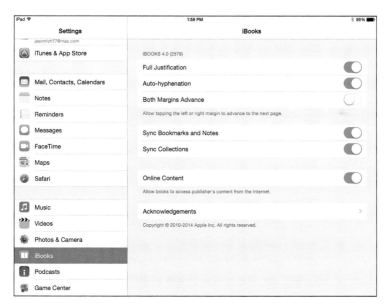

**FIGURE 15.1**

*From within Settings, it's possible to customize a handful of options related to the iBooks app.*

To turn on the iCloud syncing functions for iBooks, turn on the virtual switches associated with Sync Bookmarks and Notes, as well as Sync Collections.

> **TIP** One of the great things about reading an eBook is that it can be updated quickly by the book's author or publisher. By turning on the Online Content option that's part of the iBooks menu within Settings, your iPhone or iPad will automatically update eBooks you've already acquired if new content related to a previously published book becomes available.

You need to customize the Settings options that are associated with iBooks only once, but you can return to Settings at any time to adjust the customizable options as you see fit.

iBooks enables you to store and manage a vast library of eBooks on your iOS device, the size of which is limited only by the storage capacity of the device itself. Plus, all of your iBookstore purchases automatically get saved to your iCloud account. Thus, you can easily download eBook titles you've previously purchased via iCloud when you want to access a particular eBook that is not currently stored on your device.

## ORGANIZE YOUR PERSONAL eBOOK LIBRARY

When you launch iBooks, the main Library screen is displayed (shown in Figure 15.2). Thumbnails of the book covers in your digital eBook library are depicted. Tap on the All Books option that's found near the top center of the screen to determine which eBook titles are displayed.

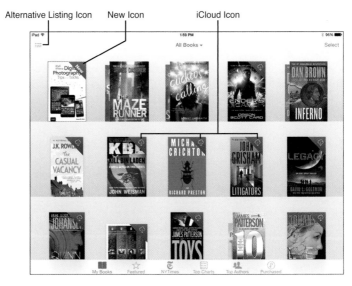

**FIGURE 15.2**

*Tap on the My Books icon at the bottom of the iBooks screen to see your virtual bookshelf, which displays your eBook titles.*

NOTE   When you have not yet opened an eBook in iBooks, a blue-and-white New banner appears on its cover thumbnail on the Library screen.

Select the All option to display all eBooks you've acquired, including titles that are stored in your iCloud account but are not currently stored in your actual iPhone or iPad. These titles display an iCloud icon in the top-right corner of their thumbnail (refer to Figure 15.2).

To hide the eBooks that are stored in your iCloud account and only display eBooks that are currently available on your iPhone or iPad, turn on the virtual switch that's displayed near the bottom of the Collections window, which appears when you tap on the All Books option.

From this Collections menu (shown in Figure 15.3), it's also possible to manually sort your eBook library into separate Collections, each of which can have a custom name. To do this, tap on the Edit option that's displayed to the right of the Collections heading, or tap on the "+ New Collection" option that's listed as part of the Collections menu.

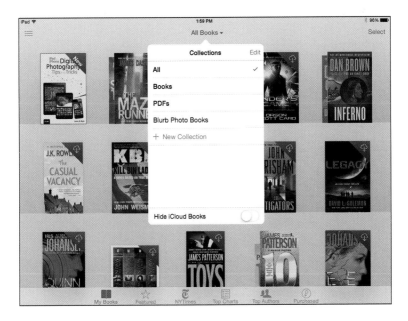

**FIGURE 15.3**
*From the Collections menu, you can create new Collection folders, each of which can have a custom title, like Summer Reading or Blurb Photos Books.*

Once you've created additional Collections, you can easily move your eBooks into a specific Collection to organize them. To do this, return to the main Library screen, and tap on the Select option. Next, tap on one or more eBook thumbnails that you want to transfer from the default All Books Collection into a specific Collection. As each eBook title is selected, a blue-and-white checkmark icon appears in the lower-right corner of its thumbnail.

Next, tap on the Move icon, and when the Collections menu appears, tap on the name of the Collection you want to move the selected eBooks into.

**TIP** In addition to eBooks that have been formatted to be read using the iBooks app, this same app can also be used to view PDF files. When PDF files are transferred into the iBooks app, they automatically get placed in a separate Collection, called PDFs.

You can create separate Collections to separate Work or Personal-related eBooks, create a Collection based on a favorite author's name, or separate your eBooks by categories you create, like Vacation Reading or Romance.

To delete eBooks stored in your iPhone or iPad (but keep them in your iCloud account), from the Library screen, tap on the Select option, tap on the eBook(s) you want to delete, and then tap on the Delete option that's displayed near the top-left corner of the Library screen.

**TIP** A cellular or Wi-Fi Internet connection is needed to load eBooks into the iBooks app from the App Store. However, after an eBook is loaded into the app, the Internet connection is no longer needed. Thus, you can read eBooks on airplanes, cruise ships, or while traveling overseas (where an Internet connection is not readily available), as long as you've preloaded the books into your iPhone or iPad.

# THE iBOOKS MAIN LIBRARY SCREEN

If you've never used the iBooks app before on any of your Macs or iOS mobile devices, when you launch iBooks for the first time, the app's main Library screen is displayed, but it is empty. If eBooks are stored in your iCloud account, they are automatically listed when you launch the iBooks app.

Displayed along the bottom of the Library screen are five (iPhone) or six (iPad) command icons. The My Books option, which displays the Library screen, is selected by default.

To start shopping for eBooks from Apple's iBookstore, tap on the other command icons to begin browsing for books or to find the exact book title you're looking for. An Internet connection is required for this.

> **NOTE** Throughout this chapter, the term *purchased* eBooks refers to eBook titles you already have purchased from iBookstore, as well as free eBooks you've acquired through iBookstore. These are eBooks already stored in your iCloud account that can be reloaded at anytime. This could also include eBooks purchased by a family member that are available to you using iCloud's Family Sharing option.

## FIND eBOOKS USING THE COMMAND ICONS DISPLAYED WHEN USING AN iPHONE

Displayed along the bottom of the Library screen within the iBooks app are five command icons (shown in Figure 15.4). Here's how to use several of these options to find the eBook(s) you're looking for from Apple's online-based iBookstore:

**FIGURE 15.4**
*These five command icons are displayed at the bottom of the screen when using an iPhone.*

- **My Books**—Tap on this icon to return to the Library screen and view your personal eBook collection.
- **Featured**—Access iBookstore and browse through books that Apple considers to be "featured" titles (shown in Figure 15.5). Here, you'll often see special categories of books being promoted, such as "Coming Soon," "Popular on iBooks," "Books Made into Movies," or "Author Spotlight." These categories change regularly. Tap on any book listing to access that eBook's Description, as well as to purchase/acquire that eBook.

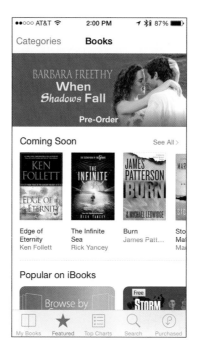

**FIGURE 15.5**

*The Featured screen in iBookstore showcases eBooks that Apple chooses to highlight.*

> ☑ **TIP**   After tapping on the Featured button, scroll to the bottom of the
> screen to access the Apple ID [Your Username] button, the Redeem button,
> and the Send Gift button. Tap on the Apple ID button to manage your Apple ID
> account. Tap on the Redeem button to redeem iTunes Gift Cards and add credit
> to your Apple ID account. Tap Send Gift to send someone you know an eBook as a
> gift. You must know the recipient's email address to do this.

- **Top Charts**—Tap on this option to display the charts listing the bestselling
  eBooks within iBookstore. Near the top of the screen, three tabs are
  displayed. Tap on the Books tab to discover two different charts, including
  a chart for Paid eBooks and Free eBooks. Tap on the NYTimes tab to display
  the current *New York Times* Bestseller list. Only titles from this bestsellers list
  that are available from iBookstore are listed. Tap on the Top Authors tab to
  view an alphabetical listing of popular authors who have books available
  from iBookstore.

- **Search**—Tap on the Search option to reveal a Search field, within which you can type any book title, author name, keyword or phrase that helps you locate a specific book. Tap on any listing to view the Description for that book.

- **Purchased**—Tap on this option to quickly find and reload any eBook you've previously purchased. At the top of this screen are two tabs. Tap on the All tab to view a comprehensive listing of all eBooks you've acquired on any of your computers or devices. Tap on the Not On This… tab to display eBooks you've previously acquired that are not currently loaded into the device you're using.

## FIND eBOOKS USING THE COMMAND ICONS DISPLAYED WHEN USING AN iPAD

When using an iPad, displayed along the bottom of the Library screen within the iBooks app are six command icons (shown in Figure 15.6). Here's how to use each of these options to find the eBook(s) you're looking for from Apple's online-based iBookstore:

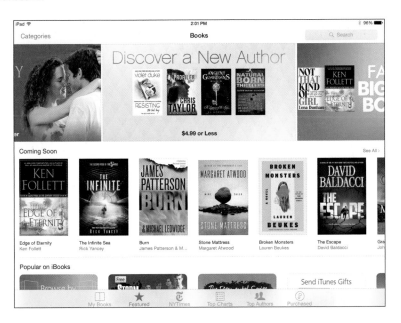

**FIGURE 15.6**

*As you'd expect, the Featured screen when viewed on the iPad reveals a lot more information than what you see when viewing the same screen on an iPhone.*

> **☑ TIP** Displayed in the top-right corner of the screen is the Search field. Tap on it anytime if you know the title of a specific book you're looking for. In this field, you can also search for eBooks based on an author's name, keyword, genre, or any search phrase. Tap on any listing to display that book's Description. If you already know what you're looking for, using the Search field is typically the fastest way to find it.

- **My Books**—Tap on this icon to return to the Library screen and view your personal eBook collection.
- **Featured**—Access iBookstore and browse through books that Apple considers to be "featured," titles (refer to Figure 15.6). Here, you often see special categories of books being promoted, such as "Coming Soon," "Popular on iBooks," "Books Made into Movies," or "Author Spotlight." These categories change regularly. Tap on any book listing to access that eBook's Description, as well as to purchase/acquire that eBook.
- **NYTimes**—Display the *New York Times* Bestsellers list for both fiction and nonfiction books. Only titles from this bestsellers list that are available in eBook form from iBookstore are listed.
- **Top Charts**—Tap on this option to display the charts listing the bestselling eBooks within iBookstore, including a chart for Paid eBooks and Free eBooks (shown in Figure 15.7).

**FIGURE 15.7**
*Shown here is the main Top Charts listings for Paid and Free eBooks.*

> ✅ **TIP** The Top Charts list can be customized to show titles from a specific category or genre. To choose a specialized Top Chart listing, first tap on the Categories option and select a specific Category.

- **Top Authors**—Tap on this option to display an alphabetical listing of popular authors who have eBooks available from iBookstore. When you tap an author's name on the left side of the screen, a listing of that author's available work is displayed on the right side of the screen.

- **Purchased**—Tap on this option to quickly find and reload any eBook you've previously purchased. At the top of this screen are two tabs. Tap on the All tab to view a comprehensive listing of all eBooks you've acquired on any of your computers or devices. Tap on the Not On This… tab to display eBooks you've previously acquired but that are not currently loaded into the device you're using.

> ✅ **TIP** When viewing the Purchased screen, tap on the Sort option that's displayed near the top-right corner to organize the listing based on Most Recent or Name.

> 🗒 **NOTE** It is possible to download and read eBooks acquired from sources other than iBookstore using iBooks; however, the eBooks must be a compatible file format. The iBooks app works with PDF files (or eBooks in PDF format), as well as eBooks created in the industry-standard ePub format.

## LEARN MORE ABOUT SPECIFIC eBOOKS WHILE VISITING iBOOKSTORE

As you add books to your eBook library, the cover art for each title is displayed in the Library screen. Tap on the My Books icon displayed near the bottom of this screen to view the Library screen.

To see an alternative listing view of the Library screen, tap on the Listing icon that's displayed in the top-left corner of the Library screen. The icon is comprised of three horizontal lines (shown in Figure 15.8). To return to the default Thumbnail view, tap the icon showing six squares.

**FIGURE 15.8**

*Sort and then view your eBook collection using this alternative listing format, as opposed to viewing eBook covers on a virtual bookshelf.*

> **TIP**   From the Library screen's Listing view screen, tap on the Most Recent, Titles, Authors, or Categories tab (displayed at the top center of the screen) to sort your eBook collection. To search this listing on an iPhone, tap on the Search field that's displayed below the tabs. On the iPad, to make the Search field appear, place your finger near the center of the screen and swipe downward.

## HOW TO FIND A SPECIFIC eBOOK—FAST

Although you can use the various command buttons and spend hours browsing through eBook titles, just as you can spend an equal amount of time perusing the shelves of a traditional bookstore, here are some simple strategies for quickly finding a specific eBook title you're looking for.

Use the Search field to enter the eBook title, author's name, subject, or keyword that's associated with what you're looking for. Entering a specific book title reveals very specific search results. However, entering a keyword relating to a topic or subject matter reveals a selection of eBook suggestions that somehow relate to that keyword.

Tap on any listing to reveal a more detailed description relating to a particular eBook. As you review a description for an eBook, look carefully at its ratings and its written reviews, especially if it's a paid eBook.

## LEARN ABOUT AN eBOOK FROM ITS DESCRIPTION

A typical eBook listing includes the eBook's cover artwork, its title, and author. An eBook's description, however, is divided into several sections. Tap on the Details, Reviews, and Related tabs to view all information pertaining to a specific eBook.

On both an iPhone and iPad, displayed near the upper-left corner of a typical eBook description, as shown in Figure 15.9, is the eBook's cover artwork. To the right of this is the book's full title, author, publication date, page length (related to the printed edition), and average star-based rating.

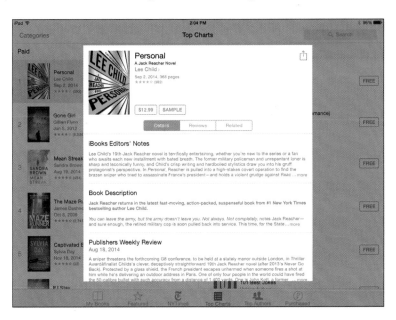

**FIGURE 15.9**

*Read a detailed description of an eBook before making your purchase and/or downloading it.*

The book's Price button and Sample button are also displayed near the top of the description.

A Share icon appears at the upper-right corner of an eBook description. Tap on it to share details about the eBook description with others via test message, email, Twitter, or Facebook. In the Share menu, there is also a Gift button. Tap on this to purchase and send the eBook as a gift for someone else. To do this, you need to know her email address.

> **TIP** You can preview an eBook before paying for it. As you're looking at a book's description, tap on the Sample button to download a free sample of that eBook. The length of the sample varies and is determined by the eBook's publisher. It is usually between a few pages and a full chapter.

Tap on the Details tab to view a detailed description or summary of the book (under the heading Book Description). There's also an informative Information section that displays the Language, Category, Publisher, Seller, Publication Date, File Size, and Print Length of the book (refer to Figure 15.9).

Tap on the Reviews option (shown in Figure 15.10) to access the iBookstore Ratings chart, which showcases the book's average star-based rating and how many ratings the book has received. You can also see this average star-based rating broken up to see exactly how many stars (from one to five) the book has received from your fellow iBookstore customers. Below the star-based ratings are more detailed, text-based reviews written by other iBookstore customers.

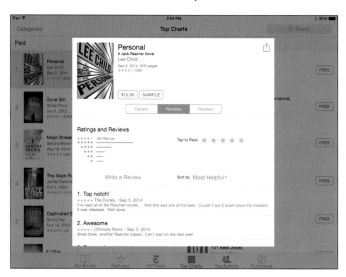

**FIGURE 15.10**

*From the Reviews section within an eBook's description are the book's star-based ratings and additional detailed reviews.*

From this Reviews screen, it's also possible to add your own star-based rating. Tap on the Write a Review option to compose and publish your own review of that book, which will then appear on iBookstore.

Tap on the Related option to view other books by that same author or similar books that Apple recommends.

To exit an eBook description screen on the iPhone, tap on the left-pointing arrow icon in the upper-left corner of the screen. The label on this icon depends upon the screen from which you entered the eBook description screen, such as Books or Featured. On the iPad, tap anywhere on the tablet's screen that is outside the Description window.

eBooks available from iBookstore are rated in much the same way apps are reviewed in the App Store. As a result, don't just pay attention to an eBook's average star-based rating, but also to how many people have rated it. After all, it's harder to get a good idea of a book's true quality if it has a five-star rating but has been rated by only a small number of people, versus a book with dozens or hundreds of five-star ratings.

To help make a purchase decision, scroll down below the customer ratings and take a look at the more detailed text-based customer reviews. Here, people who have theoretically read the book have written their own (sometimes lengthy) reviews.

## PURCHASING AN eBOOK

To quickly purchase and download an eBook, tap on the Price button displayed in its description. When you tap on a price button, it changes to a Buy Book button. Tap this button to confirm your purchase decision. You then need to enter your Apple ID password to begin the download process. If your iOS mobile device is equipped with a Touch ID sensor, you can approve your acquisition using a fingerprint.

If you're downloading a free eBook, tap on the Free button that is displayed instead of a Price button. Then, instead of a Buy Book button, a Get Book button appears. Tap on it, enter your Apple ID password, and download the free eBook. If your device has a Touch ID sensor, you can use your fingerprint to complete the transaction.

It typically takes between 10 and 30 seconds to download a full-length eBook to your iPhone or iPad, depending on the speed of your Internet connection and the size of the eBook's digital file. As soon as it's downloaded and ready to read, the book's front cover artwork is displayed as part of the Library screen in the iBooks app.

# CUSTOMIZE YOUR eBOOK READING EXPERIENCE USING iBOOKS

To begin reading an eBook that's stored in your iPhone or iPad, from the Library screen of iBooks, tap on a book cover thumbnail to open the eBook and start reading it. While reading eBooks, you can hold the iPhone or iPad in portrait or landscape mode. Then, as you're reading an eBook, tap anywhere on the screen to make the various command icons and buttons appear (shown in Figure 15.11).

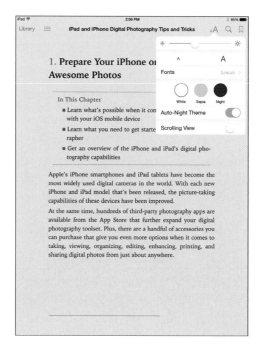

**FIGURE 15.11**

*Tap on the "aA" icon to customize the appearance of the text in the eBook you're reading.*

> 📋 **TIP**   Tap on the Library button that's displayed near the upper-left corner of the screen to automatically bookmark your location in that eBook and return to iBooks' Library (My Books) screen.

Located to the right of the Library button is the Table of Contents icon. Tap on it to display an interactive table of contents for the eBook you're reading (as shown in Figure 15.12).

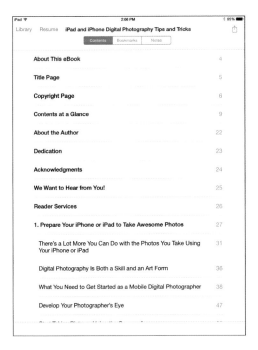

**FIGURE 15.12**
*The Table of Contents screen for eBooks is interactive. Tap on the chapter number or chapter title to jump to the appropriate page.*

As you're looking at a table of contents, tap on any chapter number or chapter title to immediately jump to that location in the book. Or, near the top center of the Table of Contents screen, tap on the Bookmarks option to see a list of manually saved bookmarks you have previously set as you were reading that eBook. Tap on the Notes tab to review the notes you've manually added to pages as you were reading.

> **TIP** Whenever you tap on the Library button while reading an eBook or press the Home button to return to the device's Home screen, your current location in the book is automatically bookmarked and saved.
>
> At any time, however, you have the option to manually add a virtual bookmark to as many pages in the eBook as you want. Then, by tapping on the Table of Contents icon and then on the Bookmarks tab, you can see a complete list of manually placed virtual bookmarks in that eBook, and return to any of those pages quickly.

To exit the Table of Contents screen and return to reading your eBook, tap on the Resume button in the upper-left corner of the screen.

Three command icons appear to the right of the eBook title. Tap on the "aA" icon to reveal a pop-up window (refer to Figure 15.11). It offers a screen brightness slider and a small and large "A" button that are used to instantly decrease or increase the font size in the book you're reading.

Tap on the Fonts button to change the text font, or tap on the Themes button to change the theme that's used to display the text and background color in the eBook you're reading.

Your theme choices include White, Sepia, and Night. Each displays the text and background in a different color combination. Choose the theme that is best suited for the lighting available and that is visually pleasing to you.

(iOS 8) **WHAT'S NEW**   If you turn on the virtual switch that's associated with Auto-Night Theme, your iPhone or iPad measures the ambient light in the area where you're reading, and then turns on the Night theme if you're reading in a dark or dimly lit area.

**TIP**   You can also switch between normal Book viewing mode, Full Screen mode (iPad only), or the Scroll mode. The Book viewing mode shows each page of the book you're reading, as well as icons on the top of the page, and page number information on the bottom. Full Screen mode gets rid of some of this onscreen clutter, so you can just focus your eyes on the eBook's page. The Scroll mode enables you to scroll up or down continuously within an eBook, as opposed to turning pages.

Tap on the Search icon (which is shaped like a magnifying glass) to display a Search field. Use this feature to locate any keyword or search phrase that appears in the eBook you're currently reading.

As you're reading, to turn the page, swipe your finger from right to left (horizontally) across the screen to move one page forward, or swipe your finger from left to right to back up one page at a time.

> **TIP**  To turn the page, you can also tap on the right side of the screen to advance or the left side of the screen to go back on the page. However, if you have the Both Margins Advance option activated (which can be done in Settings), tapping either margin advances to the next page.

Displayed at the bottom of the screen is the page number in the eBook you're currently reading, as well as the total number of pages in the eBook. The number of pages remaining in the current chapter is displayed to the right of the page number.

> **TIP**  As you're reading an eBook, hold your finger on a single word. A group of six command tabs appears above that word labeled Copy, Define, Highlight, Note, Search, and Share.
>
> Use your finger to move the blue dots that appear to the left and right of the word to expand the selected text to a phrase, sentence, paragraph, or entire page, for example.
>
> Tap on the Copy tab to copy the selected text into iOS 8's virtual clipboard. You can then paste that text into another app or into a Note within iBooks.
>
> Tap on the Define tab to look up the definition of a selected word. (Internet access is required to use this feature.)
>
> Tap on the Highlight tab to highlight the selected text. It's possible to choose the color of your highlights or underline the selected text by tapping on the yellow circle icon displayed above the word. Tap on the white circle (with a red line through it) to remove highlights, or tap on the Note icon to create a new note.
>
> The Share option also appears above the selected text after you tap on the Highlight option, as do the Copy, Define, and Search options, if you tap on the right-pointing arrow.
>
> When you tap on the Highlight option, you're given the option to choose a highlight color. The last highlight color you selected determines the color of the sticky note that appears when you tap on the Note option. This enables you to easily color-code your highlights and/or notes.
>
> If you tap on the Note tab, a virtual sticky note appears on your device's screen, along with the virtual keyboard. Using the keyboard, type notes to yourself about what you're reading. When you're finished typing, tap anywhere on the screen outside the sticky note box. A sticky note icon appears in the margin of the eBook. You can later tap on this icon to read your notes or annotations.

Tap on the Search tab to enter any word or phrase and find it in the eBook. A search window appears below the Search field. References to each occurrence of your keyword or search phrase are displayed by chapter and page number. Tap on a reference to jump to that point in the book.

When you tap on the Share option, a Share menu appears, giving you the option to email, text/instant message, tweet, or send the selected text to your Facebook friends. From the Share menu, you can also copy text to the virtual clipboard and then paste it elsewhere.

## READ PDF AND ePUB FILES WITH iBOOKS

The iBooks app can also be used to read PDF files you download or transfer to your iPhone or iPad. When you receive an email with a PDF file as an attachment, tap on the PDF thumbnail in that email so the file downloads to your iPhone or iPad. Next, tap and hold your finger on that same PDF thumbnail for a few seconds, until a menu window appears. The options in this window are Quick Look, Open in iBooks, and, if applicable, Open In [Compatible App].

The Open in iBooks command automatically launches the iBooks app and enables you to read the PDF document as if you're reading an eBook you downloaded from iBookstore. It's also possible to use the Open in iBooks command to read eBooks published in the ePub format that were acquired from another online bookseller.

**NOTE** If applicable, the Open In command enables you to open a PDF file using another third-party app. When you tap on this menu option, a list of compatible apps for viewing, printing, sharing, and/or annotating PDF files that are currently installed on your iPhone or iPad is displayed. These apps include PDFpen, Adobe Reader, PDF Reader, or GoodReader 4, for example.

When a PDF file opens in iBooks, you see command icons displayed along the top of the screen, as well as small thumbnails of the PDF document's pages displayed along the bottom of the screen.

Tap on the Library button that's displayed near the upper-left corner of the screen to return to iBook's main Library screen. When you do this, however, the Bookshelf displays all the PDF files stored on your device—not eBooks downloaded from iBookstore. To once again access your eBooks, tap on the PDFs button on the iPhone or the Collections command icon on the iPad, and then select the All Books option.

> **TIP** As you're viewing a PDF file in iBooks, next to the Library icon is the Table of Contents icon. Tap on it to display larger thumbnails of each page in your PDF document, and then tap on any of the thumbnails to jump to that page. Or tap on the Resume icon to return to the main view of your PDF file.

To the immediate right of the Table of Contents icon (near the upper-left corner of the iBooks screen as you're reading a PDF file) is a Share icon that enables you to email or print the PDF document you're currently viewing. Near the upper-right corner of this screen are three additional command icons. The sun-shaped icon enables you to adjust the brightness of the screen. The magnifying glass–shaped icon enables you to search a PDF file for specific text in the document, and the Bookmark icon enables you to bookmark specific pages in the PDF file for later reference.

> **TIP** As you're viewing a PDF file using iBooks, you can zoom in on or out from the page using a reverse pinch or pinch finger motion on the touchscreen display, or by double-tapping on the area you want to zoom in or out on.

Also, as you're reading a PDF file, you can hold the device in either a vertical or a horizontal position. If you tap anywhere on the screen (except on a command icon or page thumbnail), the icons and thumbnails on the top and bottom of the screen disappear, giving you more onscreen real estate to view your PDF document. Tap near the top or bottom of the screen to make these icons and thumbnails reappear at any time.

## CREATE YOUR OWN eBOOKS USING APPLE'S iBOOKS AUTHOR SOFTWARE

If you want to create your own content to be viewed using the iBooks app on the iPhone or iPad, create a PDF document, and then load it into iBooks. However, if you want to create interactive and visually compelling eBooks for the iPad, use Apple's free iBooks Author software for the Mac, available from the Mac App

Store. To learn more about what this software can do, visit www.apple.com/ibooks-author.

> **NOTE** It's possible to create and view eBooks using the ePub file format with other eBook creation software, but these books can't offer the interactive elements that are possible when using iBooks Author to create and publish eBooks.

## ALTERNATIVE METHODS FOR READING YOUR eBOOKS

Although Apple has worked out distribution deals with many major publishers and authors, the iBookstore does not offer an eBook edition of every book in publication.

> **TIP** In some cases, eBook titles are available from Amazon.com or Barnes & Noble (BN.com) but not from iBookstore. Or if Amazon.com, BN.com, and iBookstore offer the same eBook title, the price for that eBook might be lower from one of these other online-based booksellers.
>
> So, if you're a price-conscious reader, it pays to shop around for the lowest eBook prices. Just because you're using an iPhone or iPad does not mean you must shop for eBooks exclusively from iBookstore.

Perhaps you previously owned a Kindle, Nook, or Kobo eBook reader before purchasing your iPhone or iPad and have already acquired a personal library of eBooks formatted for that device. If you want to access your Kindle, Nook, or Kobo eBook library from your iPhone or iPad, download the free Kindle, Nook, or Kobo Reading apps from the App Store.

These apps prompt you for your Amazon, Barnes & Noble, or Kobo account information to sync your purchased content to the app. To purchase new Kindle- or Nook-formatted eBook titles, you must visit Amazon.com or BN.com using Safari or your primary computer. After you make your purchase, your eBooks can be automatically synced to the Kindle or Nook app on your device.

> **☑ TIP** Available from the iTunes Store is a vast library of audio books, which you can listen to using the Music app. If you're interested in listening to audio books, another service to check out is Audible.com. A free and feature-packed Audible app is available from the App Store. Hundreds of thousands of popular and bestselling books, from all categories and genres, are available as audio books from the iTunes Store and Audible.com.

# ACQUIRE DIGITAL EDITIONS OF NEWSPAPERS AND MAGAZINES WITH THE NEWSSTAND APP

Many local, regional, and national newspapers, as well as popular consumer and industry-oriented magazines, are now available in digital form and accessible from your iPhone or iPad via the Newsstand app. This app comes preinstalled with iOS 8.

## WORKING WITH THE NEWSSTAND APP

Not to be confused with the iBooks app, which is used for eBooks, the Newsstand app is used to manage and access all of your digital newspaper and magazine single issues and subscriptions in one place. However, the iBooks and Newsstand apps have a similar user interface, so after you learn how to use one, you'll have no trouble using the other.

> **📝 NOTE** Many of the world's most popular newspapers, including *The New York Times*, *The Wall Street Journal*, and *USA Today*, are now published in digital form, as are popular magazines, such as *Entertainment Weekly*, *TIME*, *Newsweek*, *Vogue*, *National Geographic*, *US Weekly*, *Reader's Digest*, *The New Yorker*, *Wired*, *Sports Illustrated*, *GQ*, and *People*.

After you launch Newsstand (shown in Figure 15.13), tap the Store button (shown in Figure 15.14) and browse through the ever-growing selection of digital newspapers and magazines that are available. With the tap of an icon, you can subscribe to any publication or, in most instances, purchase a single current or back issue.

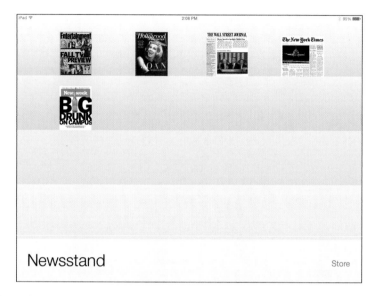

**FIGURE 15.13**

*The main Newsstand screen displays thumbnails for all newspaper and magazine issues currently stored on your iPhone or iPad.*

**FIGURE 15.14**

*Apple's online-based Newsstand offers hundreds of digital publications, including popular newspapers and magazines.*

The Newsstand is broken up by category. When you find a publication you're interested in, tap on its listing. This reveals a detailed description screen, which is very much like what you'd see in the App Store when shopping for apps. The description screen has Details, Reviews, and Related tabs that enable you to learn more about a publication.

> **NOTE** The online digital newsstand operated by Apple, which is compatible with the Newsstand app, is actually part of the App Store. Access it by tapping on the Store button in the Newsstand app, or launch the App Store app, tap on the Featured button (near the bottom of the screen), and then, tap the Categories button followed by the Newsstand option. From the Newsstand category option, you can choose a specific genre, such as Automotive or Fashion & Style, or select the All Newsstand option.

All purchases you make are automatically billed to the credit or debit card you have on file with your Apple ID account, or you can pay using iTunes gift cards.

After you purchase a digital newspaper or magazine subscription (or a single issue of a publication), it appears on your Newsstand shelf in the Newsstand app. Tap the publication's cover thumbnail to access the available issue(s).

If you've subscribed to a digital publication, Newsstand automatically downloads the most current issue as soon as it's published (assuming your phone or tablet has a Wi-Fi Internet connection available), so when you wake your iPhone or iPad from Sleep mode each morning, the latest edition of your favorite newspaper can be waiting for you.

> **NOTE** Each digital publication has its own proprietary app associated with it. These publication-specific apps are free and automatically installed on your iOS mobile device when you select a publication in Newsstand. All of these publication-specific apps are then accessible in Newsstand, plus they have their own unique functionality and allow for publication-specific interactive content.

> **TIP** To use a cellular data network to automatically download digital publications, you must turn on this feature in the Settings app. Launch Settings, select the iTunes & App Stores menu option, and then turn on the virtual switch associated with the Use Cellular Data option.

Also from within Settings, tap on the Newsstand option to turn on the virtual switches associated with each specific newspaper or magazine subscription that's listed. After you do this once, when using a Wi-Fi connection, your iPhone or iPad automatically downloads all new publication content when it becomes available, without using up your monthly wireless data allocation.

A Home screen icon badge and/or the Notification Center notifies you immediately whenever a new issue of a digital publication is automatically downloaded to your iOS device and is ready for reading. When you access Newsstand, you also see a thumbnail of that publication's cover on the main Newsstand shelf screen.

# READING DIGITAL PUBLICATIONS

Every publisher utilizes the iPhone's or iPad's display in a different way to transform a traditionally printed newspaper or magazine into an engaging and interactive reading experience. Thus, each publication has its own user interface.

In most cases, a digital edition of a publication faithfully reproduces the printed edition and features the same content. However, sometimes the digital edition of a publication also offers bonus content, such as active hyperlinks to websites, video clips, animated slide shows, or interactive elements not offered by the printed edition.

Reading a digital publication is very much like reading an eBook. Use a finger swipe motion to turn the pages or to scroll up or down on a page. Tap the Table of Contents icon to view an interactive table of contents for each issue of the publication. When viewing some publications, you can also use a reverse pinch, pinch, or double-tap finger motion to zoom in or out on specific content. Depending on the publisher, you might be able to access past issues of a publication at any given time in addition to the current issue. An additional per-issue fee may apply.

# MANAGING YOUR NEWSPAPER AND MAGAZINE SUBSCRIPTIONS

If you opt to subscribe to a digital publication, you often need to select a duration for your subscription, such as one year. However, almost all digital subscriptions acquired through the Newsstand app are auto-renewing. Thus, when the subscription ends, unless you manually cancel it, Newsstand automatically renews your subscription and bills your credit or debit card accordingly.

To manage your recurring subscriptions, launch the Newsstand app and tap the Store button. From the Newsstand store, tap the Featured command button that's located near the bottom of the screen. Scroll downward and tap the Apple ID [Your Username] button. When prompted, enter your Apple ID password.

Next, from the Account Settings window that appears, tap the Manage button that's displayed under the Subscriptions heading. Displayed on the Subscriptions screen is a listing of all publications to which you've subscribed. Tap any publication's listing to see the expiration date of your subscription, to cancel a subscription, or to renew your subscription.

## NEWSSTAND QUICK TIPS

- The publication-specific app related to the digital edition of a newspaper or magazine is free; however, in most cases, you must pay for individual issues or for a subscription to a publication. From Newsstand, to determine the per-issue or subscription cost, tap on a publication listing, tap on the Details tab, and then scroll toward the button of the screen. Tap on the option called In-App Purchases.

- To entice you to become a paid subscriber, some publishers offer free issues of their digital newspaper or magazine that you can download and read before actually paying for a subscription. Some publications, however, give away the digital edition of their publication for free to paid subscribers of the print edition.

- When actually reading a publication using a proprietary app (via Newsstand), you'll often see several command buttons displayed near the bottom of the page, including Store and Library buttons. Tap on Store to acquire additional single issues or a subscription to that publication, or tap on Library to reopen issues you've already purchased.

- Although you can download a digital publication and then read it offline, an Internet connection might be required to access interactive content that's exclusive to that digital publication. Look for interactive speaker or movie icons in a publication, and tap on them to experience this extra content.

---

(iOS 8) **WHAT'S NEW**   In addition to using the Newsstand app, an independent service called Next Issue (www.nextissue.com) enables you to pay a flat monthly fee ($14.99), and then read more than 140 popular magazines, including *Entertainment Weekly*, *Macworld*, *TIME*, *The New Yorker*, *Sports Illustrated*, *People*, *Vogue*, and *Men's Health*, on an unlimited basis.

To use this service from your iOS mobile device, you need to download the free Next Issue app from the App Store and then subscribe to the service. A free one-month trial period is offered.

# SET UP YOUR NEW iPHONE OR iPAD

If you purchased a brand-new iPhone or iPad (after September 19, 2014), iOS 8 came preinstalled; otherwise, you must upgrade your iOS mobile device from iOS 7 to iOS 8 to take full advantage of the latest features and functionality that your iPhone or iPad is capable of, and that you've been reading about in this book.

> **TIP** To upgrade to iOS 8, make sure your iOS mobile device is connected to the Internet via a Wi-Fi connection. Also, confirm the battery is fully charged or that your iPhone or iPad is connected to an external power source. Next, use iCloud Backup or iTunes Sync to back up your device.
>
> When you're ready to upgrade the iOS, launch Settings, tap on the General option, and then tap on the Software Update option. Follow the onscreen prompts to download and install iOS 8. The process takes about 15 minutes.

!CAUTION    To upgrade to iOS 8, your iPhone or iPad must have up to 6.9GB of available internal storage space (depending on the device). If not enough space is available, you'll be instructed to access the device's Usage settings to delete apps content, photos, and/or data (see Figure A.1).

Before deleting data, documents, or files, however, be sure this content is backed up. Any of your apps or purchased content can be reloaded after the iOS update is completed. However, if you have rented movies stored in your iOS mobile device (from the iTunes Store), these movies cannot be reloaded.

**FIGURE A.1**

*When you attempt to upgrade to iOS 8, your iPhone or iPad must have at least 6.9GB of available storage; otherwise, you'll be instructed to delete content to free up space.*

(iOS 8) WHAT'S NEW    Throughout the Setup and Activation process, depending on which device you're using, several options are offered in addition to the ones outlined in the following section. For example, if you're using an iOS mobile device with a TouchID sensor, during Setup you're prompted to scan your fingerprint and activate this feature.

Likewise, if you're setting up an iPhone 6 or iPhone 6 Plus, you're asked to choose between the Standard and Zoomed Display mode. These and other device-specific options can be set up during the initial Setup and Activation process, or they can be adjusted at anytime from within Settings.

# HOW TO ACTIVATE YOUR NEW iPHONE OR iPAD

To set up your brand-new iPhone or iPad that's already running iOS 8, follow these steps:

1. Unpack the iPhone or iPad and charge its battery. (Right out of the box, the device should be partially charged.)

2. Turn on your iPhone or iPad by holding down the Power button until the Apple logo appears.

3. When the device is turned on, the Hello screen is displayed (shown in Figure A.2). Swipe your finger from left to right across the Slide To Set Up slider.

**FIGURE A.2**

*From the Hello screen, slide your finger across the Slide To Set Up slider to get started using your iPhone or iPad.*

> **⌁ NOTE** If you're activating a new iPhone and transferring service from your older iPhone, you're prompted to confirm your iPhone's phone number, billing address's ZIP code, and the last four digitals of your Social Security number at the beginning of this process.
>
> If you're activating brand new service on a new iPhone, the Apple Store, cellphone store, or consumer electronics store where you purchased the iPhone must activate it for you.
>
> For iPad Cellular+Wi-Fi users, you're promoted to either transfer your existing cellular data service plan from your old tablet or set up a new month-to-month plan using a credit or debit card.

4. Select your language by tapping on a menu option. English is listed first.

5. From the Select Your Country or Region screen, tap on the appropriate option (shown in Figure A.3).

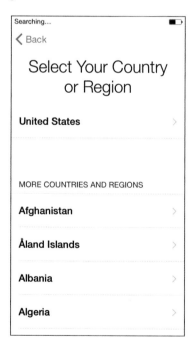

**FIGURE A.3**

*Select your home country or region, where you'll primarily be using your iPhone or iPad.*

6. When the Choose a Wi-Fi Network screen appears (shown in Figure A.4), tap on an available Wi-Fi network (hotspot). If applicable, you can tap on the Use Cellular Connection option to enable your mobile device to access a 3G/4G LTE cellular data network and complete the setup process.

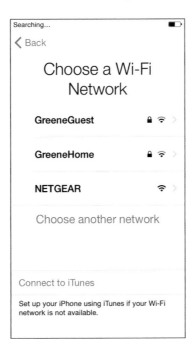

**FIGURE A.4**
*Choose an available Wi-Fi network so your mobile device can connect to the Internet.*

7. Your iOS mobile device will now be activated. When the Location Services screen appears, tap on Enable Location Services to turn on this feature and enable your iPhone or iPad to pinpoint your location.

8. From the Set Up iPhone (or iPad) screen (shown in Figure A.5), you're given three options: Set Up as New iPhone (or iPad), Restore from iCloud Backup, or Restore from iTunes Backup.

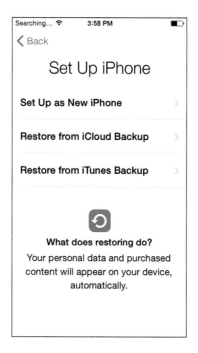

**FIGURE A.5**

*If you are upgrading from an old iPhone to a new iPhone, or an older iPad to a new iPad, and want to restore your data from an existing iCloud backup or iTunes backup, select one of these options. Otherwise, choose the Set Up as New iPhone (or iPad) option.*

**NOTE** When you select the Restore from iCloud Backup or Restore from iTunes Backup option, the setup process automatically restores your personal settings, apps, files, photos, and documents to the new iPhone or iPad using content from your backup files. If you're setting up a new iPhone or iPad and have no previously created backup files to restore, select the Set Up as New iPhone (or iPad) option.

9. From the Apple ID screen, you can either sign in with your Apple ID or create a free Apple ID. If you already have another Apple device (or you're replacing an existing one), use the same Apple ID username and password, so that all of your Macs and iOS mobile devices can sync information via iCloud, as well as share iTunes Store, App Store, iBookstore, and Newsstand purchases. As soon as you enter your Apple ID information, any related content is transferred from iCloud to your new mobile device. See Chapter 4, "Sync,

Share, and Print Files Using AirDrop, AirPlay, AirPrint, and Handoff," for more information about iCloud's features.

10. Accept the Terms and Conditions by tapping on the Agree option that's displayed near the bottom-right corner of the screen. When the Terms and Conditions pop-up window appears, tap on the Agree button.

11. You now have the option of setting up and activating the Passcode option. To do this, create and enter a four-digit passcode, and then when prompted, enter the passcode again. To skip this step, tap on the Don't Add Passcode option. If you skip this step now, you can activate this feature in the Settings app later.

12. To turn on and activate the Siri feature on your iOS mobile device, tap on the Use Siri option from the Siri screen. Then, from the Diagnostics screen, tap on either the Automatically Send or Don't Send option, based on your personal preference.

13. The Welcome to iPhone (or iPad) screen appears when the setup process is just about completed (shown in Figure A.6). Tap on the Get Started option to begin using your iOS mobile device.

**FIGURE A.6**

*The Welcome to iPhone (or iPad) screen is one of the last things you see before the setup process is fully completed.*

**14.** The Home screen appears (shown in Figure A.7). You can now begin using your newly set up and activated iPhone or iPad. If your device needs to restore app-specific data, third-party apps, and photos, this continues in the background when the Home screen appears.

**FIGURE A.7**

*When the Home screen is displayed, you now have full use of your iOS mobile device and all of the apps installed in it.*

> ✎ **NOTE**  If you've chosen to restore a backup file created from an older iPhone or iPad onto a new iPhone or iPad, some of your app-specific passwords do not transfer over. You might need to reenter your username and/or password the first time you relaunch the app on your new device.
>
> It is also necessary to confirm your iCloud Keychain function on the new device before you're permitted to access this information. This confirmation can be done from another Mac or iOS mobile device that's linked to your iCloud account or by having Apple send your iPhone a text message with a confirmation code.

From the Home screen, you can launch any of the apps that come preinstalled with iOS 8 (as well as any third-party apps that have been installed from a previous backup). Swipe from right to left across the Home screen to access additional Home screens.

Displayed near the top-left corner of the screen is the cellular data network and/or Wi-Fi signal strength indicator. As long as one or both of these options are displayed, your iOS mobile device can freely access the Internet.

Using the App Store app, it's now possible to find, purchase, download, and install new apps. Or using the iTunes Store app, you can acquire content, such as music, TV shows, movies, ringtones, music videos, or audiobooks, that you can enjoy using your iPhone or iPad.

**TIP** When your mobile device is set up and functional, be sure to use Settings to customize the functionality of your iPhone or iPad. This is covered in Chapter 1, "Tips and Tricks for Customizing Settings."

**NOTE** Apple periodically updates the iOS and the apps that come pre-installed on the device. For example, in Fall of 2014, when the Apple Pay feature launched, an update to iOS 8 was released.

To check for and install any new iOS updates (which are free), launch Settings, tap on the General option, and then tap on the Software Update option. If the message "iOS 8.0 Your Software Is Up To Date" is displayed, you already have the most current version of iOS 8 installed. However, if an update is available, a message appears on the Software Update screen, and you're walked through the step-by-step update process when you tap on the Install Update option.

Now is the perfect time to turn on the Find My… feature from within Settings, so if your device gets lost or stolen, you'll have tools available to help retrieve it or at least lock it down and erase its contents. To set up this feature, launch Settings, tap on the iCloud option, tap on the Find My option, and then turn on the virtual switch associated with the Find My iPhone (or iPad) option.

This must be done in advance,  before your iPhone or iPad actually gets lost or stolen. Turning on the Find My iPhone (or iPad) feature needs to be only done once.

(iOS 8) **WHAT'S NEW** From the Find My... submenu screen in Settings, also turn on the Send Last Location option. This enables your mobile device to automatically send its location to you before its battery dies.

Also set up the iCloud Backup feature so that your iPhone or iPad automatically creates a backup of its contents via iCloud on a daily basis. To set up this feature, launch Settings, tap on the iCloud option, and then tap on the Backup option. From the Backup submenu screen, turn on the virtual switch associated with iCloud Backup. This needs to be done only once.

Finally, if you have not already done so, consider purchasing AppleCare+ for your device from Apple. In addition to providing you with two years of free technical support, AppleCare+ also covers repair and replacement costs when a wide range of otherwise costly problems arise. For more information about AppleCare+, visit www.apple.com/support/products/iphone.html.

AppleCare+ does not, however, cover the loss or theft of your device. For this type of coverage, you can purchase third-party insurance from a company like Worth Ave. Group (www.worthavegroup.com) or SquareTrade (www.squaretrade.com).

# INTRODUCTION TO APPLE WATCH

As this all-new fourth edition of *iPad and iPhone Tips and Tricks* was being written, Apple announced the Apple Watch (also referred to as Watch). Available starting in early 2015 at a starting price of $349, Apple Watch will revolutionize how technology can be worn and utilized in our daily lives. While Apple Watch will be a wearable device that offers a wide range of features and functions, beyond just telling time, it is designed to seamlessly integrate and communicate wirelessly with your iPhone to exchange information and access the Internet. In fact, being an iPhone 5 (or higher) owner is a prerequisite for using Apple Watch.

🔍 **MORE INFO**  This appendix discusses some of the ways you'll be
able to use the Apple Watch as a standalone device, as well as with your iPhone.
In early 2015, when the Apple Watch is actually released and readily available to
the public, this appendix will be updated with tips and tricks on how to use the
Apple Watch. This updated content will be made available as a free download
online from Que Publishing's website. To access this content after it's published,
please visit www.informit.com/title/9780789753557.

# APPLE WATCH UTILIZES APPS, JUST LIKE YOUR IPHONE

Just like the iPhone and iPad, Apple Watch will come with a handful of preinstalled
apps. However, additional apps from Apple and third parties can be installed onto
the wearable device to greatly expand its capabilities. Ultimately, how you utilize
the Apple Watch in your daily life depends on what apps you ultimately install,
how you personalize the device, and what other equipment you use the watch to
exchange data with.

✓ **TIP**  Starting in early 2015, with the launch of Apple Watch, the author
of this book will expand his blog, called "Jason Rich's Featured App of the Week"
(www.FeaturedAppOfTheWeek.com) to include in-depth Apple Watch app
reviews. To access "Jason Rich's Featured Watch App of the Week," visit
www.WatchAppReview.com.

# APPLE WATCH OFFERS MULTIPLE MODELS, WITH DOZENS OF STYLE CONFIGURATIONS

Apple Watch comes in three models: Apple Watch, Apple Watch Sport, and
Apple Watch Edition. All three models offer exactly the same functionality. The
differences are the outside watch casing, casing size, and the watchband options
that are offered with each model.

Apple Watch is the basic watch model. The casing for this watch is constructed
from cold-forged stainless steel or space black stainless steel, and it has a scratch-
resistant sapphire crystal covering over the Retina Multi-Touch display. This
watch model is durable, but it's designed to coordinate perfectly with everyday

casual wear or more formal business attire. For the band, you can choose from 18 fashionable unisex options, including three different leather bands, a link bracelet, a Milanese loop, or one made from what Apple refers to as "high-performance fluoroelastomer" (which is a rubber-like material that's soft, durable, and comfortable to wear).

Apple Watch Sport is designed for people who are athletic and need a more durable watch design that matches their active lifestyle. These watch casings are constructed from lightweight and extra strong anodized aluminum and are available in a silver or space gray finish.

The displays on this watch are protected using a strong and scratch-resistant Ion-X glass, and the fluoroelastomer bands come in five colors: white, blue, green, pink, and black. Thus, between the color and the two case size options, 10 different styles of the Apple Watch Sport are initially being offered.

For those who are more style-conscious than action-oriented, Apple Watch Edition is designed to resemble a stylized luxury designer timepiece that's made from 18-karat yellow and rose gold that Apple's metallurgists developed to be twice as hard as traditional gold. Six versions of this higher-end version of the watch are available, with several different color accent options that are built in to the casing and that compliment the available band options.

Each of these unisex Apple Watch models is available in two case sizes (38mm and 42mm). While the outer construction materials of each watch model differs, it's important to understand that the technology built in to all the Apple Watch models, including the actual Retina Multi-Touch display and the proprietary Apple S1 processor chip, along with the multifunction digital crown and the Taptic Engine, are identical. Thus, the functionality of the Apple Watch, Apple Watch Sport, and Apple Watch Edition is the same, and the watches all utilize apps in the same way.

Beyond just choosing the design of your Apple Watch, however, the watch face can be fully customized to display your personality, as well as the time and date, plus additional information you want at your fingertips.

**NOTE** The Taptic Engine that's built in to the Apple Watch enables the watch to provide the wearer with physical feedback that feels like a light tap on the wrist. This is in addition to a wide range of visual and audio feedback that's possible. This Taptic Engine will be utilized by app developers in a variety of different ways, as will the watch's built-in heart rate monitor and accelerometer. The watch can also utilize your iPhone's GPS and Location Services functionality to keep tabs on your exact location, and utilize that information as it's needed.

> ✏ **NOTE** Prior to the release of Apple Watch, Apple indicated that the watch could be used in and around water but did not make any announcements about whether the watch is water resistant or fully waterproof.

# DISCOVER APPLE WATCH'S FEATURES AND FUNCTIONS

Like the iPhones and iPad, the Apple Watch has the equivalent of a Home button that takes you to the Home screen, which is displayed on the watch's full-color multitouch screen. From the Home screen, you can launch apps by tapping on the screen. By default, your watch displays the time, date, and other information you select. The Home screen, which displays your installed app options as well as access to other watch functionality, is only one touch away.

> ✏ **NOTE** One really nice feature of the Apple Watch is that you never need to manually set the time and date. The watch automatically adjusts to the time zone you're in and, when necessary, takes daylight saving time into account.

What's interesting about the Apple Watch is that it has a handful of sensors built in. It can monitor your activity and heart rate, for example. Thus, the watch can collect this data, figure out things such as calories burned, and then wirelessly transfer this data to the new Health app that comes preinstalled with iOS 8 on the iPhone. However, the watch itself is designed to be a full-featured exercise and workout tool unto itself, thanks to the Workout app and other built-in apps.

Plus, in addition to collecting and sharing information, Apple Watch is designed to receive all sorts of information from the iPhone. As a result, the watch notifies you of incoming calls to your iPhone and enables you to answer those calls or send them to voicemail without touching the iPhone.

The watch can also display incoming emails and text messages and utilize your iPhone's Internet connection in order for you to respond to these incoming communications directly from your watch, or even initiate a call, email, or text message from the watch. Apple Watch has Siri and Dictation functionality, so you don't need access to a virtual keyboard to compose messages.

The watch can be set up to offer stopwatch and timer functionality, display stock quotes, keep you up to date with sports scores, show the weather forecast, or update you about breaking news headlines, based on how you set up the main customizable watch face.

It's possible to control a wide range of other iPhone functions directly from the watch, such as the Music, Maps, and Camera apps. Plus, Apple Watch can be used to wirelessly control or exchange information with a wide range of Bluetooth devices, ranging from external speakers and wireless headphones to fitness equipment. It can also be used as a remote control for Apple TV and the iTunes software that's running on your Mac or PC.

The built-in Photos app is fully compatible with the Photos app that comes preinstalled on the iPhone, iPad, and that will be replacing iPhoto on Macs in early 2015. Thus, you can use the watch to view your favorite digital photos.

Yet another cutting-edge function of the Apple Watch involves its compatibility with Apple Pay, which by the time you read this chapter will already be supported by hundreds of thousands of retail stores and dining establishments throughout the United States. Instead of using your traditional debit or credit card to make purchases, you'll be able to pay for purchases at participating retailers and restaurants (including popular fast food establishments) by tapping your watch while using the Apple Pay app when you approach the cash resister. Your purchases will be charged to your existing debit or credit card; however, each secure transaction will be handled wirelessly by your Apple Watch.

# APPLE WATCH'S EVOLUTION HAS ALREADY BEGUN

When Apple Watch is officially made available to consumers in early 2015, it will be capable of handling a wide range of functions right out of the box. However, just as the iPhone and iPad have evolved over time, so will Apple Watch, from hardware, operating system, and app standpoints.

# Index

## G

## H

## I

# K

# N

## S

 quepublishing.com

Browse by Topic ▾ | Browse by Format ▾ | USING | More ▾

Store | Safari Books Online

# QUEPUBLISHING.COM
## Your Publisher for Home & Office Computing

**Quepublishing.com** includes all your favorite—
and some new—Que series and authors to help you
learn about computers and technology for the home,
office, and business.

Looking for tips and tricks, video tutorials, articles and
interviews, podcasts, and resources to make your life
easier?  Visit **quepublishing.com**.

- **Read the latest articles and sample chapters**
  by Que's expert authors

- **Free podcasts** provide information on the
  hottest tech topics

- **Register your Que products** and receive updates,
  supplemental content, and a coupon to be used
  on your next purchase

- **Check out promotions and special offers**
  available from Que and our retail partners

- **Join the site** and receive members-only offers
  and benefits

QUE NEWSLETTER
quepublishing.com/newsl

 twitter.com/
quepublishing

 facebook.com/
quepublishing

 youtube.com/
quepublishing

 quepublishing.com
rss

 Que Publishing is a publishing imprint of Pearson

# REGISTER THIS PRODUCT
# SAVE 35%*
## ON YOUR NEXT PURCHASE!

## 🖥 How to Register Your Product

- Go to quepublishing.com/register
- Sign in or create an account
- Enter the 10- or 13-digit ISBN that appears on the back cover of your product

## 🔓 Benefits of Registering

- Ability to download product updates
- Access to bonus chapters and workshop files
- A 35% coupon to be used on your next purchase – valid for 30 days

    To obtain your coupon, click on "Manage Codes" in the right column of your Account page

- Receive special offers on new editions and related Que products

*Please note that the benefits for registering may vary by product. Benefits will be listed on your Account page under Registered Products.*

*We value and respect your privacy. Your email address will not be sold to any third party company.*

*\* 35% discount code presented after product registration is valid on most print books, eBooks, and full-course videos sold on QuePublishing.com. Discount may not be combined with any other offer and is not redeemable for cash. Discount code expires after 30 days from the time of product registration. Offer subject to change.*

quepublishing.com

# MAKE THE MOST OF YOUR SMARTPHONE, TABLET, COMPUTER, AND MORE!

ISBN 13: 9780789753489

ISBN 13: 9780789753618

ISBN 13: 9780789753939

ISBN 13: 97807897487

## Full-Color, Step-by-Step Guides

The "My..." series is a visually rich, task-based series to help you get up and running with your new device and technology and tap into some of the hidden, or less obvious features. The organized, task-based format allows you to quickly and easily find exactly the task you want to accomplish, and then shows you how to achieve it with minimal text and plenty of visual cues.

### Visit quepublishing.com/mybooks to learn more about the My... book series from Que.

quepublishing.com